Li Da and Marxist Philosophy in China

Li Da and Marxist Philosophy in China

Nick Knight

Routledge
Taylor & Francis Group
New York London

For Jill

First published 1998 by Westview Press

Published 2018 by Routledge
605 Third Avenue, New York, NY 10017
2 Park Square, Milton Park, Abingdon, Oxon OX14 4RN

Routledge is an imprint of the Taylor & Francis Group, an informa business

Copyright © 1998 Taylor & Francis

All rights reserved. No part of this book may be reprinted or reproduced or utilised in any form or by any electronic, mechanical, or other means, now known or hereafter invented, including photocopying and recording, or in any information storage or retrieval system, without permission in writing from the publishers.

Notice:
Product or corporate names may be trademarks or registered trademarks, and are used only for identification and explanation without intent to infringe.

Library of Congress Cataloging-in-Publication Data
Knight, Nick.
  Li Da and Marxist philosophy in China / by Nick Knight.
    p. cm.
  Includes bibliographical references and index.
  ISBN 0-8133-3639-2
  1. Philosophy, Marxist China. 2. Communism China 3. Li, Ta,
d1890 1966. I. Title.
B809.82.C5.K65   1996
181'.11 dc20   96-13928
                                                                                       CIP

Frontispiece photo of Li Da from Li Zhenxia, ed. *Dangdai zhongguo shi zhe*. Beijing: Huaxia chubanshe, 1991.

ISBN 13: 978-0-8133-3639-8 (pbk)

Contents

Preface		vii
1	The Life of a Philosopher During an Era of War and Revolution	1
2	Marxist Philosophy and Social Theory: The Origins of Li Da's Thought	30
3	Li Da and Marxism, 1919–23	62
4	Li Da and Marxist Theory, 1923–32	90
5	Translation and the Dissemination of Marxism in China	112
6	Li Da's *Elements of Sociology* and Marxist Philosophy in China	151
7	*Elements of Sociology*: The History, Laws and Categories of Dialectical Materialism	179
8	*Elements of Sociology*: Epistemology and Logic	209
9	Li Da and Mao Zedong Thought	230
10	Writings on Marxist Philosophy and Theory of the 1950s and 1960s	257
11	Conclusion: Li Da and Marxist Philosophy in China	295
Bibliography		305
Index		318

Preface

In the first chapter of his *Main Currents of Marxism*, Leszek Kolakowski identifies one of the major theoretical dilemmas confronting the historian of ideas.[1] Should the historian of ideas concentrate on the ideas themselves, investing them with some degree of immunity from the effect which the context (either its own or different successive contexts) might have on those ideas, or should ideas be regarded as largely emanations of concrete historical contexts, as epiphenomena to the real theatre of history? An affirmative response to the former allows concentration on the ideas themselves. From this perspective, it is the big and enduring questions of politics and philosophy posed by a body of ideas, and the responses to those questions, which are the primary consideration. An historian of ideas of this theoretical persuasion might be interested in how a doctrine or philosophy has influenced successive generations of believers, but would be less interested — if interested at all — in the possible impact of different historical contexts on the doctrine or philosophy. The focus here is on continuity, on genealogy. An affirmative response to the latter, however, necessitates perceiving ideas as the product of limited and specific historical contexts. From this perspective, one closely aligned to the sociology of knowledge, it is the context which is dominant, and the focus is the social origins of ideas — and particularly the social and political interests which ideas are generated to serve. It is the context which prevails over ideas, and as context alters, ideas are accordingly transformed; ideas originating in another time and place are necessarily adapted to the particular requirements of different social contexts. The emphasis here is on discontinuity, on the transformative effects on ideas of changed social context.

Kolakowski's response to this dilemma is to opt for the middle ground, to give due recognition to the links Marxism had to earlier philosophies and to the continuity of its core elements in eras subsequent to Marx's own, while recognising the influence that different social conditions have exercised on those who have described themselves as Marxists. The task of analysis, for Kolakowski, is to achieve an appropriate recognition of both continuity and change, to explore Marxism in all its diversity while retaining the notion of powerful core themes which survived the erosive effects of changed time and place.

Unlike Kolakowski, my analysis of the philosophical and theoretical thought of Li Da does not seek the middle ground. My interest in Li Da grew not so much out of an interest in Li Da, the individual, as in his contribution to the elaboration and dissemination of Marxism in China. I became aware of Li Da's significance to the development of Marxism in China through earlier research on the origins of the philosophical thought of Mao Zedong.[2] The conclusion of that research was that Mao had been deeply influenced by the interpretation of Marxist philosophy endorsed in the Soviet Union in the early 1930s, which had found its way to the Chinese revolutionary movement through the translations and writings of Li Da and other Chinese intellectuals. I also discovered that Mao had been deeply influenced by a volume on philosophy by Li Da entitled *Elements of Sociology*, which itself drew heavily on Soviet Marxist philosophy. This suggested to me that the philosophical and theoretical writings of Li Da could serve as a useful medium through which to explore the origins of Marxism in China, and its relationship with the Marxism of Europe and the Soviet Union, a relationship which is, I believe, much stronger and more intimate than many commentators would have us believe. Analysis of Li Da's philosophical and theoretical writings might thus serve, I thought, as a useful corrective to those views of Marxism in China which perceive it as a quaint and exotic off-shoot of Marxism, one which drew more from the cultural and social peculiarities of the Chinese context than it did from orthodox Marxism.

My interest in Li Da was thus motivated primarily by an interest in the sources of his Marxism and the way in which he elaborated Marxism for a Chinese audience. The focus of this book is thus the continuity of ideas, the continuity which exists between the theoretical and philosophical tenets of orthodox Marxism of Europe and the Soviet Union on the one hand and the theoretical and philosophical dimensions of Marxism in China on the other. By the same token, I have not entirely ignored the historical context within which Li Da lived and wrote, and there is a biographical theme running through the book which lightly situates his philosophical and theoretical writings within the social and political environment within which he lived. Indeed, the book commences with a brief biography of Li Da. I felt this to be necessary as Li is hardly known in the West. Despite being a founding member of the Chinese Communist Party and one of the most important of China's twentieth century intellectuals, there is virtually nothing written on him in English. The biographical theme is also important as one of the objectives of the book is to explore the philosophical relationship between Li Da and Mao Zedong, for it was through his influence on Mao that Li was able to exert such a powerful influence on Marxist philosophy in China more generally. Nevertheless,

Preface　　　　　　　　　　　　　　　　　　　　　　　　　　　　　　　　　ix

in general, the life and times of Li Da take a back seat to his ideas, in particular his elaboration of dialectical materialism and important themes within the materialist conception of history.

These are complex subjects, and the reader unfamiliar with Marxist theory may find some of the language used by Li Da abstruse. There is no escaping the fact that dialectical and historical materialism are a very dense thicket, one difficult to penetrate and comprehend. Yet, if we are to make judgments about the origins and development of Marxism in China, the effort to do so must be made. The very complexity of the task is one possible reason why Western commentators on Marxism in China have given less than adequate recognition to its similarity to its European and Soviet counterparts. I argue that the more closely we look at Li Da's elaboration of dialectical and historical materialism, the more evident it becomes that Marxist theory in China (of which Li was a major figure) is in many significant respects the same as orthodox Marxism. Analysis of Li Da's philosophical and theoretical writings can thus serve to correct common misconceptions about Marxism in China.

Many people have helped me with the research for this book. Darrel Dorrington organised the search of various libraries in Beijing for material on Li Da. Wang Yuping assisted my understanding of Li Da's use of the Chinese language and also spent many hours discussing his philosophy with me. Dr. Hiroko Wilcock of Griffith University kindly identified the names of the Japanese authors whose work Li Da translated. Li Junru, Zhang Caiyun and Qian Hongming, of the Institute of Philosophy at the Shanghai Academy of Social Sciences, introduced me to contemporary Chinese evaluations of Li Da, and also helped me track down many of the texts which Li Da translated. Without their help, Chapter 5 could not have been written. Professor Reng Wuxiong, of the Memorial Hall of the First Congress of the Chinese Communist Party, discussed with me the early theoretical and political activities of Li Da. Wang Jin, Li Yong and Dai Liyong, graduate students of the Philosophy Department at Wuhan University, gave me a great deal of practical assistance and made my stay at Wuhan University a very pleasant one. Professors Chen Zuhua, Tan Zhen and Duan Qixian, also of Wuhan University's Philosophy Department, shared with me their recollections of Li Da and spent many hours of their valuable time discussing the philosophical and theoretical issues which are the subject of this book. I am very grateful for their hospitality and kindness. Professor Song Jingming, of the Politics Department of Wuhan University and one of Li Da's biographers, despite ill-health, discussed Li Da's life with me and shared with me his many publications. Professor Yuan Jingxiang, of Wuhan University's English Department and one of China's best known translators, gave me his views on Li Da's approach to translation. Sun Aidi, of Wuhan University's Law Department, introduced me to Russian writings on Li Da. Professor Wang Jionghua, of the Philosophy Department of the Huazhong University of Science and Technology and one of China's foremost authorities on Li Da's philosophical thought, spent many hours with me discussing Li's life and work; he and his wife also gave me an excellent lunch. Jennilyn Mann, of the Publications Unit of the Faculty of Asian and International Studies at Griffith University, did a marvellous job formatting the manuscript. Similarly, Sue Jarvis did a fine job editing and proofreading the manuscript. She also prepared the index.

To these kind and helpful people I offer my sincere gratitude. Their help made the writing of this book possible; it also made the task of research and writing, often a lonely and frustrating business, much more enjoyable than it otherwise would have been. If they do not always agree with the interpretation offered here, they can rest assured that their contribution to my understanding of the complex issues of Li Da's life and work was a very significant one.

Finally, to Jill Kenny, my deepest gratitude and affection. Her love and support over many years has made it possible for me to concentrate my energies on my research and teaching. This book is dedicated to you, Jill, with love and thanks.

Nick Knight
Griffith University
Brisbane, Australia

Notes

1. Leszek Kolakowski, *Main Currents of Marxism: Its Origins, Growth and Dissolution — I. The Founders* (Oxford: Oxford University Press, 1978), pp. 9–10.

2. See Nick Knight (ed.), *Mao Zedong on Dialectical Materialism: Writings on Philosophy, 1937* (Armonk, New York: M.E. Sharpe, 1990); also Nick Knight, "Soviet Philosophy and Mao Zedong's Sinification of Marxism", *Journal of Contemporary Asia*, Vol. 20, No. 1 (1990), pp. 89–109.

1

The Life of a Philosopher During an Era of War and Revolution

Introduction

While this book is primarily a study of the origins, structure, development and influence of Li Da's philosophical and theoretical thought, this first chapter is devoted to a brief biography, with the purpose of introducing Li Da. Although very widely known and admired in China, Li Da is almost unknown in the West, and is rarely mentioned even by scholars of Chinese history and ideology.[1] This chapter draws primarily on Chinese biographical accounts,[2] but also on interviews with some of his former colleagues[3] and with Chinese scholars who have specialised in the study of his life and thought.[4]

Li lived through a number of turbulent chapters in Chinese history — the decline and fall of the Qing dynasty, the early Republican period and the rise of warlordism, the formation of the Chinese Communist Party, the initial cooperation and later deadly hostility between the Communist Party and the Guomindang (Nationalist Party), the anti-Japanese War, Communist victory in the 1945–49 civil war, the years of socialist construction of the 1950s and early 1960s, and the opening salvos of the Cultural Revolution. This was the historical backdrop against which Li rose to prominence as one of China's most influential Marxist philosophers. While the influences on his philosophical thought did owe significantly to philosophical developments in the Soviet Union and elsewhere, as we shall observe in subsequent chapters, the course of events in China and Li's involvement in those events are not altogether incidental to our understanding of his contribution to the elaboration and dissemination of Marxist philosophy and theory in China. Like many of China's intellectuals of his generation, Li Da was not only a philosopher, he was also an activist — one who put his impressive intellect to the service of the Chinese revolution. Throughout Li's voluminous writings, whether on legal issues, problems of financial administration, analyses of Chinese society, the issue of women's emancipation, or the philosophical and sociological issues which are the main concern of this study, there runs a commitment to the cause of social change in pursuit of a communist victory in China. Everything Li wrote was written with a political purpose. This applies even to his extended writings on some of the most arcane formulations of dialectical materialism, the philosophical basis of Marxism. For Li's major purpose in writing textbooks on philosophy such as *Shehuixue dagang* (Elements of Sociology, 1935/37) was the widespread dissemination of Marxist perspectives and concepts among the ranks of intellectuals and activists within the revolutionary movement, and the consequent facilitation of a Marxist analysis of Chinese society and the formulation of revolutionary strategies which could transform that society.

However, while the Chinese context within which Li Da lived and wrote is significant, it is also important to bear in mind the international context which prevailed during Li's lifetime, and most importantly, the situation which emerged in the Soviet Union during the 1920s and early 1930s, in both the political and philosophical realms, for this was to have a dramatic impact on Li's political career, and on his perspective on Marxist philosophy and theory. A number of episodes stand out and will be explored in detail in both this and the following chapter. The first is the intervention of the Comintern in the internal affairs of the Chinese Communist Party (CCP) in the early 1920s to bring about the realisation of what is now known as the First United Front, the policy of cooperation between the CCP and the Guomindang (GMD) in which members of the CCP entered the GMD (a strategy known as the bloc-within), and in which the CCP was very much the junior partner of the larger and more powerful GMD. Li's implacable opposition to the form that this policy took was to contribute to his decision to quit the CCP, the party which he had worked so hard to establish. The implications of this action for his subsequent career as philosopher for the revolutionary movement need to be explored.

The second — very important — episode was the upheaval in philosophical circles in the Soviet Union which was to lead, from 1931, to the formulation of a revised interpretation of dialectical materialism, one which espoused the subordination of philosophy to the needs of the Communist Party. The emergence of this philosophical orthodoxy, sanctioned by Stalin, was to have a dramatic impact on Li's understanding of Marxist philosophy and, through his efforts, the development of Marxism in China. For this reason, the history of dialectical materialism in the Soviet Union, including the political struggles over its interpretation and function, will occupy our attention in the next chapter.

As well as events and intellectual developments in the Soviet Union, there is also the Japanese connection to be considered. As we shall see, Li's periods of study in Japan during the 1910s gave him most importantly a fluency in Japanese which he later exploited to translate Japanese Marxist texts into Chinese; the interpretations of Japanese Marxists and socialists such as Kawakami Hajime and Sugiyama Sakae were thus an influence which we will need to explore. It was from their Japanese translations that Li was to translate into Chinese many works of European and Soviet Marxism. His sojourn in Japan also provided him with an international perspective, one not always shared by his revolutionary comrades in China, and one which predisposed in him a willingness to accept as orthodoxy a reading of Marxist philosophy which derived from beyond the Chinese context.

The Early Years

Li Da (whose alternate names were He Ming [*hao*] and Yong Yang [*zi*]) was born into a tenant farming family in Lingling county in Hunan province on 2 October 1890. Although his father, Li Furen, had been born into a peasant family, he had studied for several years and, as well as working in the fields, taught in a primary school and engaged in business. From the age of five, Li Da learnt Chinese characters with his father, and was fortunate enough to gain the kindly attention of his father's intellectual companion, Hu Xieqing, who was a *xiucai*, having passed the imperial examination at the county level. In 1905, Li entered Lingling county's Yongzhou middle school, and it was here that a number of incidents occurred which aroused patriotic sentiments in him. The first was a letter, received at his school, written in blood. Its author, Xu Teli (later to become Mao Zedong's teacher at the First Normal School in Changsha), employed this emotive technique to exhort students to support the movement to resist Japan and save the Chinese nation. The second was the boycotting of Japanese goods by his fellow students, and the burning of Japanese-produced stationery in the schoolyard. The irony of this latter incident was that the matches employed to set fire to the stationery were themselves made in Japan, but these had to be preserved as there would be nothing to ignite the next lot of Japanese products if these Japanese matches were themselves consigned to the flames.[5]

In 1909, Li Da entered the Beijing Higher Normal School, and it was here that his thoughts turned to using education to save China. However, following the 1911 revolution, and under the influence of Sun Yat-sen's injunction to create a rich and powerful Chinese nation, he decided to switch from education to science and technology, and transferred to a trade school in Hunan. In 1913, having passed the provincial scholarship examinations for study abroad, he proceeded to Japan as a government-sponsored student. Unfortunately, as a result of an attack of tuberculosis, he was compelled to return to China. In 1917 he returned to Tokyo for the second time, and took courses in mining and metallurgy at Tokyo's Imperial University. During these years, a number of historical events occurred which were to have a profound influence on Li's subsequent political and philosophical career. The first of these was Japan's growing imperialist designs on China. The "Twenty-one demands" presented to the Chinese government by Japan in 1915 would, if implemented, have had the effect of turning China into a virtual Japanese colony. The Chinese overseas students in Japan reacted to this with a mixture of shame and hostility to Japan's actions, but — and as Li himself recalls — they remained very uncertain about the appropriate path China should take.[6]

The second event from this period dramatically dispelled any uncertainty Li may have felt. The victory of the Russian Revolution in 1917 was greeted with great excitment by Li, for he perceived in it the revolutionary path that China should travel. It also led to an interest in the ideology which had inspired the Russian Revolution, and using sources drawn from Japanese magazines, books and journals, he commenced what was to be a life-long study of and commitment to Marxism. This dramatic influence of the Russian Revolution on Li's thinking and his immediate search for an understanding of Marxist and Leninist theory is very significant as he was one of the first of the Chinese radicals to convert to Marxism. As Arif Dirlik has persuasively argued, the Russian Revolution did not have the profound influence on China's young intellectuals that has been presumed by many historians. Rather, they responded to the problems of Chinese society and, in particular, the threat posed by Japanese imperialism, by turning initially to anarchism rather than Marxism; it was often only after an apprenticeship in anarchism that they gravitated to Marxism.[7] Mao Zedong, for example, did not convert to Marxism until some time in 1920, and had earlier been influenced, amongst other doctrines, by anarchism, and in particular the Russian anarchism of Kropotkin.[8] However, while Dirlik's interpretation of the anarchist roots of Chinese communism holds true for many Chinese intellectuals and activists at this time, it does not do so for Li Da. Some of his earliest published writings deal with the opposition between anarchism and Marxist socialism, and he is quite critical of the claims of anarchism. For this reason alone, the trajectory of development of Li's thought stands as an interesting and significant contrast to the general tendency of the time, which was an attraction by Chinese intellectuals to the radical claims of anarchism.

Following the 1918 accord between the Japanese government and the Chinese government headed by Duan Qirui, which would have allowed Japanese troops to enter Manchuria, the Chinese overseas students in Japan established their own branch of the Save China Association; they boycotted classes, and began to return to China. Li Da took a prominent role in these activities, and was amongst the first of the Chinese students to leave Japan. In May he returned to Beijing as the representative of the Japanese branch of the Save China Association, and immediately plunged into student activities designed to oppose the Duan government. The failure of this movement left a deep impression on Li, for the political actions it had pursued, such as petitioning the government, had produced no effect. Success, he came to realise, would only come when the people rose and overthrew the reactionary government, as they had in Russia; to follow that road, it was necessary (as he recalled in 1961) "to study Marxist-Leninist theory, to study the revolutionary experience of the Russian people".[9]

With this new conviction, he returned to Japan in June 1918 for the third time. However, he abandoned his study of science and, under the guidance of the famous Japanese scholar of Marxist economics Kawakami Hajime, specialised in the study of Marxist theory. Included amongst the works studied by Li were Marx's *The Communist Manifesto*, Volume I of *Capital*, the "Preface" to *A Contribution to the Critique of Political Economy*, Lenin's *State and Revolution*, and a number of introductory texts on Marxist theory. He also translated into Chinese *An Explanation of the Materialist Conception of History* by the Dutch Marxist Hermann Gorter, *An Overview of Social Problems* by Takabatake Motoyuki and *The Economic Doctrines of Karl Marx* by Karl Kautsky. His translations were subsequently published in China — indeed, Li's translation of Kautsky's *The Economic Doctrines of Karl Marx* was one of the texts studied by the Marxist study group established by Li Dazhao in March 1920. It is evident that Li Da perceived very early on the importance of translating Marxist texts into Chinese as the first step in the dissemination of Marxist theory amongst Chinese radical intellectuals, particularly as there was, at the time of the May Fourth Movement and throughout the 1920s and 1930s, a dearth of Marxist material in the Chinese language. Li's contribution to the introduction of Marxist theory to China through his translations is of considerable significance for an understanding of the type of Marxism which took root in China, and we will return in a subsequent chapter to a more detailed consideration of this aspect of his political and philosophical career

When the May Fourth movement of 1919 broke out, Li was still in Japan and he took no direct part in it. However, this movement and the subsequent June Third movement motivated Li to express his political views, and he proceeded to write a series of articles on the nature and goals of socialism, on Chen Duxiu and the new thought movement, and on the situation of the European socialist movement in the pre-war period.[10] In certain important respects, these first articles, published almost immediately in China, set the tone for Li's subsequent enormous literary output. First, they focused on theoretical issues concerned with socialism, and left-wing politics and thought, and it is entirely consistent with his later writings that his first two publications are entitled "What is socialism?" and "The objectives of socialism". Second, these essays are didactic in character, providing explanations of complex events, issues and concepts in a way designed to facilitate the ready comprehension and dissemination of the information contained within them. Third, these early writings demonstrate clear evidence of an intellectual whose political emotions and values are very deeply engaged. It is this latter characteristic which anticipates most forcefully the general tenor of Li's prolific literary career, for everything he subsequently wrote was written with a political objective in mind. Li's impressive capacity as an author and his skills as a translator were thus, from the very beginning, deployed in the service of the political goals of communism to which he remained committed to the end of his life.

The Formation of the Chinese Communist Party and Its Aftermath

In the summer of 1920, Li travelled to Shanghai, where he engaged in discussions with Chen Duxiu.[11] Li and Chen, together with Li Hanjun, Chen Wangdao and others, established what was later termed the Shanghai Committee for the Establishment of the Chinese Communist Party (*Zhongguo gongchandang Shanghai faqizu*).[12] This committee not only liaised with various regions of China in preparation for the establishment of a Communist Party, it established in November 1920 what was to be the CCP's first journal, *Gongchandang* (The Communist), and appointed Li Da as its editor. This journal dedicated itself to the cause of socialist revolution, and propagandised Marxism-Leninism, in particular the theories of proletarian revolution, the dictatorship of the proletariat and party building; it also criticised "opportunism", provided information on the achievements and experiences of the Russian Revolution, gave news of the international communist movement, and discussed problems of the Chinese and world revolutions. *The Communist* became an important medium for the dissemination of Marxist theory, its circulation exceeding five thousand; one of its subscribers, Mao Zedong, was to refer to the journal approvingly as a "bright flag".[13] Although this journal ceased publication in July 1921 after seven issues due to financial problems,[14] it filled an important theoretical role at a crucial juncture in the development of the communist movement in China. As its editor, Li had to work under very difficult conditions, often singlehandedly performing the work of writing and examining drafts, proofreading, publication and distribution. He wrote a regular column for the journal entitled "Brief words" (*duanyan*), in which he presented short, punchy essays on Marxism and the revolutionary movement. Li also was involved in editorial work for *Xin qingnian* (New Youth) after it became a publication for the Party, and he contributed essays and translations to *Shaonian Zhongguo* (Young China), *Laodongjie* (The World of Labour), *Juewu* (Consciousness) and other journals. These essays again dealt with issues of basic Marxist-Leninist theory, and countered anarchist attacks on Marxism which were prevalent at this time. Looking back on this period of his life, Li commented in his autobiography (1949) that his two major tasks following the establishment of the Shanghai Committee for the Establishment of the CCP were "first, propaganda, and second, organising the workers".[15]

In the first half of 1921, Li was heavily involved in the preparatory work for the First Congress of the CCP. On behalf of the Shanghai Committee, he contacted the groups in Beijing, Jinan, Changsha, Guangzhou, Wuhan and Tokyo to send two delegates apiece to the Congress. Li Da and Li Hanjun represented the Shanghai group.[16] In the latter half of July (probably 23 July), the Congress convened in Shanghai. However, because of harrassment by French police, the first session of the Congress was adjourned. Wang Huiwu, Li Da's wife and a native of Jiaxing, arranged for the closing session of the Congress to be held on a pleasure boat on the South Lake in Jiaxing, Zhejiang province.[17] As a result of the First Congress, Li was elected to the Provisional Central Executive Bureau, and appointed head of the Party's Propaganda Department.[18]

In September 1921, the Party established its first publishing house, The People's Publishing House, with Li as its Director. Li's plan was to publish a series of works by Marx, Lenin and other authors. He again threw himself into the work of writing, translating, proofreading, publishing and distribution, and within the space of a year, this new publishing house had succeeded in publishing fifteen volumes, including *The Communist Manifesto*, *Critique of the Gotha Program*, *An Introduction to Marx's Capital*, *Wage Labour and Capital*, and two books by Lenin. In October of that year, Li also became headmaster of a school for girls (*Pingmin nuxiao*), established by the Party in Shanghai. He set up and edited a journal entitled *Funu sheng* (Women's Voice), and he contributed many articles and translations on women's issues to this and other journals.

At this time, Li also wrote a large number of articles addressed to members of the working class, with the purpose of spreading information on socialism and Marxism amongst them. He also wrote, in essays such as "Russia's New Economic Policies", about the current situation in the Soviet Union, and translated a lengthy monograph on the working class and peasantry in Russia.

In July 1922, Li chaired the Second Congress of the CCP in Shanghai,[19] and in November of that year, he received an invitation from Mao Zedong to take up the position of principal of the Self-Study University (*Zixiu daxue*) in Changsha in his native Hunan province, and to be editor of the university's journal, *Xin Shidai* (New Age).[20] The Self-Study University taught not only members of the Party, but "advanced elements" from the working class and youth. Mao introduced Li to the university as "the Director of the Party's Propaganda Department, whose understanding of Marxism-Leninism is profound, and who has come specifically to help everyone study Marxism-Leninism".[21] Li lectured on the materialist conception of history, the theory of surplus value, scientific socialism and other basic Marxist theories; he also compiled an anthology of teaching material entitled *An Explanation of Marxist Terminology*. During this period, Li Da and Mao Zedong were constantly in each other's company, and discussed Marxism and problems of the Chinese revolution. According to Chinese biographers, the two revolutionaries forged a "militant friendship".[22] Between April and July 1923, four issues of *New Age* were published, and they contained a large number of Li's essays and translations, including amongst the latter Marx's famous "Critique of the Gotha Program".

The First United Front and Li Da's Departure from the CCP

In "Marxism Restored", written in late 1920 and published in *Xin Qingnian* in early 1921, Li had referred to the importance of establishing appropriate organisations for the working class; of these, the political party was of great significance.[23] Li stressed the importance of the independence of such a party in its dealings with the organisations of other classes; to lose this independence would spell "its death" (*siwang*). Here is an early indication of Li's tenacious belief in the importance of the organisational independence of the Communist Party, for the Party had the function of schooling its members for the struggle against capitalism in pursuit of socialist goals.[24]

Li's concern for the independence of the Communist Party appears also in an important essay in *New Age*, "Marxist Theory and China" (May 1923). Here, Li addressed the pressing issue now confronting the CCP, an issue which was to have a dramatic impact on his own future.[25] Under pressure from the Third Communist International (Comintern), which the CCP had formally joined at its Second Congress, the Party had been exploring the possibility of an alliance with the GMD. The issue of the relationship between communist and bourgeois parties in colonial countries had been a contentious one since the Second Congress of the Comintern of July 1920.[26] At this Congress, Lenin had clashed with the Indian delegate M.N. Roy, arguing that communist parties "must enter into a temporary alliance with bourgeois democracy in colonial and backward countries, but must not merge with it and must under all circumstances uphold the independence of the proletarian movement even if in its most rudimentary form".[27] Lenin appeared therefore to be sanctioning the concept of a united front with bourgeois parties, but insisting by the same token that the independence of proletarian parties and movements had to be maintained. Roy had vehemently objected to this formulation, arguing that it was not the task of the Comintern to be advocating collaboration with the class enemy, but rather developing a purely communist movement which would not have to rely on potentially dangerous partners in the revolutionary venture.[28] The Dutch Communist, Hendricus Sneevliet (alias Maring), who was to play such a prominent role in the formulation and implementation of the CCP's united front strategy, spoke in defence of Lenin's position, admitting that, although it might be difficult in theory to formulate the precise relationship between the parties of the proletariat and bourgeoisie, in practice the two had no alternative in the colonial context but to cooperate.[29]

Maring had gained considerable experience in united front tactics in the Dutch East Indies. Between 1914 and 1918 he had master-minded the infiltration of the large but loosely organised religious-nationalist party, the Sarekat Islam, by members of the diminutive Indonesian Social Democratic Association (ISDV), a strategy which came to be known as the "bloc within". The strategy was ultimately so successful that ISDV members managed to gain control of many key regional branches, to radicalise the objectives of the Sarekat Islam, and to recruit followers among the masses to the cause of socialism. The success of the strategy can also be seen by the fact that, by 1922, the Indonesian Communist Party (PKI), formed in 1920, and its affiliated organisations had some 50,000 members and controlled much of the trade union movement.[30]

The parallels between China and the Dutch East Indies were obvious. Here was a recently formed and tiny communist party, with a membership of only 195 at the time of its Second Congress in 1922. Its potential partner in any united front strategy, the GMD, was a large and poorly organised party. The GMD had, however, a lengthy revolutionary history and widespread popular support, and was led by

Sun Yat-sen, widely regarded as the father of the 1911 revolution. The GMD thus appeared as the natural leader of the Chinese revolution, at least for the forseeable future. Should the CCP ally with the GMD, and if so, what form should such a united front adopt? Should members of the CCP join the GMD, and how and to what extent should the independence of the CCP be maintained?

In "Marxist Theory and China" (May 1923), Li quoted extensively from *The Communist Manifesto* by Marx and Engels to reinforce the view that an alliance between a communist party and bourgeois political parties was appropriate in certain circumstances, particularly where the principal enemy was feudalism and its political representatives. Li argued that, in the Chinese case, both the propertied class (*youchan jieji*) and the proletariat were the victims of international oppression by imperialists and their agents in China, the warlords. However, he recognised that, while the propertied class (that is, the bourgeoisie) was, like the proletariat, oppressed and exploited by the feudal class, it in turn oppressed and exploited the proletariat; any alliance between the parties of the proletariat and bourgeoisie had therefore to recognise its temporary character and also its potential dangers. A communist party should therefore never lose sight of the importance of both maintaining its independence and encouraging the proletariat to a recognition of its own class interests. Li here quotes approvingly from the *Communist Manifesto*:

> But they [the German Communists] never cease, for a single instant, to instil into the working class the clearest possible recognition of the hostile antagonism between bourgeoisie and proletariat, in order that the German workers may straightway use, as so many weapons against the bourgeoisie, the social and political conditions that the bourgeoisie must necessarily introduce along with its supremacy, and in order that, after the fall of the reactionary classes in Germany, the fight against the bourgeoisie itself may immediately begin.[31]

The proposition that there be an alliance between the CCP and the GMD to overthrow warlord politics was, Li thus inferred, founded on Marxist theory. But a number of conditions attended any such alliance: that the CCP attempt to inculcate left-wing views into the various categories within the GMD membership (for Li, capitalists, intellectuals and workers); when the democratic revolution had matured, the CCP must lead the next stage, the proletarian revolution; the CCP must emphasise the work of organising the proletariat as a class; and the CCP must protect its own independence and avoid being influenced by the other party. For Li, the latter condition was the most important. At the Second Party Congress in 1922, he had advocated a "bloc without" strategy — that is, an alliance of the two parties at a party-to-party level. The independence of the CCP had to be protected, and he consequently vehemently opposed the excessive subordination of the CCP to the GMD; the CCP could not effectively perform its role of radicalising the proletariat or leading the subsequent stage of the revolution if its independence were compromised.

It was with these strongly held views in mind that Li travelled, in the summer of 1923, from Hunan to Shanghai to hold talks with Chen Duxiu on the question of cooperation between the CCP and GMD. It was not a happy meeting. According to Chinese sources, Li could not accept Chen's view (also held by Maring) that "all [Party] work should be done with the approval of the Guomindang".[32] Li believed that this position, now labelled a "Right deviationist" line by Party historians, hopelessly compromised the independence of the Party. According to Li's later recollection, on hearing Li's views, Chen stormed and railed at Li, banging the table and smashing a teacup, and threatening him with expulsion from the Party. It was a vain threat, for Li determined, on the basis of Chen's overbearing behaviour and their differences over policy, to leave the Party. He refused to participate in any further overt Party activities in Changsha, such as parades or demonstrations,[33] and on returning to Changsha he severed his connections with Chen and the Party centre and in the autumn of 1923 he left altogether the Party he had helped establish.[34]

This act of angry opposition to Chen's position on the united front is one of the very few aspects of Li's long political and philosophical career to draw criticism from historians and biographers in post-Mao China. While they concede the correctness of Li's opinion that the independence of the CCP had to be maintained, they chide him for not adopting appropriate methods of struggle with Party comrades. It is interesting, too, that this act of defiance — one which was to have such important personal and professional implications for Li — is only dealt with superficially, if at all, by most of his Chinese biographers; one perceives a sense of embarrassment that this admired figure of Chinese Marxism, one of the founding members of the CCP, should have departed the Party in a fit of pique.

Another perspective on Li's departure from the Party is provided by Professor Reng Wuxiong, an expert on the Party's early history.[35] In Reng's view, it would be a mistake to perceive Li's departure from the Party as the act of an isolated individual. Li was not alone in his opposition to the united front policies of Chen Duxiu, and his act of defiance was a reflection of the views held by a significant number of other Party members. Professor Reng also argues that the differences between Li and Chen were not only over the issue of cooperation with the GMD. Li was first and foremost a theorist who believed that the principal task of the Party during the early phase of its existence was the study and dissemination of Marxist theory in China. He consequently invested most of his time and effort in research, writing, translating and publishing in order to raise the theoretical level of the early Chinese Communist movement. Chen, on the other hand, was a "politician" (*zhengzhijia*), one who felt that the emphasis should be put on practical political action and struggle. This interpretation of the reasons for Li's departure from the Party is supported by a number of comments in Li's own later writings. In his 1928 essay, "The Revolution which China Needs", Li stated: "At that time I advocated that a great deal of study of Marxist theory be carried out within the Party, and I myself worked hard studying Marxist theory and Chinese economic conditions; I requested that we gain a thorough understanding of revolutionary theory. However, the others within the Party emphasised practical action, and put no emphasis on study, demanding rather, 'Marxist practitioners and not Marxist theorists'." Indeed, after the Party's Second Congress in 1922, Li quit his post as Director of the Propaganda Department and became an ordinary Party member so that he could concentrate his attention and energies on study and writing. According to Song Jingming, one of China's foremost authorities on Li Da's life and writings, this difference over the degree of emphasis to accord to theoretical as opposed to practical work was as important to Li's decision to quit the Party as the disagreement over the united front policy.[36]

The Non-Party True Believer

Li's departure from the Party had the potential to drastically alter the context within which he worked and wrote, freeing him from the strict discipline which had become a hallmark of communist parties of the Bolshevik persuasion. Here, for the first time in a number of years, Li was a free agent, at liberty (should he so choose) to defy Party pressures to conform to orthodox interpretations of Marxist theory and philosophy; he could think, say and write what he liked, mindless of disapproval or censure from Party authorities. Moreover, he was no longer, in any organisational sense, obliged to support the Party in its operational work or accept tasks from it. Other founding members of the Party, such as Chen Gongbo and Zhou Fohai, were to leave the Party and go over to the GMD; Liu Renjing was to become a Trotskyist. Yet Li Da's response to his resignation from the Party was quite different, and it is one of the great enigmas of his political and philosophical career that, in his long period of self-imposed exile from the Party (he did not rejoin until 1949), he continued — often at considerable inconvenience and danger to himself — to write and publish works of Marxist theory of the most unimpeachable orthodoxy, to recruit among his students for the Party, to accept work and instructions from the Party, and to maintain good relations with some within its leadership, including Mao Zedong. In fact, despite Dong Biwu's inaccurate categorisation of Li in 1937 as "now a liberal who became a professor",[37] Li remained a committed Marxist in his theoretical views, and to a large extent also in practice.

This firm commitment to Marxism while no longer a formal member of the CCP provides an important insight into Li's character. From his conversion to Marxism in 1918-19, his commitment was first and foremost to the integrity of Marxism, and particularly its integrity as a theoretical system. It is significant that one of the issues over which he quarrelled with Chen Duxiu was the independence of the CCP, for Chen's "Right deviationist" views were a threat, not only to the Party as an organisational structure, but to its capacity to develop and disseminate Marxist theory free from the restrictions and impediments which Chen's conception of the united front made likely. This commitment to the integrity of Marxism as a theoretical system remained a driving force behind Li's subsequent career for, while he never completely abandoned political action, he regarded teaching, writing and translation as the media through which he could most effectively serve the cause of revolution in China, and all evidence points to the orthodox character of the content of his lectures, books and articles on Marxist theory. Indeed, being outside the Party paradoxically made it possible for Li to remain more orthodox, more of a purist, than had he remained within it; for he was not constrained to tailor his interpretations of Marxism to the shifting tide of Party policy. It is thus possible to perceive in his writings after 1923 a broader and firmer grasp of Marxism, one less immediately tied to the concerns of Party policy and strategy, than is evident in the writings of many of his Party contemporaries. While this characteristic of his work has led to criticisms that he failed to "Sinify" Marxism,[38] his philosophical stature in contemporary China rests, in large part, on the fact that his philosophical writings do engage extremely abstract and complex issues of theory which transcended the particular strategic and tactical concerns of the Party.

Life Outside the Party: The "Fellow Traveller"

While Li Da had cut his links with the Party centre, he continued to work with the Party organisation in Hunan, and continued to research and propagate Marxist theory. He also frequently recommended progressive students for membership of the Party to the Changsha Party authorities. During this period, he published his first major book on Marxist theory. Titled *Xiandai shehuixue* (Contemporary Sociology), this volume was published in June 1926, and comprised eighteen chapters and some 170,000 characters. *Contemporary Sociology* represents a compilation of lectures written by Li in the previous three years for delivery at the Hunan Self-Study University and Hunan University, and subsequently revised for publication. Written in the classical *wenyan* style, it addresses the fundamental principles of the materialist conception of history and scientific socialism; it examines the world revolution and the revolution in China, and critiques various anti-Marxist trends of thought. We will return to a more detailed consideration of the contents of this important volume in Chapter 4, for it provides useful insights, not only into Li Da's understanding of Marxist theory and philosophy, but also the extent to which the revolutionary movement in China did have access to Marxist theory; it casts doubt on the assumption that the early Communist movement in China was largely isolated from the theoretical currents and developments of mainstream Marxism, and was consequently theoretically rather immature. For the moment, it suffices to note that the publication of *Contemporary Sociology* identified Li Da as one of the foremost Marxist philosophers in China, and the book enjoyed wide popularity amongst the ranks of the revolutionaries.[39] Indeed, Chinese commentators have described it as the first independently created systematic theoretical work in the history of the development of Marxist philosophy in China.[40] The book's publication also made Li Da more vulnerable to attack from his political enemies, particularly those within the GMD, and he was listed in 1928 on the Hunan register of wanted criminals; similarly, in the same year, the criminal list for his hometown of Lingling listed his name, and mentioned *Contemporary Sociology* as his major publication and the propaganda use to which this volume was being put.[41]

In October 1926, following the occupation of Wuhan by the Northern Expeditionary Forces, Li travelled to Wuhan from Changsha where he served as chairperson of the Editorial Committee of the Military and General Political Department, and also lectured on social science at the Military and Political College of which he was the principal. In the spring of 1927, he was also appointed to a committee to advise on questions concerning the peasantry. Mao Zedong subsequently asked Li Da to return to Changsha to make preparations for the establishment of a Provincial Party School whose task would be the training of cadres for participation in the agrarian revolution. However, the events of 1927, culminating in the breach between the Left GMD and the CCP in Wuhan and the subsequent massacre of CCP members and supporters, prevented the completion of this project. Li Da was forced to flee, firstly to Lingling, but following news that the Hunan provincial authorities were seeking his arrest, he was forced into hiding, and he subsequently fled, first to Wuchang where he narrowly avoided execution when the military police surrounded Wuchang's Zhongshan University (where Li had been teaching) and began killing revolutionary teachers, and in the winter of 1927 moving secretly to Shanghai.

For the next few years, Li Da remained in Shanghai, and despite the great personal danger that attended any involvement in left-wing activities, he remained active in the dissemination of Marxist theory through his writing, translating, publication and teaching activities. In 1928, with Deng Chumin and others, he established the Kunlun Publishing House which published numerous works of Marxist theory, as well as many of Li's own translations. In 1929, he published *Zhongguo chanye geming gaiguan* (A Survey of China's Revolution in Property), *Shehui zhi jichu zhishi* (Fundamental Knowledge of Society) and *Minzu wenti* (The Nationality Problem). Between 1928 and 1930 he translated Marx's *A Contribution to the Critique of Political Economy*, Hozumi Shigeto's *Outline of Jurisprudence*, A. Thalheimer's *The Modern Worldview*, Sugiyama Sakae's *A Survey of Social Science*, Kawakami Hajime's *The Fundamental Theories of Marxist Economics* (Li Da translated the section entitled "The Philosophical Basis of Marxism"), Luppol's *Basic Problems of Theory and Practice in Social Science* and Kawanishi Taichirō's *Theories on the Agricultural Question*, and other works. Li's Chinese biographers note, that Li Da's purpose in translating these works into Chinese, as revealed in his translator's prefaces and postscripts, was "to provide the broad masses with a weapon with which to comprehend the Chinese revolution".[42]

In 1930, through an introduction by the secretary of the left-wing League of Social Scientists, Zhang Qingfu (who was an underground member of the CCP), Li gained a teaching position at the Shanghai Institute of Law and Politics, and in 1931, again through the good offices of Zhang Qingfu, he also held the position of departmental head of the Sociology Department of Jinan University. In these teaching positions, he continued to lecture on Marxist philosophy and political economy, and to analyse problems of the Chinese revolution. His lectures drew large audiences, with the lecture halls in which he lectured frequently filled to overflowing; in this way he influenced a number of young intellectuals to join the revolution. As a result, he became the target of right-wing attack. His house was searched and he was set upon after one lecture by right-wing agents, resulting in a broken shoulder and collar bone; he was subsequently hospitalised for seven weeks. This setback did not deter Li, however, and he continued to use his classes as a medium for spreading the revolutionary message. Eventually, in February 1932, under the pretext of moving the university to another location, Li was dismissed, and his position in Shanghai became impossible. In May of that year, and at the instigation of the CCP, he moved to Taishan, in Shandong province, where he joined with a number of other professors to teach the former warlord, Feng Yuxiang, together with his wife and members of his study group. Li spoke to them of Leninism, the materialist conception of history, revolution, political economy and the Chinese and external situation. Feng recorded in his diary that these lectures filled him with happiness and astonishment that scholars of Li Da's erudition should come to talk with him of the most recent theories of revolution.[43] Li's Chinese biographer suggests that Li's lectures had a major impact on Feng's subsequent political activities,[44] but the wily and eclectic Feng was also reading works on Christianity at the time Li lectured on Marxism-Leninism and revolutionary theory.[45]

The Beiping Years

In August 1932, Li Da moved to Beiping. From then until June 1937, he taught at the Institute of Law and Commerce at Beiping University, where he held the post of departmental head of the Department of Economics. He remained under surveillance by the Beiping GMD military authorities, but he was protected by the CCP underground and by progressive teachers and students. Despite this rather threatening environment, he continued to research, write and lecture on questions of Marxist philosophy and economic theory. Indeed, this five-year period was to be the most important and prolific period in Li's lengthy career as an author, and the books and articles he wrote at this time were to establish his reputation as one of China's pre-eminent left-wing philosophers and social scientists. His translations from this period, especially of the "new philosophy" emanating from the Soviet Union, were also to have an important impact on the dissemination of orthodox Marxist philosophy within China.

The first of Li's books from this Beiping period was *Jingjixue dagang* (An Outline of Economic Theory), which was published by the Institute of Law and Commerce in 1935. Li posted a copy of the book to Mao, who subsequently recommended it to theoretical circles in Yan'an. Mao later claimed to have read the book "three times, and I intend to read it ten times".[46] In the "Preface" to this volume, Li made it clear that his purpose in writing a book on economic theory was not just an academic one, but to promote China's economic development. He was thus at pains to establish the "particular laws of development of the Chinese economy".[47] The three processes he discerned at work in China's contemporary economy were the intervention and impact of imperialism, the decline in national capital and the collapse of feudal agriculture. Given the predations of international imperialism, how should China respond? Li's response was that the problem of the oppression and bankruptcy of the Chinese economy could not be solved by economic means alone; rather, Li's analysis led to a political conclusion, one in which China's people must struggle to seek liberation and economic survival.

As well as another economics text on currency, Li also wrote two books dealing with problems of Marxist philosophy and social theory, *Shehui jinhua shi* (A History of the Evolution of Society) and *Shehuixue dagang* (Elements of Sociology). The latter massive tome is, it could be argued, the most important text on Marxist philosophy to have been written by a Chinese philosopher. It not only provided a comprehensive coverage of dialectical and historical materialism, it did so from the perspective of the orthodoxy which had emerged in the Soviet Union following the overthrow of the Deborinite school of philosophy in 1931. *Elements of Sociology* thus provided Marxists in China with detailed information on the current line on Marxist philosophy within the international communist movement. The book was to have a significant impact on the development of Marxist philosophy in China, both directly and through the influence it was to have (along with a number of other influential philosophical texts) on the development of Mao Zedong's philosophical thought in 1936–37.[48] The importance of this text has been recognised by the editors of Li Da's writings, for *Elements of Sociology* now occupies the entire second volume of *Li Da Wenji* (Collected Writings of Li Da). We will return, in Chapters 6, 7 and 8, to a detailed evaluation of the sources, content and influence of *Elements of Sociology*, for this philosophical text can tell us much about the origins, development and degree of orthodoxy of the philosophical dimensions of Marxist philosophy in China. As well as being heavily involved in researching and writing on Marxist theory and philosophy, Li also continued to engage in political activities instigated by the CCP. In January 1933, he again went to see Feng Yuxiang in an attempt to persuade him to enter an alliance with the CCP to resist Japan.

The Anti-Japanese War

After the invasion of China in July 1937, Li was obliged to move to Guilin to seek employment at Guangxi University. However, he was not able to take up a teaching post until his former superior at the Beiping Legal and Commercial Institute, Bai Pengfei, became vice-chancellor of Guangxi University in the spring of 1938. He then commenced teaching and functioned as the head of the Department of Economics, and continued to lecture on Marxist philosophy and economic theory. In January 1939, Li received an invitation from Feng Yuxiang to again give lectures on Marxist philosophy to Feng and the members of his study group. This time, Li, along with members of the CCP within Feng's study group, were able to persuade Feng to cooperate with the CCP. In September 1939, Li returned to Guilin expecting to pick up his teaching duties, only to discover that Bai Pengfei had been dismissed and that Li himself was now without work. However, Zhou Enlai sent a message of support and some economic assistance to Li Da, and Li gave classes to cadres of the Guilin office of the CCP's Eighth Route Army.

In the autumn of 1940, Li Da took up a teaching post at Zhongshan University in Guangdong province, but in July of 1941, the GMD Education Department sacked him and, being without employment, he had no option but to return to his hometown. He there continued to research and write until July of 1944, when Lingling county was overrun by the Japanese. Li Da was forced to hide from the Japanese army, and he fled into the mountains where he became a victim of banditry, all of his drafts of work from this period and his letters from Mao Zedong being stolen. Only with the surrender of Japan was he able to return to his hometown. In February 1946, Li established a primary school there, which he named after his father, Li Furen. Almost singlehandedly, and without resources of any kind, Li Da got the Furen primary school going, and acted as its principal. In this modest establishment of some seventy students in five grades, Li put into practice his philosophy of education. He believed that teachers and students were equal, and he eschewed compulsion and punishment in favour of patience and persuasion; his students were also encouraged to participate in classroom discussions.[49]

Li Rejoins the Communist Party

In the spring of 1947, through the good offices of the CCP underground organisation in Hunan, Li gained a teaching position in the Law Department of Hunan University. Throughout this period, he was kept under surveillance by the GMD authorities, his lectures monitored, his visitors recorded and his name placed on a blacklist. However, Li continued to lecture on sociology and legal theory from a Marxist perspective, and to meet young students in his own home to persuade them to participate in revolutionary struggle. It was also during this period that, despite serious health problems,[50] he completed *Falixue dagang* (Outline of Jurisprudence), in which he employed a Marxist standpoint to analyse the law. Law, he asserted, had to be perceived from a class perspective, for it was employed by the dominant class to protect prevailing property relations.

The period from November 1948 to April 1949 brought Li Da directly into the attempts by the CCP's Hunanese underground organisation to persuade General Cheng Qian, at that time commander of the GMD's Headquarters for the Pacification of the Region, to capitulate to the communists. Li Da was asked by the CCP to persuade Cheng Qian to go over to the communists, a venture which was not without great personal risk to Li. General Cheng requested Li to report to Mao Zedong on the situation in Hunan, and on Cheng's desire to see a peaceful liberation of the province. The strategy was ultimately successful insofar as Cheng and the governor of Hunan, Cheng Mingren, did go over to the communists, although the governor appointed to replace him did resist militarily the southward advance of Lin Biao's forces.

In 1948 Mao Zedong had sent word via the CCP's Hunanese underground organisation to invite Li Da to Beijing, and on 16 April 1949, Li left Changsha and travelled secretly via Hong Kong, arriving in Beijing on 14 May. There he met with Mao Zedong, Liu Shaoqi, Zhou Enlai, Zhu De and other Party leaders. He talked late into the night with Mao Zedong, reporting on the situation in Hunan and re-establishing his old friendship with Mao. Because of his support for the CCP over many years, even though not formally a member, Li was invited to rejoin the Party, with Mao Zedong, Liu Shaoqi, Li Weihan and others testifying as to his suitability for Party membership (*lishi zhengmingren*), and Liu Shaoqi acting as his sponsor (*jieshaoren*). In December 1949, Li Da was readmitted to the Party that he had left some twenty-six years before.

Philosophy and Politics in Post-Liberation China

After the establishment of the People's Republic of China, Li Da was heavily involved in both educational and political work. He was, at various times, the deputy principal of the Central Party Political and Legal School, and the vice-chancellor of Hunan and Wuhan Universities. He was a delegate to the First, Second and Third National People's Congresses, and was a member of the Standing Committee of the Third National People's Congress; he was also a delegate to the Eighth Party Congress of the CCP. He was elected a member of the Philosophy and Social Science Department of China's Academy of Science, and he was the president of China's Philosophical Association.

It is clear, however, that Li did not rise to the political status which he might have attained had he not left the Party over a policy dispute in 1923. By doing so, Li had contravened the fundamental principle of intra-Party discipline which was the hallmark of a Leninist party such as the CCP. And while he performed sterling service for the Party as a "fellow traveller" between 1923 and 1949, there can be no doubt that his angry departure over the issue of the united front policy was to cost him dearly in political terms. The tough and independent streak in Li's character made the unquestioning discipline of the Party a difficult proposition, and even after his readmission to the Party his outspoken manner saw him at odds with those with far greater power in the Party than Li could ever hope to possess; this propensity was eventually to cost him dearly. By the same token, although there can be no doubt that Li was of an uncompromising nature, his work on Marxist philosophy and social theory, as we will have cause to note frequently as our analysis unfolds, never strayed far from orthodoxy, as Li interpreted this. And if we are to remember Li for anything, it is his major contribution to the dissemination in China of a form of Marxist philosophy and social theory which carried with it strong traces of orthodoxy. Similarly, after Liberation, Li worked hard to elaborate the philosophical thought of Mao Zedong as the new orthodoxy, one which itself had deep roots in the orthodox Soviet Marxist philosophy of the early-1930s which Li had been partly instrumental in introducing to Mao. Yet, even here, Li retained a degree of critical independence, and shortly before his death he was to publicly oppose Lin Biao's theory of Mao Zedong Thought as the ultimate pinnacle of Marxism-Leninism. What this and his earlier transgressions of Party discipline suggest is that Li argued for his perception of orthodoxy, not just because it was orthodoxy, but because Li believed it to be true. In circumstances where a new (and from Li's perspective, false) orthodoxy emerged, as was the case with the onset of the Cultural Revolution, Li had no hesitation in opposing it, even at the risk of considerable personal hardship and danger.

Although in poor health during the 1950s and early 1960s as a result of recurring stomach troubles and diabetes, he kept up a gruelling regime of research, writing and lecturing. His important philosophical works from the early 1950s include explanatory guides to Mao Zedong's "On Practice" and "On Contradiction" (subsequently published as a single volume).[51] In February 1953, Li Da assumed the position of vice-chancellor of Wuhan University, a post he was to hold until his death in August 1966, and it was here that he was to work on the many articles and books on philosophy which constitute his post-Liberation corpus. The Philosophy Department at Wuhan University was, under his leadership, to become one of the most influential centres for the study of Marxist philosophy in China. In 1954–55 Li became involved in the anti-Hu Shi campaign and wrote a book and a number of articles criticising Hu Shi's philosophy of pragmatism. Li Da's Chinese biographer Wang

Jionghua is critical of this episode in his philosophical career, for Li failed, Wang argues, to take account of the positive significance of Hu's introduction of pragmatism to China and his positive contribution to the New Culture Movement during the May Fourth period. Wang suggests that Li's critique suffered from "arbitrariness" (*duduanzhuyi*), showing manifestations of the politicisation of philosophy which Li absorbed from the Soviet philosophy of the 1930s. Li was to lend his pen to other such attacks on philosophical and intellectual figures, especially during the Hundred Flowers period of 1957, an action which his biographer deems "inappropriate".[52] We will return to a consideration of these controversial episodes in Li's life in Chapter 10.

Wang Jionghua is also critical of Li's initial support for the Great Leap Forward of 1958, and his approval of the policy of sending teachers and students to the countryside (*xiaxiang*) to engage in labour. Li personally went with the staff and students of Wuhan University's Philosophy Department to Hubei's Hongan county, where he lived and worked. At that time, Wang asserts, Li had not perceived the leftist errors of Mao and the Party. However, it appears that this stint in the countryside convinced Li that Mao was placing too much emphasis on the subjective dynamism of the masses and was moving towards communist goals too quickly. In October of 1958, during Mao's inspection tour of Hubei province, Li met with the Chairman and they engaged in an evening of spirited philosophical debate which bore on the issue of the Great Leap Forward. The slogan "dare to think, dare to speak, and dare to do" (*gan xiang, gan shuo, gan gan*) was not in itself inappropriate, Li suggested to Mao. However, like all things, this slogan had two aspects: if the slogan suggested developing the subjective dynamism of the people, that was entirely rational; but if it suggested that what one wanted to achieve could be achieved immediately, then that was unscientific. Was the slogan to be affirmed? Li and Mao then proceded to debate the problem of affirmation and negation in relation to the question of the role of human subjective dynamism. Mao reminded Li of the Long March, and what had been achieved through the subjective dynamism of the Red Army. Li responded that he did not believe that subjective dynamism should be perceived as that extensive, and that to affirm the slogan of the Great Leap Forward was to imply that the subjective dynamism of the people was limitless, a mistake in Li's view. "The development of the subjective dynamism of humans cannot be divorced from definite conditions ... human subjective dynamism is not limitless," Li warned Mao.[53] Li went on to suggest that the Chairman was suffering from a fever of the brain (that is, was getting carried away), and that this would lead to disaster for China. Although agitated by Li's words, Mao controlled himself, but retorted: "You say I have a fever, but I say you have a fever, one of a 100 degrees. At the

Chengdu Conference, I said that the brain needs to be both hot and cold."[54]

Li's overt disagreement with Mao over the Great Leap Forward and his subsequent support for Peng Dehuai, disgraced at the Lushan Plenum of 1959, is further evidence of Li's uncompromising character. It is also symptomatic of Mao's high regard for Li, both as a philosopher and as an old and trusted comrade, that his reaction to Li's views on the Great Leap Forward was as restrained as it was. Indeed, at about this time, Mao referred glowingly to Li as the "Lu Xun of the world of theory", high praise indeed, and he continued to recommend, read and annotate works by Li.

Li was to meet with Mao again in August 1961. In a long conversation, Mao reaffirmed his view that Li Da's *Elements of Sociology* was the first Marxist text on philosophy to have been written by a Chinese, and that it had had a major impact, Mao himself reading it ten times and writing many annotations on it. He suggested to Li that *Elements of Sociology* had contemporary significance, and that it should be revised and republished. Li responded that this was a mammoth task and that his health may not allow him to undertake it. Mao responded that Li could use research assistants within his own Philosophy Department to assist him with this task. Li consequently assembled a group of research assistants under Tao Delin, the present vice-chancellor of Wuhan University, and divided the work of revision among them. The political and philosophical significance of this project will be considered in Chapter 10.

The Final Chapter

During the early 1960s, Li was in very poor health and obliged to take regular medication and have daily injections.[55] Despite his failing health, Li continued to work hard on the draft of *Makesizhuyi zhexue dagang* (Elements of Marxist Philosophy), and in the autumn of 1962, a preliminary draft of the first volume of this work, *Weiwubianzhengfa dagang* (Elements of Dialectical Materialism), was completed and used by the students in Wuhan University's Philosophy Department. This volume went through a series of drafts and became a completed book in 1965. This volume persisted with the logical structure of *Elements of Sociology*, but introduced new theoretical content, in particular the contributions which Mao Zedong Thought had made to Marxist philosophy. A hundred draft copies of the book were printed and sent to Mao Zedong, Zhou Enlai, Liu Shaoqi and other Party leaders for comment. Unfortunately, the Cultural Revolution intervened, and it was only after the overthrow of the "Gang of Four" in 1976 that Li Da's personal assistant, Tao Delin, was able to make the necessary revisions to the book envisaged by Li, and it was eventually published in May 1978, some twelve years after Li's death. However, Li was not able to complete the ambitious project to thoroughly revise and expand *Elements of Sociology* to incorporate developments in Marxist philosophy, and only the first volume of this work was ever published.

In March 1966, Li Da responded to Lin Biao's theory that Mao Zedong Thought was the pinnacle of Marxist-Leninist theory in characteristically forthright manner. On being informed — possibly rather nervously — by one of his research assistants that this theory originated from Vice Chairman Lin, Li responded:

> I realise that, and I don't agree! This notion of a 'pinnacle' is unscientific, and does not conform to dialectics. Marxism-Leninism is developmental, and so is Mao Zedong Thought. If you compare them to a pinnacle, then there is no direction in which they can develop from there. How can Marxism-Leninism have a 'pinnacle'? I can't agree with violations of dialectics, regardless of who utters it.[56]

It was this sort of indiscrete utterance, his criticisms of Mao during the Great Leap Forward, and his earlier breach with the Party in 1923, which put him at odds with the Cultural Revolutionary authorities, particularly Lin Biao and Kang Sheng. He was branded a "criminal element", "traitor" and "landlord element", and his so-called "anti-Party, anti-socialist, anti-Mao Zedong Thought" research material and papers picked over, page by page, for evidence of his transgressions.[57] Wuhan University split into two Red Guard factions, the "Dragon" and the "Tiger" factions; membership of these factions was largely determined by support for or opposition to Li Da. The "Tiger" faction, which was the radical faction opposed to Li, ultimately prevailed, and at least half of the members of the Philosophy Department were branded the "Black Gang" for their support for Li.[58] In the face of these bitter attacks and criticisms, Li remained defiant, adamant that he was a loyal Party member, and a firm believer in Mao Zedong Thought. On June 1 1966 (August according to Wang Jionghua), Li Da was expelled from the Party, an illegal act according to post-1978 commentaries on his life.

Li had been in very poor health for many years with serious problems (diabetes, ulcers and a stroke) which required constant medication. The vilification and abuse which he suffered in the first half of 1966 no doubt made this medical condition worse. However, his enemies, and in particular Lin Biao, were to show him no mercy, and despite Li petitioning Mao by letter to save his life (*jiuming*), his medication was stopped.[59] He died in hospital, without being provided with the appropriate medical treatment, on 24 August 1966. According to Wang Jionghua, Mao saw Li's *jiuming* on 10 August, a fortnight before Li's death. Mao apparently took no other action other than to direct it to Wang Renzhong, then leader of Hubei province, for his attention. Mao was later (some time after the Ninth Party Congress) to concede that Li Da had been correct in his opposition to Lin Biao's theory of Mao Zedong Thought as the "pinnacle" of Marxism-Leninism.[60] In January 1974, a commemorative service was held by staff and students of Wuhan University to honour Li's memory, and in November 1980, Li Da was rehabilitated, the verdict of the Cultural Revolution overturned and his Party membership posthumously restored.[61]

Since 1978, Li Da has been honoured in China as one of the most outstanding Chinese Marxist philosophers and theorists of the twentieth century. Numerous articles and books have been written analysing his contribution to the dissemination of Marxist philosophy and social theory in China, the structure and characteristics of his philosophical thought and his role in the formation of the CCP. Many of his writings were reissued in the 1980s in the four-volume *Li Da wenji* (Collected Writings of Li Da) and in other volumes. The brief biography in the *Li Da wenji* sums up his life in the following appropriate style:

> Comrade Li Da was one of the earliest to pioneer the dissemination of Marxism in China, and one of the founders of the Chinese Communist Party. For over a half a century, and to the very end of his life, he persevered in the study and spread of Marxism. Not only did he attain a deep mastery in Marxist philosophy, economics and social science, in the areas of jurisprudence, the study of currrency, history and so on, he also made significant achievements. His theoretical activities were closely attuned to the pulse of the Chinese revolution; and his huge corpus of writings reflects half a century of Chinese intellectual history, and is a valuable legacy. He is an influential figure in the history of culture in contemporary China. A study of his works is essential in order to attain a deep understanding of the dissemination of Marxism in China, the history of the development of intellectual thought in our country, including the early establishment of theory in the history of our Party. Because of the historical conditions and his own limitations and personal characteristics, his writings are sometimes not mature, and do contain imprecisions and errors. However, his achievements and shortcomings, contributions and failures, are in themselves a genuine reflection of the tortuous progress described by the path of revolution, and in this too lies the value of his writings.[62]

In subsequent chapters, we will look in some detail at Li Da's contribution to the introduction and dissemination of Marxist philosophy and social theory in China. We will pay particular attention to the origins, content and development of Li Da's Marxism, and by so doing, raise broader questions about the nature of Marxism in China. For it is often suggested in Western accounts that Marxism in China is an aberrant form of Marxism, one which owes far more to the influence of the Chinese tradition and the contemporary realities of the Chinese revolutionary context than it does to mainstream and orthodox forms of Marxism, particularly those emanating from Europe and the Soviet Union. Marxism in China, from this perspective, is only distantly related to "orthodox" Marxism. This stubborn resistance to taking seriously the Marxist-Leninist origins of Marxism in China has even descended, in some accounts, to an Orientalist disinclination to accept that the Chinese could possibly comprehend Marxism, a theory originating in Europe.[63]

Our evaluation of Li Da's Marxism and the important role he played in introducing Marxist philosophy and social theory to China will demonstrate that such accounts are quite misleading. Li Da was a Marxist to his bootstraps, and no slouch as a philosopher and theorist. He had a firm grasp of Marxist philosophy and theory and worked hard to ensure that Marxism in China had its roots firmly embedded in the soil of orthodox European and Soviet Marxism. We will be tracing a number of major themes through Li Da's writings to demonstrate this proposition. The first of these is the philosophical dimension of Marxism, often referred to as dialectical materialism; the second is an important dimension of Marxism's social theory, namely its aetiology of social change (in particular, the relationship between economic base and superstructure). Both of these themes have been employed by critiques of Marxism in China to demonstrate its heterodoxy, and they therefore constitute a significant medium for evaluating its orthodoxy.

In the next chapter, we turn to a brief construction of the genealogy of the concepts and issues in Marxist philosophy and social theory which we will explore in Li Da's writings. This exercise will provide us with a compass to navigate Li's vast corpus, for we have no intention of addressing the entirety of issues considered by Li in his long and very productive intellectual life; our purpose is a more limited one, and we will be restricting our gaze to these central themes in Marxist theory and Li's usage of them. Our genealogical detour will also create the foundation on which will be constructed judgments regarding the nature and orthodoxy of Li Da's Marxism, and of Marxism in China more generally.

Notes

1. There is almost no mention of Li Da in the only major study of the philosophical debates over dialectical materialism in China during the 1930s. See

Werner Meissner, *Philosophy and Politics in China: The Controversy Over Dialectical Materialism in the 1930s* (London: Hurst and Company, 1990). Similarly, Li Da is not mentioned at all in Arif Dirlik's otherwise superb *Revolution and History: Origins of Marxist Historiography in China, 1919–1937* (Berkeley: University of California Press, 1978), although he is mentioned in Dirlik's *The Origins of Chinese Communism* (New York: Oxford University Press, 1989). Michael Y.L. Luk refers in passing to Li Da as a theorist "of first-rate importance" and "extremely important in helping to outline the initial framework of the party's ideology"; see *The Origins of Chinese Bolshevism: An Ideology in the Making, 1920–1928* (Hong Kong: Oxford University Press, 1990), pp. 58, 232. For short references to Li Da in English, see Howard L. Boorman and Richard C. Howard, *Biographical Dictionary of Republican China* (New York and London: Columbia University Press, 1968), Volume II; also O. Briere, *Fifty Years of Chinese Philosophy, 1898–1948* (New York: Praeger, 1965).

2. Li Da tongzhi shengping shilue" (A Biographical Sketch of Comrade Li Da), *Li Da wenji* (Beijing: Renmin chubanshe, 1980), pp. 3–20; Wang Jionghua, "Li Da: yi wei Puluomixiusishi bohuozhe" (Li Da: A Prometheus Who Sowed Fire), in Li Zhenxia (ed.), *Dangdai Zhongguo shizhe* (Ten Philosophers from Contemporary China) (Beijing: Huaxia chubanshe, 1991), pp. 1–49; Wang Jionghua, *Li Da yu Makesizhuyi zhexue zai Zhongguo* (Li Da and Marxist Philosophy in China) (Hubei: Huazhong ligong daxue chubanshe, 1988); Tao Delin et al., "Li Da yijiusijiu nianqian lilun huodong ji zhuzuo biannian" (The pre-1949 Theoretical Activities of Li Da and a Chronicle of His Works), in *Zhongguo zhexue*, Vol. I (1979), pp. 345–72; and Song Jingming, *Li Da zhuanji* (The Life of Li Da) (Hubei: Hubei renmin chubanshe, 1986).

3. Including Chen Zuhua, Tan Zhen, Song Jingming, Wang Jionghua, Duan Qixian and Yuan Jinxiang.

4. In particular, Song Jingming and Wang Jionghua. For a list of their publications on Li Da, see the Bibliography.

5. Ye Yonglie, *Hongse de qidian* (Red Beginnings) (Shanghai: Shanghai renmin chubanshe, 1991), p. 124.

6. Li Da, "Yanzhe shiyue geming de daolu qianjin" (Forward Along the Road of the October Revolution), *Zhongguo qingnian*, Nos 13–14 (1961).

7. Arif Dirlik, *The Origins of Chinese Communism*.

8. See Mao's reference to Kropotkin and Marx in "The Great Union of the Popular Masses", in Stuart R. Schram (ed.), *Mao's Road to Power: Revolutionary Writings, 1912–1949: Volume I, The Pre-Marxist Period, 1912–1920* (Armonk, New York: M.E. Sharpe, 1992), p. 380.

9. Li Da, "Yanzhe shiyue geming de daolu qianjin".

10. These articles can be found in Volume I of *Li Da wenji*.

11. For further details on Li Da's activities at the time of the founding of the CCP, see Li Qiju, "Zhongguo gongchandang chuangshiren zhi yi: Li Da de jiandang huodong" (One of the Founders of the Chinese Communist Party: Li Da's Party Building Activities), *Henan shifan daxue*, No. 2 (1981).

12. The actual founding of the Chinese Communist Party is given by Li as occurring in August 1920. See Li Da, "Qiyi huiyi" (Reminiscences of the First of July), *Qiyi yuekan*, No. 1 (1958), pp. 11–12. See also Tony Saich, *The Origins of the*

First United Front in China: The Role of Sneevliet (alias Maring) (Leiden: E.J. Brill, 1991), Vol. I, p. 46.

13. In a letter to Cai Hesen, 21 January 1921; *Mao Zedong shuxin xuanji* (Selected correspondence of Mao Zedong) (Beijing: Renmin chubanshe, 1983), pp. 15–16.

14. Li's biography in *Li Da wenji*, p. 5, gives the discontinuation of *Gongchandang* as "after the Second Congress" (1922). However, see Saich, *The Origins of the First United Front in China*, p. 51. See also Li Da, "Zhongguo gongchandang de faqi he diyici, dierci daibiao dahui jingguo de huiyi" (Reminiscences on the initial period of the Chinese Communist Party and the First and the Second Party Congresses), *Yida Qianhou* (Beijing: Renmin chubanshe, 1980), Vol. 2, pp. 6–18.

15. See Li Siju, Wang Jionghua and Zhang Dixian (eds), *Makesizhuyi zhexue zai Zhongguo* (Marxist philosophy in China) (Shanghai: Renmin chubanshe, 1990), p. 90. See also Li Da, "Li Da zizhuan (jielu)" (Autobiography of Li Da (extracts)), in *Hunan dangshi renwu zhuanji cailiao xuanpian* (Selected biographical materials on persons in the history of the Hunan Communist Party) (Hunan: Zhong gong Hunansheng weidangshi cailiao zhengji yanjiu weiyuanhui, 1987), Vol. 2, pp. 1–11.

16. Sun Qinan and Li Shizhen, *Mao Zedong yu mingren* (Mao Zedong and the famous) (Jiangsu: Jiangsu renmin chubanshe, 1993), Vol. 1, p. 315.

17. Shao Weizheng, "The First National Congress of the Communist Party of China: A verification of the date of convocation and the number of participants", *Social Sciences in China*, Vol. 1, No. 1 (March 1980), pp. 116–18.

18. *Li Da wenji*, Vol. 1, p. 5; also Saich, *The Origins of the First United Front in China*, p. 68.

19. Indeed, the first session of the Second Congress was held at Li Da's family home. Unable to find it, Mao Zedong did not participate in the Congress. See Sun Qinan, "Mao Zedong yu Li Da jaiowang de qianqianhouhou" (The ins and outs of the relationship between Mao Zedong and Li Da), *Qilian xuekan*, No. 4 (1992), p. 80.

20. *Xin shidai* commenced publication on 15 April 1923. Its first issue carried an article by Mao Zedong entitled "Waili, junfa yu geming" (External forces, the warlords and revolution). This text is reproduced in *Mao Zedong wenji* (Collected writings of Mao Zedong) (Beijing: Renmin chubanshe, 1993), Vol. 1, pp. 10–14.

21. Sun Qinan and Li Shizhen, *Mao Zedong yu mingren*, p. 316.

22. *Li Da wenji*, Vol. I, p. 9.

23. For a more detailed summary and analysis of this important essay, see Chapter 3.

24. *Li Da wenji*, Vol. I, p. 37.

25. Ibid., pp. 202–15. See Chapter 3.

26. For extracts of this debate, see Hélène Carrère d'Encausse and Stuart R. Schram (eds), *Marxism and Asia: An Introduction with Readings* (London:Allen Lane, The Penguin Press, 1969), pp. 149–67.

27. V.I. Lenin, *Lenin on the National and Colonial Questions: Three Articles* (Peking: Foreign Languages Press, 1967), p. 27.

28. See Carrère d'Encausse and Schram (eds), *Marxism and Asia*, pp. 150–52.

29. Ibid., 164–65.

30. See Michael William, "Sneevliet and the Birth of Asian Communism", *New Left Review*, No. 123 (September–October 1980).

31. *Li Da wenji*, Vol. I, pp. 211–12; the translation here is from Karl Marx, *The Revolutions* of 1848 (Harmondsworth: Penguin, 1973), p. 98.

32. Party History Research Centre of the Central Committee of the Chinese Communist Party, *History of the Chinese Communist Party — A Chronology of Events (1919–1990)* (Beijing: Foreign Languages Press, 1991), p. 20. Li Da's relations with Sneevliet are also said to have been characterised by a "marked lack of cordiality". See Saich, *The Origins of the First United Front in China*, Vol. 1, pp. 58–59, also pp. 62, 73.

33. Wang Jionghua, "Li Da", in *Dangdai Zhongguo shizhe*, p. 7.

34. Edgar Snow states that Li left the Party during the 1927 repression. See *Red Star over China* (Harmondsworth: Penguin, rev. edn, 1972), p. 546. The date of Li's actual departure from the Party is complicated by the conflicting testimony left by Li himself. In the autobiography written shortly before his readmittance to the Party in 1949, he wrote that he had left the Party in September 1924, and in another part of the same autobiography he gives the date as early 1924. In an essay in 1928, he gave the date as the autumn of 1923. This date is accepted by one of Li's biographers, Song Jingming, who provides perhaps the most probing analysis of this important episode in Li's life. See Song Jingming, *Li Da zhuanji* (The life of Li Da) (Hubei: Hubei renmin chubanshe, 1986), pp. 69–71.

35. Interview with Professor Reng Wuxiong, 24 September 1993. Professor Reng is attached to the Memorial Hall of the site of the First National Congress of the Communist Party of China.

36. Song Jing Ming, *Li Da zhuanji*, pp. 69–71. The quote in this paragraph is taken from p. 69. See also Xu Quanxing, "Zhongguo Makesizhuyi zhexuejie taidou" (Struggle Within the Philosophical Realm of Marxism in China), in Zhongguo xiandai zhexue shi yanjiuhui et al. (eds), *Jinian Li Da yibai zhounian* (Commemorate the Hundredth Anniversary of Li Da's Birth) (Changsha: Hunan chubanshe, 1991), pp. 39–41. Xu concurs with Li Da's judgment that the orientation of the Party lacked balance and that Chen Duxiu gave insufficient attention to the study and dissemination of Marxist theory.

37. Shao Weizheng, "The First National Congress of the Communist Party of China", p. 121.

38. See Xu Quanxing, "'Shijianlun','Maodunlun' yu 'Shehuixue dagang'" ("On Practice", "On Contradiction" and *Elements of Sociology*), *Mao Zedong zhexue sixiang yanjiu dongtai*, No. 2 (1984).

39. *Zhongguo zhexue*, I, p. 359.

40. Zhao Dezhi and Wang Benhao, *Zhongguo Makesizhuyi zhexue qishinian* (Seventy Years of Marxist Philosophy in China) (Liaoning: Liaoning daxue chubanshe, 1991), p. 53.

41. Ibid.

42. *Li Da wenji*, Vol. I, p. 14.

43. Song Jingming, *Li Da zhuanji*, pp. 86–88.

44. Ibid., p. 87.

45. James E. Sheridan, *Chinese Warlord: The Career of Feng Yu-hsiang* (Stanford: Stanford University Press, 1966), p. 269.

46. *Li Da wenji*, Vol. I, p. 15.

47. Ibid., p. 16. See also Li Da, *Jingjixue dagang* (An Outline of Economic Theory) (Wuhan: Wuhan daxue chubanshe, 1985), pp. 3–11.

48. For an assessment of the influences on the development of Mao Zedong's philosophical thought during the late 1930s, see Nick Knight (ed.), *Mao Zedong on Dialectical Materialism: Writings on Philosophy, 1937* (Armonk, New York: M.E. Sharpe, 1990), Introduction.

49. Tang Qunyuan, "Li Da yu Furen xiaoxue" (Li Da and Furen Primary School), *Lingling shizhuan xuebao*, No. 2 (1982).

50. Li Da suffered from diabetes and a number of other medical complaints which had been exacerbated during the years of privation of the Anti-Japanese War. These medical problems were to dog Li for the rest of his life, and he finally succumbed to them during the early stages of the Cultural Revolution in 1966.

51. Li Da, *"Shijianlun" "maodunlun" jieshuo* (Beijing: Sanlian shudian, 1979).

52. Wang Jionghua, "Li Da", pp. 32–35.

53. Sun Qinan and Li Shizhen, *Mao Zedong yu mingren*, p. 329.

54. Wang Jionghua, "Li Da", pp. 37–38. See also Sun Qinan and Li Shizhen, *Mao Zedong yu mingren*, pp. 329–30.

55. Chen Zuhua, Li Da's former research assistant and now a professor of philosophy at Wuhan University, worked on the project to revise *Elements of Sociology*. He described Li's ill-health in an interview with me on 4 October 1993. Chen said that Li Da's hands shook so badly that he was scarcely capable of holding a pen.

56. Wang Jionghua, "Li Da", p. 46.

57. See *Wuhan fengyun renwu*, pp. 38–40.

58. Discussions with Wang Jionghua and Song Jingming, Wuhan University, October 1993.

59. Li Da's *jiuming* to Mao can be found in *Wuhan fengyun renwu*, p. 40.

60. Wang Jionghua, "Li Da", p. 47.

61. For the notice of Li Da's rehabilitation, published in *People's Daily*, see *Hunan dangshi renwu zhuanji ziliao xuanpian*, p. 153.

62. *Li Da wenji*, Vol. I, p. 20.

63. The worst of these is Werner Meissner, *Philosophy and Politics in China: The Controversy over Dialectical Materialism in the 1930s*.

2

Marxist Philosophy and Social Theory: The Origins of Li Da's Thought

Li Da was one of the most influential of the philosophers and social theorists to introduce Marxism to China. As we saw in the previous chapter, he was amongst the first of the May Fourth generation of Chinese radicals to convert to Marxism,[1] and for the rest of his life he strove tirelessly to propagate his version of Marxism amongst Chinese intellectuals and activists. His major works on Marxist philosophy and social theory, especially *Contemporary Sociology* (1926) and *Elements of Sociology* (1935/37), were instrumental in bringing to many Chinese the contemporary interpretation of orthodox Marxism, and they explained in great detail issues and concepts central to Marxist theory. Because of their centrality, these issues and concepts were also of considerable sensitivity, many fierce polemics having been fought over their definition and elaboration. Two major themes had been (and in fact still are) the subject of controversy within the Marxist tradition, and it is these that we will pursue through the voluminous writings of Li Da. Our purpose in doing so is to understand the origins, content and development of Li's Marxism. We are particularly concerned with its genealogy and its relationship to mainstream European and Soviet forms of Marxism. This evaluation will allow a clearer understanding of the origins of the theoretical and philosophical dimensions of Chinese Marxism, from its introduction to China in the late 1910s to its manifestations in the China of the 1990s, for it is no exaggeration to suggest that the ideological system referred to in China today as Marxism-Leninism-Mao Zedong Thought still contains very strong genealogical connections to the orthodox Marxism propagated by Li Da in the 1920s and 1930s. We will return later in the book to a consideration of the influence of Li Da on Marxist theory and philosophy in post-Mao China, and raise questions about the trajectory which Marxism in China has described over the three-quarters of a century since its introduction to China.

The first of the themes we will be pursuing through Li Da's writings is the philosophy of Marxism, often referred to as dialectical materialism. This philosophy has been the subject of considerable and at times very bitter controversy, for it is the articulation of the core ontological and epistemological assumptions upon which the entire Marxist theoretical system rests. Dialectical materialism thus poses questions about the very nature of reality. How are we to understand the universe and its inner workings? Is there an objective reality beyond human consciousness, and if so, of what is it constituted? Is the universe — and the objects which comprise it — subject to natural laws, and again, if so, how are these to be understood and categorised; how are these laws to be discovered? How is human knowledge of reality derived, and how are true human perceptions of reality to be distinguished from those which are false? What is the relationship between human thought and external reality? How are movement and change to be explained and is there purpose and direction in change?

All philosophies must pose these or similar questions, for they deal, at a very abstract level, with the relationship between humans and the world. Marxism is different insofar as it does not perceive philosophy as an isolated and disinterested inquiry into this relationship; rather, philosophy has a political purpose, and that is to demonstrate the certainty of the ultimate realisation of the telos of human history, the realisation of the higher form of communism as the final goal of social development. The laws of nature which govern movement and change in the universe are to be employed as a rational premise on which extrapolations regarding the direction and speed of change in human society can be based. Philosophical laws are thus of immediate relevance to an understanding of why the proletariat — the class nominated by Marx as the "universal class" — will, in the fullness of time, triumph. The deep and intense interest in philosophy within the Marxist tradition has grown from this certainty that philosophy holds the key to an understanding of movement and change, in the universe more generally, but in human society as well. Philosophy is thus not seen as separate from history or from politics. Rather, philosophy has been perceived within the Marxist tradition (although not necessarily by Marx himself) as the indispensable tool of the revolutionary, and it is no coincidence that philosophy was to hold a considerable fascination for prominent Marxist leaders such as Lenin and Mao, as well as Marxist theorists like Lukács and Korsch.[2]

The second theme we will explore in Li Da's writings is the aetiology of social change. This has been another central and very controversial issue within Marxist theory, and one which has been central to debates within Marxism in China. How is social change to be explained? If it is the economic realm which is the causal locus of change, how is this realm to be defined? If it is constituted from the productive forces of society (its objects and instruments of labour and associated technological skills) and the relationships which emerge amongst humans on the basis of the process of production (class relationships), which of these has causal dominance? If there is a dialectical relationship between them, how does this operate? What is the relationship between the economic and non-economic realms of society; does the latter (usually referred to as the superstructure) have any causal effectivity and, if so, of what magnitude is it and in what sorts of historical contexts does it operate?

In this chapter, we turn to a brief analysis of these intellectual themes within Marxism which were to have a profound influence on the development and structure of Li Da's thought. It will become apparent that, as a Marxist philosopher and theorist, Li Da was confronted by a series of theoretical choices in searching for answers to the questions we have outlined above. Marxism is not, and never has been, a unified intellectual tradition; there are different and competing currents within it, each claiming legitimacy as the appropriate interpretation. Even the conception of "orthodoxy", against which claims to legitimacy are frequently measured, is contested; "orthodoxy", like all versions of the truth, is a construction, but one which normally possesses the power of enforcement through the agency of organisational sanctions. While "orthodoxy" may be claimed as the "true" interpretation by its adherents, its status as truth relies ultimately on its relationship with power, for it is power that sanctifies truth and employs it for its own ends.

The notion of "orthodoxy" as a construction, and not a given, is extremely important in any consideration of Marxism in China, for there has been an unfortunate tendency on the part of many Western China scholars to evaluate Chinese Marxism against an orthodoxy which is for the most part assumed and given, and one which is also static — and that orthodoxy is often employed in a way which demonstrates the supposedly wide gulf which separates Marxism in China from its European and Soviet counterparts.[3] In the analysis below, I will attempt a reconstruction of the "orthodoxy" which was to have the most profound effect on Li Da's thought and, through him, on the structure and development of Marxism in China. It will become evident that the distance which separated Li Da's Marxism and mainstream European and Soviet variants of Marxism was far less significant than one would gather from secondary accounts of Marxism in China; indeed, we will have frequent occasion to note the considerable congruence existing between the structure of Li's thought and the structure of the Marxism which Li believed to be orthodox.[4]

Marx and Engels on Social Change and Philosophy

While some commentators perceive the origins of dialectical materialism in the general project of Western philosophy from earliest times to explain the nature of reality and movement and change within it,[5] others have argued strongly and often critically that its origins can be found in the attempt by Engels to formulate a *Naturphilosophie* from which the history of human society might be deduced.[6] The latter viewpoint thus takes issue with the assumption, so important to the establishment of dialectical materialism as an orthodoxy, that the ideas of Engels and Marx can be readily equated,[7] that Marx knew and approved of Engels' project to provide a philosophical basis for the materialist conception of history.[8] Rather, Engels' forays into philosophy (contained in such works as *Anti-Dühring*, *Ludwig Feuerbach and the End of Classical German Philosophy* and *Dialectics of Nature*) diverged from Marx's approach in a number of fundamental respects, the most important of these being that Marx did not perceive human history as an expression of nature, a nature governed by general philosophical laws external to human society. Human history was, to the contrary, a history of human interaction with nature and not a passive reflection of the laws of nature. Marx accordingly abandoned philosophical attempts to explain human history, developing in its place his characteristic political economy within which humans are attributed, according to Lichtheim, with critical reason, the capacity to interact with and change nature in a dynamic way.[9]

Marx's abandonment of philosophy occurred, according to his own recollections, in the mid-1840s, at which time he embraced political economy as the means by which the contradictions and laws of motion of capitalism could be explained. As Marx recalled in 1859:

> The first work which I undertook to dispel the doubts assailing me was a critical re-examination of the Hegelian philosophy of law; the introduction to this work being published in the Deutsch-Franzosische Jahrbücher issued in Paris in 1844. My inquiry led me to the conclusion that neither legal relations nor political forms could be comprehended whether by themselves or on the basis of a so-called general development of the human mind, but that on the contrary they originate in the material conditions of life, the totality of which Hegel, following the example of English and French thinkers of the eighteenth century, embraces within the term "civil society"; that the anatomy of this civil society, however, has to be sought in political economy.[10]

However, despite Marx's explicit repudiation of philosophy as the key to an understanding of the development of human history, there remained in his mature work significant traces of his earlier commitment to it. As Maurice Dobb points out, "If Marx's economic analysis was distinguished by its historical setting, his historical interpretation had deep philosophical roots — roots originating in the Hegelian philosophy."[11] First, it is apparent from Marx's writings on political economy that he premised his entire theoretical system on the assumption of the materiality of reality; there is thus an ontological premise at work within the materialist conception of history, and this derived from his largely philosophical repudiation of the idealism of the Hegelian philosophical system. Second, there inevitably exists within Marx's writings an epistemology, a mechanism for "knowing" the origins and nature of capitalist society, and at times these epistemological assumptions appeared on the surface of the Marx texts, such as the "Introduction" to the *Grundrisse* and his "Marginal Notes" on Adolph Wagner's text on political economy.[12] Third, Marx clung strongly to the belief that social change was subject to laws of motion, and that the regularities apparent in social change were a manifestation of certain laws, laws which he had derived largely from the Hegelian system. These dialectical laws dictated that movement and change were not and could not be random; there was purpose, progress, advance, direction. One of the primary reasons for the purposive direction of change was the existence and behaviour of contradictions within things, for the appearance and resolution of contradictions followed a pattern which was, in theory, discoverable.

While limitations of space preclude a more detailed analysis of these philosophical traces within the writings of the mature Marx, the point remains that, even following his supposed repudiation of a philosophical investigation into the history, structure and development of capitalism, Marx drew on modes of thought and analysis which possessed a strong philosophical dimension. His writings consequently could and indeed did give comfort to those who later sought to delineate and elaborate the *philosophy* of Marxism. The comparative absence of purely philosophical texts in the writings of the mature Marx suggests, however, that he may not have approved of the project to create, in his name, a highly structured philosophical system premised on a limited number of fundamental laws and principles; still less would he have approved of the enforcement of this philosophical system through its complete subordination to the dictations of the political realm, a situation which was to emerge in the Soviet Union after 1931.

If Marx was therefore disinclined to elaborate a philosophical system which he then applied to analysis of human society and its history, his friend and collaborator Frederick Engels demonstrated no such disinclination. In a number of texts explicitly on philosophy, Engels elaborated the basis of what was later to be designated the Marxist philosophy of dialectical materialism. Moreover, although some of these texts were written after Marx's death, Engels in each case claimed the approval of Marx for the project to articulate their philosophical position. For example, some three years after Marx's death, Engels published *Ludwig Feuerbach and the End of Classical German Philosophy*, and in the "Foreword" to the book edition of this work (1888), Engels invoked Marx's early interest in philosophy as one reason for providing "a short, connected account of our relation to the Hegelian philosophy, of how we proceeded from as well as separated from it".[13] Similarly, in the second "Preface" to *Anti-Dühring*, written some eleven years after Marx's death, Engels claimed that he had "read the whole manuscript [of *Anti-Dühring*] to him [Marx] before it was printed".[14] In addition, Engels had written to Marx in May 1873, providing him with an outline of his ideas on the philosophy of natural science, ideas which were to form the core of Engels' unfinished manuscripts later entitled *Dialectics of Nature* and published only in 1925; there is no evidence of Marx objecting to this foray of Engels into the philosophy of nature and science.[15] Engels thus provided plentiful ammunition to those who wished to conflate the writings of Marx and Engels in the realm of philosophy and, on that basis, create a unified philosophy as the foundation of the Marxist theoretical system.

Engels argued in *Anti-Dühring* that nature and history are governed by the same laws of dialectics, and that these laws ultimately emerge too in the realm of human consciousness; thus nature, history and thought are actually elements of a universe whose laws of motion and change are dialectical. The purpose of philosophy is the discovery of these laws of dialectics,[16] and the process of discovery is based on a largely inductive and empirical approach in which dialectical laws are the final result of investigation, and not the starting point.[17] Observation of reality confirms that the universe (nature, history, thought) is in motion, a form of motion which is dialectical, allowing for both movement and stasis. Stasis can, however, only be a relative phase in the absolute imperative of change, for even during stasis internal changes occur within phenomena which dictate the reappearance of overt change.[18] The demiurge which creates this imperative for change and motion is internal contradiction, for all things contain contradiction; it is the ceaseless emergence of contradictions and the struggle between them which dictate that stasis can only ever be a relative condition. As Engels points out, "as soon as we consider things in their motion, their change, their life, their reciprocal influence ... we immediately become involved in contradictions".[19]

The ubiquity of contradictions, their interaction and the results of their interaction are expressed as a series of laws which are, Engels asserts, deduced from nature and history and not "foisted" on them. In *Dialectics of Nature*, Engels summarises these as follows:

It is, therefore, from the history of nature and human society that the laws of dialectics are abstracted. For they are nothing but the most general laws of these two aspects of historical development, as well as thought itself. And indeed they can be reduced in the main to three:
The law of the transformation of quantity into quality and vice versa;
The law of the interpenetration of opposites;
The law of the negation of the negation.[20]

The expression of these laws in reality leads to a "spiral form of development".[21] We will comment below on the interpretation of these dialectical laws in Soviet Marxism, and we will examine in considerable detail the explanation of them provided by Li Da in his voluminous writings on philosophy. For the moment, it suffices to say that Engels had provided the basis on which a systematised philosophy of Marxism could be built, one premised on the centrality of the laws outlined above. However, Engels' scattered and often polemical writings on philosophy also created fertile ground for differing and sometimes incompatible interpretations of these laws and the relative significance of them; nor could Engels have anticipated the political uses to which philosophy would be put, especially in its guise as orthodoxy.

As we have seen, Engels insisted that the laws of dialectics existed in nature, human society and thought, and had to be discovered. One of the central problems of philosophy, as Engels saw it, was how this dialectical reality could be known. In *Ludwig Feuerbach and the End of Classical German Philosophy*, Engels suggested that the "great basic question of all philosophy ... is that concerning the relation of thinking and being", and he articulated the fundamental questions of epistemology as follows: "in what relation do our thoughts about the world surrounding us stand to this world itself? Is our thinking capable of the cognition of the real world? Are we able in our ideas and notions of the real world to produce a correct reflection of reality?"[22] In response to these epistemological questions, Western philosophy had divided into two great camps, according to Engels — those of idealism and materialism. Idealism believed that thought or spirit was dominant in relation to being or nature; materialism, on the other hand, regarded being or nature as dominant. In support of this latter position, Engels points to practice (experiment and industry) as the most telling refutation of such "philosophical crotchets" as idealism,[23] for "we simply cannot get away from the fact that everything that sets men acting must find its way through their brains ... The influences of the external world upon man expresses themselves in his brain, are reflected therein as feelings, thoughts, impulses, volitions."[24]

One of the major problems with the materialist epistemological position articulated by Engels, and one which has continued to exercise subsequent Marxists, Li Da amongst them, is the issue of how a true reflection of reality is achieved. After all, every human engages in practice of one sort or another, and yet — as Engels is only too well aware — many of them are clearly the bearers of false, unscientific reflections of reality. How is this to be explained, particularly if the reflection theory of epistemology, alluded to by Engels and later taken up with a vengeance by Lenin, is invoked? This is never satisfactorily answered by Engels, and the issue of the criteria by which true reflections of reality may be distinguished from the false has remained a controversial issue around which a number of highly charged philosophical polemics of considerable political significance have been fought.

In his *Elements of Sociology*, Li Da was to expend considerable energy recounting his understanding of the problem of reflection within Marxist epistemology, and we will note, in Chapter 8, that his response relies heavily on the importance of practice, and the dialectical relationship between thought and being (or nature) via the mediation of practice. Li, following the Soviet texts on Marxist philosophy which were his most important influence during the early 1930s, thus perceived the interaction of human thought with nature through practice as a dynamic process, practice being the best guarantee that reflections of reality in the human brain are correct. Wedded to this notion is the historicist suggestion that the context of human thought can place limitations on its veracity; thus it is only with the rise of modern industry and science that the exploitative character of class society can be faithfully reflected in the brains of members of the industrial proletariat. But does the industrial proletariat gain a complete understanding of capitalism in one fell swoop; can the totality of reality be reflected in the human brain immediately? Here, as we will see, Li Da invokes the distinction articulated by Engels and later Lenin between absolute and relative truth; the aggregation of the myriad relative truths will, in the fullness of time, provide absolute truth, for the accumulation of "eternal truths", as Engels calls them, is a process — one which proceeds unevenly in different areas of human inquiry.[25]

Li Da was also, in his many books on sociology, to ponder and elaborate the problem of the aetiology of social change within Marxist theory. The conventional interpretation — one which had gained widespread currency during the period of the Second International — was that the economic structure or base of society possessed absolute causal dominance; other social realms — political and legal institutions and ideologies, cultural practices and beliefs, including religions — were superstructural insofar as their emergence and continued existence were dependent on developments within the economic base and possessed little if any effectivity to initiate social change. Support for this supposedly materialist interpretation drew sustenance from Marx's "Preface" to *A Contribution to the Critique of Political Economy*. Here

Marx had identified the causal preeminence of the economic realm as follows:

> In the social production of their existence, men inevitably enter into definite relations, which are independent of their will, namely relations of production appropriate to a given stage in the development of their material forces of production. The totality of these relations of production constitutes the economic structure of society, the real foundation, on which rises a legal and political superstructure and to which correspond definite forms of social consciousness. The mode of production of material life conditions the general process of social, political and intellectual life. It is not the consciousness of men that determines their existence, but their social existence that determines their consciousness ... The changes in the economic foundation lead sooner or later to the transformation of the whole immense superstructure. [26]

While Marx was obviously, in this famous "Preface", providing only a thumbnail sketch of his political economy, many facets of which he elaborated in great detail in his extended theoretical critique of capitalism, the passage quoted above has become the *locus classicus* for the economic determinist interpretation of Marxism.[27] But what does this passage signify? What did Marx mean when he suggested that the "mode of production of material life *conditions* the general process of social, political and intellectual life"? Does the term "condition" denote the absolute causal priority of the "economic foundation"; was Marx suggesting that the "legal and political superstructure and ... definite forms of social consciousness" had no causal role to play in the process of social change? Or is it possible that he allowed the superstructure some role, changes in the superstructure only following those in the economic foundation "sooner or later"?

The point here is that Marx's "Preface", like all texts, is ultimately an empty vessel which can be filled with different meanings by different readers.[28] There can be no doubt, however, that the "Preface" has given great comfort to those, Marxist and non-Marxist alike, who wish to construct as Marxist orthodoxy an economic determinism in which the various elements of the superstructure are attributed with no effectivity whatsoever. And this determinist interpretation of the Marxist theory of social change has been employed to make invidious comparisons and negative judgments regarding the heterodox character of interpretations which diverge from economic determinism. But what is the result if a different reading of Marx's theory of social change is derived from the Marx texts, one which perceives some role for the superstructure and a dialectical relationship of action–interaction between economic base and political-ideological superstructure? Is such a reading unorthodox, un-Marxist?

Protagonists of this latter position have drawn on texts written by Marx himself,[29] but also on texts written by Engels who attempted to qualify the apparent economic determinism of the "Preface". As Engels was to point out in his letter to Joseph Bloch of September 1890:

> According to the materialist conception of history, the *ultimately* determining element in history is the production and reproduction of real life. Neither Marx nor I have ever asserted more than this. Therefore if somebody twists this into saying that the economic factor is the *only* determining one, he is transforming that proposition into a meaningless, abstract, absurd phrase. The economic situation is the basis, but the various components of the superstructure ... also exercise their influence upon the course of the historical struggles and in many cases determine their *form* in particular. There is an interaction of all these elements...[30]

We can see at a glance the fertile ground for differing interpretations of the aetiology of social change within Marxist theory. Our primary concern, though, is with the interpretation taken by Li Da from Marx, Engels, Plekhanov and Lenin, but particularly from the Soviet philosophers and theorists of the early 1930s, and introduced into China. We will notice that the materialist conception of history enunciated by Li Da, particularly in his major books *Contemporary Sociology* and *Elements of Sociology*, allowed that, while the economic base retained overall dominance, a dialectical relationship existed between economic base and superstructure in which the superstructure possessed the capacity to react back upon the economic base, thus having some influence on the general tenor and direction of historical change. We will have cause to note that this position, which was to become so influential in Marxism in China, particularly through Mao's endorsement of it in "On Contradiction", was in all essential respects a reflection of the approved version contained in Soviet Marxism; and in making this observation, we will problematise the oft-repeated categorisation of Marxism in China as unorthodox because of its concession to the superstructure of a capacity to effect historical change.

Plekhanov and Lenin: The Establishment and Defence of Orthodox Marxism

While there is, in my view, some justification for perceiving dialectical materialism as originating with Engels rather than Marx, the point remains that the emergence of an orthodox Marxist philosophy relied on the assumption of an identity of thought between the two. It is clear from the writings of some of the earliest systematisers of dialectical materialism that they perceived Engels' writings on philosophy as logical extensions of Marx's own thought. To that extent, the emerging philosophical orthodoxy could claim lineage to Marx and thus assert its legitimacy.[31]

One of the most important figures in the establishment of an orthodox Marxist philosophy was the Russian Marxist George Plekhanov (1856–1918). Indeed, Plekhanov is credited by some with being the first to coin and use the term "dialectical materialism" (possibly in 1891).[32] He was also to follow in the footsteps of Engels' *Anti-Dühring* by perceiving the political significance of philosophy, and consequently writing about philosophy in a highly polemical way. This is clearly in evidence in Plekhanov's writings such as *Materialismus Militans* (1908) and *The Materialist Conception of History* (1897), which are charged with personal invective against those such as A.A. Bogdanov, a follower of Mach and Avenarius, who had criticised the philosophical, and in particular the epistemological, dimensions of Marxism. There was, according to Plekhanov, an orthodox and correct way of thinking about philosophy, and those who did not conform were beyond the pale. The following passage from *Materialismus Militans* is characteristic of the polemical tone of a good deal of the philosophical writings of the Russian Marxists; one can see in it, too, the construction of an orthodoxy whose tenets could be employed to attack and exclude the Bogdanovs and Deborins whose views were perceived as a threat:

> You are terribly mistaken, dear Sir [Bogdanov], if you imagine that I am throwing out more or less obvious hints to the effect that you should be, if not hanged, at least "banished" from the confines of Marxism at the earliest possible moment. If any one intended to treat you in this way, he would first of all have to come up against the utter *impossibility of fulfilling* his harsh design ... no ideological Pompadour could possibly "banish" from the confines of a particular teaching a "thinker" who was already *outside them*. And that you are outside the confines of Marxism is clear for all those who know that the whole edifice of this teaching rests upon *dialectical materialism*, and who realise that you, as a convinced Machist, do not and cannot hold the materialist viewpoint.[33]

It is indeed interesting that the formulation of dialectical materialism as the orthodox interpretation of Marxist philosophy grew out of Plekhanov's polemic with the Russian Narodniks or populists, particularly Mikhailovsky, who had been attacking Marxism in the early 1890s. In response to these attacks, Plekhanov wrote his famous treatise In *Defence of Materialism: The Development of the Monist View of History* (1894). Plekhanov here reiterates Engels' suggestion that the history of philosophy is the history of the struggle between materialism and idealism. However, while staunchly defending materialism,[34] Plekhanov argues strongly for the dialectical method contained in Hegelian idealist philosophy, particularly the notion "that every phenomenon is transformed into its own opposite" and that development proceeds through the transformation of quantity into quality and vice versa; motion is inherent in all phenomena.[35] Indeed, it was Plekhanov who was to alter the sequence of the three dialectical laws outlined by Engels in *Dialectics of Nature*, and to give prominence to the law of the interpenetration of opposites, a practice followed by Lenin, and subsequently by Soviet Marxism until the publication of Stalin's *Dialectical and Historical Materialism* in 1938.[36]

However, Hegel's ideas were, according to Plekhanov, guilty of mysticism in perceiving reason as the demiurge of history, reason unrelated to the material conditions of existence of human beings. The dialectical method in Hegel's philosophy ("the examination of phenomena in their development, in their origin and destruction") had to be combined with a materialist appreciation of the significance of the process of production in the unfolding of history. In this, according to Plekhanov, lies Marx's genius.[37] Marx recognised the overwhelming importance of the productive forces in historical development: "On the basis of a particular state of the productive forces there come into existence certain relations of production, which receive their ideal expression in the legal notions of men and in more or less 'abstract rules,' in unwritten customs and written laws."[38] But, while quoting approvingly from Marx's "Preface" of 1859,[39] Plekhanov dismisses the idea that superstructural institutions can have no influence on the economic foundation of society; their influence is, however, limited. "Interaction between politics and economics exists," Plekhanov insists, for "[p]olitical institutions influence economic life. They either facilitate its development or impede it."[40] He makes it very clear, however, that the starting point of historical analysis is the productive forces, for while political institutions may facilitate or impede the development of economic life, major historical transformations are a function of developments within society's economic foundation. As he insists in his attack on Mikhailovsky, "Dialectical materialism says that it is not the consciousness of men which determines their being, but on the contrary their being which determines their consciousness; that it is not in the philosophy but in the economy of a particular society that one must seek the key to understanding its particular condition."[41] Consequently, "Dialectical materialism is the highest development of the materialist conception of history."[42]

Plekhanov's most systematic exposition of dialectical materialism appears, however, in *Fundamental Problems of Marxism* (1908), one of his last works.[43] In this book, Plekhanov asserts the identity of the philosophical views of Marx and Engels, an important premise, as we have seen, for the construction of dialectical materialism as the orthodox philosophy of Marxism.[44] He continues by elaborating the debt owed by Marx and Engels to Feuerbach; however, the latter, in struggling against the speculative and idealist character of Hegelian philosophy, had not appreciated nor made use of its dialectical element. Marx and Engels were to fill this gap, and to grasp the importance of combining Feuerbach's stress on materialism with the dialectical method of Hegel, for only thus could the motion, change and development of human history be explained.[45] Plekhanov emphasises the centrality of motion to dialectical materialism, and also the connection between motion and contradiction: "The movement of matter underlies all the phenomena of nature. But motion is a contradiction."[46] He also suggests that the contradictions which exist in concepts are "only the reflection, the translation into the language of thought, of contradictions which exist in phenomena owing to the contradictory nature of their common foundation, namely movement".[47]

The issue of how contradictions in reality could be faithfully reflected in human thought was a contentious one for both Plekhanov and Lenin. In *Materialismus Militans*, Plekhanov made the conventional dualistic distinction between thought and objects in material reality, but believed that the latter could be reflected in human thought, not just as the result of the impressions (sensations) they made on the human nervous system, but as a result of practice (experience) which allowed humans to test their concepts; if this is done, then "our perceptions conform to the objective nature of the things perceived".[48] In *Materialism and Empirio-Criticism*, written at the same time as *Materialismus Militans* and for the same purpose of defending "orthodox" Marxism against the philosophies of the followers of Mach such as Bogdanov and Bazarov, Lenin also expended considerable energy articulating the epistemology of dialectical materialism. Lenin asserted that "the materialist theory, the theory of the reflection of objects by our mind, is here presented [in Engels' 'Introduction' to *Socialism: Utopian and Scientific*] with absolute clarity: things exist outside us. Our perceptions and ideas are their images. Verification of these images, differentiation between true and false images, is given by practice."[49] Lenin recognised, however, that the attainment of a true reflection of reality requires a dialectical process, one in which numerous relative truths combine to provide, ultimately, absolute truth; the process of knowledge thus possesses an historical dimension, one in which the practice of the human subject within a social context is central.[50]

While *Materialism and Empirio-Criticism* is primarily concerned with the epistemological dimensions of dialectical materialism, in his later *Philosophical Notebooks* (1914–15), Lenin explored the dialectical component of Marxist philosophy in considerable detail, arguing the centrality of contradictions and their struggle to all phenomena and processes. As he pointed out in "On the Question of Dialectics" (1915):

> The identity of opposites ... is the recognition (discovery) of the contradictory, *mutually exclusive*, opposite tendencies in *all* phenomena and processes of nature (*including* mind and society). The condition for the knowledge of all processes of the world in their *"self-movement,"* in their spontaneous development, in their real life, is the knowledge of them as a unity of opposites. Development is the "struggle" of opposites ... The unity (coincidence, identity, equal action) of opposites is conditional, temporary, transitory, relative. The struggle of mutually exclusive opposites is absolute, just as development and motion are absolute.[51]

In his "Conspectus of Hegel's Science of Logic", Lenin summarised this view as follows: "In brief, dialectics can be defined as the doctrine of the unity of opposites."[52] He also provided a list of the elements of dialectics which incorporated, as had Engels in the *Dialectics of Nature*, the laws of the negation of the negation and the transformation of quantity into quality and vice versa.[53] Lenin's endorsement of these laws and categories of dialectics was to have a marked influence on the variant of dialectical materialism which became orthodox after 1931, and his views were widely quoted in Soviet philosophical texts of the early 1930s.

Lenin agreed with Plekhanov, too, in rejecting the idea that Marxism allowed no historical role to the superstructure. Like Plekhanov, Lenin accepted the materialist foundation of Marxist theory, believing that economic forces (forms of production and class relationships) exercised a predominant effect in historical change. This is evident in both his *The Development of Capitalism in Russia* and *Imperialism, the Highest Stage of Capitalism*.[54] However, Lenin believed that the struggle between classes, while rooted in the material conditions of existence within society and operating initially at an economic level, eventually gave rise to a political struggle, one which incorporated the political organisations and parties of the various contending classes. The success of such organisations and parties in their political struggle could have a significant, and in some contexts decisive, influence on the outcome of the class struggle at the economic level. Lenin believed that the materialist theory established by Marx recognised the importance of political struggle, and he was able to invoke many of Marx's writings (such as *The Eighteenth Brumaire of Louis Bonaparte* and *The Civil War in France*) in rejecting a deterministic reading of Marx which allowed no significance to human political action in the historical process. As Lenin pointed out, "Marx gave brilliant and profound examples of materialist historiography, of an analysis of the position of each individual class, and sometimes of various groups or strata within a class, showing plainly why and how 'every class struggle is a political struggle'."[55] This view led logically to the conclusion that those engaged in the class struggle had to devote considerable time and energy to problems of political organisation and tactics, for without successful prosecution of the struggle at the political level, the struggle at the economic level would lack coherence and direction. Most important for Lenin was the establishment of a revolutionary party which could pursue the class interests of the proletariat, for without such a party, the cause of the proletariat would be jeopardised; and central to Lenin's conception of the revolutionary party was his insistence on the need for forceful leadership, for "without the dozen tried and talented leaders ... professionally trained, schooled by long experience and working in perfect harmony, no class in modern society can wage a determined struggle".[56]

Lenin and Plekhanov were therefore both prepared to concede a degree of effectivity to the superstructural realm in their reading of historical materialism. What divided them was not whether Marxists should be involved in political activity or not, for both agreed that they should. Rather, the disagreement centred on the extent to which political action could, in the context of Russia in the early years of the twentieth century, precipitate and consolidate a revolution which had socialist intentions. Plekhanov, on the basis of a reading of Russian history which stressed its Asiatic past, advocated a gradualist form of political action which accommodated Russia's comparative lack of industry and bourgeois culture. Lenin, on the other hand, perceived Russia as thoroughly permeated by the contradictions of capitalism,[57] and argued the possibility of dramatic change being effected through concerted political action by a revolutionary party committed to the socialist cause. In the event, it was Lenin's view of the dynamics of social change, rather than Plekhanov's, which prevailed in the revolutionary movement, and the Bolshevik victory in the Russian Revolution served to reinforce Lenin's claim to have interpreted correctly the Russian historical context; it also reinforced the claimed orthodoxy of Lenin's reading of dialectical and historical materialism.

Dialectical and Historical Materialism in Soviet Marxism

By the time of the Russian Revolution, the idea had become well entrenched that there was an orthodox philosophy of Marxism and that philosophical speculation and debate were legitimate preoccupations of Marxist theorists.[58] However, during the early 1920s — and despite Lenin's strongly held and defended views on the definition of orthodox

Marxist philosophy[59] — considerable debate continued over philosophical issues. As Ahlberg notes, "In the first half of the twenties the principles of Marxist philosophy had by no means been fully elaborated."[60] Some of the major figures in these debates were Minin and Encmen, who endorsed the view, later to be attacked by Bukharin as "vulgar materialism", that philosophy was itself an anachronism left over from class society and that it should be discarded in favour of science;[61] Bogdanov, whose empiriomonism attempted to unite subject and object on the basis of the sensations of the subject;[62] and Stepanov and Timiryazev, who represented the "mechanical materialists", with their belief in mechanical motion, external causality and linear forms of development. It was against this latter philosophical tendency that the proponents of "dialectical materialism" were to struggle, and it was their victory over the mechanists in 1929 which was to set the scene for the emergence of the philosophical orthodoxy of the years 1931–36 which was to have such a dramatic influence on Marxism in China through the writings and translations of Chinese scholars like Li Da.

A major figure in the emergence of dialectical materialism as the orthodox philosophy of Soviet Marxism was Abram Deborin, described by his biographer Rene Ahlberg as the "forgotten philosopher".[63] It was Deborin who led the attack against the "mechanistic materialists" during the years 1925–29, and who accelerated the process of formalising and systematising the philosophy of dialectical materialism. Deborin and the dialectical materialists quarrelled with the mechanistic materialists over a number of basic philosophical postulates. The latter, drawing on a particular interpretation of Engels' writings, had adopted a strictly determinist perspective which favoured an evolutionary view of development, one founded on a belief in external causation; it was openly hostile to dialectics, regarding it as "scholasticism", and urged the abolition of philosophy and dialectics as subjects to be studied and taught in the Soviet Union, arguing that these should be replaced by the positive sciences.[64] Deborin violently opposed this attack on dialectics. Following in the footsteps of Hegel and Plekhanov, Deborin perceived the dialectic as a combination of logic, ontology and epistemology, and as such, the dialectical method constituted the foundation of the natural sciences. Deborin insisted that development proceeded in a dialectical manner, that leaps in development were caused by contradictions inherent within phenomena; indeed, he perceived dialectic's law of the unity of opposites as so fundamental to an understanding of the natural world that he insisted it be made the basis of theoretical physics.[65]

The staunch defence and further elaboration of dialectical materialism's basic propositions (unity of opposites, internal causality, development in leaps) by Deborin and his supporters was not only pursued in the realm of theoretical debate. During the latter half of the

1920s, adherents of dialectical materialism as propounded by Deborin successfully strove to gain increasing control in key organisations such as scientific institutes (the prestigious Soviet Academy of Sciences being a prime example),[66] universities and professional associations. Of the latter, the Society of Militant Materialists and Dialecticians, directed by Deborin, had by 1929 established an organisational network covering almost all of Russia; Deborin was also the chief editor (from 1926–30) of *Under the Banner of Marxism*, the major philosophical journal.[67] The increasing influence within such organisations of supporters of dialectical materialism was accompanied by, and was in part a manifestation of, the increasing control exercised by the Communist Party over philosophy and science; these realms were progressively regarded as too significant to the goals of the Party to remain autonomous. The judgment rendered by the Party on mechanistic materialism in April 1929 — that it was an "obvious deviation from the position of Marxist-Leninist philosophy" — consequently foreshadowed the end of philosophy as a realm of free debate, and anticipated the idea, to become entrenched from 1931 on, that the Party would be the ultimate determiner of which variant of Marxist philosophy was to be regarded as orthodox.[68]

Soviet Marxist Philosophy: Dialectical Materialism as "Orthodoxy", 1931–36

The status of orthodoxy which dialectical materialism thus attracted in 1929 with the victory of the Deborinites over mechanistic materialism was therefore in part a function of a belief that a dialectical rather than mechanistic variant of materialism accorded more closely with the philosophical tradition of Marxism. After all, while the mechanists might invoke the positivist and evolutionary themes in Engels' writings, dialectical materialists could appeal with equal if not greater justification to their dialectical elements, as well as appealing to the ideas of Plekhanov and Lenin, both of whom regarded a dialectical materialism which drew heavily on both Hegel and Marx as "orthodox" Marxism. The ascendancy of dialectical materialism thus rested in part on the ideological authority of its earlier famous proponents (Engels, Plekhanov, Lenin), as well as on the persuasiveness of its ideas and concepts.[69] In this regard, there can be no doubt that Deborin, influenced heavily by the philosophies of Hegel and Plekhanov, firmly believed in the superiority of dialectical materialism, and functioned as an energetic and effective advocate of its ideas, one who was able to convince through his writings and activities an emerging generation of Soviet philosophers.[70] He was also to influence philosophers in China, Li Da among them. Li was later to concede, after Deborin had fallen from grace, that his ideas had been influenced, perhaps too much, by the Hegelian dimension of Deborin's interpretation of dialectical materialism.

However, the establishment of dialectical materialism as orthodoxy in the Soviet Union was not only a function of the intellectual persuasiveness of Deborin's interpretation of Marxist philosophy. It was also a function of increasing control of key organisations by its proponents, and ultimately of intervention by the Party; for it was the Party — now firmly under the control of Stalin — which determined that philosophy, science and history were realms of intellectual inquiry too important to socialism to permit the existence of ideas which might be inimical to its needs as the Party perceived these. This increasing and ultimately complete domination of philosophy by the Party not only explains the triumph of Deborin and the dialectical materialists over the mechanists in 1929, it explains why Deborin himself was to fall from grace in January 1931. As early as April 1930, the Deborinites had been attacked by members of the Institute of Red Professors Mark Mitin, Pavel Yudin and Vasili Raltsevich. Significantly, the attack was directed not so much at the theoretical arguments mounted by Deborin and his followers, but at their disinclination "to give immediate sanction to the Party's practical measures". In an article published in *Pravda* in June 1930, they were accused of "a lack of party-mindedness", of "extreme formalism and the malicious separation of philosophy from the practical problems of the country". Deborin's views were finally branded by Stalin as "Menshevizing idealism" in December 1930, as having been influenced too heavily by the ideas of Hegel and Plekhanov.[71] However, the basic tenets of Deborin's philosophy were not repudiated after 1931, although in practice they were interpreted in a less Hegelian spirit.[72] What did distinguish Soviet philosophy after 1931 was its complete domination by the Party. "Orthodoxy" was now defined and enforced politically; this was to lead to the complete formalisation of dialectical materialism, a process in which speculative and innovative thought disappeared and in which there was constant repetition of the approved principles of this philosophy.[73]

The formalistic and repetitive nature of the orthodoxy which prevailed in Soviet philosophy during the early 1930s serves to make a comparison with Li Da's reading of dialectical materialism more straightforward, and we will pursue that comparison in subsequent chapters. Let us turn firstly to a necessarily brief reconstruction of this orthodox Soviet dialectical materialism. Our attention will be focused on the basic premises of this philosophy, its laws and the relative significance attributed to these, its epistemology, and its approach to the problem of social change. This will function as a basis from which judgments regarding the source and degree of orthodoxy of Li Da's interpretation of Marxist philosophy can be made.

According to Mitin, who became the pre-eminent spokesperson for Soviet philosophy after the fall of Deborin, the basic premise of dialectical materialism is that the universe is a material one and that the objects of which it is constituted are composed of matter existing independently of human consciousness.[74] Drawing heavily on Engels, Mitin argued that the behaviour (motion, change, development) of this material universe is governed by a number of fundamental natural laws. The first of these is the law of the unity of opposites (sometimes described as the law of the unity and struggle of opposites).[75] This law posits within all objects and processes the existence of opposites (or contradictions). The identity which exists between the opposites which constitute an object is the ontological premise for its existence; but the existence of opposites is at the same time the premise for the change and development of that object, for while there is identity between opposites, there is at the same time struggle, ensuring that no object in the universe is free from the imperative which drives change. The fundamental cause for motion, change and development is thus internal. As the existence of opposites (contradictions) provides the original impulse for change and motion in the material universe, the law which describes this — the law of the unity of opposites — is designated the most important of the laws of dialectics. In *Dialectical and Historical Materialism*, Mitin asserts:

> Consequently, the law of the unity and mutual penetration of opposites becomes the most fundamental, the most important law of dialectics, and the law of determinative significance ... In his *Philosophical Notebooks* Lenin described the unity of opposites as the kernel of dialectics ... The law of the unity of opposites is the most universal law of the objective world and of cognition.[76]

The same judgment appears in other Soviet texts on philosophy from the early to mid-1930s. Shirokov and Aizenberg's *A Course on Dialectical Materialism*, translated by Li Da into Chinese in the early 1930s,[77] referred to the law of the unity of opposites as "the fundamental law of dialectics" and its "determining element".[78] Similarly, Razumovisky, writing in Mitin's *Outline of New Philosophy*, commented on the determinative and general significance of this law;[79] yet another Soviet text, *An Outline of Dialectical Materialist Philosophy*, asserted the principle of the unity of opposites to be the basis of dialectics and dialectical logic.[80] We can thus conclude that a central element of the orthodox version of Soviet Marxist philosophy from this period was the belief that, of the various laws and categories of dialectical materialism, the law of the unity of opposites occupied a pre-eminent position.

The second and third of the laws of dialectical materialism are the law of the mutual transformation of quantity and quality and the law of the negation of the negation. While the law of the unity of opposites describes the ontological basis of change and development, these two laws are concerned with the process of change itself and the reasons why change proceeds in leaps rather than gradually and uniformly. The first of these two laws, according to Mitin, suggests that change takes different forms: change which is gradual, cumulative and does not alter the essential nature of the phenomenon is quantitative change; such quantitative change will, however, eventually reach a point at which the nature of the phenomenon will be altered to become something qualitatively different. A new phenomenon is thus created which does, however, retain elements of the old phenomenon. The reasons for this are explained by the law of the negation of the negation, perceived by Mitin and other Soviet philosophers as a concrete manifestation of the law of the unity of opposites.[81] The law of the negation of the negation describes the manner in which the struggle of the contradictions within a phenomenon proceeds. Of the two contradictory elements, one represents stability and that which is old, whilst the other represents that which is new, change and progress; the resolution of the struggle between them leads ultimately to the overcoming of the former by the latter, the negation of the old by the new (the negation of the negation), resulting in progress, in the emergence of a new phenomenon which nevertheless retains elements of the old. This is expressed by Mitin in the form of the Hegelian triad — thesis, antithesis, synthesis — in which synthesis represents at the same time the negation *and* retention of elements of both the thesis and antithesis.[82] The law of the negation of the negation explains, according to Mitin and other Soviet philosophers, the periodicity of the process of change and the reasons why the direction of change is not random but progressive.[83]

The issue of epistemology is also prominent in the Soviet philosophical texts of the early 1930s. Closely following Lenin, Mitin and other Soviet philosophers stress the dialectical character of the process of knowledge. Knowledge of reality comes about through a process of reflection in which reality is reflected in the brain of the subject; this reflection does not occur immediately but proceeds through a cycle of stages which leads the subject to a deeper understanding of reality, its internal connections, its laws of motion and development. Rational knowledge or concepts develop on the basis of perceptions; these latter are the raw material of rational knowledge. But how are we to know that concepts correctly reflect reality? The answer is practice, for practice is the foundation of the movement of knowledge: it is the criterion of truth.[84] Rational knowledge, which derives from perceptual knowledge, must be tested through practice, and the most important form of practice is social practice. Both Plekhanov and Deborin are criticised for giving insufficient emphasis to the social practice of the subject of cognition. For Mitin, social practice is not only the basis of the knowledge process, it introduces the importance of the "Party character" of knowledge, for knowledge must not only be true, it must be useful, and for it to be useful, it must serve the needs of society which, in the context of the Soviet Union, means the social needs and goals defined by the Communist Party.

For much the same reason, a strictly economic determinist reading of Marxism was also frowned on in post-1931 Soviet Marxism. "Economic materialism", as it came to be known in Soviet historical debates, argued for the decisive role of the economic base in historical change and development. However, this position (defended by the famous historian Pokrovsky, who built his interpretations entirely on economic factors) came to be seen by the Party as out of step with the actual role and significance of the superstructure since 1917, in particular the role of the state and its planning agencies in the process of socialist reconstruction. Consequently, the orthodoxy which emerged after 1931 recognised the "active role of the superstructures" and their "reciprocal influences on the base",[85] and the defenders of economic materialism were forced to recant. In 1930, Pokrovsky conceded that "[a]ccording to a purely economic explanation, if appeal were made exclusively to the laws of economics ... it would have been impossible to foresee what actually happened — that we *would break through to socialism*, through every law, in defiance of narrowly economic laws".[86] Indeed, the concept of "economic materialism" was linked to the ideas of both Trotsky and Bukharin, its proscription thus becoming the more urgent. In 1938, in his *Dialectical and Historical Materialism*, Stalin summarised the view which had emerged amongst Party theorists during the early 1930s and his own opposition to "economic materialism" as follows:

> After the new productive forces have matured, the existing relations of production and their upholders — the ruling classes — become that "insuperable" obstacle which can only be removed by the conscious action of the new classes, by the forcible acts of these classes, by revolution. Here there stands out in bold relief the *tremendous role* of new social ideas, of new political institutions, of a new political power, whose mission it is to abolish by force the old relations of production. Out of the conflict between the new productive forces and the old relations of production, out of the new economic demands of society, there arise new social ideas; the new ideas organize and mobilize the masses; the masses become welded into a new political army, create a new revolutionary power, and make use of it to abolish by force the old system of relations of production, and to firmly establish the new system.

The spontaneous process of development yields place to the conscious actions of men ...[87]

We have seen that this reading of the aetiology of social change could find comfort in passages taken from the writings of Engels and Plekhanov, who had both conceded some significance to the superstructure in the process of historical change. Similarly, Lenin's emphasis on the role of the party as an agent of revolutionary change, and on the political dimensions of class struggle, facilitated a reading of Marxist social theory which was far more activist in its political implications than an evolutionary, economic determinist reading of Marxism would allow.[88]

Dialectical Materialism: The Japanese Connection

The tension between activism and determinism, between economic base and superstructure, was also an issue which exercised Japanese Marxists. The early introduction of Marxist theory to Japan, under the rubric of "scientific socialism", had stressed its deterministic and mechanical aspects, particularly those evident in Engels' writings. For "scientific socialism", the economic base was regarded as the overwhelmingly decisive factor for change, the superstructure little more than a pale reflection of the impulses at work within the "real foundation". In this guise, Marxism was regarded as an economistic theory. However, a number of the more influential Japanese Marxist theorists recognised the two apparently conflicting themes within the corpus of Marx's writings, between the evolutionary, deterministic theme evident in his economic writings, particularly *Capital* (translated into Japanese in 1920) and the political theme which stressed the conscious and active role of human beings in the process of social change.[89] The latter theme was prominent in such writings as *The Communist Manifesto*, one of the first of the Marx texts to be translated into Japanese (in 1904 by Sakai Toshihiko),[90] and *The Eighteenth Brumaire of Louise Bonaparte*. The tension between determinism and conscious action is particularly evident in the famous passage from this latter text, a passage usually employed to validate the political reading of Marx's view of social change: "Men make their own history, but not of their own free will; not under circumstances they themselves have chosen but under the given and inherited circumstances with which they are directly confronted."[91]

Which reading of Marx's theory of social change was the correct one? Was it necessary to make a choice, or was it possible, through an exercise in thinking dialectically, to reconcile the apparent tension between them?⁹² The response of Japanese Marxists to this dilemma bears on our analysis of Li Da's contribution to the process of the dissemination of Marxist philosophy and theory in China for, as we have seen, Li first commenced his study of Marxism in Japan and under the influence of Japanese Marxists. Much of the first wave of Marxist theory reached China from Japan, and it was Li Da and a number of other Chinese radicals who translated Marxist texts into Chinese, not from their original German or Russian, but from their Japanese translations.⁹³ Moreover, Li continued to translate the writings of Japanese Marxists into Chinese long after his departure from the Party in 1923, and this remained a continuing source of influence on the development of Marxism in China.

One of the most famous of Japanese Marxists was Kawakami Hajime (1879–1946), under whom Li Da studied in the late 1910s. Many of Kawakami's writings on Marxism were translated into Chinese (some by Li), and indeed they were amongst the first writings on Marx and Marxism to be introduced to China.⁹⁴ While Kawakami came to recognise the importance of economic factors in the creation of poverty and social injustice, and spent many years studying Marx's *Capital*, he could not accept an entirely economic reading of Marxism's theory of social change, for this left no role for the conscious and independent role of the human actor. Kawakami was very concerned with the importance of ethical behaviour, of self-sacrifice, duty and restraint, as human virtues which could allow a rational response to social injustices. As Kawakami argued, revolution was not just a matter of blind natural forces, but of human action; "since social organization consists of the association of individuals, changes in social organization are different from natural phenomena, and *both the construction and the destruction must be done by human power and deed* ... It is not a natural change."⁹⁵ Kawakami's study of the Russian Revolution in the early 1920s also reinforced his belief that Marxism did recognise the importance of conscious human will in the shaping of history.⁹⁶

Kawakami's concern with the economic determinist interpretation of Marxism was shared by other prominent Japanese Marxists. Yamakawa Hitoshi, in an article translated by Li Da and published in *Xin Qingnian* in 1921, argued that Marx's economic theory was only one component of his complete theory; there was also the activist element which perceived the need for a revolutionary proletariat and class struggle.⁹⁷ Similarly, Sugiyama Sakae's *An Introduction to the Social Sciences* (1929), translated into Chinese by Li Da and Qian Tieru and published in Shanghai in 1930, devotes considerable attention to the possibility of the political, legal and ideological superstructures possessing the capacity to react on the economic base. This interesting explication of the materialist conception of history represents an early and quite detailed attempt to reconcile economic determinism with the importance of political action and correct consciousness. The outcome is a mode of analysis which stresses the interrelatedness of the various elements of society and their mutual causal interaction, while at the same time attempting to retain a degree of causal priority for the economic base. Sugiyama's explication of the materialist conception of history was thus clearly an attempt to elaborate the concept contained in Engels' 1890 letter to Bloch of economics as determinant in the last instance. We will turn to a more detailed analysis of the contents of this volume in Chapter 5, when our focus shifts to Li Da's activities as a translator.

There can be no doubt that the concerns of some Japanese Marxists over the tension between determinism and conscious human action in Marxism communicated themselves to Li Da, and at the very least, the recognition of the political dimension of Marxism by influential Marxists such as Kawakami and Yamakawa must have impressed on Li the possibility of a reading of Marxism other than one which was purely economistic and determinist.[98] We will explore in subsequent chapters what he made of this and other influences.

The growing importance of the philosophical dimension of Marxism was also reinforced by Japanese Marxists such as Kawakami and Sugiyama Sakae. Kawakami had grappled with the German idealism of Hegel during the mid-1920s in order to make sense of the new philosophical material emanating from the Soviet Union, but also to arrive at a comprehensive understanding of Marxism, one which integrated economics and philosophy.[99] This is apparent in his *The Philosophical Basis of Marxism* (1929) and *The Basic Theory of Marxist Economics* (written in 1929 and translated by Li Da and others in 1930), which contained a substantial section on the philosophy of Marxism. Written before the repudiation of "Menshevising idealism" in the Soviet Union in 1931, the latter book quotes approvingly from the works of Deborin and Plekhanov, and also emphasises the significance of Hegel and the dialectic to Marxist philosophy; it consequently contains sections on the laws of the unity of opposites, the mutual transformation of quantity and quality and the negation of the negation.[100] The inclusion of a section on philosophy in this book on economic theory signifies that Kawakami had recognised, as Bernstein points out, that the dialectical mode of thought was the basis of Marxist economics.[101] Similarly, Sugiyama Sakae's *An Introduction to Social Science* contained a section on dialectical materialism, indicating a belief that philosophy was the basis of social science.[102]

Li Da and "Orthodoxy"

The purpose of this chapter has been threefold. The first has been to provide a schematic representation of the concepts within Marxist discourse which we will pursue, in considerable detail, in subsequent chapters, through Li Da's writings on philosophy, history, sociology and political economy. The major concepts of dialectical materialism and Marxism's aetiology of social change have been introduced and will function as our compass as we navigate the extensive and complex structure of Li Da's corpus. The second has been to provide, again rather schematically, a genealogy, in order to portray these central concepts of Marxism as possessing a history. Concepts and themes within Marxism have never been static; their definition has been a source of struggle, interpretations have been contested, and Marxism has become — like all major systems of thought — differentiated on the basis of different readings. We are interested in Li Da's reading of Marxism and the way this reading influenced the development of Marxism in China.

Our third purpose has been to introduce the notion of "orthodoxy" and, in particular, to suggest that "orthodoxy", like all readings of Marxism, is a construction and never a given. What constitutes "orthodox" Marxism has been, as we have seen, a matter of contention. The short-lived "orthodoxy" of the Deborinite period in Soviet philosophy (1929–31) gave way, after an intense political struggle, to the "orthodoxy" of the "New Philosophy" under Mitin; this was an "orthodoxy" which specified more overtly the subordination of philosophy to the goals of the Party, and one which modified the Hegelian dimensions of dialectical materialism. Similarly, proponents of "economic materialism" found themselves, in the climate of the 1930s in the Soviet Union, the subject of criticism as Marxism's theory of social change was interpreted to attribute greater effectivity to the superstructure and its various institutions. What distinguished these different readings of Marxist theory? Can a distinction be drawn on the basis of whether they did or did not conform to the content of Marx's writings; in other words, is there an external and absolute set of criteria by which the "orthodoxy" of readings of Marxism can be evaluated and judged? The distinction derives not from the presumed truth content of one reading of Marxism as opposed to another, but rather from the relationship to power of the reading which became dominant. The concept of "orthodoxy" thus implies the capacity for political enforcement, through the imposition of sanctions or the distribution of rewards. "Orthodoxy" is the reading favoured by power, for its tenets reinforce power's assertions of legitimacy; and "orthodoxy" is true because power decrees that it should be so. But power is unstable and finite, and so too are orthodoxy's verities. What passes for truth soon gives way to a rival account favoured by those who now carry the leader's baton.

Li Da had a long and intimate relationship with "orthodoxy", but a relationship strongly tinged with ambiguity. A significant portion of his writing is polemical in character, from his early critiques of anarchism and the revisionism of Bernstein to his attacks on Hu Shi and Fei Xiaotong in the 1950s; the purpose of these verbal sorties was to defend a reading of Marxism (or Mao Zedong Thought) which Li Da considered to be true, a viewpoint very frequently shared by leading figures in the political hierarchy of the Comintern or Chinese Communist Party. Indeed, one commentator has identified Li Da as one of the earliest defenders of Marxist "orthodoxy" in China.[103] Yet Li Da was not by any means, as we observed in the previous biographical chapter, a mere toady to power. He supported a particular view of Marxism, but not from any desire for rewards or fear of sanctions; his support rested very largely on a strongly held personal conviction of the truth of this viewpoint. In 1923 and again in 1966, he defied authority in pursuit of his vision of the truth, and in both cases, defiance was to extract a heavy cost in personal and political terms. His altercation with Mao over the policies of the Great Leap Forward is further evidence of a steely determination to speak the truth as he saw it, no matter what the cost.

Li Da's reading of Marxist philosophy and social theory was thus very often "orthodox", but not always so. We will concentrate in particular on the convergence between Li Da's reading of dialectical materialism and the "orthodoxy" which prevailed in Soviet philosophical circles of the early 1930s, for this particular "orthodoxy" was to have a dramatic impact on the development of Marxism in China, partly as a result of Li's efforts. We will also analyse Li's elaboration of the "orthodoxy" which emerged in post-1949 China, through an investigation of his writings on Mao Zedong Thought, and particularly its philosophical dimensions. But we will pause as well to consider areas of divergence from "orthodoxy" (whether new or old) and contemplate their significance for the development of Li's thought.

Our inquiry commences in the May Fourth period. The young Li Da is still in Japan, struggling to master Marxism. He takes up his brush to give voice to the words inside him, words which he hopes will illuminate the revolutionary path for like-minded Chinese incensed at China's humiliation at the hands of foreign powers, and the poverty and injustice suffered by her people.

Notes

1. Li's early conversion to Marxism has not been given sufficient recognition by historians of the early Chinese Communist movement; moreover, he was not, like many of the other early converts to Marxism in China, first attracted to anarchism. See the otherwise excellent studies by Michael Y.L. Luk, *The Origins of Chinese Bolshevism: An Ideology in the Making, 1920–1928* (Hong Kong: Oxford University Press, 1990); also Arif Dirlik, *The Origins of Chinese Communism* (New York: Oxford University Press, 1989).

2. See Karl Korsch, *Marxism and Philosophy* (London: NLB, 1970); also Georg Lukács, *History and Class Consciousness: Studies in Marxist Dialectics* (London: Merlin Press, 1971).

3. See, for example, Benjamin I. Schwartz, *Chinese Communism and the Rise of Mao* (New York and London: Harper and Row, 1951); also *Communism and China: Ideology in Flux* (New York: Atheneum, 1970). See also Stuart R. Schram, *The Political Thought of Mao Tse-tung* (Harmondsworth: Penguin, 1969, revised edn); also *Mao Zedong: A Preliminary Reassessment* (Hong Kong: The Chinese University Press, 1983); and *The Thought of Mao Tse-tung* (Cambridge: Cambridge University Press, 1989). See also Maurice Meisner, "Utopian Socialist Themes in Maoism," in John W. Lewis (ed.), *Peasant Rebellion and Communist Revolution in Asia* (Stanford: Stanford University Press, 1976), pp. 207–52; also "Leninism and Maoism: Some Populist Perspectives on Marxism-Leninism in China", *China Quarterly*, Vol. 45 (January–March 1971), pp. 2–36; and *Mao's China and After: A History of the People's Republic of China* (New York: The Free Press, 1977, 1986).

4. I have argued elsewhere that certain themes within Mao Zedong's thought were also more "orthodox" than most secondary accounts suggest. See Nick Knight (ed.), *Mao Zedong on Dialectical Materialism: Writings on Philosophy, 1937* (Armonk, New York: M.E. Sharpe, 1990), Introduction; also "'On Contradiction' and 'On New Democracy': Contrasting Perspectives on Causation and Social Change in the Thought of Mao Zedong", *Bulletin of Concerned Asian Scholars*, Vol. 22, No. 2 (1990), pp. 18–34.

5. See, for example, Loren R. Graham, *Science and Philosophy in the Soviet Union* (New York: Alfred A. Knopf, 1972), esp. Chapter 2.

6. See Z.A. Jordan, *The Evolution of Dialectical Materialism: A Philosophical and Sociological Analysis* (London: Macmillan, 1967), p. 11.

7. A primer on dialectical materialism published recently in the Soviet Union explicitly makes this point and rejects assertions to the contrary as the work of "bourgeois ideologues and revisionists of all stripe". Dialectical materialism was

"founded by Marx and Engels" and is an "integral doctrine". See V. Krapivin, *What is Dialectical Materialism?* (Moscow: Progress Publishers, 1985), pp. 91–96.

8. See also George Lichtheim, *Marxism: An Historical and Critical Study* (London: Routledge and Kegan Paul, 1961), Chapter 4; also Lucio Colletti's "Introduction" to Karl Marx, *Early Writings* (Harmondsworth: Penguin, 1975), pp. 14–16; also Gustav A. Wetter, *Dialectical Materialism: A Historical and Systematic Survey of Philosophy in the Soviet Union* (New York: Praeger, 1958), pp. 280ff, and passim; also Terrel Carver, *Marx and Engels: The Intellectual Relationship* (Brighton: Wheatsheaf Books, 1983), passim; Norman Levine, *The Tragic Deception: Marx Contra Engels* (Oxford and Santa Barbara: Clio Books, 1975); Richard T. De George, *Patterns of Soviet Thought* (Ann Arbor: University of Michigan Press, 1966), esp. pp. 107–8.

9. Lichtheim, *Marxism: An Historical and Critical Study*, esp. pp. 246–47; see also Henri Lefebvre, *Dialectical Materialism* (London: Jonathon Cape, 1968), pp. 13–19.

10. Karl Marx, *A Contribution to the Critique of Political Economy* (London: Lawrence and Wishart, 1971), Preface.

11. Ibid., p. 6.

12. Karl Marx, *Grundrisse: Foundations of the Critique of Political Economy (Rough Draft)* (Harmondsworth: Penguin Books, 1973); and Karl Marx, "Marginal Notes on A. Wagner, *Lehrbuch der Politischen Ökonomie*", in *Theoretical Practice*, No. 5 (1972).

13. Karl Marx and Frederick Engels, *Selected Works* (Moscow: FLPH, 1951), Vol. II, p. 325.

14. Frederick Engels, *Anti-Dühring (Herr Eugen Dühring's Revolution in Science)* (Peking FLP, 1976), p. 9.

15. Frederick Engels, *Dialectics of Nature* (Moscow: FLPH, 1954), pp. 5–6, 8.

16. Engels, *Anti-Dühring*, pp. 12–13.

17. Ibid., p. 43.

18. Ibid., p. 77.

19. Ibid., pp. 152–53.

20. Engels, *Dialectics of Nature*, p. 83, see also p. 27.

21. Ibid., p. 27.

22. Engels, *Ludwig Feuerbach*, pp. 334–35.

23. Ibid., p. 336.

24. Ibid., p. 341.

25. Engels, *Anti-Dühring*, pp. 105–20.

26. Marx, *A Contribution to the Critique of Political Economy*, pp. 20–21.

27. For a very lengthy and none too positive elaboration of what this text "means", see John Plamenatz, *German Marxism and Russian Communism* (London: Longmans, Green, 1954). For a more positive assessment, see Derek Sayer, *The Violence of Abstraction: The Analytic Foundations of Historical Materialism* (Oxford: Basil Blackwell, 1987).

28. For my views on the problem of "reading", see Nick Knight, "The Marxism of Mao Zedong: Empiricism and Discourse in the Field of Mao Studies", *The Australian Journal of Chinese Affairs*, No. 16 (July 1986), pp. 7–22.

29. See, for example, Karl Marx, *Capital, Volume I* (Harmondsworth: Penguin, 1976), pp. 915–16: "But they all employ the power of the state, the concentrated and

organized force of society, to hasten, as in a hothouse, the process of transformation of the feudal mode of production into the capitalist mode, and to shorten the transition." See also Karl Marx, "The Eighteenth Brumaire of Louis Bonaparte", in *Surveys from Exile* (Harmondsworth: Penguin, 1973), pp. 142-249; also (with Frederick Engels), "The Communist Manifesto", in *The Revolutions of 1848* (Harmondsworth: Penguin, 1973), pp. 62-98.

30. Karl Marx and Frederick Engels, *Selected Letters* (Peking: FLP, 1977), p. 75. Emphasis in original.

31. Jordan, for example, has argued that the notion "that dialectical materialism was formulated once and for all in its final and perfect form by Marx and Engels is an idea deeply embedded in Soviet philosophy". Z.A. Jordan, *The Evolution of Dialectical Materialism: A Philosophical and Sociological Analysis* (London: Macmillan, 1967), p. x.

32. Graham, *Science and Philosophy in the Soviet Union*, p. 25; see also Tom Bottomore and Maximilan Rubel (eds), *Karl Marx: Selected Writings in Sociology and Social Philosophy* (Harmondsworth: Penguin, 1963), Introduction; and Jordan, *The Evolution of Dialectical Materialism*, p. 184. However, John Gerber claims that it was Joseph Dietzgen (1828-86), the German "worker-philosopher", whose thought Marx praised, who first coined the term "dialectical materialism". See Gerber's Preface to Serge Bricianer, *Pannekoek and the Workers' Councils* (Saint Louis: Telos Press, 1978), p. 4.

33. George Plekhanov, *Materialismus Militans* (Moscow: Foreign Publishers, 1973), p. 8, emphasis in original.

34. See, however, Jordan, *The Evolution of Dialectical Materialism*, pp. 185-88. Jordan suggests that Plekhanov did not endorse Engels' absolute materialism, for, aware of the implications of Kant's critique of pure reason for all metaphysical speculation, including materialism, Plekhanov endorsed what Jordan calls a "genetic materialism".

35. George Plekhanov, *In Defence of Materialism: The Development of the Monist View of History* (London: Lawrence and Wishart, 1947), pp. 91-107.

36. See Jordan, *The Evolution of Dialectical Materialism*, pp. 188-90.

37. Plekhanov, *In Defence of Materialism*, p. 138.

38. Ibid., p. 180.

39. Ibid., p. 175.

40. Ibid., pp. 185-86. Emphasis in original.

41. Ibid., p. 292.

42. Ibid., p. 291. Emphasis in original.

43. George Plekhanov, *Fundamental Problems of Marxism* (London: Martin Lawrence Ltd, n.d.).

44. Ibid., pp. 3-4.

45. Ibid., pp. 26-27.

46. Ibid., p. 113.

47. Ibid., p. 119.

48. *Materialismus Militans*, pp. 57-59, quoting Engels.

49. V.I. Lenin, *Materialism and Empirio-Criticism* (Peking: FLP, 1972), p. 119.

50. Ibid., pp. 152-53.

51. V.I. Lenin, *Collected Works* (London: Lawrence and Wishart, 1963), Vol. 38, p. 360. Emphasis in original.

52. Ibid., p. 223
53. Ibid., pp. 221–22.
54. See Lenin, *Collected Works*, Vol. 3; and V.I. Lenin, *Imperialism, the Highest Stage of Capitalism: A Popular Outline* (Peking: FLP, 1969).
55. Lenin, *Collected Works*, Vol. 21, p. 59. Emphasis in original.
56. V.I. Lenin, *What is to be Done?: Burning Questions of Our Movement* (Peking: FLP, 1975), p. 149.
57. "There is not a single economic phenomenon among the [Russian] peasantry that does not bear this contradictory form, one specifically peculiar to the capitalist system." *Collected Works*, Vol. 3, p. 172.
58. For the development of the conception of philosophy within the Bolshevik Party before 1917, see Joravsky, *Soviet Marxism and Natural Science, 1917–1932* (New York: Columbia University Press, 1961), pp. 24–44.
59. The second edition of Lenin's *Materialism and Empirio-Criticism* was published in September 1920. Lenin expressed the hope, in the Preface to this second edition, that the book would "prove useful as an aid to an acquaintance with the philosophy of Marxism, dialectical materialism": Lenin, *Materialism and Empirio-Criticism*, p. 8.
60. Rene Ahlberg, "The Forgotten Philosopher: Abram Deborin," in Leopold Labedz (ed.), *Revisionism: Essays on the History of Marxist Ideas* (London, George Allen & Unwin, 1962), p. 129.
61. See Werner Meissner, *Philosophy and Politics in China: The Controversy over Dialectical Materialism in the 1930s* (London: Hurst and Co., 1990), pp. 16–17.
62. See Graham, *Science and Philosophy in the Soviet Union*, p. 43.
63. Rene Ahlberg, "The Forgotten Philosopher", pp. 126–41.
64. Ibid, pp. 129–32.
65. Ibid., p. 134.
66. For an analysis of the increasing domination of the affairs of the Academy by political and ideological considerations, see Loren R. Graham, *The Soviet Academy of Sciences and the Communist Party, 1927–1932* (Princeton: Princeton University Press, 1967).
67. Ahlberg, "The Forgotten Philosopher", p. 132.
68. Ibid., p. 134.
69. It is fashionable in much Western literature to belittle dialectical materialism as a philosophy. However, for a reasoned defence of it, see Graham, *Science and Philosophy in the Soviet Union*, Chapter 2.
70. Indeed, Lenin had read and been influenced by Deborin's *Introduction to the Philosophy of Dialectical Materialism*, written in 1908; see Ahlberg, p. 126. For Lenin's critical annotations on Deborin's article of 1909, "Dialectical Materialism", see Lenin, *Collected Works*, Vol. 38, pp. 477–85.
71. Deborin had in fact left the Bolshevik Party in 1907 and become a Menshevik. He did not rejoin the Communist Party of the Soviet Union until 1928.
72. See Eugene Kamenka, "Soviet Philosophy, 1917–67," in Alex Simirenko (ed.), *Social Thought in the Soviet Union* (Chicago: Quadrangle Books, 1969), p. 95; also Ahlberg, "The Forgotten Philosopher", pp. 136–40. The pejorative term "Menshevizing idealism" appears frequently in the Soviet texts on philosophy from the early 1930s which Li Da was to read and translate; he was thus left in no doubt as to Deborin's outcast status in the world of Marxist philosophy.

73. On the issue of repetition in Soviet philosophical writings, see Kamenka, "Soviet Philosophy, 1917-1967", p. 95; also De George, *Patterns of Soviet Thought*, p. 193.

74. M.B. Mitin, *Bianzhengweiwulun yu lishiweiwulun* (Dialectical and Historical Materialism), translated by Shen Zhiyuan (n.p.: Shangwu yinshuguan, 1936), pp. 160-61.

75. Ibid., p. 212; also W.N. Kalosikov, *Sulian Makesi lieningzhuyi zhexue shi gangyao (sanshi niandai)* (A Commentary on the History of Soviet Marxist-Leninist Philosophy During the 1930s) (Beijing: Qiushi chubanshe, 1985), p. 55.

76. Mitin, *Dialectical and Historical Materialism*, p. 222; see also pp. 212-13.

77. Knight (ed.), *Mao Zedong on Dialectical Materialism*, pp. 31-35, 267-77, and passim.

78. M. Shirokov and A. Aizenberg et al., *Bianzhengfa weiwulun jiaocheng* (A Course on Dialectical Materialism), translated by Li Da and Lei Zhongjian (Shanghai: Bigengtang, 1935), pp. 15, and 309. Li Da was to take this Soviet text on philosophy which he had translated into Chinese as a model for his own *Shehuixue dagang* (Elements of Sociology). In this text, also read and annotated by Mao, Li Da refers to the law of the unity of opposites as the "basic law" of dialectics which incorporated all other laws and categories of dialectical materialism. See *Li Da wenji* (Collected Writings of Li Da) (Beijing: Renmin chubanshe, 1981), Vol. 2, p. 132.

79. M.B. Mitin (ed.), *Xin zhexue dagang* (Outline of New Philosophy), translated by Ai Siqi and Zheng Yili (n.p.: Dushu shenghuo chubanshe, 1936), p. 238.

80. Kalosikov, *A Commentary on the History of Marxist-Leninist Philosophy During the 1930s*, p. 62.

81. Mitin, *Dialectical and Historical Materialism*, p. 247; also Shirokov and Aizenberg, *A Course on Dialectical Materialism*, p. 348.

82. Mitin, *Dialectical and Historical Materialism*, p. 253.

83. See also Shirokov and Aizenberg, *A Course on Dialectical Materialism*, pp. 271-76, 321-48.

84. Shirokov and Aizenberg, *A Course on Dialectical Materialism*, pp. 193-211; also Mitin, *Dialectical and Historical Materialism*, pp. 172-86; and Mitin, *Outline of New Philosophy*, pp. 341-411.

85. Kolosikov, *A Commentary on the History of Marxist-Leninist Philosophy in the Soviet Union During the 1930s*, pp. 111-13.

86. Konstantin F. Shteppa, *Russian Historians and the Soviet State* (New Brunswick, New Jersey: Rutgers University Press, 1962), pp. 67, 101, 112.

87. J.V. Stalin, *Problems of Leninism* (Peking: FLP, 1976), pp. 871-72.

88. V.I. Lenin, *What is to be Done?: Burning Questions of Our Movement*.

89. Although the extent to which the Japanese Marxists pursued the political theme within Marxism-Leninism, even after the Russian Revolution, is doubtful. See Gail Lee Bernstein, "The Russian Revolution, the Early Japanese Socialists, and the Problem of Dogmatism", *Studies in Comparative Communism*, Vol. IX, No. 4 (Winter 1976), pp. 327-48.

90. Germaine A. Hoston, *Marxism and the Crisis of Development in Prewar Japan* (Princeton: Princeton University Press, 1986), p. 43.

91. In Karl Marx, *Surveys from Exile* (Harmondsworth: Penguin, 1973), p. 146.

92. Georg Lukács, for example, argued that "Fatalism and voluntarism are only mutually contradictory to an undialectical and unhistorical mind. In the dialectical view of history they prove to be necessarily complementary opposites." *History and Class Consciousness*, p. 4.

93. Although, in translating Japanese translations of German texts, Li compared the Japanese with the German original. See his translator's postface to Hermann Gorter, *Weiwushiguan jieshuo* (An explanation of the materialist conception of history), translated by Li Da (Shanghai: Zhonghua shuju, 1920), appendix, p. 7. Li did, however, concede his debt to his friend Li Hanjun, whose German was better than his own.

94. See Dirlik, *The Origins of Chinese Communism*, pp. 99–103. Dirlik suggests that Kawakami's influence was very pervasive among Chinese radicals at this time: "it may not be an exaggeration that Chinese thinking on Marxism in the immediate May Fourth Period was shaped by Kawakami. His emphases became theirs, his doubts appeared as theirs" (p. 105).

95. Note, however, that Kawakami was criticised by other Japanese Marxists for his ethical views "and was driven by his critics to purge his interpretations of unorthodox ideas in order to become a 'pure' Marxist": Bernstein, "The Russian Revolution, the early Japanese Socialists", p. 340. See also Gail Lee Bernstein, *Japanese Marxist: A Portrait of Kawakami Hajime, 1879–1946* (Cambridge Mass.: Harvard University Press, 1976), pp. 119–23; the quote is taken from p. 120, emphasis in original.

96. Bernstein, *Japanese Marxist*, p. 124.

97. Luk, *The Origins of Chinese Bolshevism: An Ideology in the Making, 1920–1928*, p. 49.

98. Li Da also acknowledged the influence of Japanese political economists in the preparation of his research into the Chinese economy. See his preface to *Zhongguo chanye geming gaiguan* (A General Survey of China's Revolution in Production) (Shanghai: Kunlun shudian, 1930), pp. 1–3.

99. Bernstein, *Japanese Marxist*, pp. 137–43; also Germaine A. Hoston, *Marxism and the Crisis of Development in Prewar*, p. 47.

100. See *Mao Zedong zhexue pizhuji* (Philosophical Annotations of Mao Zedong) (Beijing: Zhongyang wenxian chubanshe, 1988), pp. 453–92.

101. Bernstein, *Japanese Marxist*, p. 143.

102. Sugiyama Sakae, *Shehui kexue gailun* (An Introduction to Social Science), trans. Li Da and Qian Tieru (Shanghai: Kunlun shudian, 1929), see the translators' preface, pp. 1–3.

103. "Chen Duxiu and Li Da wrote emphatically on the uncompromising differences between Bolshevism, which they described as the only correct interpretation of Marxism, and all such schools of 'opportunism' as Bernstein, Social Democracy, and Menshevism, which they all rejected. Thus, a concept of correct thought was firmly established at this early date." Luk, *The Origins of Chinese Bolshevism: An Ideology in the Making, 1920–1928*, p. 213, see also pp. 59–60.

3

Li Da and Marxism, 1919–23

Li Da had returned to China from Japan in May 1918 as a representative of the Save China Association. The month he spent in China working to alter the pro-Japanese policies of the Duan Qirui government convinced him that reformist policies, such as petitioning the government, were of little if any use. He returned to Japan in June, abandoning his science studies to immerse himself in the study of Marxism-Leninism, and to translate works on Marxism into Chinese. It was during this subsequent year of study that his conversion to Marxism occurred. The outbreak of the May Fourth movement and the subsequent June Third movement prompted Li to write a number of essays on the subject of socialism. We commence our analysis of Li Da's understanding of Marxism, and in particular its philosophy and social theory, with these essays.

What Is Socialism?

Although Li does not mention Marxism in either of these essays on socialism (1919), it is clear from their contents that he wrote them from the perspective of Marxism.[1] The first essay, "What is Socialism?", spells out in simple terms the ideals and values of socialism. Socialism opposes individual competition and supports mutual co-operation; socialism opposes the power of capital and supports the power of labour; socialism opposes the monopolisation of things by individuals and supports common ownership; socialism breaks down economic impediments and restores the freedoms of the masses. Li then spells out the distinction between socialism and communism. Socialism advocates common production and distribution, while communism advocates life in common (*gongtong de shenghuo*); socialism advocates the abolition of all capital, but not all private property, whereas communism desires the abolition of all private property, with all property to be held in common by society. It is apparent that Li had, by this time, grasped that communism represented the final goal of revolutionary activity, and that to employ the values of communism to guide a socialist movement in the present would be premature. It is possible that Li drew this distinction from his reading of Lenin who, in *The State and Revolution* (which Li had already studied), had cautioned against the utopian idea of thinking that communism could be established without proceeding through the phase of socialism.

When Li turns his attention to the distinction between socialism and anarchism, a similar form of logic is at work. Anarchists desire the immediate abolition of the state, whereas socialists desire a government which will represent the whole of society, the abolition of state power only becoming possible with the realisation of communism. Significantly, Li concurs that socialism shares with the more extreme forms of anarchism a belief in the methods of violence (*baoli*) and assassinations, although he admits that many socialists are more moderate in their approach than the extreme anarchists. Li's admission that socialism employs force to achieve its ends indicates that he had, from the outset, accepted an important credo of the political dimension of Marxism: that the achievement of the goals of socialism is dependent, at least in part, on human action, and is not just a function of economic forces entirely beyond human control.

The second essay, "The Goals of Socialism", provides a brief history of socialism, which is, Li suggests, a product of the nineteenth century. The French Revolution had swept away the monarchy and the aristocratic class, but the successes of this revolution were only political, and an investigation of the economic realm reveals that there was still inequality, a wide gulf between labourers and capitalists, and it was this which had given rise to socialism. Socialism at its simplest, Li asserts, is a doctrine which seeks to rectify inequality in the economic realm — this is its fundamental aim. But it also has the goal of restoring genuine equality in the realms of thought, of consciousness.

The theme of equality emerges in another of Li Da's early essays, "On the Liberation of Women" (*Nuzi jiefanglun*, 1919),[2] and the issue of equality between the sexes and opposition to the subordinate status of women in Chinese society continues as a powerful theme in his subsequent early writings.[3] While we will not be pursuing Li's interest in gender equality, these preliminary explanations of the causes of women's oppression are of interest as they bear on the issue of his understanding and application of Marxist social theory. Did Li employ a materialist, class analysis to comprehend the subordination of women in Chinese society? Did he perceive the subordination of women in morals, habits and customs, in law and in politics,[4] as a function of a class society?

Indeed, this essay argues that the oppression of women had an economic origin; in particular, the decline in women's status had been a function of their loss of independent economic status with the onset of settled forms of agriculture and animal husbandry. The liberation of women required certain economic conditions ("economic independence for women"), but also their "spiritual independence", for their spiritual oppression had been even more severe than their economic oppression; in the realm of morality and the acquisition of knowledge, women had been stifled. As economic and material factors altered, these spiritual impediments to the liberation of women would also be transformed. But the most pressing task was for women to engage in labour, and to realise their capacity for economic independence. In this respect, the struggle for socialism and the struggle for gender equality intersected, for only with the economic conditions created by socialism could women achieve the economic independence Li perceives as necessary for their liberation.

Marx and Marxist Theory Explained

In his first major essay on Marxist theory, "Marx Restored" (*Makesi huanyuan*),[5] written in December 1920 in Shanghai and published in *Xin Qingnian* in January 1921, Li argued that Marx had explained the principles and methods of social revolution by reference to seven major points. First, all relations of production and property relations are the basis (*jichu*) of the social system; all the institutions of religion, philosophy, law and so on are determined by this economic base. Second, when the material productive forces of society develop to a certain stage, they come into conflict with the prevailing relations of production and property relations. Under capitalism, capitalists extract surplus value from labourers, the result being that the rich get richer and the poor get poorer, thus splitting society into two great classes, the propertied and the propertyless. Third, the history of humankind is the history of class struggle. Capitalism develops to a certain stage at which the vast mass of the proletariat and the minority propertied class confront each other. There emerges among the labourers a class mentality (*xinli*) and consciousness, and they unite and organise to become an immense class, and proceed to engage in a fierce struggle with the propertied class. Fourth, capitalism has international tendencies, and the battle waged by the proletariat implies international cooperation. No proletariat can be completely liberated while class oppression and class struggle persist anywhere in the world. Fifth, proletarian revolution, in overthrowing the power of the propertied class, establishes a workers' state and institutes a dictatorship of the proletariat. Sixth, when the proletariat becomes the dominant class, it expropriates all capital from the capitalist class and concentrates the instruments of production in the hands of the workers' state; with maximum speed, it then develops the forces of production. Seventh, the state is an institution for the oppression of one class by another. After the dictatorship of the proletariat has completely taken over the operation of the economy and has transformed the instruments of production into publicly owned state property, then the interests of the labouring class become the interests of society as a whole; there are no more class distinctions, the productive forces are fully developed, and all people will achieve freedom. Under such circumstances, the state naturally withers away (*xiaomie*), and a free society naturally appears.

Li sums up by asserting Marxist socialism to be a revolutionary, uncompromising, and internationalist doctrine, one which advocates the dictatorship of the proletariat. Marxism is a science, he continues, incorporating five major principles: the materialist conception of history, the theory of the concentration of capital, the theory of the collapse of capital, the theory of surplus value, and the theory of class struggle. Marxist theorists must also be practitioners; errors emerge as a result of a separation between theory and practice, from which a distinction between "orthodox" (*zhengtong*) Marxism and revisionism emerges. Li categorises the reasons for the degeneration (*duoluo*) of Marxism into errors of practice and errors of theory. Errors of practice had derived most importantly from the reformist policies advocated by the followers of Lasalle amongst the German socialists, with their belief in the possibility of using the existing capitalist state to further the interests of the working class. This approach was based on the possibility of economic and political reform following the securing of a parliamentary majority through the electoral process. Even though the Social Democratic Labour Party, formed after the Unity Congress of 1875, included many Marxists, its policies were premised on the possibility of the harmonisation of classes, rather than class struggle. The influence of the followers of Lasalle was evident in the Gotha Program, and they remained a strong force in this new party. Although Marxist rhetoric was often employed at the level of theory, this was out of step with the reformist policies employed, policies based on "statism" (*guojiazhuyi*). Marxism in Germany had thus degenerated, at the level of practice, from class struggle and opposition to parliamentarianism, to class conciliation and support for the parliamentary system.

The degeneration of Marxism was also a function of theoretical failure. According to the materialist conception of history, at a certain stage in the development of the capitalist system, the productive forces come into conflict with capitalism's social form (*shehui xingshi*); capitalism's monopoly becomes a fetter on the forces of production, the centralisation of production and the socialisation of labour become incompatible with capitalism, and a new social organisation emerges to replace it. In explaining this process, Li refers to the important role played by human spirit and consciousness; without these factors, Marxism's historical materialism becomes a mechanistic theory of history.[6] The oppression of the proletariat by the capitalist develops, sooner or later, a class consciousness among the proletariat; on the basis of this class consciousness emerges a class mentality, and it is only with the appearance of this that class organisation and a class movement are possible. The final result of class struggle is the victory of the proletariat and the overthrow of capitalism. The materialist conception of history thus explains, on the one hand, the process of the development of the capitalist system while, on the other, emphasising the emerging strength of the proletariat within contemporary society. To ignore or de-emphasise class consciousness and mentality in this process is to hinder the class struggle, and the social revolution will consequently not occur.

One further important reason for the theoretical degeneration of Marxism, according to Li, is that some Marxists had come to doubt Marx's predictions regarding the concentration of capital and the increasing polarisation of the classes. Rather than a revolutionary overthrow, there would be an evolutionary emergence of the new society, achieved through reformism. This shift from a revolutionary to an evolutionary perspective had been accompanied by a shift, in art and literature, from naturalism to neo-romanticism, and in philosophy, from positivism to neo-idealism (*xinlixiangzhuyi*). This latter philosophy had threatened to replace Marxism's materialist conception of history, and had been accompanied by the attempted Kantianisation (*Kangdehua*) of Marxism.

Li then provides a very interesting interpretation of the political limits of a Marxist political movement. Referring to the ten "measures" in the *Communist Manifesto*, Li notes that their achievement relies heavily on the use of the state. The revisionists of Marxism have perceived in this a sanction for reformism, but Li stresses that all social questions are class questions, and a question of the communication between classes. In some circumstances, the overthrow of the propertied class is a necessity; in others, there is the possibility of some cooperation between the classes (*xieshou*, literally "hand in hand"). This movement is a political movement, and political movements must use the state. However, the revisionists err in giving too much emphasis to the political movement, to the possibility of communication between the classes, and hence restrict the opposition between classes within the sphere of the political movement. Once this occurs, Marxism degenerates from a revolutionary doctrine to reformism. Nevertheless, Li emphasises that a political struggle and political organisation are part and parcel of the struggle by the proletariat to overthrow capitalism. He insists that the independence of the organisations of labour must be maintained, otherwise they will perish, for these organisations represent the school of socialism — one within which workers struggle against capitalism, and whose end result will be the achievement of socialism. It is only if it can form from within its own ranks a genuine working class party that the working class will gain the strength to oppose capitalism.

In the realm of theory, Li concludes, Marxism is complete (*wancheng*); in the realm of fact, it can also become complete. Here Li provides the example of the new Russia of the labourers and peasants which, under Lenin, was building a dictatorship of the proletariat (*laodong zhuanzheng*). Lenin is not, according to Li, a creator of Marxism (*chuangzaojia*), but is one who has put Marxism into practice (*shixingjia*), and this is his great achievement.

It is apparent from "Marxism Restored" that Li rejected an evolutionary and reformist interpretation of Marxism. He accepted, rather, a revolutionary perspective, one grounded in a materialist conception of the underlying impulses leading to historical change, one which nevertheless perceived a role for conscious political action (in the form of organisation and policies) based on the class interests of the proletariat. Conscious political action could thus be a significant factor in the eventual overthrow of capitalism and the establishment of a socialist society. Li perceived no contradiction between the economic and political readings of Marxism; as he points out, at the level of theory, Marxism is "complete". By the same token, he was well aware that correct practice is essential, for as circumstances change and as the extent and intensity of class struggle varies, so policies will need to alter. Economics provides the framework, but within this framework the proletariat and its political party must exploit all possible opportunities to advance their cause, as long as revolutionary goals are not compromised.

Li's acceptance of both the economic and political dimensions of Marxism as components of one "complete" theoretical system is also evident in a short speech delivered at the same time he wrote "Marxism Restored". In "The Labourer and Socialism" (*Laodongzhe yu shehuizhuyi*),[7] Li explains the oppression and exploitation of labour under capitalism by the emergence of a new social system premised on the industrial use of machinery. The machinery belongs to the capitalist; the labourer, without resources, has no option but to toil for the capitalist for wages that are barely able to sustain the labourer. The miserable economic conditions of labour are thus explained by reference to the form of production and economic divisions characteristic of capitalism. In pondering how this inequitable situation can be overturned, Li again invokes the necessity of class consciousness among the working class, one which would allow the working class to perceive the exploitation and oppression of capitalism and to establish itself into unions and other organisations of resistance. On this basis, the capitalists can be opposed; the stronger is the organisation of labour, the greater is its strength. Initially, the struggle of the organisations of the working class involves a demand for shorter working hours (four or five hours a day is enough, according to Li) and more pay (the more the better); however, with the increased strength of the organisations of labour, open battle can be joined with the capitalists, and with their eventual overthrow the final goal of socialism will be achieved.

Deliberation on Social Revolution

Li Da wrote a number of revealing polemical essays prior to the establishment of the Chinese Communist Party which target doctrines such as anarchism and "false socialism", doctrines he regarded as antithetical to Marxism. These essays tell us much about Li's position on Marxism's theory of social change, for in critiquing these (from Li's perspective) spurious doctrines, he was compelled to elaborate his own views. One of the most significant of these polemical essays is "Deliberation on Social Revolution", published in the *The Communist* in December 1920 (under the *nom de plume* Jiang Chun).[8]

In this essay, Li queries whether those who participated in the French Revolution had mastered Rousseau's theories, and whether those who participated in the Russian Revolution had all mastered Marxism. Li responds that these revolutionaries were responding primarily to economic and political oppression. For people to grasp the theories of Rousseau and Marx, these theories first had to be explained. Li's explanation of Marxism runs as follows. The foundation (*jichu*) of social structure is the material production and exchange of human life. All causes of revolution are to be found in the methods of production and exchange, and are not to be explained by reference to human wisdom or abstract truths. Put simply, Li asserts, social revolution does not derive from philosophy, but from changes in the economic conditions of contemporary society.

Li then introduces the importance of class by quoting the famous sentence from the *Communist Manifesto*: "The history of all hitherto existing society is the history of class struggles." There are those, he says, who suggest that China has no class distinctions, that there are no landlords and capitalists, and that social revolution is not possible. Li responds that, since ancient times, China has had a class structure made up of those who owned land and those who were tenants. The latter had no choice in the matter; their lives were difficult, labour was harsh, their living conditions were poor, and the lot of many of them was starvation as every year they were compelled to hand over more than half of their harvest to the landlords. Their suffering is there for anyone who has eyes to see, but some cannot see it, Li complains. The same harsh working and living conditions are also the lot of the working class, a class clearly in evidence in China as a result of the revolution in production China was experiencing. Although China's industry had not developed to the extent occurring in Europe, America or Japan, the lives of the Chinese proletariat were even more tragic than the lives of their counterparts in these more industrially developed countries. And while the confrontation between labour and capital might on the surface seem different in China, in actuality it was no different. The commodities produced by European, American and Japanese, and to a lesser extent Chinese, factories entered the Chinese market and undercut Chinese handicrafts. Unable to compete, Chinese artisans had no option but to enter the factories of (usually) foreign capital in China's large cities and become slaves to the machines within them. The influence of foreign capital was felt on agriculture too, and many peasants were forced into the ranks of the unemployed where they faced the prospect of death from starvation and cold. Rather than there being no labouring class, China had a surplus of labour. The increasing misery of the proletariat and the increasing wealth of the propertied classes meant that the opportunity for social revolution had arrived.

But how is this revolution to be achieved? Li canvasses a number of possible options. The first he considers is the parliamentary strategy — that is, working to elect members to parliament who will represent the interests of the working class by introducing laws of benefit to labour. Li dismisses this option. After all, political power is in actuality the organised force of one class for the oppression of other classes. The capitalists will not allow their position of power to be substantially threatened by the actions of parliament; the parliamentary representatives of labour will thus be forced into all sorts of compromises and will not achieve their socialist objectives. Li again uses the example of the German Social Democratic Party as an illustration of the uselessness of this strategy. The second strategy considered by Li is that of the union movement. Here he makes a distinction between reformist trade unions, which adopt the means of class conciliation, and revolutionary unions which are socialist and adopt class struggle in order to transform the current system. One of the means open to such unions is the industrial strike, but strikes of this sort on their own will not fundamentally alter the current system, nor the relationship between labour and capital. General strikes have a more revolutionary ambition and potential, but there are limitations here also. Nevertheless, Li endorses the organisation of labour into unions and the education of the working class to its revolutionary role. However, it is the third strategy, that of the "direct movement" (*zhijie yundong*) based on class struggle, which is the most important. Examples of direct movements are, according to Li, the 1871 Paris Commune, the 1904 Italian workers' movement, the 1917 Russian Revolution, and the 1918 rice riots in Japan led by the proletariat. The May Fourth and June Third movements in China were similar, but had some incorrect characteristics. Nevertheless, the situation in China was now such that there existed the opportunity for large-scale movements, and Li calls for the organisation of a great union (*tuanti*) of workers, peasants and soldiers to grasp this opportunity, to launch such a movement, to seize political power and to establish socialism.

Li concludes by asserting that social revolution is inevitable when the capitalist system has developed to a certain point. Importantly, he adds that this process can be speeded up through "human force" (*renwei shili*), through uncompromising class struggle. This was the reason why revolution broke out in Russia and not in Britain or America, where the capitalist systems and union movements were ten times more developed than in Russia. In Russia, the force exerted by the revolutionary party far exceeds any comparable action in Britain or America. The same is required in China, but it can only be achieved, Li suggests, through the expenditure of great effort in the realm of practice.

"Deliberations on Social Revolution" reinforces an important theme in Li's Marxism which had been present from virtually his first published writings: that an explanation of revolution is to be sought initially and primarily in large-scale economic changes, such as the rise of industrial capitalism, and the consequent transformations in the social system with their increasingly intense class contradictions. This, for Li, was the basis of a materialist explanation of the process of social revolution. However, this was not, and could not be, the end of the explanation, for this resulted only in a mechanistic and evolutionary view of the process of social change. Rather, once the conditions which made revolution possible had developed, other factors emerged as necessary for the successful realisation of this revolutionary potential. Of these, the organisation of the proletariat into unions and a political party, and the heightening of class consciousness and mentality amongst the working class, were the most significant. On the basis of successful organisation and a mature consciousness of its own exploitation and oppression, the proletariat could launch "direct movements" which threatened the very basis of the existing economic system, and which hastened the progress of historical change towards the goal of socialism. For Li, as we have already observed, there existed no tension between a recognition of massive economic forces as the demiurge of history and the significant role that political action and consciousness could play once these economic forces had reached a particular stage of development. These were dimensions of the one unified and "complete" theoretical system of the materialist conception of history.

Contra Liang Qichao, Contra the Anarchists

"Deliberations on Social Revolution" also reinforces the tendency, again evident from Li's very earliest writings, to elaborate his understanding of Marxism through a critique of doctrines which he regarded as false. Li was thus appealing to a conception of Marxism that he regarded as "orthodox", and his often polemical writings, directed at persons and doctrines both in China and beyond, were important, as Luk has observed, in instilling in the early Chinese communist movement a perception that there was a "correct" reading of Marxism and that those who did not adhere to its truths were legitimate targets for criticism.[9]

One of the targets of Li Da's criticism immediately prior to the establishment of the Chinese Communist Party was the famous scholar and reformer Liang Qichao.[10] In a lengthy essay published in *Xin Qingnian*, Li again detailed his view that the socialist movement could be explained only by reference to the revolution in China's production. As in Europe, where the emergence of industrial capitalism created the class conditions within which a socialist movement could emerge, so in China the apppearance of factory-based production, within which the exploitation of the new working class could occur, had led to a socialist movement whose goal was the overthrow of capitalism and the establishment of a socialist society based on public ownership of production. But how was this goal to be achieved? Li again emphasises the importance of organising the workers into unions, establishing schools within which socialist ideas can be propagated, studying how to manage the organs of production, and following appropriate training, adopting the strategy of the direct movement to institute a social revolution. It is not, as Liang Qichao had suggested, a matter of raising the status of the workers, but a transformation of the entire economic system.

In order to improve the economic situation of the working class, it would be necessary to expand production by establishing new productive enterprises. But should this be under the control of capitalists or socialists? Their methods, Li contends, are entirely different. Under capitalist control, the worker is nothing more than a wage slave; the surplus produced by the worker goes to the capitalist, and in times of over-production, the worker faces the prospect of unemployment. This is the unavoidable result of production unsupervised by politics. Under socialism, the organs of agricultural and industrial production are publicly owned, and there is equitable distribution of the results of production; the producer is not oppressed by the product and competition between humans will be completely eliminated. There will be no economic hardship and no danger of unemployment. Economic production under capitalism is characterised by an anarchic lack of order, while there is order and state direction under socialism. However, what Liang Qichao forgets, according to Li, is that capitalism is an unavoidable process, one essential for the creation of the consciousness of the working class. Nevertheless, society's future economic organisation must be socialist, and although China's productive enterprises were in their infancy, much less developed than in Europe, America or Japan, it would be foolish to merely replicate their unhappy experiences. China could learn, moreover, from the hard work and sacrifice of the movements in these places which sought to transform society, for the transformation of China should rely on the new and rational ideals of those inspired by socialism.

It is important to remember, Li argues, that capitalism is an international system, and the methods used to oppose it must also be appropriately international, and in particular must rely on the unity of the working class internationally. The working class has no country, and it must oppose capitalism wherever it oppresses workers. It is not appropriate to oppose foreign capitalism and to support Chinese capitalists, as some Chinese do. As Li points out, capitalists are "tigers", and they eat workers wherever they are. In opposing these tigers, Li again rejects the reformist parliamentary strategy. What is needed is the organisation of the workers into a labour movement which will facilitate strike action and educate the workers in the management of organisations. However, more important still is the strategy of the "direct movement". This can take one of two forms. The first is a direct movement of the form taken by Bolshevism (*laonongzhuyi de zhijie yundong*),[11] and the second is syndicalism. The latter advocates the use of strikes to implement revolution; the former unites the vast majority of the proletariat, thus increasing its fighting strength, allowing it to initiate an intense and general mass movement, to seize state power and allow the proletariat to become the dominant class. It is this Bolshevik strategy which is endorsed by Li; it succeeded in Russia, which was an agricultural country much like China, and it should be the strategy of the revolutionary movement in China also.

In May 1921, Li also returned to his earlier attack on anarchism. In an essay published in *The Communist*, he details and refutes the tenets of a number of different strands of anarchism.[12] The most significant part of this essay, for our purposes, is his critique of the anarchism of Bakunin and Kropotkin. Li agrees with Bakunin's proposition that humans are not independent entities and that they live socially; they are conscious creatures whose mission is to create the world. However, Li demurs at Bakunin's suggestion that all states are inevitably the creatures of the privileged classes. In Russia, power had shifted into the hands of the working class and in Germany attempts had been made to establish a social democratic state. Bakunin's opposition to all states is thus arbitrary. Li similarly objects to Kropotkin's suggestion that the state, politics and law are created by and invariably operate to the benefit of a small minority; rather, the state, politics and law of a socialist society will be welcomed by the working class, as they have been in Russia. Basic to Li's opposition to anarchism is his belief that politics and the state are not intrinsically evil; politics can be employed to change oppressive social systems, and in the hands of the working class, the state can organise production so that it runs both efficiently and to the benefit of the workers. Li sums up his opposition to the anarchists by insisting that society, economics and politics had developed historically, and could not be transformed on the basis of mere sentiment or opinion, as the anarchists wrongly believed; appropriate social conditions which created a new power were necessary for this revolutionary goal to be realised, and only Marxism could provide an understanding of this process.

Marxist Socialism

In the June 1921 edition of *Xin Qingnian*, Li returned to a consideration of the nature of Marxism.[13] A number of variants of Marxism had emerged, and it was therefore necessary to consider these in order to understand what constituted "true" Marxism.

According to Li, Marxism spread in the mid-1800s to various countries in Europe, and those who believed in Marxism enthusiastically endorsed and anticipated an early social revolution. They wanted to implement Marxist theory, and worked hard to that end; they refused to compromise, and engaged in direct movements. Their goal was the fundamental transformation of the existing system, and not its reform. Their tactics involved the uniting of the proletariat, and the building of the organisations of class struggle. They instituted a revolutionary political movement and, on the basis of the doctrine of communism, sought the establishment of a communist society. They opposed leniency towards their opponents, opposed seeking economic reforms through legislative means, and opposed cooperation with the capitalist class and exclusive reliance on the industrial movement. The Marxist movement at that time thus employed the tactic of the direct movement of the proletariat, and those involved in the socialist movement sought to thoroughly implement Marxism.

However, social revolution is, Li asserts, an entirely proletarian affair, and only if the proletariat is conscious of its mission could there be any hope for the development of the revolutionary movement. Although capitalism continually expanded and the size of the working class continually grew, the consciousness and mentality of the working class remained very much in its infancy and, as a result, the organisation and movement of the working class did not develop to any great extent. Despite the evolution of production and the tendency for concentration of ownership, these did not eventuate with the speed anticipated by Marx. Small and medium-sized enterprises appeared to increase, and the experience in agriculture ran counter to Marx's expectations, with the numbers of landlords increasing rather than decreasing; nor did the crisis in commerce eventuate as frequently as was thought. Confronted by this situation, socialists recognised that their efforts to raise the consciousness of the working class had not been successful and, contrary to Marxist theory, altered their approach in the realms of both theory and practice. Li again provides the example of the history of the German Social Democratic Party, which altered its orientation to embrace parliamentarianism, and which, while still superficially embracing Marxism, in reality had become a democratic party. There ensued, at the end of the nineteenth century, a conflict among Marxists, and there emerged two factions: the "orthodox" Marxists and the revisionists. The so-called "orthodox" Marxists naturally endorsed "pure" (*chuncui*) Marxism, but there existed a basic error in their understanding of Marxist theory, an error illuminated by their support for democracy and the parliamentary strategy. For Li, whether or not Marxists should adopt democracy and the parliamentary strategy was a recent question of great moment for Marxists. The writings of Kautsky and Lenin were relevant to this discussion, but whoever has studied Marxism and read the writings of these two would definitely understand which of them was the true (*zhenzheng*) Marxist.

Li does not bother to spell out his own conclusions, but it is very clear from his subsequent criticisms of the evolutionary and reformist doctrines of revisionism, and syndicalism's excessive reliance on union organisations, that his sympathies lie with Lenin's Bolshevist interpretation of Marxism. For Li, the dictatorship of the proletariat is a key criterion in the determination of what constitutes true Marxism. In response to Kautsky's denials, Li returns to Marx and, quoting from *The Civil War in France*, *Critique of the Gotha Programme* and the *Communist Manifesto*, insists that this concept did originate in Marxism. Moreover, democracy is not an absolute concept, and it is not appropriate to counterpose democracy to the dictatorship of the proletariat, as Kautsky does. Rather, democracy, as Lenin has demonstrated, is class democracy. The goal of the democracy of the working class (that is, the dictatorship of the proletariat) is the overthrow of the democracy of the capitalist class. But what is the essence of the dictatorship of the proletariat? On this issue, the opinions of Lenin are, according to Li, at one with those of Marx and Engels. Lenin, building on Marx and Engels' view of the state, argued that the state is a product of class antagonism, and an expression of the irreconcilability of the interests of the classes. The dictatorship of the bourgeoisie can only be superseded by the dictatorship of the proletariat, and it is the goal of the latter to eradicate the dominance of capitalist thought, customs and habits, to abolish the institutions which the capitalists had employed to oppress the working class, to seize the armed forces of the capitalists and to arm the working class, to suppress all counter-revolutionary forces, and throughout this political transitional period, to consolidate the foundations of the new society.

While Li evidently endorses Lenin's interpretation of Marxism over Kautsky's, he is uncertain about the applicability of Bolshevism to Chinese conditions. The timing of the social revolution and the sort of socialism it adopts will depend on Chinese circumstances and the characteristics of the Chinese people. It is not possible to anticipate in advance what strategy will be used; consequently, "we would not dare to say that China should implement Bolshevism, or dare to say that China is definitely appropriate for Bolshevism".

Marxist Theory and China

The issue of the applicability of Marxist theory to China was the central focus of Li's last major essay before he left the Chinese Communist Party in mid-1923.[14] "Marxist Theory and China" is a very significant essay, and we will follow the logic of Li's argument closely. It is significant for a number of reasons. First, the essay demonstrates that, in the two years since the founding of the Party, Li had given considerable thought to the issue of the relevance and applicability of Marxism to Chinese conditions. Second, the essay reveals a growing mastery of Marxist theory, to the extent that Li does not merely rehearse well-worn arguments and theoretical concepts; rather, he moves forward to an application of Marx's historical method (as Li understood it) to analysis of China's economic and political circumstances, and discussion of the sorts of strategies which are suggested through this historical analysis. Third, it provides a clue to Li's angry and somewhat intemperate departure from the Chinese Communist Party just a month or so later, an act which had ramifications that extended to the end of his life.

Li commences by summarising the Manifesto passed at the Party's Second Congress in 1922. According to this Manifesto, the goal of the Communist Party was to organise the proletariat, to employ the tactic of class warfare, to establish a dictatorship of workers and peasants (*laonong zhuanzheng*), and to strive for the establishment of a communist society. The Party's current political strategy was to lead the proletariat in assisting the democratic revolution, to cooperate with China's democratic revolutionary parties (among which was numbered the Guomindang) and to overthrow warlord politics. The issue of what policies to pursue was vital because Marxism had, according to Li, moved from the period of its introduction to China to the period of its implementation.

Li divides his discussion into three sections. In the first, he poses the question of whether present-day China can use Marxist theory to transform society. In responding to this question, Li suggests that it is first necessary to understand what Marxist theory actually understands by social revolution, and how and at what stage it can be initiated. According to Marx's materialist conception of history (and here Li quotes from the famous 1859 "Preface"):

> At a certain stage of development, the material productive forces of society come into conflict with the existing relations of production or — this merely expresses the same thing in legal terms — with the property relations within the framework of which they have operated hitherto. From forms of development of the productive forces these relations turn into their fetters. Then begins an era of social revolution. The changes in the economic foundation lead sooner or later to the transformation of the whole immense superstructure.[15]

Li interprets this passage to imply the complete disintegration (*jieti*) of the organisation of society. But how is social revolution to be implemented? If the passage from the "Preface" is closely analysed, Li suggests, the answer is that social revolution results from the proletariat employing political revolution to seize political power. The emergence and development of industry based on machines saw the propertied class employ the means of concentration so that large-scale production resulted. This concentration of labour within the factory, where many workers collectively manufactured products, was social, but the benefits of the results of this concentrated labour were not social, becoming as they did the private property of the capitalists. The propertied class employed prevailing property relations to greatly expand the productive forces and to concentrate capital; production, trade and distribution could not, of course, be regulated and the result was a series of economic crises, each one worse than the last, with the conditions of wage labourers deteriorating. With the oppression of the middle class by large capital, its members too were forced into the ranks of the proletariat. Society divided into two great classes: the propertied and the propertyless. At this stage, the property relations inhibit the further development of the forces of production and there ensues a conflict between capitalists and the proletariat. The proletariat develops a class consciousness, and from this springs class struggle, the final result of which is the victory of the proletariat. The proletariat employs political power to return all productive organs to common ownership by society. Production, trade and distribution are fully regulated and the rights of the individual and labour are fully protected. Thus, although changes in political organisation follow changes in the economic base, political changes can be accomplished sooner than the changes in the economic base, and the motivating force behind these political changes is the proletariat.

Social revolution is, therefore, accomplished through the initiation of political revolution by the proletariat, and its seizure of political power. Is this a true reading of Marxism? From first to last, Li argues, Marx held unwaveringly to this idea. To support this contention, Li quotes from the *Communist Manifesto, Critique of the Gotha Program* and Marx's writings for the *Neue Rheinische Zeitung*. One can visualise from reading these passages, he says, the terrible scenes of death and violence, as if one can hear the din of class warfare, the crash of firearms. The proletariat's political revolution allows no room for compromise. Neither do these passages leave any room for doubt that Marx believed firmly that the proletariat would use political revolution to realise the social revolution.

Li then moves forward to a consideration of the question of timing. According to the *Communist Manifesto*, he suggests, the social revolution will probably pass through three periods. The first is the preparatory period, and during this period it is the task of a communist party to propagandise its perspectives, goals and directions, and then to organise the proletariat so that it becomes a class. The second period is that of the dictatorship of the proletariat (*laogong zhuanzheng*), and during this period the task of the communist party is to overthrow the power of the propertied class and assist the proletariat to seize power. The third period is concerned with the development of production, and during this period the proletariat uses its superior power to wrest the capital from the capitalist and to centralise control of all the instruments of production in the hands of the state. According to Li, these are the three periods through which a social revolution must pass; the duration of any one of these periods will be determined by the circumstances of each society and the extent of development of its production. In this lies the key to the length of time that this process will take. Here Li quotes Marx to the effect that no new social organisation may emerge until all of the productive forces of the old society have been fully developed. In other words, Li says, in order for the proletariat to realise the social revolution through political revolution, it must attend the full development of all the productive forces. However, the determination of when the productive forces are developed is not something that can be ascertained with mathematical precision. Even Marx himself was not able to correctly determine the extent to which the productive forces in the society of his own time had developed, and his conclusions were that the era of social revolution in European society had already arrived. Li uses the example of the textile industry. Although the textile industry in England had reached what seemed the peak of development, the textile industry in France and Germany was still in its infancy, perhaps not much more advanced than the China of Li's own day. However, Marx clearly believed that the society of his own time had reached a point at which no further development could occur, and thus advocated revolution.

Li then poses the pertinent question: is China ready for revolution? The answer he eventually arrives at is that the possibility is there. However, he responds initially by introducing a number of factors to explain why Marx's predictions of revolution had not been realised in Europe. The first was the inadequate organisation of the working class, their courage to wage class warfare not yet having reached "white heat". Moreover, the propertied class had postponed its fate by extending the development of production overseas, by getting rid of its surplus products in the colonies and semi-colonies which it had seized. Consequently, capitalism could continue to develop, and it did so, passing from the age of textiles to the age of the steel industry. The problem for Marx had been in determining whether the expansionary impulses within capitalism had reached their limit, but he was certainly not wrong in advocating that the proletariat employ political revolution to realise the social revolution. The extent of development of a society had to be evaluated along with the organisation of the proletariat and its fighting spirit, for these were the determining factors. Interestingly, Li here quotes Trotsky to the effect that the possibility of the proletariat seizing power is not determined by the degree of development of the productive forces of capitalism, but by class struggle, by the international situation and particularly by all sorts of subjective factors, such as the courage and determination of the proletariat to fight. For Trotsky, the suggestion that there is an automatic correlation between the level of development of a country and the possibility of the establishment of a proletarian dictatorship represents a naive understanding of the materialist conception of history, one which bears no relationship to Marxism. Trotsky's view, Li opines, is a new and different one, yet one which truly captures the essence (*jingsui*) of Marxist theory. The possibility of the realisation of social revolution through political revolution is thus determined by these sorts of factors. Consequently, in Russia, the Communist Party was able to achieve the consolidation of the organisation of the proletariat and to use its courage to fight, to exploit the crisis created by the European war for Russian imperialism, and overthrow the weakened propertied class, and so establish a dictatorship of the proletariat. By contrast, a social revolution was still difficult to realise in England and America, and it was not because the time for revolution had not eventuated. Rather, the organisation of the proletariat had not been consolidated, revisionist (*huangse*, literally "yellow") leadership had led the working class astray, and the courage of the proletariat to do battle was not particularly intense. Moreover, the propertied classes of these countries repeatedly employed their superior international status and power to plunder the flesh and blood of the peoples of the colonies and semi-colonies, and in so doing extended the evil existence of capitalism. But its final grave had, according to Li, already been dug.

Here again, we can see that Li's understanding of the materialist conception of history was premised on a recognition of the importance of long-term social and economic factors on the one hand, and the significance of more immediate political factors such as the organisation and will of the proletariat on the other. The former created the context within which a political revolution could become a possibility, but without the latter, no revolution could occur, regardless of how propitious the social and economic context might appear. Li perceived no deviation from Marx's intent in this interpretation of the materialist conception of history; rather it truly captured the "essence" of Marxist theory.

Having outlined his analytical premises, Li turned to a specific analysis of China's economic and political conditions. For the past two thousand years, China's economy had been a purely agricultural one, and on this economic base had been constructed the politics of feudalism. During this feudal era, economics had not undergone any substantial change and, despite periodic changes of dynasty, there was consequently no significant change in the political realm either. After the Opium War, capitalism gradually infiltrated China, and China's economy had been completely ruined. China then entered the era of revolution in production. The products of international capitalism sold widely throughout China, whose own textile industry was still in its infancy, and China's handicrafts had been destroyed; the great majority of Chinese had become wage slaves or had become unemployed.

Li reminds us that politics is constructed on an economic base, and that as the latter changes, the organisation of politics becomes no longer appropriate, and must also change. When China's economy altered from an agricultural to an industrial economy, its politics changed from the politics of feudalism to the politics of democracy. Those advocating democracy availed themselves of the opportunity presented by the collapse of the Qing dynasty to strive for democratic politics. However, the early industrial and commercial class in China could not, because of the oppression of imperialism, become a revolutionary capitalist class. Moreover, the Guomindang, which claimed to be a revolutionary party, was inspired by the ideals of Rousseau and hatred for the Manchus. The revolution of 1911 was thus based on sentiment, rather than on a firm economic foundation; such sentiment is a transitory thing, and the goals of the 1911 revolution were eventually derailed by the feudal warlord faction of Yuan Shikai. China's politics was thus characterised by the opposition between those who strove for democracy and the feudal warlords.

Li then turns his attention to the relationship between imperialism and China. In the previous eighty years, China's diplomatic history was the history of invasion by imperialism. Control of China's finances was entirely in the hands of foreign capitalists, and the bulk of China's railroads, mines, forests and communications, and many enterprises, were also under foreign control. The Beijing government was indirectly controlled by foreign capital. In short, China had become a semi-colony of imperialism.

On the basis of this elaboration of the international and internal political and economic situation, Li constructs a chart which depicts the opposition between classes as follows.

International	The oppressing classes (Imperialists and minority Chinese warlords)	→	Oppressed classes (China's capitalists and proletariat)
Within China	Feudal class (already matured)	→ Capitalists (just forming)	→ Proletariat (just forming)

The Parties which represent these classes:
The Northern faction → Guomindang → Chinese Communist Party

It can be seen from this, Li explains, that China's proletariat suffers a threefold oppression: by China's capitalists in the economic realm, China's feudal class in the political realm, and internationally from imperialism. China's capitalists suffer a twofold oppression: by feudalism and imperialism. Given these economic and political circumstances, the Chinese Communist Party must avail itself of the opportunity to organise the proletariat, and to attempt the social revolution, for both in theory and in reality there is a genuine basis for doing so. But how to proceed? Here Li quotes extensively from the *Communist Manifesto* to demonstrate that an alliance between a communist party and a party representing capitalists can, under certain circumstances, be a valid strategy; the oppression of the capitalists in China by imperialism and feudalism, both common enemies of the proletariat, makes such an alliance conceivable. The proposed alliance between the Chinese Communist Party and the Guomindang to overthrow warlord politics thus had a basis in Marxist theory. Li urges the Chinese Communist Party to pay particular attention to two factors in any proposed alliance between the two parties. First, the Guomindang is, Li asserts, similar to a social-democratic party, having members who are capitalists, intellectuals and workers, and the strategy of the Communist Party should be to influence them to move towards the left. With the maturation of the democratic revolution, the Communist Party should lead the revolution forward to a proletarian revolution. Second, the Communist Party should pay special attention to the work of organising the proletariat to become a class, and it must constantly protect its independent existence, avoiding the influence of the other party.

But what policies should be pursued if and when the proletariat is able to seize power? Li responds that the policies enacted by this new state will be determined by the circumstances of production and the cultural level achieved; in this, the state of the propertied class is no different from a proletarian state. Li then lists the ten measures suggested by Marx in the *Communist Manifesto*, measures which could only be enacted by the most developed states of the time. These measures could likewise be enacted only by the most developed of proletarian dictatorships. However, times had changed since Marx and Engels wrote the *Communist Manifesto*; and policies which may have been appropriate in 1848 were not so in 1875 when Marx wrote his *Critique of the Gotha Program*. Marx here castigated the leaders of the German Workers' Party for not recognising that several of the measures enunciated in the *Communist Manifesto* were no longer relevant; not only had the economy and culture developed, but some of these policies had already been adopted by capitalist states.

Li continues that, when Lenin analysed the characteristics of Russia's economic evolution, he came up with five factors:

1. patriarchal, based on primitive peasant production;

2. small-scale commodity production (including the selling of grain by the vast majority of the peasants);
3. private capitalism;
4. state capitalism; and
5. socialism.

If Lenin's analysis is applied to China's economic and social conditions, Li suggests, what is apparent is that the first three factors on Lenin's list are evident, but private capital is the most representative. Consequently, if China's proletariat were to seize power it would naturally use political power to speed the change from private capitalism to state capitalism. Li then suggests his own set of twelve measures which, on the basis of Marxist theory and the circumstances of China's production and cultural level, the proletariat should enact:

1. those who do not work, neither will they eat;
2. equality of land ownership and the opening up of waste land;
3. banks to be state-owned;
4. transport and communication to be state-owned;
5. foreign trade to be state-owned;
6. abolition of all taxes, and implemention of a heavy progressive income tax;
8. conditional importation of foreign capital;
9. implementation of free and compulsory education below middle school;
10. enactment of laws which guarantee work;
11. unconditional right for workers and peasants to elect and be elected; and
12. equality for women, economically, politically and socially.

This is, Li concludes, just a general program, the more detailed items not being included.

Conclusion

"Marxist Theory and China" develops a number of themes already evident in Li Da's earlier writings. The most important of these is the belief that the Marxist theory of social change is not a mere evolutionary theory premised on the overwhelming causal dominance of economic forces largely beyond human influence. Li does indeed recognise the significance of the economic realm as the starting point in any historical analysis, and he quotes extensively from Marx, particularly the 1859 "Preface", to reinforce this position. The productive forces and their level of development, and the existence of economic classes, are invariably Li's first concern when posing questions of historical interpretation. The economic base, Li repeatedly affirms, determines the superstructure. But this, Li is adamant, is only one dimension of the materialist conception of history. Marxism is above all a theory of revolution. While history might have periods of evolutionary development, its dominant motif is revolutionary, the major social changes deriving from revolutionary transformations in the social fabric. Moreover, this process of social revolution is not immune from human intervention. At certain stages in history — and the period following the rise of capitalism is of immediate concern to Li — class struggle in the realm of politics can have a decisive influence on the pace of change. Changes to the organisation of politics initially follow changes in the economic realm, but once created, the political organisation and the strategies of the proletariat can exert a decisive influence. Thus, while the context created by changes in the economic base made the political revolution possible, the revolution at the political level ensured the realisation of the tendencies for fundamental social change. Li clearly perceived some sort of dialectical relationship between the economic base and the political superstructure, the latter representing far more than a passive reflection of the former, it being in some sense the midwife of historical change. The political superstructure could not of itself initiate the massive changes set in motion by the economic base, but once set in motion, its impact on channelling and accelerating these changes could be decisive.

Li believed strongly that the level of class consciousness of the working class, its class "mentality", was of very great significance to the chances of success of the proletariat in the revolutionary struggle. As we have seen, Li suggested that the economic and social conditions for revolution had existed in Europe in the latter half of the nineteenth century. However, the level of consciousness of the European proletariat and its courage to wage class warfare were insufficient to the task of political revolution. It was thus vital, particularly for the newly created Communist Party in China, to adopt as one of its principal functions the raising of the class consciousness of the proletariat, arming it with an awareness of its oppression and exploitation, and mentally preparing it for the realisation of its historical mission, the overthrow of capitalism and the establishment of a socialist society. This emphasis on the role of consciousness as a medium for change in Li's early writings anticipates Gramsci, although in Li's writings the idea is not pursued with the same degree of theoretical complexity and sophistication with which the Italian Marxist explored problems of consciousness. Nevertheless, the appearance of these themes in Li Da's writings underlines once again that he was no mechanistic Marxist; for Li, humans were not the mere creatures of history, pushed along by the tide of change, inert, passive, unresponsive. Rather, they were the dynamic medium through which forces for economic, social and political change were realised. Change might well be generated by the forces of production, within the economic base, but without human awareness, a consciousness of the need for change, the full potential of the tendencies within the economic base may never be realised. The failure of the political revolution in Europe could be explained, at least in part, by failures at the superstructural level in the human dimension.

Where did this interpretation of the materialist conception of history come from? Were the ideas of the young Li Da merely derivative, drawing readily on the activist inclinations of the Leninist reading of Marxism? The response cannot be so straightforward. While Li does invoke Lenin at points in his elaboration of the Marxist theory of social change, it is to Marx, much more so than Lenin, that Li turns to validate his perception of a dynamic, reactive relationship between economic base and political and ideological superstructures. Li draws in particular on the *Communist Manifesto*, but he draws too on the *Critique of the Gotha Program* and Marx's writings from the *Neue Reinische Zeitung*. These are often categorised as Marx's "political writings", as opposed to the supposedly "economic" writings of his critique of political economy. We know from biographical accounts that Li had studied Volume I of *Capital* while in Japan, and the writings of both Kautsky and the Dutch Marxist Hermann Gorter, both of whom drew on Marx's political economy, and he quotes approvingly from the famous "Preface" of 1859. Li was thus clearly cognisant of the economic dimensions of Marx's theoretical approach. But he did not recognise a fundamental distinction or opposition between the economic and the political themes in Marx's writings. They were, rather, integral aspects of a "complete" theory. Li could point easily — and did so — to the Marx texts to validate this interpretation, an interpretation he believed to be a true reading, one which captured the "essence" of Marxism. His certainty of the rectitude of his own reading of Marxism is reflected too in the often polemical tone of his writings, his own ideas frequently emerging in response to the supposed fallacies of other interpretations. The revisionism of the German socialists was a favourite target, and Li used their deviations as a stalking horse for illuminating the integrity of his own version of Marxism.

However, while Marx's influence is strongly present in Li's reading of the materialist conception of history, Lenin's voice is certainly not absent. As we observed, Li draws on Lenin in his "Marxist Theory and China" to justify a particular analysis of China and the sorts of goals that the Chinese Communist Party should work towards; his many references to the successes of the revolution in Russia and its newly formed workers' state leave no possible doubt that Li greatly admired Lenin's achievements and stature as a Marxist, particularly as a Marxist practitioner. It is also clear that he recognised that Marx's ideas were not eternally true, that they required development to keep them attuned to the developments in capitalism, and that Lenin had played a significant role in this area. Nevertheless, Li also demonstrated that he was no slavish imitator of Lenin and the Bolsheviks, and it is instructive that he concludes "Marxist Theory and China" with the reservation that Bolshevism may not be appropriate to Chinese conditions; as he says here and elsewhere, different circumstances require different strategies.

In terms of Li Da's theoretical influence, there can be no doubt that his prolific writings in such key journals as *Xin Qingnian* and *The Communist* were widely read by members of the early Chinese communist movement; his grasp of Marxist theory and the history of European socialism was apparent to his readers in his extended essays as well as the shorter "*Duanyan*" commentaries. His understanding of Marxism's theory of social change could not but have had an impact on the hungry minds of those, like Mao Zedong, whose theoretical level did not yet match their political ardour. Moreover, his role as editor of influential journals not only ensured a degree of control of the interpretation of Marxism that infiltrated China (in the form of both essays and translations), his initial organisational role as head of the newly formed Party's Propaganda Department provided him an ideological and theoretical status which ensured a receptive audience for his ideas. And Li was tireless in pursuit of the goal of the dissemination of Marxism in China; his output, large even in these early years, was oriented entirely to this goal. Through sheer weight of publications alone, Li's impact on the theoretical development of the communist movement in China was considerable.[16] Li's contribution in this area has been widely recognised and lauded in China, but largely ignored in the West.[17] And while it is true that there were other major figures in the early theoretical development of Marxism in China (Qu Qiubai, Li Dazhao, Chen Duxiu), Li Da's contribution was in many respects as important, if not more so, than these other high-profile political figures, and his contribution, as we shall see, was to be much more enduring, for he remained a major theoretical presence in China until the mid-1960s.

Li's important role in disseminating Marxism in China during the formative years of the communist movement raises the question of the "orthodoxy" of his interpretation of Marx's materialist conception of history. As we observed in the previous chapter, Chinese Marxism, particularly in the guise of Mao Zedong Thought, has frequently been categorised — and as often castigated — by Western commentators for its emphasis on the capacity of the superstructural levels to effect historical change. We commented too that judgments of this sort are inevitably premised on assumptions regarding the nature of "orthodoxy", the judgments rendered on Chinese Marxism often premised on a mechanistic, economistic and evolutionary reading of Marxism. It has thus been a very easy matter to draw out invidious distinctions between "orthodox" Marxism on the one hand and a reading of Marxism which recognises the role of human agency in historical change on the other. However, it is possible, as we have seen, to demonstrate that Marx and many subequent influential Marxists did not perceive history as evolutionary change driven by economic forces from which human consciousness and action were excluded. The writings of Marx, Engels, Plekhanov and Lenin all carry strong activist traces; by the same token, they also emphasise the primary importance of the economic realm as the demiurge of history. A central theoretical challenge of Marxism has been the integration of these two potentially divergent impulses into a complete and coherent theoretical system.

Evaluation of the Marxism of the early Li Da must be situated in this theoretical context. It is clear, as we have observed in the course of this chapter, that Li did not perceive any necessary contradiction between the political economy of Marxism, with its emphasis on the relations and forces of production, and its revolutionary, activist theme. Changes in the economic realm create changes in the political and ideological superstructures; however, the latter are not passive reflections, but possess the capacity for reactive influence, becoming a significant factor in the successful realisation of the impulses for change in the economic base. There was thus a dialectical relationship between social and political revolution. Was this reading of Marxism by Li "orthodox" or "unorthodox"? The answer depends, of course, on which orthodoxy we select as the touchstone for evaluation. It is clear, however, that Li found no difficulty locating precedence for his rendition of the materialist conception of history in the writings of the major theoretical figures of Marxism; it was a reading which had, over time, attracted a certain validity, particularly with the success of the revolution in Russia. This reading became "orthodox" because powerful figures and organisations decreed it to be so. In this sense, the form of Marxism introduced by Li to the early communist movement in China was "orthodox", and Li was, as we have seen, prepared to defend it staunchly in the face of deviations, revisions and attacks from all quarters. We can thus conclude that Li was instrumental in introducing a particular version of orthodoxy to the early Chinese communist movement, both through the content of his theoretical elaborations and through his polemics which reinforced this "orthodox" reading of Marxism. His influence was thus considerable.

Li's influence during these early years, those prior to his departure from the Party, did not, however, extend to the philosophical dimension of Marxism. Largely absent from his early writings is any elaboration of Marxist philosophy. The role of disseminator of Marxist philosophy to the early Chinese communist movement was performed by Qu Qiubai.[18] Li Da does, in his early writings, indicate an awareness of the inroads on Marxist philosophy attempted by the neo-Kantians, but he does not elaborate this. Indeed, his primary focus during this period is on the materialist conception of history and the relationship between the social and political revolutions. It is not until the publication in 1926 of his first major book, *Xiandai shehuixue* (Contemporary Sociology), that the issue of Marxist philosophy is raised, and even here it appears in the shadow of his much more extended explication of the materialist conception of history. By the late 1920s and early 1930s, however, the importance of the philosophical dimension of Marxism had impressed itself forcefully on Li. Through his translations of Japanese Marxists such as Kawakami Hajime and Soviet authors such as Thalheimer, and Shirokov and Aizenberg, it became evident to him that a comprehension of Marxist philosophy was essential to the communist movement in China. In his characteristically tenacious manner, he proceeded to master this complex area, and wrote what was to become one of the great classics of Marxist theory in China, *Elements of Sociology*, more than half of which is concerned with the philosophy of dialectical materialism.

In the next chapter, we will pursue the themes of philosophy and social change through Li's writings published following his departure from the Party in 1923. Our attention will focus on the contents of Li's complex book *Contemporary Sociology*, but will also draw on his other writings of the late 1920s and the early 1930s. Did his departure from the Party lessen his commitment to Marxism? Did it alter his conception of the process of historical change? How did he integrate the realm of philosophy into his reading of the materialist conception of history? And how did he relate to "orthodoxy" as a non-Party theorist? To a consideration of these questions, we now turn.

Notes

1. *Li Da wenji*, Vol. I, pp. 1–5.
2. Ibid., pp. 9–23.
3. In this respect, Li's concerns parallelled those of Mao Zedong. For Mao's early writings on the oppression of women, see Stuart R. Schram (ed.), *Mao's Road to*

Power, Revolutionary Writings, 1912–1949: Volume I, The Pre-Marxist Period, 1912–1920 (Armonk, New York: M.E. Sharpe, 1992), pp. 421–49.

4. In "On the Liberation of Women", he states: "The bulk of the history of women in the world, has been the history of their subjugation by men. During this period, in morals, in customs and habits, in law, in politics and in economics, the position women invariably occupied was subordinate to men." Li Da wenji, vol. I, p. 9.

5. Ibid., pp. 30–39.

6. In his column, "Duanyan" (Brief Words), in issue no. 5 of The Communist which he edited, Li spoke of the "two missions" which confronted a communist party in China: "one is the economic mission, the other is the political mission". The political mission involved transformation of the politics and political parties which had grown up on the basis of capitalism; unless politics, law, education and state finances were transformed, the political mission could not be accomplished (Duanyan, nos 1, 3). See also Li Siju, Wang Jionghua and Zhang Dixian (eds), Makesizhuyi zhexue zai Zhongguo (Marxist Philosophy in China) (Shanghai: Renmin chubanshe, 1991), pp. 100–101.

7. Li Da wenji, Vol. I, pp. 40–41. "The Labourer and Socialism" was first published in Laodong Jie (The World of Labour) in November 1920. See also Li Da wenji, vol. I, pp. 42–45 for Li's glowing paean to the virtues of labour and the working class.

8. Ibid., pp. 46–56.

9. This is evident in his critiques of Zhang Dongsun and Liang Qichao. See Li Da wenji, vol. I, pp. 24–26, 57–74. See Michael Y.L Luk, The Origins of Chinese Bolshevism: An Ideology in the Making, 1920–1928 (Hong Kong: Oxford University Press, 1990), p. 60.

10. Li Da wenji, vol. I, pp. 57–74.

11. The term "Bolshevism" was translated variously in early Chinese Marxist texts. Li later moved from this translation to duoshuzhuyi. For his comment on the translation of this term, see Li Da wenji, vol. I, p. 91.

12. Ibid., pp. 78–90.

13. Ibid., pp. 91–104.

14. Ibid., pp. 202–15.

15. I have employed the translation in Karl Marx, A Contribution to the Critique of Political Economy (London: Lawrence and Wishart, 1971), p. 21.

16. One bibliography of Li's work lists seventy-five essays, chapters and translations, some of book length, between 1919 and mid-1923. See Zhongguo dangdai shehui kexuejia (Social Scientists of Contemporary China) (Beijing: Shimu wenxian chubanshe, 1983), pp. 131–34.

17. An exception is Luk, who refers to Li Da as a "theorist of first-rate importance". The Origins of Chinese Bolshevism, p. 59.

18. There can be no doubt that Qu Qiubai was far more important than Li Da in terms of introducing Marxist philosophy to the early Chinese communist movement. In 1923, Qu had written a major treatise on Marxist philosophy which demonstrated his deep familiarity with contemporary debates on the origins and content of dialectical materialism. See Qu Qiubai, "Shehui zhexue gailun" (A Survey of Social Philosophy), in Qu Qiubai wenji (Collected Writings of Qu Qiubai) (Beijing: Renmin chubanshe, 1988), vol. 2, pp. 310–485. For a Chinese evaluation of the relative theoretical importance of the early leaders of Chinese communism,

which judges Qu Qiubai to be the most important for the elaboration and dissemination of Marxist philosophy in China, see Song Zhiming and Zhao Dezhi, *Xiandai Zhongguo zhexue sichao* (Philosophical Trends in Contemporary China) (Beijing: Zhongguo renmin daxue chubanshe, 1992), pp. 36–53.

4

Li Da and Marxist Theory, 1923–32

In "Marxist Theory and China", published in May 1923, Li had put two conditions on the collaboration between the Communist Party and the Guomindang. The first was that the Communist Party must propagandise members of the Guomindang to persuade them to a more left-oriented perspective; the second was that the independence of the Communist Party must not be compromised. As Li put it, the Communist Party must "at all times protect its independent existence, and avoid the influence of the other Party".[1] Li thus supported the strategy of the united front and could perceive great benefits deriving from it, but he was adamant that a strategy of alliance with the Guomindang must not weaken the independence of the Communist Party, nor weaken its capacity to commence the proletarian revolution on the successful completion of the democratic revolution. He thus supported the general tenor of the "Resolution on the Relationship between the Chinese Communist Party and the Guomindang", adopted by the Communist International in Moscow in January 1923.[2] What he could not accept, however, was the way in which Chen Duxiu and the Comintern agent Maring (Sneevliet, with whom Li had developed a rather antagonistic relationship)[3] were prepared to diminish the independence of the Communist Party to achieve an alliance with the Guomindang. Their position was that "all work should be done with the approval of the Guomindang",[4] a position which Li felt could only weaken the independence of the Party. In his celebrated confrontation with Chen Duxiu in mid-1923, Li gave vent to his anger at what he considered Chen's supine position and promptly left the Party.

Li's departure from the Party could well have been the occasion for a change in theoretical perspective, perhaps a diminution in his commitment to Marxism. However, his writings and translations from the period 1923–32 indicate that this was certainly not the case. His publications, while not so numerous in number (almost certainly a function of the closure of access to Party periodicals and journals), consist in the main of works of book length which display, if anything, a deepening commitment to Marxism and a far greater sophistication in his understanding of its theoretical dimensions. Important from this period are such works as *Xiandai shehuixue* (Contemporary Sociology, 1926), *Zhongguo chanye geming gaiguan* (A Survey of China's Revolution in Production, 1930), *Shehui zhi jichu zhishi* (Fundamental Knowledge of Society, 1929) and *Minzu wenti* (The Nationality Question, 1929). He also published a considerable number of book-length translations which were to greatly expand the textual basis from which Marxism in China could develop. Such translations also included, for the first time, in-depth studies of the philosophical dimensions of Marxism by such authors as the Japanese Marxist Kawakami Hajime and the Soviet Marxist philosophers Luppol and Thalheimer.

We will turn to a consideration of the content and influence of these and other translations in the next chapter. In this chapter, we will be pursuing the themes outlined in Chapter 2 and applied in the previous chapter to an evaluation of Li's writings of 1919–23. In this chapter, our focus will be on Li's writings from the years 1923–32 — that is, from his departure from the Party to the commencement of his "Beiping period" in 1932. Once again, we will be tracing and evaluating Li's understanding of Marxism's theory of social change, and also his interpretation of the philosophical dimensions of Marxism.

Contemporary Sociology: Social Structure and Social Change

Perhaps the most important of Li Da's publications from this period, and the one which exerted the most influence on the revolutionary movement, was *Xiandai shehuixue* (Contemporary Sociology). His first major monograph on Marxist theory, *Contemporary Sociology* was published in June 1926, and was based on his lectures on the materialist conception of history at various universities during the previous three years.[5] Divided into eighteen chapters, the book runs to 170,000 characters. Somewhat surprisingly, *Contemporary Sociology* is written in the old-fashioned *wenyan* style, but this did not seem to lessen its appeal, with almost every revolutionary possessing a copy, according to Deng Chumin.[6] By 1933, this book had been republished fourteen times[7] and made, according to Chinese commentaries, "a major contribution to the dissemination of the materialist conception of history in China", with "some people" gaining their first understanding of Marxism as a result of *Contemporary Sociology*, this "setting them on the path to revolution".[8] Indeed, once the reader gets past the title of the book, it reveals itself very clearly as a major work of Marxist theory, rather than a conventional sociology textbook. The inclusion of "sociology" in the title of this book and that of its famous successor *Elements of Sociology* (1935/37) was intentionally deceptive. In order to distract the reactionary authorities from the contents of the book and thus reduce problems of publication and distribution, Li employed "sociology" as a euphemism for the materialist conception of history, which is in fact the major preoccupation of *Contemporary Sociology*.[9]

In the "Preface" to *Contemporary Sociology*, Li stresses the class character of sociology.[10] It is the task of sociology, he argues, to study the principles underlying the evolution of society; and on the basis of an understanding of the history of society's evolution, to understand present-day society and to predict the future. The ideals of a future society will be those of human equality. Looked at in this way, Li asserts, the class character of sociology becomes evident, and it is evident too that truth has a class component. Those who would study sociology must study the sociology of Marx, for it was he who formulated the materialist conception of history; it was Marx who discovered the "nucleus" (*hexin*) of social organisation and the direction of social evolution, and who provided the guiding principles for transforming society. Sociology must, therefore, be premised on the materialist conception of history.

Much of *Contemporary Sociology* is consequently concerned with an elaboration of the materialist conception of history.[11] Li counterposes this theory to three other, incorrect, theories: contract social theory, organic social theory and idealist social theory. Each of these, Li argues, has been used to defend capitalism. Contract theory implies a rational agreement on the part of all humans to society's organisation and a willingness to comply with its demands; the organic (or biological) theory perceives capitalism as an inevitable consequence of the development of nature; and idealist theory is premised on the psychology, the customs and habits of people, with change in society deriving from a change in these. It is the mission of *Contemporary Sociology*, Li declares, to expose the errors of these three theories, and to advocate the social theory of the materialist conception of history.[12]

Central to the materialist conception of history is the concept of society as a structure, and this structure can be divided into two components: the economic base and the superstructure. The first task, Li suggests, is to understand the structure of the economic base, then the superstructure which "stands on" (*liyu*) the economic base, and finally the relationship between the two. Society's foundation is composed of the economic relations; the superstructure is comprised of the political system and forms of consciousness. As the productive forces change, the economic relations of which they are a constituent part also change, and so too do the political system and forms of consciousness. Li divides human relations into material relations (namely those which are economic) and spiritual (*jingshen*) relations, which include the relationships of politics, law, science, art and literature, morals, religion, philosophy and so on. All of these relationships structure the totality of social life and all relationships of a spiritual nature make up the superstructure of society.

Before humans can establish superstructural relationships, Li contends, they must first of all provide themselves with the material necessities of existence. The production of the latter involves relations of production, relations in which humans must work on nature and work with each other. Humans are enmeshed in relations; in the process of labour, through the use of certain instruments of labour and through the exchange of their labour, humans are part of productive relationships. A society's relations of production must, Li argues, be appropriate to its forces of production for development to occur in those forces of production. But harmony between relations and forces of production is only one form of their relationship; the other is disharmony, and when this occurs, the social basis becomes unstable. In order for the productive forces to develop, the techniques and methods of labour must change; moreover, the conditions of labour must also change. It is only when the techniques and methods of labour change that new forces of production can emerge, and it is only when this latter situation occurs that the relations of production are transformed. Changes to the relations of production mean a change in the basis (*jichu*) of society, and a fundamental transformation of society's entire structure.[13]

Having established the premise for his interpretation of the materialist conception of history, Li turns his attention to the structure and function of the superstructure.[14] Society's political and legal superstructure and its forms of consciousness emerge, he says, as a result of its economic relationships, and function to maintain those relationships. The nature of a society's political thought and political orientation is determined by the nature of its social life; similarly, political organisation is the result of class struggle. The state is thus an institution of the ruling class, its purpose being the oppression of the producing classes, the state having served this purpose in slave, feudal and contemporary capitalist societies. The state emerged initially because the contradiction between the ruling and producing classes could not be resolved. The law too is a manifestation of property relations, and functions to protect those relations; it serves to legitimate the right of the dominant class to exploit the lower classes.

Li perceives science as a part of the superstructure too. It is a tool humans employ to subordinate and transform nature, but it is a form of consciousness closely related to developments in the techniques of production. Art and literature are also a manifestation of social life, an expression of human emotion and a record of the relationships between humans; as these relationships alter, art and literature change accordingly. Much previous art and literature had been a product of the dominant class, for it had only been its members who had enjoyed sufficient leisure and opportunity to be involved in such pursuits. Similarly, morals and morality are social products, and as the forces of production change, so too do morals; in class society, morality performs a class function, rationalising the domination of one class by another. The world of religion is also a reflection of the real world, according to Li, and the mysteries of religion are to be explained by reference to real life. The worship of nature was appropriate to primitive society, Christianity to feudal society, and the new religions to capitalism. Like morality, religion performs a class function, being employed by one class to control another.

Another element of the superstructure is philosophy. The object of philosophy, Li suggests in one of his first major references to it, is to understand the basic principles of life and nature. All of the concepts of philosophy have their genesis in the material world, and the systems of philosophy are the organised forms of the ideas of ordinary people, ideas which are influenced by the social and economic environment. There is an intimate relationship between human thought and social organisation; the forms of human thought which develop in a particular society are essentially depictions of the economic conditions of that society, and are appropriate to the needs of its classes. Philosophy comes into being in this way, and philosophy is consequently the philosophy of particular classes; it can have no independent existence.

Li concludes that, while the superstructure is created by the relations and forces of production, it has the capacity to influence them. The structure of society is determined by the forces of production, and the change in its form is also determined by changes in the forces of production. The superstructure can influence this change in quantitative terms, but cannot be the primary force for qualitative economic change.[15]

What makes humans distinctive, Li continues, is not so much that they are social animals, for other animals possess highly structured forms of social organisation; the distinction lies, rather, in the capacity of humans to create instruments and tools and use these in a purposeful way to transform and control their environment. Humans are also able to accumulate experience, to improve their techniques of production, and hence allow progress. As the instruments of production change, human life undergoes major change, and as life changes, consciousness also alters accordingly. However, in turn, new forms of consciousness are able to invent new instruments. It is for this reason that the principles (*faze*) which govern socially organised animals do not apply to human society.¹⁶

Li then turns his attention to the function of language and thought. The development of these is closely bound up with the invention of instruments of production, and the consequent development of human society. Language in particular is an indispensable medium of communication and, unlike animals, humans are able to employ language to express emotion as well as to describe things. Language and thought are closely connected, and thought (*sixiang*) has played a major part in human progress. Those who study sociology, Li suggests, should not underestimate the significance of thought; unlike the psychologists who perceive thought as mere manifestation of matter, thought must be seen as reacting on matter. The separation of humans from animals verifies this; humans are able to develop goals and to pursue and satisfy these, particularly through the conscious use of instruments and tools. Humans are able, through the exercise of their capacity for thought, to strive to achieve their goals through action (*xingwei*), and through the continued use and development of instruments, humans are able to control their environment and to increase their capacity for thought and reflection. There is thus an intimate connection between the development of the instruments of production and an increase in the capacity of human thought; the former gives rise to the latter, but the latter in turn facilitates the further development of the former. The result is that society progresses.¹⁷

Contemporary Sociology: Social Development and Social Consciousness

The development of society, Li suggests, is characterised by increasing complexity and an expansion in the capacity (*fanwei*) of society; complexity of social life arises from complexity in the relations of production, whereas increased capacity is a result of expansion of the capacity of production and exchange. Those who seek the increased complexity and capacity of society, Li suggests, must work for the development of the forces of production. The development of the forces of production has two causes. According to the original edition of *Contemporary Sociology*, these are increase in population and growth in human aspiration (*yuwang*). Li concedes that the Malthusian population theory is partially correct insofar as an increase in population dictates an increase in the material necessities of human existence, and thus an increase in production. Humans also will work hard to fulfil their aspirations, and this too impacts on the forces of production, increasing their capacity and pushing them forward.

However, in the revised edition of *Contemporary Sociology*, Li explains the development of the forces of production by reference to the two following factors: the socialisation of labour and the development of the methods (*shouduan*) of production. (In the original edition, these two factors are cited as the methods by which the forces of production are developed, rather than their underlying causes.) The first factor, the socialisation of labour, occurs on the basis of the increasing division of labour. The movement from primitive forms of industry, such as handicrafts, to more complex industries, such as textiles, required not only a far more complex division of labour, but also far greater cooperation for the production of commodities; in turn, this form of production developed more complex forms of trade and exchange, which in turn prompted new forms of the division of labour. Under capitalism, workers are concentrated within a factory to produce under a conscious plan; the organisation of large-scale heavy industry is based on a highly complex division of function which at the same time operates to allow cooperation in production. This advanced division of labour, and the consequent specialisation in production, functions to promote the development of the forces of production. The second factor, development of the methods of production, comes about because humans are, says Li quoting Franklin, tool-making animals, and the development of tools serves to extend human control over nature. From simple tools, which humans used directly on the objects of labour, humans developed complex machines made up of many smaller instruments. The improvement in the performance of these machines and the methods of their propulsion has greatly increased the capacity of production, and hence the forces of production.[18]

When he turns his attention to social change, Li commences with the premise that revolution is central to social change.[19] He repeats his earlier observation that revolutionary social change occurs as a result of the obstruction of the forces of production by social organisation; the forces of production come into conflict with the relations of production, or with the legal manifestation of these, the property relations. Li emphasises that social change must be evaluated on the basis of the material changes of society, rather than on the basis of social consciousness, for changes in social consciousness follow and are the result of material changes.[20] Social consciousness was nevertheless a very important issue for Li, and he devoted an entire chapter of *Contemporary Sociology* to it.[21] Through an elaboration of his views in this chapter, we will gain a clearer understanding of his perception of the dialectical relationship between the economic realm and the superstructure, a relationship within which the economic base nevertheless retained dominance.

In the attempt to fulfil their economic aspirations, Li argues, humans must, directly or indirectly, enter relationships with other humans, and these take on the character of relationships of production; at the same time as these economic relationships emerge, so too do appropriate forms of consciousness. The synthesis of all the economic relationships constitutes the base (*jichu*) of society, while the various forms of consciousness combined create social consciousness (*shehui yishi*). All human beings must belong to society, and must consequently be subject to social consciousness. However, following the emergence of class society, social consciousness is characterised by the class which dominates society. In feudal society, social consciousness is not the consciousness of the peasants and the poor but of the landed aristocracy, although the peasants and the poor are subject to this social consciousness; the same is true of capitalist society, with the workers subject to a form of consciousness emanating from the capitalist class.[22]

But what is the function of social consciousness? According to Li, social consciousness functions to dominate the consciousness of individuals and thus to preserve the existing society. The restraint imposed on individuals by social consciousness takes two forms. The first is the one which is internalised, with the individual not conscious that he or she is following the directions of social consciousness. The second is the external form, manifest as a legal system able to compel submission from individuals. The beneficiaries of this restraint are, according to Li, members of the class which enjoys economic dominance; those who are oppressed may not even be aware that they are oppressed, because of the domination of their thinking by social consciousness.

However, Li continues, society is not unchanging, and as the economic organisation becomes unstable, there gradually emerges a change in the content of social consciousness. The traditions and customs which constitute social consciousness nevertheless change only slowly, and can continue to exert an influence even while new forms of social consciousness are emerging. This can be seen in capitalist society, where the proletariat had been strongly influenced by the social consciousness of the capitalist class; with the growth in the importance of the proletariat within capitalism, however, a realisation grew amongst the working class that this social consciousness was "unreasonable" (*bu heli*), and a new form of consciousness emerged whose content reflected the interests of the proletariat. The consciousness of the proletariat is based on the desire for socialism, and as the numbers of capitalists decline and the ranks of the proletariat swell, the force for change grows; eventually capitalism will be overthrown, to be replaced by a socialist society. With the eventual realisation of a classless society, social consciousness will revert to the form it had taken in ancient classless society, to a consciousness appropriate for each person, rather than just the dominant class.[23]

In a later section of *Contemporary Sociology*, Li returns to the issue of consciousness and its role in social change. Thought, he stresses, is created by particular classes, but in general, the form of consciousness which predominates in a society is the consciousness of the dominant economic class. However, with the emergence of new class forces, new forms of consciousness arise, and at times of instability and change, the new forms of thought also become a factor for change, becoming a "subsidiary factor" (*zizhu*) in the destruction of old customs and habits.[24] The picture which emerges from Li Da's interpretation of the historical role of thought and social consciousness is clearly premised on a materialist conception of social structure and change. He invariably relates the emergence of forms of consciousness to particular societies and their characteristic forms of economic production and relationships. Consciousness is, he stresses, related to class, and the class which enjoys dominance in the economic realm is dominant too in the arena of social consciousness. In morals, philosophy, religion, art and literature, and legal systems, the customs, beliefs, habits and practices which prevail are those which serve to maintain the existing social and economic structure. It is only with the emergence of new economic practices and relationships that new forms of consciousness can emerge, but even then, the old traditions and habits can persist in the face of change; it is only at times of social instability and change that new forms of consciousness are able to exert a significant influence, and this influence does not approach the significance of the influence exerted by forces for change in the economic realm.

Class, Law, Politics

Class, Li argues, emerges as a result of the process of production, and the sort of class structure to emerge is dependent on the nature of production. It is the forces of production which determine the relations of production.[25] The division of society into two major classes between which there has been opposition has meant that all members of society are invariably members of a class. For Li, the issue of the distribution of resources, the means of production, is crucial to an understanding of where a member of society stands in relation to the class structure. Those who own the means of production occupy a directive, managerial role, whereas those who are propertyless must be involved in labour; the rewards which flow from this differentiated structure are in turn very different, the labourer under capitalism receiving a wage while the capitalist receives the profit from the enterprise.

For Li, therefore, class is an economic category. However, class is at the same time a legal and a political category, for the legal system and the nature of politics within a society emerge as a result of, and must be consistent with, the nature of that society's class relations. The very different status of the owning and non-owning classes within the realm of the relations of production is reflected in the realm of law, and the law functions to maintain the economic interests of the owning class. This is a theme which permeates Li's voluminous writings on jurisprudence. As he points out in a later volume on law, *Elements of Jurisprudence* (1947), the property relations which exist in law are, at the economic level, relations of production, and are dependent on the existence of private property; the most fundamental relations which exist within law are class relations.[26]

In the same way, the opposition between classes is the premise for political life and the relationships which exist in political life. For Li, the most important institution in the political realm is the state,[27] and Chapter 8 of *Contemporary Sociology* is devoted to an exploration of the distinction between state and society, the essence and development of the state, and finally the withering away of the state. As one would expect, Li argues that the basis of the state is the opposition between classes.[28] An explanation for the emergence and character of particular types of state is thus dependent on an explanation of the economic evolution of society, and the sorts of class structures which have emerged in the course of this evolution.[29] Li provides examples of states within different class societies to demonstrate that their structure and the laws they enact reflect the nature of the production process, and the interests of the dominant economic class. The state which characterised late feudal society, for example, was premised on a shift from the forms of agriculture and economic production characteristic of early feudalism. The growth in population, the advent of new agricultural techniques, the expansion of manorial land, the rapid growth of handicrafts, emergence of large-scale trade and commerce between countries, the increasing importance of large cities and in particular the capital city as the centre of industry and commerce all presaged a shift from a decentralised political structure to one in which political institutions and power became centralised, and the power of the monarch greatly increased. This power was, of course, employed to reinforce the structure of class relationships which had emerged alongside the economic changes within feudalism, and was a state of the feudal lords (*lingzhu*). Similarly, the state in capitalist society was premised on the forms of economic activity characteristic of capitalism. Industry and commerce now supplanted agriculture as the dominant economic activity.

Production was now based on machines, and this necessitated a class which would operate these machines for wages; the workforce was centralised in cities, and a system of free economic competition between privately owned enterprises emerged. The old feudal state was overthrown to be replaced by a state which would represent the interests of the newly dominant capitalist class. The object of this state was to legitimise and reinforce the exploitation of the working class by the owners of capital; its laws and policies were all directed towards the protection of the power of this dominant class, and a major function was consequently the moderation of the class struggle generated by the inequalities inherent in the class structure of capitalism.

However, capitalist society is the final stage in the historical development of class society, Li asserts, and the state which has emerged during this period of intense class struggle is, like the capitalist society which spawned it, reaching the point of collapse.[30] When economic development reaches its maximum capacity, the necessity for classes will disappear, and they will wither away; the state, which was premised on the existence of classes, will also wither away. To achieve that end, the proletariat must seize the state, and use its power to socialise productive enterprises, but when class distinctions disappear, the state will become a state for the whole people, and in doing so will lose its character as a state.

Li's quite detailed foray into state theory leaves the impression that the political realm is merely a reflection of economic conditions, and indeed he states on several occasions that it is the forces of production which generate economic classes, and it is classes and their antagonism which create the basis for the state. However, Li had emphasised in his early writings the importance of the political revolution for the realisation of the social revolution, and this theme re-emerges in Chapter 14 of *Contemporary Sociology*, and serves to modify the rather economistic reading of the state in that volume. Marxism, he asserts, is made up of three theories: the historical, the economic and the political. The first two belong to the theoretical realm of Marxism; the latter belongs to the realm of practical policy (*shiji zhengci*).[31] This latter realm, it is clear, was of great significance to Li, for the success of organisation and policies here could have a dramatic impact on the success of the revolution in the economic realm. Indeed, he argues that in order for the economic revolution to be fully realised, the political revolution must first be implemented.[32] With the successful seizure of power, the proletariat can move to the completion of the revolution in the economic realm: the centralisation of control of the means of production in the hands of the state, and the rapid development of the forces of production.

Li thus perceived politics and the state as possessing a capacity to influence the economic realm, but it is also clear that politics and the state could do no more than realise the potential for change inscribed on the economic structure of society. In the same way, social consciousness could react on its material basis, but was categorised by Li as a "subsidiary factor". His conception of social change thus had a dialectical flavour to it, but it remained in the final analysis a reductionist theory, one which perceived the forces of production, and developments within them, as the demiurge of history.

Dialectics and Philosophy

While his conception of social change may have been dialectical insofar as it perceived a degree of reactive influence between the economic realm and the various elements of the superstructure, Li Da had not, by the mid-1920s, provided a focused interpretation of the dialectical philosophy of Marxism for his many readers. Indeed, it had been Qu Qiubai (1899–1935), rather than Li, who had written most prolifically on Marxist philosophy in the early 1920s. In a series of publications written while he was head of the Sociology Department at Shanghai University in 1923, Qu had demonstrated a familiarity with dialectical materialism lacking in the writings of other early Chinese Marxist theorists. In particular, his *Shehui zhexue gailun* (A Survey of Social Philosophy) contains an interesting introduction to the laws of dialectical materialism. Here he argues, in his explanation of the law of the unity of opposites, that contradictions within things and their motion constitute the "most fundamental principle" (*zui jiben yuanli*) of dialectics; without contradictions, there could be no mutual transformation of contradictions, and therefore the motion of things would not be possible.[33] Qu does not, however, elaborate at any length on the relationship between the various laws of dialectics, nor the relationship between historical and dialectical materialism. He was, nevertheless, the pioneer of Marxist philosophy in China, and it was on the foundation that he laid that others, and especially Li Da, were to further elaborate dialectical materialism and disseminate information on it in their writings and translations.

In his *Contemporary Sociology*, Li had contemplated the issue of human consciousness, and had come to the conclusion that consciousness did have a role to play in social and historical change. To the extent that correct consciousness was a factor in achieving change, it was important for a communist party to elaborate and disseminate forms of consciousness which could guide and encourage the actions of members of the proletariat in the political revolution. Intellectually, the scene was thus set for Li to move to a deeper inquiry into Marxist philosophy, for here was a philosophy which claimed insight into the laws which governed movement and change in both the natural and social realms; an understanding of this complex philosophy might well provide guidance to the political movement to achieve change. Li Da's writings and translations of the late 1920s and early 1930s evince a growing fascination for the world of philosophy, although he never lost sight of its political significance. We will examine Li Da's philosophical translations from this period in the following chapter, and his major treatise on philosophy, *Elements of Sociology*, in subsequent chapters.

In the remainder of this chapter, we will briefly examine the first references to philosophy in Li Da's writings. These appear in his *Fundamental Knowledge of Society* (1929, written under the name Li Haoming), in which he devotes a short section to the history of philosophy, culminating in a discussion of dialectical materialism and its superiority over other philosophies.[34] As usual, Li here premises his elaboration of philosophy on the belief that it is the economic structure which is the basis of society, and within this basis it is the system of technology at work which determines the relations of production; as technology alters, so too do the relations of production, and ultimately the social form.[35] Nevertheless, the elements of the superstructure are not passive reflections of the economic base, but capable of exerting some influence, whether to inhibit or accelerate change generated within the economic base. Politics (in the form of the political revolution during capitalism) occupied a particularly important place in social change. Philosophy, and in particular a correct understanding of Marxism's philosophy of dialectical materialism, now also emerges as a potent force for change; philosophy thus becomes, as Li points out, "the science of sciences", for it represents a synthesis of the knowledge contained in both the natural and social sciences; it is the basis of all scientific knowledge.[36]

Philosophy, Li suggests, is concerned with such questions as human knowledge, and the relationship between knowledge and the world; it is concerned with the question of spirit and matter (namely, the relationship between thought and existence). Philosophy is the pinnacle of human spiritual activity, and its dependent relationship with the forces of production is thus naturally an exceedingly complex one. The factors which Li perceives as linking the forces of production to philosophy are, in order: the nature of the classes within society and the economy; the disposition and condition of existence of these classes; the mentality (*xinli*) of society; and the situation of the various sciences. Thus, although the connection between forces of production and philosophy is a complex one, it is evident, Li argues, that the forces of production remains the starting point for the study of philosophy.[37] Li gives as an example the lack of a coherent philosophical world view within primitive society; this can be explained, he says, by the nature of the labour process and the "realities" of life in those societies. It was in ancient Greece that the systematisation of philosophy commenced, and it commenced as natural philosophy, with philosophers such as Thales attempting to explain the basis of all things existing within the universe. Thales believed the origin of all things to be water: all things emerged from water and returned to water. However, as Greek society became more complex, its philosophy developed from a philosophy of nature to a philosophy which incorporated the concerns of human life.

According to Li, an organised world view must address the following issues: the relationships between "I" and "not-I", "knowledge" and "existence", and "spirit" and "reality"; these were the fundamental issues which concerned Greek philosophy, and they have remained the preoccupation of philosophy to the present. The various philosophies, he suggests, can be grouped into two categories on the basis of their responses to these issues. The first category includes those philosophies which take the object, nature and reality as their starting point; that is, they perceive nature or reality as the basis, existing independently of humankind, with spirit or thought a product of nature or the material world. The second category incorporates philosophies which regard the subject, spirit and thought as the starting point — that is, they perceive spirit and thought as the basis, existing independently of nature, with nature and the object a product of thought or the spiritual world. The former category is materialism, the latter idealism. Philosophies which attempt to harmonise materialism and idealism are described by Li as eclecticism.

The history of philosophy, Li contends, is the history of the opposition and struggle between materialism and idealism. The creator of idealist philosophy was Plato, whose subjective idealist philosophy argued that the only truly existing things are concepts, that all knowable objects and phenomena are nothing more than the images (*yingxiang*) of concepts. During the Middles Ages, philosophers took Plato's concepts and suggested that God originally created all material things, and in the last century, the English philosopher Berkeley stated that all existing things are spirit, everything else being only appearance. Hegel established the philosophy of dialectical idealism by perceiving the existence of objective reason in the dialectic's own development, suggesting that all things are a manifest form of the development of the dialectic.

The combination of dialectics and materialism, Li continues, gives dialectical materialism, which is the philosophy of the revolutionary class. The materialist element of dialectical materialism has, he suggests, the following premises:

1. Only nature is real.
2. Nature exists independently of the subject (spirit).
3. Spirit is a minor part of nature.
4. Nature precedes life, matter precedes spirit.
5. Spirit emerges only when matter has appeared in a definite form.
6. Spirit cannot exist apart from matter, but matter can exist without spirit.
7. Knowledge emerges from experience.
8. Consciousness is determined by the external world.
9. Reality is the only object of knowledge, and only when our knowledge is consistent with reality is it truly objective.

When Li turns his attention to the dialectical component of dialectical materialism, he commences by identifying the origins of dialectics in the mode of philosophical discourse characteristic of ancient Greek philosophy. In disputation, the discourse of the first speaker would be negated by the discourse of the second, a synthesis of elements of both discourses resulting ultimately in the truth. As well as a mode of dialogue, it is as well, Li adds, a method of thought with which humans can think about things. Hegel stated that objective reason develops through the dialectical principle of thesis, antithesis and synthesis; it is therefore necessary to investigate things in motion, in change, in life and through their interconnections.

Li argues that materialist dialectics perceives dialectics as the laws of development of contradictions, of change and motion of matter, and of change and motion in nature and society. The dialectical mode of thought, he asserts, is the only method for grasping the dialectics of nature, and it is therefore the only scientific method. Idealist philosophy seeks truth in thought, but dialectical materialism seeks it in practice; idealism concentrates on abstractions divorced from life, whereas materialism regards the realities of life as pre-eminent. Idealism and materialism are thus the manifest forms of consciousness of two classes; idealism is a world view of the class separated from the direct process of production, from the practice of production, whereas materialism is the world view of the class which engages in the practice of production.[38]

We can identify, in this section on philosophy from *Fundamental Knowledge of Society*, many of the themes and concepts which Li Da was to explore in such detail over the next few years. His explorations in philosophy were to culminate in the publication in 1935 (second revised edition, 1937) of *Elements of Sociology*, in which he provides a detailed elaboration of dialectical materialism. It would be a mistake, however, to give the impression that Li perceived the study of philosophy as separate from the study of other dimensions of social life and activity. Indeed, it is clear that he came to regard Marxist philosophy as providing the concepts, categories and modes of analysis which could facilitate comprehension of social realms as diverse as law and currency. In particular, he mobilised the categories of essence and phenomenon, which he drew from dialectical materialism, to comprehend and explain the distinction between the stated purpose of the law (its "phenomenon") and its real purpose (its "essence"). In *Elements of Jurisprudence* (written in 1947),[39] Li suggests that all things are a unity of essence and phenomenon; and knowledge of an object represents an understanding of this unity, which is a unity of contradictions (*maodun de tongyi*). The unity of essence of a phenomenon represents both identity and "not-identity", compatability and lack of compatability; and a phenomenon is both able and not able to completely manifest essence. In the final analysis, it is essence which determines phenomenon; phenomenon is the manifest form of the connections of the various aspects internal to an object, and essence represents the fundamental connections contained within phenomenon. The essence of an object is that which permits and defines its existence (*wei meijie er cunzai*), but essence develops through phenomenon; phenomenon represents an object's development, essence its relative stability. The contradiction between phenomenon and essence, Li continues, is the premise for scientific knowledge; if there were to be complete consistency between phenomenon and essence, science would be useless. Phenomenon is the direct reflection of an object at the level of perceptions, whereas essence is hidden deep within an object, requiring the exercise of thought for its discovery. Consequently, to know an object, one cannot stop at its phenomenal surface, but must penetrate deep below the phenomenon to discover its hidden essence. The discovery of essence within phenomenon is the starting point of scientific knowledge.[40]

Li then applies this dialectical distinction between phenomenon and essence to an analysis of law. The phenomenon of law manifests itself as the protection of the liberties of the individual, and gives the appearance of assuring equality to all people. The constitution, for example, guarantees legal equality to all citizens regardless of their gender, religion, ethnicity, class, and party affiliation.[41] But the essence of the law is very different; its essence is a class relationship, its class character, and it serves to maintain a particular class structure.[42] Similarly, in his writings on the economy and currency of the early 1930s, Li applies the distinction between phenomenon and essence to the analysis of money. Money, in essence, is a general concretised expression of the value of a commodity and a manifestation of the social productive relations of the producers of commodities; it is a necessary form of motion of the contradictions of a commodity economy. In its phenomenal form, money becomes a medium of exchange for commodities of unequal value, this medium allowing the resolution of the contradiction between the value of a commodity (the amount of socially necessary labour time embodied within it) and its use value (that is, the price that will be paid for it). A distinction must thus be drawn between the world of the commodity and the world of money, although the essence of money is to be found in the world of the commodity, for it is here that value resides.[43]

Conclusion

The interest in Marxist philosophy which emerges in Li Da's writings of the late 1920s may have been triggered by his translation of a number of important works on philosophy into Chinese. In the same year as Li's *Fundamental Knowledge of Society* appeared (1929), he published his translation of Thalheimer's *Introduction to Dialectical Materialism*, which had originated as a text for the Sun Yat-sen University in Moscow. The following year, Kawakami Hajime's *Fundamental Theories of Marxist Economics* was published in Chinese, Li having been one of its translators. This volume contained a lengthy section on the philosophy of Marxism, a section which Li had translated. Li also published his translation of the Soviet philosopher Luppol's *The Fundamental Questions of Theory and Practice in the Social Sciences* in 1930, which was largely an elaboration of Lenin's exposition of Marxist philosophy. These and other translations by Li will be examined in the next chapter.

More broadly, Li's interest in philosophy was a reflection of the growing interest in philosophy within the Soviet Union. The heated polemic which occurred between the proponents of mechanical materialism and the advocates of dialectical materialism culminated in 1929, as we observed in Chapter 2, with victory for dialectical materialism and its chief advocate Abram Deborin. This victory is significant for a number of reasons. First, it established dialectical materialism as *the* philosophy of Marxism. A number of other philosophies, including the empirio-criticism of the followers of Ernst Mach, had also proclaimed themselves as Marxist. Now, for the first time, there was an official adjudication which defined dialectical materialism as Marxist philosophy. A second and related point is that dialectical materialism, as defined by the Deborinites, became *orthodox* Marxist philosophy. The status of orthodoxy attributed to dialectical materialism was reinforced by the power of the Communist Party of the Soviet Union, and followers of rival philosophies such as mechanical materialism soon discovered that philosophy was no longer an intellectual realm of free inquiry or speculation; advocacy of philosophies deemed unorthodox attracted sanctions. Moreover, the philosophy deemed orthodox in the Soviet Union had the same status throughout the international communist movement.

The dissemination of orthodox Marxist theory and philosophy in China was a function of the translation activities and interpretive writings of Marxist intellectuals, and of these, Li Da was the most significant. As we observed in the previous chapter, Li's writings of the early 1920s on the materialist conception of history had been largely instrumental in establishing the idea that there was an orthodox Marxist theory of social change. With the appearance of philosophy in his writings and translations from the late 1920s, we can observe the same process at work. While his writings of the late 1920s contain only brief sections on philosophy, these are indicators of a growing interest in dialectical materialism as well as a growing concern that the philosophy disseminated to the revolutionary movement in China should be the orthodox version. This interest and concern would culminate, in the mid-1930s, with the publication of Li's magnum opus *Elements of Sociology*, the first half of which is devoted to an explication of dialectical materialism. It is significant that the elaboration of dialectical materialism contained in *Elements of Sociology* does not employ the Deborinite version as its point of departure; it is, rather, the post-1931 version of dialectical materialism which Li explicates, for the mantle of orthodoxy worn by Deborin had by then passed to Mark Mitin, his successor as philosophical commissar. Li's reading of the post-1931 Soviet writings on philosophy convinced him that Deborin had been guilty of Hegelian excesses and a lack of "party-mindedness", and he ensured that his own writing would not suffer from the same defects.[44] In doing so, Li provided the Chinese Communist Party with a recipe for orthodoxy in the realm of philosophy, one which was to have a powerful and sustained influence.

When we turn our attention to Li's writings on the Marxist theory of social change of the late 1920s, the most striking impression we derive is of his commitment to a materialist explanation which located causal primacy within the forces of production, and in particular within its sphere of technology. The nature and level of sophistication of the technological dimension of production has, according to Li, an overwhelming impact on the way in which society changes, for these establish the necessity for certain forms of labour and relegate others to oblivion. The class structure of a particular social formation thus has its basis in the prevailing techniques of production, although there is interaction between these. Similarly, Li invariably asserts that, in the relationship between economic base and superstructure, the economic base is dominant. The various elements of the superstructure (politics, law, religion, art and literature, morality, philosophy) all derive from the economic base. Changes within the economy will ultimately lead, as Li argued at length in *Contemporary Sociology*, to changes in the structure and policies of the state; the same is true of other superstructural elements as well. However, the relationship between economic base and superstructure is not, for Li, a one-way street. Once created, the elements of the superstructure have the capacity to exert an influence on the economic base, primarily to obstruct or to facilitate the changes at work there.

Li's attribution of a degree of influence to the superstructure is manifest most clearly in his confidence in the capacity of political revolution to facilitate the realisation of social revolution. From his earliest writings, as we saw in the previous chapter, he was an advocate of such a political revolution; for he believed that, while political revolution was only possible once particular productive forces and class relationships had emerged, the political organisations and forms of consciousness they generated could function as catalyst to realise the potential for change of which these deeper economic forces were capable. Li's early explanation of the materialist explanation of history thus incorporated a strong dialectical motif, one in which base and superstructure were bound together in an interactive, though ultimately unequal, relationship, the economic base being the realm which specified the nature and capacity for influence of the elements of the superstructure.

While this motif persists in Li's writings following his break with the Communist Party in 1923, there is, if anything, a stronger emphasis on the importance of the economic realm as the starting point in historical analysis. This was a function of the more extended treatment he gave to his elaboration of the materialist conception of history. His writings of the late 1920s consist less of short polemical articles exhorting comrades to organise for and fight the political revolution (the pattern of his pre-1923 writings), and more of extended and very detailed expositions of the various theoretical dimensions of Marxism. His *Contemporary Sociology* is a prime example, and so too is his book *A Survey of China's Revolution in Production* (1930), which demonstrates only too clearly that Li perceived the possibility of political revolution in China emanating from the radical changes to the Chinese economy of the last century.[45] However, these more extended publications do not reveal any diminution in his belief in the possibility and desirability of a political revolution in China; rather, they set the call for political revolution within a more wide-ranging consideration of the broad historical forces which constituted the context within which political revolution had become possible.[46]

The deeper and more extended theoretical treatment of Marxism evident in Li Da's post-1923 writings was, somewhat paradoxically, made possible by his departure from the Party. Although still active as a non-Party revolutionary, he was no longer involved in the day-to-day administration of the Party or its propaganda work, and this left him time to pursue and extend his interests in education, social science theory and philosophy. And in so doing, he was able to conceive and write the extensive tomes on Marxist theory and philosophy which, by the mid-1930s, had established his reputation as one of China's pre-eminent Marxist intellectuals. These lengthy works of explication of Marxist theory were also, as we have suggested, to exert a major influence on the development of Marxism in China, and to provide it with a textual basis from which other more prominent political figures, and in particular Mao Zedong, could derive their own understanding of Marxism.

Li's influence on the introduction of Marxist theory to China came, however, not only through his own writings, but through his translations. From the very first, Li had perceived the urgent necessity of providing Chinese revolutionaries with an accessible corpus of writings by Marxists in Japan, Europe and the Soviet Union, and it is no coincidence that some of his earliest publications are translations. Between 1920 and 1935, Li published some thirty-two translations, ranging from short pieces such as Marx's *Critique of the Gotha Program* to enormous texts such as Kautsky's *The Economic Doctrines of Karl Marx* and Shirokov and Aizenberg's *A Course on Dialectical Materialism*. The role of translation in the dissemination of Marxism in China and its contribution to the sort of Marxism which developed there is an area which has not attracted the attention it deserves from Western scholars of Marxism in China. It is essential, however, in evaluating Li Da's contribution to the development of Marxist theory in China, to look in some detail at his translations, and it is to this task we turn in the next chapter.

Notes

1. *Li Da wenji*, Vol. I, p. 212.

2. This Resolution had specified that collaboration with the Guomindang "must not be done at the price of the C.P. of China losing its own political identity. The Party must preserve its own organisation with a strongly centralized apparatus ... In this work the C.P. of China must act strictly under its own banner and independently of any other political group ..." See Tony Saich, *The Origins of the*

First United Front in China: The Role of Sneevliet (Alias Maring) (Leiden: E.J. Brill, 1991), Vol. 2, 565–66.

3. Ibid, Vol. 1, p. 73.

4. Party History Research Centre of the Central Committee of the Chinese Communist Party (comp.), *History of the Chinese Communist Party: A Chronology of Events (1919–1990)* (Beijing: Foreign Languages Press, 1991), p. 20.

5. See Huang Nansen et al., *Makesi zhexue shi (diliujuan)* (A History of Marxist Philosophy (Volume 6)) (Beijing: Beijing chubanshe, 1989), pp. 163–74; also Zhuang Fuling (ed.), *Zhongguo Makesizhuyi zhexue chuanbo shi* (A History of the Dissemination of Marxist Philosophy in China) (Beijing: Zhongguo renmin daxue chubanshe, 1988), pp. 210–21.

6. *Zhongguo zhexue*, Vol. I (1979), p. 359. Deng Chumin was part of the group which helped Li Da establish the Kunlun publishing house in Shanghai in 1928. See ibid., p. 360.

7. *Contemporary Sociology* was published in 1926 by the Hunan xiandai congshushe. In 1928 Li Da established, with a number of like-minded intellectuals, the Kunlun shudian publishing house in Shanghai, which published a revised edition of *Contemporary Sociology*. See *Li Da wenji*, Vol. I, p. 236n; also Li Da, *Xiandai shehuixue* (Contemporary Sociology) (Shanghai: Kunlun shudian, 1928), pp. 1–2.

8. Huang Nansen et al. (eds), *Makesizhuyi zhexue shi (diliujuan)*, p. 173.

9. Song Jingming, *Li Da zhuanji* (The life of Li Da) (Hubei: Hubei renmin chubanshe, 1986), p. 72.

10. *Li Da wenji*, Vol. I, pp. 236–37.

11. For a potted summary of Li's interpretation of the materialist conception of history from *Contemporary Sociology*, see *Li Da wenji*, Vol. I, pp. 370–72.

12. Ibid., pp. 238–40.

13. Ibid., pp. 240–46.

14. Ibid., pp. 246–49.

15. Ibid., p. 249.

16. Ibid., pp. 250–55.

17. Ibid., pp. 255–57.

18. Ibid., pp. 258–63.

19. Ibid., p. 267.

20. Ibid., pp. 269–70. See also pp. 516–17; Li here emphasises the importance of developments in technology within the forces of production for social change.

21. Chapter 9 of *Contemporary Sociology*; see ibid, pp. 287–94.

22. Ibid., pp. 287–91.

23. Ibid., pp. 291–94.

24. Ibid., pp. 370–74.

25. Ibid., pp. 315–16.

26. Ibid., p. 726, also p. 508.

27. See also ibid., p. 507.

28. Elsewhere, Li suggests that, in primitive society, there was no state as there was no surplus from production and no class which monopolised surplus production. ibid., p. 507.

29. Ibid., p. 330.

30. Ibid., p. 340.

31. Ibid., p. 370.
32. Ibid., p. 381.
33. Qu Qiubai, "Shehui zhexue gailun" (A Survey of Social Philosophy), in *Qu Qiubai wenji* (Collected Writings of Qu Qiubai) (Beijing: Renmin chubanshe, 1988), Vol. 2, p. 307; see also Song Zhiming and Zhao Dezhi, *Xiandai Zhongguo zhexue sichao* (Philosophical Trends in Contemporary China) (Bejing: Zhongguo renmin daxue chubanshe, 1992), pp. 36–53.
34. See Li Da, *Shehui zhi jichu zhishi* (Fundamental knowledge of society) (Shanghai: Xin shengming shuju, 1929).
35. *Li Da wenji*, Vol. 1, pp. 505–7.
36. Ibid., p. 511.
37. Ibid., p. 512.
38. Ibid., pp. 511–16.
39. Ibid., p. 723.
40. Ibid.
41. Ibid., p. 724.
42. Ibid., p. 727.
43. Li Da, *Jingjixue dagang* (Elements of Economics) (Wuhan: Wuhan daxue chubanshe, 1985), pp. 186–90.
44. See Li Da's translator's Preface to Shirokov and Aizenberg's *Bianzheng weiwulun jiaocheng* (A Course on Dialectical Materialism) (Shanghai: Bigengtang shudian, 1935), pp. 1–4.
45. Li Da, *Zhongguo chanye geming gaiguan* (A Survey of China's Revolution in Production) (Shanghai: Kunlun shudian, 1930).
46. In an article of 1928, Li still spoke of the revolution which China needed. See "Zhongguo suo xuyao de geming", *Xiandai Zhongguo*, Vol. 2, no. 1 (16 July 1928).

5

Translation and the Dissemination of Marxism in China

The role of translation in the dissemination of Marxism in China is of considerable importance for the evaluation of the sources of theoretical influence on the early Chinese communist movement. It is, however, an area which has been largely and surprisingly ignored.[1] Any attempt to evaluate the theoretical maturity of the first generation of Chinese Marxists, and the nature of their understanding of Marxism, should not, however, overlook the content of translated texts, for these constituted a significant ingredient in the brew of theoretical formulations and political strategies which came to define Marxism in China. Analysis of the content of these translations can shed light on the reasons why Marxism in China adopted the theoretical trajectory that it did, and also on the vexed issue of its "orthodoxy". By bringing translation into focus as a source of theoretical and political inspiration, it opens the door to a clearer recognition of the fact that Marxism in China drew on a theoretical tradition which originated from outside the Chinese context, a tradition with its own body of concepts, modes of understanding and forms of discourse; and this recognition should weaken the unfortunately widespread tendency to regard Marxism in China as merely a distant and rather exotic cousin of supposedly mainstream (that is, European and/or Soviet) Marxism. Given its external theoretical sources, many of which came to China in the form of translations, Marxism in China could never be "hermetic", regardless of the distinct manner in which Marxists in China were subsequently to apply their understanding of this theory.[2] Marxism had a history prior to its importation into China, and that history (debates over theory, political movements and struggles) was frequently communicated to Chinese through the efforts of those, like Li Da, who assumed the onerous task of translating the Marx texts and texts on Marxism into Chinese.

Following his conversion to Marxism in the late 1910s, Li commenced a period of intensive tutelage in the basic theories of Marxism. At this time, Li was still in Japan and most of his sources were in the Japanese language.[3] Some of these documents had been written by Japanese socialists, but many were Japanese translations of texts on Marxism written by European Marxists. Documents not yet translated into Japanese were for the most part inaccessible to Li, for although he had some German and a smattering of English, his abilities in these European languages never achieved the level of his mastery in Japanese.[4] From the very commencement of his career as a Marxist theoretician, Li was thus made aware of the problem of access to the texts of the Marxist tradition, and the fundamental problem this posed for the dissemination of Marxism in China. Translation of texts on Marxism into Chinese thus presented itself to the young Li Da as an urgent necessity, and to this demanding task he turned with a vengeance. Over the next twenty years, a stream of translations poured from his pen, over thirty books and articles, and it is no exaggeration to say that Li was one of the most important of the early Chinese translators of Marxism. Through his efforts, the infant communist movement in China was provided with a number of extremely important interpretations of Marxism, interpretations which were to exert a significant influence on the theoretical development of Marxism in China.[5]

Li Da was not, of course, the only Chinese intellectual to be involved in the translation of Marx and Marxist texts into Chinese. Others, such as Chen Wangdao, Wu Liangping, Zhang Zhongshi, Qin Bangxian, Hou Wailu, Wang Yanan and Guo Dali, also made a major contribution.[6] But Li Da stands out for a number of reasons. He was amongst the first to render into Chinese the commentaries and interpretations of influential European Marxists and Japanese socialists. An example is his translation of the Japanese version of Karl Kautsky's *Karl Marx's ökonmische Lehren* (The Economic Doctrines of Karl Marx), which contains a lucid and reasonably comprehensive summary of *Capital*, Volume I. Li's translation of this important text had a significant impact, being used by Li Dazhao's Marxist study group in Beijing.[7] Similarly, his translation of the Japanese version of the influential Dutch socialist Hermann Gorter's *The Materialist Conception of History*, published in China in 1921, contains a readable and wide-ranging account of the main themes of Marxism. Second, Li's translations often went through numerous editions, indicating that they were much sought after and widely read. Li's translation of Gorter's book, for example, had been republished fourteen times by 1932. Third, Li's translation activities stand out for both the enormous range of issues they cover as well as their sheer volume. While the focus is the theoretical and political dimensions of Marxism, Li also translated works on topics as diverse as Scandinavian literature, China's tariff system, the women's movement, and German culture and art. And it must be remembered that he maintained this impressive output of translation while writing his own books and articles, as well as being heavily involved in political and educational activities. Finally, Li's translations stand out for their influence on the development of Mao Zedong's philosophical thought. His co-translations of Shirokov and Aizenberg's *A Course on Dialectical Materialism* and Kawakami Hajime's *Basic Theories of Marxist Economics* (which contains a substantial section on Marxist philosophy) were both read and annotated by Mao, the former text being a major influence on Mao at the time of his writing "On Contradiction" and "On Practice" in 1937.[8]

Li Da's translation activities were thus an important facet of his lifelong commitment to the dissemination of Marxism in China, and any appreciation of his intellectual and political activities must include consideration of them. They are particularly important in the context of this study, for a number of the books and articles which he translated contain extended discussion of the themes we have been pursuing in his own writings; these are the philosophy of Marxism and the problem of social causation. In the analyses which follow, we will occasionally allow our gaze to dwell on other aspects of Li's translations; for the most part, however, we will concentrate our attention on these two central dimensions of Marxist thought. Through a consideration of these themes in Li's translations, the nature and range of theoretical choices open to Marxists in China will become clearer, although a comprehensive study of the influence of translation on the development of Marxism in China would, of course, need to incorporate a broader consideration than can be offered here of the translation activities of the entire cadre of translators who worked on behalf of the early Chinese communist movement.

Li Da's translation activities fall into two fairly distinct periods. The first extends from his conversion to Marxism in the late 1910s to his departure from the Communist Party in 1923. During this phase, Li translated a large number of articles, as well as three books, on different aspects of Marxist theory and politics, as well as other subjects. There is then something of a hiatus during which Li published little in the way of translations. The second major period commences with the establishment in 1928 of a publishing house in Shanghai (Kunlun shudian) by Li Da, Deng Chumin and others. The purpose of this publishing house was to make widely available translations and books on philosophy and the social sciences by progressive authors. The establishment of Kunlun shudian triggered an enormous flow of translations from Li's pen, although not all of his translations were published by it. By 1932, he had translated or co-translated thirteen books. Li Da's translation activities largely came to an end with the publication of Shirokov and Aizenberg's *A Course on Dialectical Materialism* in 1932 for, apart from one further translated book published in 1938, he published no further translations. There are a number of explanations for this. The first is that Li was, as we shall see in subsequent chapters, heavily occupied from 1932 with the writing of his own major work on Marxist philosophy and social theory, *Elements of Sociology*. Li no doubt felt that the first phase of the dissemination of Marxism in China had come to an end, and that, while there remained works by Marx and Marxist commentaries which remained untranslated, the important task now was for Chinese Marxists themselves to write texts on Marxist theory, texts which incorporated not only discussion of the universal dimensions of Marxism, but also its application to the particular social and economic conditions of China. A second and important reason for the cessation of Li's translation activities was the rise of militarism and fascism in Japan. It must be remembered that the language from which Li translated was Japanese, although he did have sufficient German to check the Japanese translation against the orginal should the original be a German text. With the emergence of a political climate in Japan hostile to the activities of Marxists and socialists, the flow of material which Li could translate dried up.[9] A third, and rather more prosaic reason, is that in 1932 Li gained regular employment at the Legal and Commercial Institute at Beiping University, and was therefore not reliant on the income which his translations had generated. In the late 1920s, Li had found himself in a precarious financial situation, Wang Huiwu and he now having two children to support, with little likelihood of employment given the political climate of reaction which prevailed following the collapse of the united front between the Guomindang and the Chinese Communist Party. Li had turned to translation partly as a means of gaining a livelihood, for translations of foreign works sold well, but by 1932 this financial imperative had passed.[10]

In the course of this chapter, we will introduce and briefly analyse a number of the more important books and articles translated into Chinese by Li. Our purpose is to investigate the response of these texts to the problems of Marxist theory which were discussed in some detail in Chapter 2. How did the Japanese, European and Russian writers Li translated formulate the problem of social causation, the relationship between the economic base and the superstructure? If they spoke of Marxist philosophy, how did they conceive of its central preoccupations, and what philosophical laws and categories did they list and in what order of importance? In responding to these questions, we can obviously provide no more than thumbnail sketches of these often very substantial volumes. Nevertheless, these brief sketches will demonstrate that these translations provided a significant quantity of information about these central theoretical problems of Marxism, and this suggests that Marxists in China were consequently not quite the theoretical babes in the wood so often implied in Western accounts of the early communist movement in China. It will become clear that the theoretical responses of European, Russian and Japanese Marxists and socialists to the problem of the relationship between the economic base and superstructure communicated to Marxists in China the possibility of theoretical choice within the Marxist tradition; also made evident to them was the possibility that there were alternatives to a mechanistic and economistic reading of the process of social change, and that these alternatives possessed a strong degree of theoretical legitimacy. The same is true of Marxist philosophy, for a range of different readings are evident in the translations, especially in texts originally published before and after the watershed of 1931 in Soviet philosophical circles.

Li Da on Translation

Before turning to his translations, however, it is important to consider the philosophy of translation adopted by Li Da. While clues to his approach to translation are scattered throughout the translator's prefaces and postfaces which he often inserted into the books he translated, Li left no substantial published discussion of the problem of translation. He did, however, give a talk on this topic at a conference in 1954, and we are fortunate that notes on this talk were taken and kept by a colleague at Wuhan University. In this talk (*Tantan fanyi*), Li Da referred to a number of criteria which should guide the work of the translator.[11] The translator should strive for three things, Li suggests: exact comprehension of the content of the original (*xin*), precise and accurate translation (*da*), and elegance of style of the translated text (*ya*). He concedes that the last of these is the most difficult to attain, and that it is sufficient if only the first two are achieved. To achieve these, translators must firstly work hard to improve their understanding of the Chinese language, for if this is deficient the original meaning of the text will be lost in the process of translation. Second, translators must improve their political level, for if this is insufficient, the translator will be able to understand neither the progressive knowledge in the text nor its basic spirit (*jiben jingshen*). All those involved in translation, Li asserts, must study Marxism-Leninism and Mao Zedong Thought, for only when they have grasped "this weapon" will their ideological (*sixiang*) and political level be raised, and only then will they be able to do the work of translation well. Third, translators should translate those things with which they are familiar. The translation of specialist texts requires that translators prepare themselves in the relevant specialist knowledge. And finally, translators must adopt an attitude of responsibility to the people (and this includes the author of the text and the readers of the translation). To do this, they must exert all efforts to do a competent job. Translators should not commence translation before they have looked at the document several times, and only when they have thoroughly understood the text's central idea and related problems should they commence translation. For Li, translation implies a deep understanding not only of the text, but its author as well:

> My own experience suggests that in order to translate the composition of a foreign author, it is necessary firstly to understand that author's life, the things he or she has written in the past, his or her particular characteristics, what status the composition has in its particular period, and so on. Next, it is necessary to examine the style of that author, and only then can one commence work on his or her composition. Of great importance is the translation of the author's style.[12]

It is clear, both from these comments and from the general tenor of his translations, that politics (the orientation of both author and translator, as well as the political level of the translator) loomed large as a criterion in the selection of a text for translation and in the mode of its translation. While Li's translations cover subjects from widely dispersed fields, the common thread that unites these is the desire to provide China's progressive intellectuals with information from abroad on important social, political and cultural issues. His translation of Shokai Shungetsu's article on Scandinavian literature (1921), for example, had the purpose of introducing Scandinavian writers to Chinese intellectuals and informing them of the progressive themes and techniques employed by writers such as Strindberg and Ibsen.[13] Similarly, his translation of Takayanagi Matsuichiro's book on the history of China's system of customs and excise (1924) alerts readers to the inequities and injustices suffered by China as a result of foreign interference in and control of China's trade.[14] Nowhere in the corpus of Li's translations does one find any concession to the idea that the function of the translator is to provide amusement or entertainment; the purpose of translation is to educate, to enlighten and, most importantly, to arouse the reader to action.

Karl Kautsky and Marxist Economics, Gorter and the Materialist Conception of History

While in Japan, Li translated three books which cover a wide spectrum of Marxist theory. One of these was *The Economic Doctrines of Karl Marx* written by Karl Kautsky (1854–1938), published first in 1887, and published by Li in Chinese translation in 1921.[15] This volume provides a readable and fairly comprehensive summary of Volume I of Marx's *Capital*, and it served for some decades after its original publication in German as a handbook of Marxist economic theory for beginners, with those who had read it being better equipped to approach *Capital* itself.[16] Kautsky follows the general outline of *Capital*, providing analysis of commodities, the way in which commodities come to have value and the exchange of commodities. He deals with money and its circulation, and the problem of price. His analysis of money incorporates consideration of the way in which money is transformed into capital, which introduces too the problem of surplus value and how labour power becomes a commodity under capitalism. He replicates Marx's discussion of the working day and the way in which surplus value is central to the generation of profit. The concept of class is introduced through a discussion of the exploitation of labour power, and the role of the industrial reserve army in depressing wages. Kautsky makes it quite clear that Marx had employed political economy to unravel the natural laws of the process of production of capital; his analysis of capitalism's "laws of motion" was thus premised on a scientific approach.

Li's translation of Kautsky's *The Economic Doctrines of Karl Marx* was employed by the Marxist study group in Beijing led by Li Dazhao and, according to Chinese sources, it consequently played an important role in disseminating the theories of Marxist political economy in China, with many readers being assisted by this book in their study of the materialist conception of history.[17] It was also to be only the first of a number of books on economics and political economy translated by Li Da, although the remainder were mainly from the second period of his translation activities.[18]

The second work on Marxism translated by Li while in Japan focused more directly on the ensemble of theories and concepts which, combined, constitute the materialist conception of history. *An Explanation of the Materialist Conception of History* (in Chinese, *Weiwushiguan jieshuo*) was written by the Dutch Marxist Herman Gorter (1864–1927), a leader of the the left faction of the Social Democratic Party and one of Holland's foremost poets.[19] This book, of fourteen chapters and 60,000 words of text, was translated by Li from the Japanese translation which was, according to Li, incomplete; his own translation compared the German and Japanese texts to ensure that the Chinese translation was complete. Because his own knowledge of German was "not so good", he obtained the assistance of his friend Li Hanjun when he ran into difficulties with the German language.[20]

An Explanation of the Materialist Conception of History commences with a discussion of historical and philosophical materialism, Gorter arguing that philosophical materialism perceives matter as eternal, with spirit emerging on the basis of matter. Philosophical materialism deals with the origins of thought, he suggests, while the materialist conception of history deals with the reasons for the changes in human thought. Consciousness is determined by social life, which is in turn constituted of the forces of production and the relations of production, and the contradiction between the two. The materialist conception of history consequently perceives class divisions and inequality as a major factor in the shaping of human consciousness, and thus in the shaping of history.[21] An example is religion, which is, Gorter contends, a product of social and economic conditions, of ignorance and fear of nature in the case of primitive societies and of exploitation and alienation in the case of class societies.[22]

According to Gorter, the materialist conception of history contains three major tenets. First, the techniques of labour, namely the forces of production, constitute the social base; the forces of production determine the relations of production, and these latter are consistent with society's property relations. The relations between humans are therefore necessarily class relations, not individual relations. Second, the techniques of production continually develop, and as there is continual change in the forces of production, so too is there continual change in class and property relations, change which is subsequently mirrored in changes in morals, religion, politics, law, philosophy and the arts. Third, when the techniques of production have progressed to a certain point, a contradiction emerges between the forces of production on the one hand and the class and property relations on the other; it is this contradiction which generates the impulse for qualitative, revolutionary change.[23] In elaborating these tenets, Gorter stresses that the labour process is the source of thought, politics, law — in short, the human spirit — but it is important to recognise too, he suggests, that *conscious* human labour is at the basis of the process of production, for it is this which allows humans to create inventions and to progress. Human spirit is thus part of the process of production.[24] Humans are animals with the capacity for thought, but human thought operates within the boundaries established by the relations of production and the property relations. Gorter points out that the forces of production and relations of production are material, and so too in its own way is spirit; what he denies is that spirit can exist independently. Spirit gives rise to new science, new techniques of production, but these do not arise from spirit as an independent entity, but as something which has evolved from society itself. Nevertheless, humans are creative animals and their consciousness is part of the process of creation.[25]

While Gorter apparently sets out from a rather mechanistic and determinist premise (the labour process determines thought), he proceeds to qualify this by insisting that the materialist conception of history does *not* incorporate the proposition that a certain sort of production will automatically give rise to a certain sort of thought. Other factors, he suggests, intervene to influence this process, and these factors vary from one society to another, and these too must be investigated. An important factor singled out here by Gorter is nationality. The history of a nation's politics, as well as its climatic and geographical conditions, can influence production and thought; the various aspects of society are interdependent and influence each other. Consequently, politics may influence economics, customs influence politics, and the arts influence science; by the same token, economics influences politics, politics influence customs, and science influences the arts. There is mutual interaction and reaction.[26]

For Gorter, then, the premise of the materialist conception of history (outlined earlier in his book, that the labour process determines thought) does not preclude the possibility that thought, once created, can have an influence on the course of history; indeed, by perceiving production as *conscious* human production, Gorter in effect perceives thought as an integral element of the forces of production. Humans are creative, and their capacity to reflect critically on their activities and formulate ideas which will improve the techniques of production represents a major factor in the initiation of historical change. This is a most interesting proposition, not only in its own right, but in terms of the perceptions which the early Chinese communists must have gained on reading it. For here is a major text by a left-wing European Marxist,[27] a text endorsed by Karl Kautsky (who wrote the Preface to Gorter's book), insisting that Marxism's theory of history is not a mechanistic and economistic doctrine: the economic realm is of great historical significance, but it is not the only causally significant factor, and human consiousness also must be recognised as a force for change; the various dimensions of human society are interrelated and there is interaction between them. As one of the first texts on the materialist conception of history to be translated into Chinese (published in China in 1921), Gorter's book provided Chinese communists with an initial view of Marxism which was both flexible and dialectical, and the book's longevity and popularity (it was republished fourteen times in China by 1932) meant that this initial impression was extended to a subsequent generation of Chinese Marxists.[28] Indeed, the contents and influence of Gorter's book (that is, a European text on Marxism) serve to query the view of Marxism in China as heterodox or aberrant for its acceptance of human thought and consciousness as a factor in historical change; the intellectual sources of Marxism in China (such as Gorter's book) suggest that this view, if extended to Marxists in Europe, would also see all but the most economistic and mechanistic of them dismissed for their heterodoxy. But this sort of parallel judgment never seems to be contemplated, for to do so would significantly weaken those evaluations of Marxism in China premised, as most of them are, on a shallow economistic reading of Marxism.

Takabatake Motoyuki and Social Problems

Gorter's suggestion that the materialist conception of history, which emphasises the economic realm of society but is not a mechanistic theory, is a theme which emerges frequently, in one form or other, in the other works on Marxist theory translated into Chinese by Li Da. It appears, although in somewhat different form, in Li Da's 1921 translation of *An Overview of Social Problems* (Shehui wenti zonglan) by the Japanese social theorist and translator of *Capital* Takabatake Motoyuki (1886–1928).[29] The focus of this three-volume, 210,000 character book is the study of social problems and their resolution through different forms of social policy.

The first volume[30] contains a detailed consideration of the source and significance of social problems. Social problems, according to Takabatake, can be divided into two types: those related to the social totality (*shehui quanti*) and those related to the problems of labour under the prevailing system of production. If the problems of labour can be solved, other social problems are comparatively easy to solve.[31] The heart of contemporary social problems lies not in agriculture, but in industry, for it is here that the problem of labour is most accute. The final stage of industrial development is the production of the commodity, and this is where the analysis of social problems must focus; Japan, like Europe and America, has reached the stage where industrial commodity production is the root cause of social problems, and central to this form of production is the struggle between labour and capital. As a basis for solving other social problems, this struggle between labour and capital must first be overcome, although Takabatake concedes that its solution will not lead to the complete solution of all other social problems.[32]

Social policy must address the two main principles of contemporary social organisation — free competition and private property — for these principles underpin the inequality which is characteristic of modern society. Germany, according, to Takabatake is the most progressive society in terms of its thinking on social policy. Here, there has been emphasis laid on the role of the state in addressing the problem of inequality; the principle of the state should be equality, as opposed to the principle of society which is inequality.[33] Various aspects of state policy, such as the restriction of the length of the working day, can work towards the goal of equality, although social policy of this sort could do no more than ameliorate the worst excesses of the inequalities generated by capitalism. A thorough remedy of the problems of capitalism requires socialism, defined by Takabatake as a change in the structure of ownership; under socialism, there would be state control and management of property.[34] Thus, while he advocates social policy, and much of the first volume is spent in discussion of this both in theory and in its application in various capitalist countries,[35] he recognises that fundamental change requires socialism. It is in this context that the ideas of Marx are introduced, for in his advocation of class struggle, Marx is presented as an opponent of social policy.[36]

The second volume[37] provides a quite detailed history of the concept of socialism, and places Marx's thought in the context of the evolution of socialist thought. While socialist thought is relatively new, according to Takabatake, dating in its modern form from only 1833, it has roots in earlier utopian socialist speculation. These earlier forms of socialist thought, such as Thomas More's *Utopia* and Harrington's *Oceania*, are introduced and discussed, and so too are the ideas of Rousseau, Locke, Montesquieu and Voltaire. Takabatake also gives particular attention to the early English socialist thinkers such as Godwin and William Thompson, and to the emergence of the Chartists and Fabians. When he turns his attention to socialist thought in Germany, Takabatake introduces the ideas of Hegel, Fichte and Schelling as precursors of the thought of Marx and Engels, for it is the ideas of these latter which are now central to contemporary socialist thought and movements.[38] Marxism, Takabatake asserts, can be equated with scientific socialism, and it is comprised of three different (though related) themes: the philosophical, the sociological and the economic. Philosophically, Marxism is a materialist doctrine; sociologically, it incorporates the materialist conception of history; and economically, it is based on the theory of surplus value. Marx's theory is based on a dialectical mode of analysis and a materialist investigation; and it is the combination of Hegel's notion of progress in history and Marx's materialism which underpins the materialist conception of history.

Takabatake explains the materialist conception of history as follows. The spiritual world is a reflection of material conditions, and human existence is not determined by human thought; rather, the conditions of human existence are responsible for the emergence of the various forms of human consiousness. The economy (the technology of production and its social relations) is the motive force for the creation of politics and spirit, and the relations and forces of production are consequently the base of society. It is from this economic realm that inevitability in history arises; society does not change in accordance with abstract principles of truth and justice, but in accordance with changes within the relations and forces of production. The causes of change are thus to be sought, not in philosophy, but in economics.[39] Having provided the conventional economistic introduction to the materialist conception of history, Takabatake, like Gorter, then proceeds to qualify its mechanistic implications. The consciousness of classes, he asserts, does become a factor for change once this has been brought into existence by the economic base.[40] Interestingly, Takabatake here refers to Engels' attempt to salvage the materialist conception of history from its vulgar economistic interpreters; elements of the superstructure, while themselves influenced by the prevailing economic relations, can and do exert an influence on historical change.[41]

Takabatake then proceeds to a discussion of revisions to Marxist thought, and particularly the ideas of Bernstein and neo-Kantianism.[42] He provides a detailed survey of the history and situation of the socialist parties in England, Russia, the United States and Italy, and gives special attention to the ideas of Bolshevism.[43] Similarly, the first half of the third volume[44] provides a detailed analysis of unionism (its history, goals, organisation, policies) in America, Russia, England, France, Germany, Switzerland, Italy and other European countries. The remainder of the book is concerned with the issue of the women's movement, and the solution to the problem of gender inequality, an issue which was of great interest to Li Da and a subject on which he was to publish a series of articles and translations in the early 1920s.[45]

Takabatake Motoyuki's *An Overview of Social Problems* is interesting for a number of reasons. First, as we have seen, the materialist conception of history is portrayed in a way which (once again) allows that non-economic factors may play some role in the process of social and historical change. Second, the comprehensive survey of socialist thought and ideas presented here puts the lie to Werner Meissner's argument that Chinese Marxist theoreticians had never "grasped the intellectual dimension of Marxism in the history of European thought", nor had they informed themselves of it from sources other than approved Soviet sources.[46] It is clear that Li Da, as the translator of this book, was well aware of Marxism's intellectual ancestry and theoretical dimensions, and it is very likely from the success of Li's translation of *An Overview of Social Problems* (republished eleven times by 1932)[47] that many Chinese Marxists also were not quite as ignorant of Marxist and other socialist thought as Meissner suggests. Third, it is very likely that Takabatake's book was one of the sources of inspiration and information on a number of the themes on which Li Da wrote so extensively in the early 1920s, in particular the history of the European socialist parties and the issue of the liberation of women.

Sugiyama Sakae's *A Survey of Social Science*

Although the texts on Marxist theory translated and published in China by Li during the early 1920s contain some reference to Marxist philosophy, it is not their primary focus. As we observed in Chapter 3, the preoccupation of Marxist theorists during this early phase (Qu Qiubai is the exception here) was with the materialist conception of history, and much less so with the purely philosophical dimensions of Marxism. This was certainly the case with Li Da's own writings which are preoccupied with the theoretical aspects of the materialist conception of history and its practical political implications, in China as well as in other countries. Indeed, it is not until the late 1920s that Marxist philosophy makes a significant appearance in Li's writings, and this coincides with his second major period of translation activities. A number of the books translated by Li between 1928 and 1932 discuss in considerable depth the premises, laws and categories of dialectical materialism, and also the debates which had occurred over their appropriate intepretation. What is interesting about this array of translations is that they fall over the 1931 watershed in Soviet philosophy; consequently, works by Deborinites such as Luppol, as well as critics of Deborin such as Shirokov and Aizenberg, are represented in Li's corpus of translations. Of the translations, it was to be Shirokov and Aizenberg's *A Course on Dialectical Materialism* which was to exert the greatest influence on the development of Marxist philosophy in China, and we will turn to an analysis of its contents in due course.

One of the first of the books dealing with philosophy which Li Da translated is the Japanese socialist Sugiyama Sakae's *Shehui kexue gailun* (A Survey of Social Science). Published in China in 1929, *A Survey of Social Science* is an interesting bridge between Li's earlier translations and writings, with their preoccupation with the materialist conception of history, and the later translations and writings in which philosophy appears as a major theme. For in Sugiyama's book, not only is there considerable attention devoted to both of these themes, but its interpretation of the materialist conception of history continues the tendency of the earlier translations to represent the relationship between economic base and superstructure in flexible and dialectical, rather than mechanistic and economistic, terms.

For Sugiyama, the laws which govern the development of society are influenced most strongly by society's productive realm (the form, instruments and forces of production, as well as the relations of production). Quoting from Engels, Plekhanov, Weber, Oppenheimer and Bukharin, Sugiyama argues that there are indeed laws of cause and effect which exist between things.[48] An example is the most fundamental of these laws, that which describes the connection between existence and consciousness. It is not consciousness which determines existence, Sugiyama reiterates, but existence which determines consciousness; it is not the form of thought which determines the forces of production, the material productive form and social relations, but the reverse.[49] The difference between the laws of the natural and social sciences, he continues, is only one of degree, not of kind. However, the laws of nature change comparatively little, whereas the laws of society are more changeable; the distinction here is that the laws of nature are created by nature, whereas the laws of society are created and discovered by humankind. The laws of society are a reflection of the forces of production and the relations of production, and as these change, so too do the laws of society. The purpose of science is not merely to reveal these laws, but to provide knowledge which will change the world. Knowledge must therefore be practical; the object of science is practice, and knowledge of an object is also determined by practice.[50]

When Sugiyama turns his attention to the philosophy of Marxism,[51] he commences by suggesting that Marx deepened Feuerbach's materialism and inverted Hegel's dialectics, and created a synthesis through combining them. Feuerbach perceived thought as determined by humans, but perceived humans as a part of nature; Marx and Engels, on the other hand, saw humans as social beings. For Marx and Engels, humans are dynamic, participating in activities which develop the world; they thus examined the relationship between humans and their social and natural environment in a dialectical way, one which perceived a mutual interaction (*huxiang zuoyong*) between them. Hegel, however, perceived spirit as primary, with universal rationality as the motive force of world history. For Hegel, the development of history takes a dialectical form: thesis, synthesis, antithesis (or in terms of logic — affirmation, negation, negation of the negation).

For Sugiyama, a basic premise of materialism is the proposition that all things can be divided into spirit (thought, consciousness) and matter (existence); spirit has no substance in time and space, whereas matter does. But which determines which? Idealism argues that thought determines existence, while materialism argues that it is existence which determines thought. A number of propositions encapsulate the materialist view of the relationship between thought and existence:

1. Humans are part of nature, and so must engage in natural production and observe the laws of nature.
2. Humans, like other animals, have evolved, and part of this evolution has been the development of thought from matter.
3. Thought is manifested as a particular form of matter, such as the brain.

4. Without thought, matter could still exist, but thought could not exist without matter.

Materialism, however, must be united with dialectics in order to provide an accurate perception of the world and its development. The basic propositions of a dialectical materialism, Sugiyama suggests, are that:

1. All things are in motion, and motion is a form of the existence of matter.
2. All things contain contradictions, which continually emerge and are resolved.

Things must therefore be grasped as in motion and as containing contradictions. In addition, dialectical materialism perceives things in their entirety and in their connection with other things.

Although Sugiyama has earlier informed us that it is the productive realm which determines thought, he returns to this theme to qualify the apparently mechanistic and economistic tone of this proposition.[52] The superstructure, he argues, emerges on society's "basis" and cannot exist apart from society. The basis is constituted of the relations of production, which are detemined by and compatible with the forces of production. Interestingly, Sugiyama posits the existence of not one, but two, superstructures. Superstructure I is made up of society's legal and political systems, while superstructure II is constituted of consciousness (*yishixingtai*). The economic structure is made up of the dominant and subordinate forms of the relations of production. While it is clear from Sugiyama's analysis of this core theoretical problem of the materialist conception of history that he perceived the economic structure of society and the forces of production as "the *ultimately* determining element in history" (indeed, he quotes Engels' words to this effect),[53] he is at pains to demonstrate that politics, law, philosophy, religion, literature and the arts have the capacity to react back on the economic base. Superstructures I and II thus are not merely passive reflections of the economic base, but play a significant role in social change. This is quite evident in Figure 5.1, taken from Sugiyama's book.[54]

It can be seen at a glance that there is, in Sugiyama's formulation, a strong and apparently reciprocal relationship between the "process of social life" (incorporating social organisation, economic structure, form of production and material productive forces) and the two superstructures (incorporating the processes of spiritual and political life); the different areas of "society" are clearly interrelated and interactive. What the diagram does not make particularly clear is which area of "society" is predominant in its causal influence. However, the text of Sugiyama's book stresses that the starting point of social investigation is the

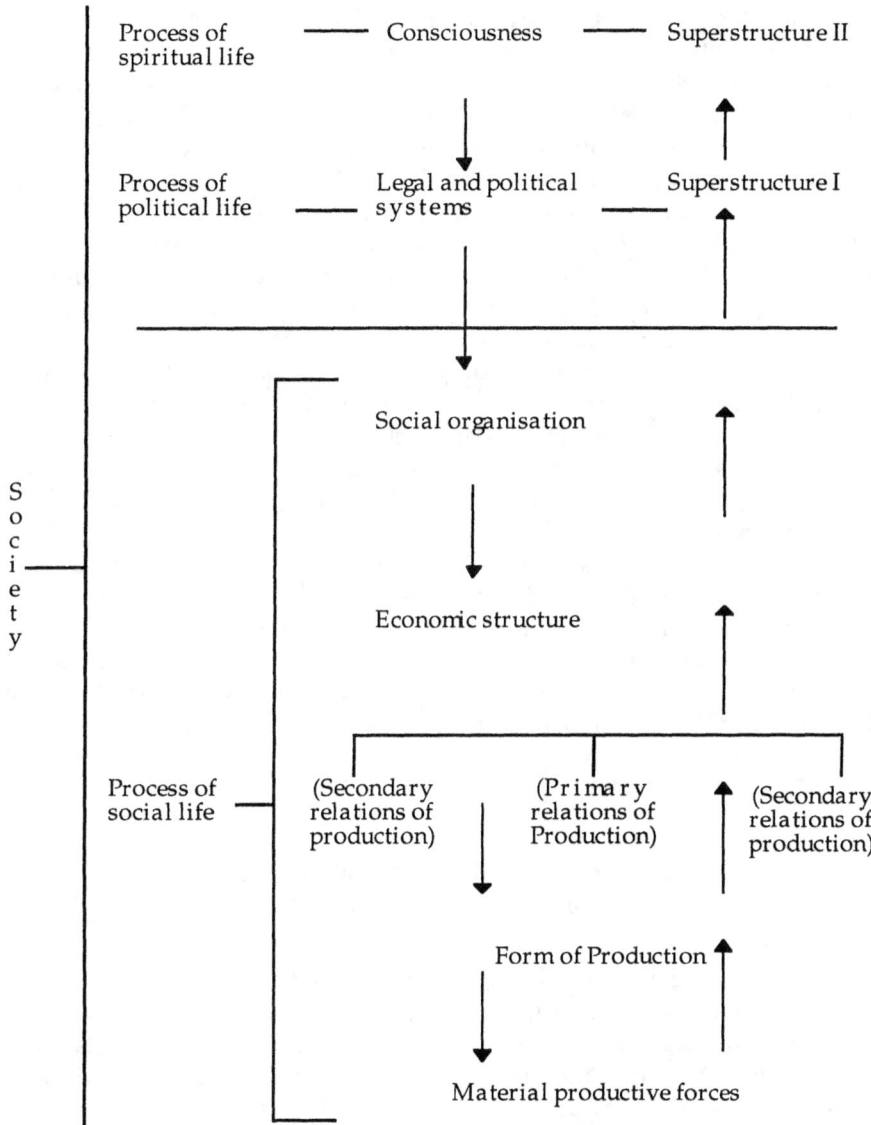

FIGURE 5.1
Source: Sugiyama Sakae, *A Survey of Social Science*

economic realm, and in particular the economic structure, for social investigation must mirror the actual character of the causal sequence within society.[55] It is not fortuitous that Sugiyama employs Engels' 1890 depiction of the economic realm as being "the *ultimately* determining element in history", for he was evidently attempting to arrive at a formulation which allowed the economic structure and form of production causal priority, while attributing the superstructures with a significant capacity for reactive influence. His interpretation of the causal sequence within the materialist conception of history is thus far from being mechanistic or dogmatically economistic; it is, rather, flexible and dialectical, while retaining a materialist perspective. In this regard, Sugiyama's *A Survey of Social Science* reinforces the interpretation of the materialist conception of history evident in Li's earlier translations of the books by Gorter and Takabatake.

There is some evidence to suggest that Li perceived Sugiyama's formulation as an appropriate interpretation of the causal relationship between economic base and superstructure. As we shall observe in subsequent chapters, not only did he provide a similarly flexible and interactive interpretation of the materialist conception of history in his key writings of the 1930s, but a diagram very similar to Sugiyama's appears in Li's writings of the late 1950s when he was to devote considerable attention to the issue of the relationship between economic base and superstructure in the context of a socialist society. It is also likely that Sugiyama's flexible understanding of the materialist conception of history was widely influential amongst other Chinese Marxists, for the book had been republished seven times by November 1931.

Thalheimer, Luppol and Kawakami Hajime on Marxist Philosophy

A number of the texts translated by Li Da and published in 1929 and 1930 dealt exclusively or in large part with dialectical materialism, the philosophy of Marxism. What is interesting about these texts is that they were written under the influence of the Deborinite interpretation of dialectical materialism, and they consequently are characterised by a rather Hegelian reading of the dialectic, something for which Deborin and his followers were to be criticised after 1931.[56]

The first of these is August Thalheimer's *Einfuhrung in den Dialectischen Materialismus (Die Moderne Weltanschauung)* (Introduction to Dialectical Materialism [The Modern Worldview]), although Li employed the subtitle, *The Modern Worldview*, as its Chinese title (Xiandai shijieguan). First published in 1927 as a textbook for Moscow's Sun Yat-sen University, Li came across its Japanese translation in 1928, and it impressed him as an excellent introduction to the philosophy of dialectical materialism. He translated it firstly on the basis of the Japanese translation, and then checked his translation against the German original which a friend had sent him. Li believed Thalheimer's book to be as important as Plekhanov's *Fundamental Problems of Marxism* and Bukharin's *Historical Materialism*.[57]

Thalheimer's exposition of dialectical materialism suggests that all things are matter in motion, and spirit too is a form of matter (such as the nervous system and the brain); there is thus an absolute unity of matter. Reality is, however, knowable by human thought, and the criterion of truth is human practice; but human knowledge is a process, for things cannot be known in their entirety at first contact, and the knowledge which results is relative knowledge. The idealists are incorrect in suggesting the absence of contradictions as a criterion of truth, for all things contain contradictions.[58] Indeed, this is a central characteristic of dialectics, which Thalheimer sums up in two related propositions:

1. All things, phenomena, and concepts are united in one absolute unity, despite their contradictions and differences.
2. There is identity between all things, while at the same time there exists absolute and unconditional opposition.[59]

The law which describes this latter condition is the law of the unity of opposites in things, which is the most common, the most basic of the laws of dialectics.[60] The law which describes the development of contradictions, and consequently the inevitable change and motion in things, is the law of the negation of the negation; the unity of opposites is the premise for the negation of the negation, for contradictions create the impulse for change and development.[61]

Dialectics, Thalheimer continues, has to be applied to the study of history. He stresses production and the economic formation of society, as well as classes and class struggle, as the starting point for analysis. However, consciousness, while created by class, does possess a reactive influence; indeed, historical materialism does not deny the effect of social groups and political parties, but it is class which is the determining factor.[62] Here again, we notice an important concession to the influence exerted by the superstructural realm, a concession which could not have gone unnoticed by Marxists in China, for the book had been republished eight times by 1942.

The second text on philosophy from this period is I. Luppol's *Lenin und die Philosophie — Zur Frage des Verhaltnisses der Philosophie Zur Revolution*, although once again Li Da employed the Japanese translation, and again altered the title, this time to *Fundamental Problems of Theory and Practice in the Social Sciences* (Lilun yu shijian de shehui kexue genben wenti). According to his translator's Preface (dated August 1930), Li altered the title because he considered the central theme of Luppol's book to be the unity of theory and practice. This book is, Li asserts, "essential reading for Marxist scholars and activists", for "the method of theory and practice of the proletariat is materialist dialectics, it is a weapon".[63]

This substantial volume (402 pages) by Luppol contains a detailed exposition of dialectical and historical materialism, but is based primarily on Lenin's thought, although it also quotes extensively from Deborin. It introduces a number of themes of considerable interest to Marxism in China. The first of these is the unity of theory and practice. Practice, Luppol argues, is the criterion of truth, and to ensure that knowledge is scientific, there must be a leap from theory to practice; in daily life, this unity of theory and practice occurs regularly. It must be recognised, however, that the acquisition of knowledge is a process, and that knowledge of reality and the objects in it comes gradually through continual practice.[64] Second, Luppol discusses Lenin's approach to the Party character of philosophy. Philosophy is not a neutral and disinterested inquiry into humans and their relationship with the world; it develops from class society and is the articulation of the interests of particular classes. Philosophy is thus, according to Luppol, a "class science".[65] Third, Luppol stresses the dialectical character of reality and development. All things, he asserts, are connected and in motion; all things are full of difference, and under certain conditions contradictions manifest themselves and change into other forms through the process of the negation of the negation.[66] In addition, Luppol provides anlayses of formal and dialectical logic, the distinction between dialectical materialism and dialectical idealism, and the problem of phenomenon and essence. Underpinning all of these themes is the view that at the basis of dialectical materialism is the unity of theory and practice.

Kawakami Hajime's *Fundamental Theories of Marxist Economics* was the third text from this period (published in China in 1930) to contain a detailed exposition of dialectical materialism.[67] Although Kawakami's volume is supposedly about Marxist economics, the first 310 pages (translated by Li himself) are devoted to materialism, dialectics and the materialist conception of history. Kawakami had spent the latter half of the 1920s wrestling with Marxist theory and attempting to integrate its philosophical and economic dimensions into a unified theoretical framework.[68] He attempted to achieve this by firstly exploring the materialist premises of Marxism, looking in detail at the history of materialism in pre-Marxist thought, and in particular the materialism of Feuerbach, for Marx and Engels' materialism was created on the basis of a deepening of Feuerbach's materialism.[69] Feuerbach had rejected the possibility that the world was a manifestation of human thought; rather, thought (consciousness, spirit) was itself created by matter. He had not proceeded past this point, however, and his entire philosophical framework rested on a simple and rather mechanistic materialism which perceived humans and their thought as solely the product of nature. Not only was this approach mechanistic, it was undialectical, for it did not allow the possibility that thought might have a reactive influence on matter. Marx and Engels consequently took the "rational" part of Feuerbach's materialism, but deepened and critically extended it by uniting it with dialectics, and through perceiving humans as social and not just natural beings. Marx and Engels, while building on the proposition that existence (reality) determines thought (spirit), recognised that this proposition could not adequately explain why human thought did not always and immediately accurately reflect existence in its entirety.[70] Important to the solution of this problem was the fact that humans, while living in society, do not share the same social experiences; in particular, humans belong to different classes, and the reflection of reality as human consciousness is consequently mediated by many other factors. Correct thought thus emerges gradually, and the truth which we gain as a reflection of reality is thus relative, rather than absolute truth; with the development of new sciences, however, human thought does gradually get closer to absolute truth.[71] The agency which allows human thought to progressively approach absolute truth is practice, and it is practice which is the basis of materialism's epistemology.[72]

When Kawakami turns his attention to dialectics,[73] he reiterates that Marx and Engels overcame Feuerbach's mechanistic materialism by reuniting materialism with dialectics to create dialectical materialism, for Marx and Engels had recognised the revolutionary dimension of Hegel's dialectic. But how could the dialectic be placed on a materialist basis? In terms of method, Marx continued many aspects of Hegelian philosophy, but he rejected the idealist dimension of its dialectic; Hegel's view that the world's development depended on the self-motion of the absolute idea was rejected by Marx in favour of a view that perceived the world's development as the self-motion of matter.[74] Nevertheless, this self-motion of matter adopts a dialectical form, and this is why there must be a union of dialectics and materialism. This in turn necessitates investigation of the self-motion of matter as a function of the struggle of opposites in things, for it is knowledge of the contradictions replete within all things which is the essence of dialectics.[75] Not only is there a unity of opposites, there is struggle and dissociation; it is therefore essential to recognise the role of negation in the process of development, for it is this which allows the emergence of new things.[76]

The investigation of reality must thus commence from the premise that the cause of a thing's existence is internal, as are the factors which impel it to move towards its opposite. The existence of contradictions within all things means that the imperative for change is ubiquitous, and there is consequently the necessity to grasp things as in a process of development, as in motion.[77] Development itself can be seen as the result of the struggle of opposites, and it is this struggle which makes development a process of qualitative as well as quantitative change, rather than merely a process of expansion or contraction; development therefore occurs through leaps, as things change from one form of quality to another through the process of the negation of the negation.[78]

Kawakami's elaboration of the materialist conception of history commences from the assumption that, while humans are a product of their natural and social environment, they are capable of transforming that environment through practice.[79] The basic contradiction in society, he argues, is that between the forces of production and the relations of production.[80] For Kawakami, the forces of production are largely equivalent to the means of production (technology, instruments of labour), but he does allow that there is a conscious dimension to the forces of production.[81] The principal cause of social change is developments within the forces of production; it is the motive force in human history. The materialist conception of history consequently commences from analysis of the forces and relations of production and the relationship between them. But the superstructure also exerts an influence,[82] and here Kawakami uses the example of the state, which emerges to control and moderate the struggle between classes.[83] He provides a lengthy quote from Lenin to demonstrate that the political superstructure emerges as a result of the needs of the economic base, but that there is also interaction and mutual influence (*huxiang zuoyong*) between them.[84] Similarly, in terms of the ideological superstructure, social consciousness reflects society, but consciousness too can exert an influence. Kawakami uses the invention of new machinery as an example of the capacity of human consciousness to influence history. He nevertheless stresses the importance of commencing historical analysis through investigation of social conditions and social existence.

Kawakami's exposition of materialism, dialectics and the materialist conception of history is replete with lengthy quotes, not only from Marx, Engels and Lenin, but also from Plekhanov, Deborin, Luppol and Thalheimer. This clearly marks this text as a work from the period prior to the 1931 break in Soviet philosophy; for after 1931, Plekhanov, Deborin and Luppol's interpretation of Marxist philosophy was only ever referred to negatively, as an example of an excessively abstract view, one which did not integrate philosophy with politics and which was preoccupied with the Hegelian dimension of the dialectic.

Shirokov and Aizenberg's *A Course on Dialectical Materialism*

The "failure" of Deborin and his followers to integrate philosophy and politics and to subordinate philosophy to the needs of the Party was criticised by Stalin in 1931 as an example of "Menshevising idealism". During the early 1930s, the new generation of Soviet philosophers, under the leadership of Mark Mitin, thus ensured that their texts on philosophy demonstrated the veracity, not just of Marxism, but of the policies of the Communist Party of the Soviet Union. These texts are, in some contrast to the three pre-1931 volumes on philosophy examined above, intensely polemical in character, with Bukharin, Plekhanov and Deborin in particular frequently employed as a whipping boy for the supposed failures of pre-1931 philosophy. The new philosophy promulgated by the Soviet philosophical texts of the early 1930s consequently became the new orthodoxy, the "correct" interpretation of Marxist philosophy, articulated by Party philosophers, disseminated by the Party and its agencies and reinforced through threat of quite palpable sanctions at the discretion of the Party.

The Soviet philosophical texts of the early 1930s are characterised too by a rather formalistic codification of the basic laws and categories of dialectical materialism. Gone is any pretence that the purpose of philosophy is speculation, or that uncertainty or scepticism may be the appropriate attitude of the philosopher. We find, rather, certainty verging on dogmatic rectitude, and elaborations of dialectical materialism which reiterate, as in a standard recipe, the core assumptions and political implications of this philosophy. There is consequently considerable repetition, and while the volumes on philosophy from this period are not identical, there exists between them an intertextual congruence which precludes any one text standing out as particularly distinct.[85]

It is this genre of Soviet Marxist philosophy which was to exert such a major influence on the development of Marxist philosophy in China, for it was its texts which were to constitute the core material from which Mao Zedong was to draw his understanding of the new orthodoxy in Marxist philosophy.[86] The philosophical texts which Mao studied so assiduously in 1936–37, prior to writing his own essays on philosophy, were drawn from this genre, or from the works of Chinese philosophers (such as Li Da and Ai Siqi) who had also come under its influence.[87]

One of the earliest of these texts to be translated into Chinese was Shirokov and Aizenberg et al.'s *A Course on Dialectical Materialism*.[88] We know that Li Da, the principal translator of this volume, could not read Russian,[89] so we must assume that he translated it into Chinese on the basis of a Japanese version.[90] First published in China in September

1932 under the title *Bianzhengfa weiwulun jiaocheng*, it was republished on several occasions throughout the 1930s. There can be no doubt that this volume, and the process of translating it, impressed very forcefully on Li the inadequacies of the previous texts on Marxist philosophy that he had read and translated. As he points out in his translator's Preface, Deborin was guilty, on numerous occasions, of "'unconditionally accepting (*rongna*) Hegel', uncritically continuing Plekhanov, and in so doing ultimately exposing his 'formalism', his Hegelian tendency, and his Menshevik colouration".[91] Li admits that he had himself uncritically adopted the views of these philosophers, and would employ the criteria provided by Shirokov and Aizenberg's *A Course on Dialectical Materialism* to "settle accounts" with the philosophy of Plekhanov and Deborin. The research in this volume is, Li declares, "our model".[92]

It is no coincidence that the opening section of *A Course on Dialectical Materialism* deals forcefully with the "Party character" (*dangpaixing*) of philosophy. The Soviet Union, Li asserts, has achieved the era of socialism and, in this context, a major target of theory is those who opportunistically oppose the correct policies of the Party; of these "class enemies", the Mensheviks are the most pernicious, for their brand of mechanistic materialism and "Menshevising idealism" represents a revisionist theme within philosophy.[93] The Mensheviks are guilty of refusing to change, even though the context had changed and the urgent needs of the Party demanded that they change. For the tasks of Marxist-Leninist philosophy in the current stage are to study the problems raised by practice in the period of the socialist transition: the relationships between the various classes in the Soviet Union, the creation of new forms of labour and other problems of contemporary significance. And such problems can only be solved through an acknowledgement of the Party's orientation, and through a struggle for the truth of Leninism.[94] Philosophy can therefore no longer be perceived as a realm of inquiry that stands apart from the urgent tasks of the day; it is, rather, a "Party science" (*dangpai de kexue*).[95]

The Mensheviks are guilty of proceeding not from "concrete reality", but from empty theoretical premises; in so doing, they produce elaborations that are subjective and non-materialist.[96] Singled out for criticism are those mechanistic materialists, like Minin, who advocate the abandonment of philosophy for natural science.[97] These advocates of the natural sciences in fact employ the premises of bourgeois philosophy, adopting a static conception of nature and society, one which ignores the dialectical character of motion and change. An instance of the latter is Bukharin's theory of equilibrium, which ignores the existence of classes and the struggle between them, and ignores the fact that development comes through leaps. This position thus rejects the law of revolutionary development which is the law of the struggle of opposites, opting rather for a perspective which views change as gradual expansion or contraction, as merely quantitative change.[98] Similarly, Menshevising idealists such as Deborin are accused of being unable to integrate theory and practice, of being unable to grasp the purpose of philosophy during its "Leninist stage".[99] It is the task of Party philosophers to struggle against these erroneous tendencies and to establish a philosophy which explains the correctness of the Party's goals and tactics, and that philosophy is the Marxist philosophy of dialectical materialism.[100]

Philosophy, Shirokov and Aizenberg inform us, can be reduced to two basic tendencies, materialism and idealism (*guannianlun*), and the distinction between them rests on their response to the basic question of philosophy, namely the relationship between the environment and human consciousness. Materialism holds that the environment determines (*jueding*) consciousness, whereas idealism holds that all of the objects of reality are created by consciousness.[101] The working class is, because of its practice and engagement in class struggle, materialist; it knows that its knowledge is an objective reflection of existing matter. Consequently, it is practice which guides materialism. But materialism must be united with dialectics, for all things are in motion and developing, and dialectics seeks the causes for motion and change within things, in the contradictions within things and processes; it is this which distinguishes dialectical materialism from mechanistic materialism.[102]

Subjective idealism, in contrast to materialism, commences not from reality, but from abstract propositions about reality. Examples of this approach are Berkeley, Kant, the neo-Kantians such as Mach and Bogdanov and, of course, Hegel. It is the last-mentioned of these philosophers who exerted such a pernicious influence on the Deborinites they are guilty of becoming separated from practice and the Party's political struggle, and their thought is consequently guilty of subjective idealism.[103] They emphasise Hegel's thought over Marx and Lenin's, and pay insufficient attention to the revolutionary struggles of the proletariat. They are obsessed with Hegel's view of the dialectic, of the symmetry of his theoretical system which appeared capable of explaining not only motion, but the direction of change as well. For change was not random, not accidental; purpose and goal were guaranteed by the existence, in Hegel's theoretical system, of an absolute spirit, and all things — the creativity of human thought, all social forms, the various forms the state adopted — were presumed to be a product of this absolute spirit and its self-knowledge. The rationality of this supposedly divine being manifested itself, according to Hegel, in human history, philosophy, science and technology, law and in the very social system itself; the changes in these were manifestations of the progression of the absolute spirit towards its final goal. The cause of this motion and development was the contradictions replete within the absolute spirit's process of development; in all things, there were consequently forces for change and progress, and others which resisted change, and it was the struggle between these (between affirmation and negation) which led to the dialectical pattern of development.

While the dialectical element of Hegel's system was rational, according to Shirokov and Aizenberg, its location of the causal impulse in the existence and development of an absolute spirit was not. Only through its union with the materialism of Marx, with his identification of the proletariat as the force for change within capitalist society, could the dialectic be salvaged from Hegel's idealism. Those guilty of "Menshevising idealism" placed too much emphasis on the dialectic at the expense of Marxism's materialist premises. Moreover, they compounded this error by perceiving Marx as the theorist and Lenin as simply a proletarian revolutionary practitioner, without perceiving the philosophical and theoretical implications of Lenin's writings and practice.[104] For Lenin, dialectics permeated every dimension of class struggle, and it was thus of great theoretical significance, but the object of analysis and investigation was not the dialectic itself, but its implications for the course of revolutionary struggle. Nevertheless, Lenin had devoted considerable attention to understanding the philosophical dimensions of Marxism; in particular, Lenin had identified the law of the struggle of opposites as the basic law of dialectics, had recognised that identity between opposites was relative while struggle between them was absolute.[105] Lenin had also recognised the unity of dialectics, epistemology and logic, and had criticised Plekhanov for addressing the problem of epistemology separately from that of dialectics.

When they address the problem of epistemology, Shirokov and Aizenberg stress the centrality of practice to the process of knowledge production, and to the unity of subject and object; the process of knowledge production is a dynamic process which incorporates the multi-faceted aspects of social practice, and of these production and class struggle are the most significant.[106] In this process, humans act on reality and, in changing it, also change themselves; practice is the basis of the motion of knowledge, and practice is the criterion of truth.[107] Knowledge production is a process, however, one which incorporates a number of stages. The first of these is perceptual knowledge, which commences from an understanding of the external dimension of things; the process then moves to the stage of rational (*lunli*) knowledge, to an understanding of the internal connections of things, to an understanding of their laws. Materialists acknowledge that the objects which constitute reality are knowable, Shirokov and Aizenberg continue, and it is through social and historical practice that they are knowable.[108] But the acquisition of knowledge involves a dialectical process in which thought, through the agency of practice, more closely approaches absolute truth. Nevertheless, truth is concrete; dialectical materialism rejects the notion of abstract truth, for only concrete truth can function as a weapon in practical activity.[109]

While attacking Plekhanov and Deborin for their excessive preoccupation with the dialectic, Shirokov and Aizenberg nevertheless devote three lengthy chapters to the laws and categories of dialectics. Chapter 3 provides a detailed elaboration of the basic laws of dialectics, the law of the mutual transformation of quantity and quality, the law of the unity and struggle of opposites, and the law of the negation of the negation. The most important thing to grasp, they assert, is that all things in reality are in motion, motion which is driven by the struggle of contradictions. It is consequently the task of science to reveal the causes and stages of this process — in other words, the laws which govern it. Shirokov and Aizenberg commence by examining the law of the mutual transformation of quantity and quality.[110] Reality is constituted of many different qualities. A multi-faceted process such as the development of capitalism has numerous qualities (such as production, distribution, accumulation), and it is the task of dialectical materialism to study the qualitatively different aspects of this process.[111] In order to reveal the causes of change in a process and why one quality may change into another, dialectical materialism must disclose the way in which quantitative change eventually culminates in qualitative change. The causes of this are internal, although all things are related and these external factors do exert an influence; however, it is the contradictions within things, and the struggle between them, which are of the greatest significance.[112] All processes are replete with contradictions, and the essence of dialectics is knowledge of the way in which the unity of an object undergoes dissociation as a result of the numerous contradictory parts which constitute that apparently unified object.[113] Indeed, the unity and dissociation of opposites is the universal law of thought, and it is the basic law of dialectics.[114] The struggle between contradictions leads to qualitative change which takes the form of a leap, and this process is covered by the third law of dialectics, the negation of the negation, which describes the way in which the negative elements within a thing are negated to allow a qualitative new and progressive thing to emerge.[115] The law of the negation of the negation is a concrete manifestation of the law of the unity of opposites.

Contradictions, Shirokov and Aizenberg assert, are constituted of different aspects; one aspect is the condition for the existence of the other aspect, and change takes place from one to the other. This interpermeation (*huxiang shentou*) of opposites exists in all processes, and it is necessary to mount a concrete analysis to reveal the nature of the contradictions, their aspects and the way in which their struggle leads to change. The identity between the aspects of a contradiction can only ever be relative, while the struggle between them is absolute. In the struggle between the aspects of a contradiction, one of the aspects is the principal (*zhudao*) aspect,[116] and in analysing a particular process, it is necessary to identify this principal aspect. In addition, it is important to be aware that the motion of contradictions exists in a process from beginning to end, and in analysing the many contradictions which exist within the process it is necessary to identify the principal (*zhuyao*) contradiction, for it is this which has a determining effect on the other contradictions in the process.[117] There is thus a principal contradiction, and there is a principal aspect of this contradiction.

Chapters 4 and 5 of *A Course on Dialectical Materialism* elaborate the various categories of dialectics. These are phenomenon and essence, form and content, possibility and reality, chance and inevitability, basis and condition, inevitability and freedom, and link and chain. Shirokov and Aizenberg stress that each of these categories is a manifestation in a particular form of the fundamental law of dialectics, the law of the unity of opposites.[118] It is for this reason that each of the categories is posed in the form of a contradiction.

The final chapter examines the opposition between dialectical and formal logic. The reasons for this opposition are made clear through Shirokov and Aizenberg's examination of the three laws of formal logic. The first of these is the law of identity which asserts the content of a phenomenon to be unchanging, the phenomenon being forever the equivalent of itself. Its formula is A equals A, and consequently does not recognise that all things change and are driven by their internal contradictions. The second law of formal logic is its law of contradiction. Unlike dialectical materialism, however, formal logic perceives contradiction as an error in thought, it supposedly being impossible for a concept to contain two contradictory meanings. The identity of an object precludes the possibility of its simultaneously containing both affirmation and negation, for only one is possible; A cannot be the equivalent of not-A. The third law, the law of the excluded middle, precludes the possibility that a thing or concept can change into something radically different; A can be equal or not equal to B, but it cannot be equal to C. According to Shirokov and Aizenberg, formal logic thus provides a set of laws which allows only a formalistic, abstract and static appreciation of the relationship between things or concepts, and dismisses the possibility that the existence of internal contradictions is the premise on which the quest for truth must be based, for formal logic perceives the existence of contradiction as an error which signifies the absence of truth. Advocates of formal logic (such as Bukharin and Plekhanov) thus do not understand that the law of the unity of opposites is the essence of dialectical materialism, or that practice is central to its epistemology. Dialectical materialism insists on a unity of theory and practice, in contrast to the passive epistemology of formal logic; moreover, dialectical materialism has revolutionary implications, for through its recognition of the contradictions inherent within things, and the ubiquity of change through leaps, it has become a weapon in the hands of the proletariat, which can use the knowledge it supplies to change society and itself.[119]

A Course on Dialectical Materialism concludes with a discussion of the movement within the process of knowledge from the particular to the universal and from the universal to the particular. In order to reveal the concrete contradictions within specific things, thought must employ judgment (or evaluation, *panduan*); and judgment, on the basis of the practice of production and class struggle, allows the observer to decide whether a concept actually reflects the motion of the contradictions within things, for it is this social practice which provides the criteria for judgment to occur. Judgment is an important stage in the motion of knowledge from the specific to the general, and it allows the formation of premises which allow inferences to be made. However, such inferences avoid the subjectivism and formalism of formal logic through their reference back to practice, for the motion of knowledge must return from universal conclusions (judgments and inferences) to concrete reality, and these conclusions tested again in practice. Similarly, analysis and synthesis, while high-level orders of cognition and seemingly very abstract, must, like judgment and inference, return to practice to ensure that generalisations, laws and principles do reflect reality. It is this constant motion, from the particular to the universal and from the universal to the particular, which makes possible a reflection in thought of a constantly changing and developing reality; for change and development are not merely random, and thought can achieve ever-closer approximations of their law-like regularities and, on this basis, can formulate predictions about the future development of natural and social realities.[120]

Translation and the Dissemination of Marxism in China

While our thumb-nail sketch of the contents of Shirokov and Aizenberg's *A Course on Dialectical Materialism* can do no more than identify the main lines of argument in what is a very large (582 pages) and complex volume, it serves to establish some basis for comparison with Li Da's own massive philosophical tome, *Elements of Sociology*, the history and contents of which we will subject to sustained scrutiny in the next three chapters. It will become evident that Li's own elaboration of dialectical materialism was heavily influenced by *A Course on Dialectical Materialism*, just as Mao Zedong was to be influenced by it in late 1936 and early 1937 prior to writing his own essays and lectures on Marxist philosophy.[121]

The influence of this Soviet text on philosophy highlights the significance of translation for an understanding of the process of the dissemination of Marxist philosophy in China, for it forcefully underscores the importance of recognising that Marxists in China drew heavily on foreign sources for their understanding of Marxist theory. Concepts, laws, principles, modes of discourse and debate characteristic of Marxist thought in other countries entered the vocabulary of Marxism in China largely (although not entirely) via the agency of the translated text.[122] Judgments regarding the level of theoretical maturity of Chinese Marxists in the 1920s and 1930s, and the extent to which Marxism in China did or did not develop at variance to Marxist theory formulated elsewhere, therefore need to be based on a closer familiarity with the source and content of these translations. For we have seen, through an examination of just a portion of Li Da's extensive translation activities, that Marxists in China did indeed have access to a wide variety of information on Marxist theory and movements in other parts of the world. A broader study of the translation activities of the first generation of China's translators of Marxism would undoubtedly reinforce this judgment.

One of the dimensions which this broader study would need to consider is the importance of the Japanese connection to the dissemination of Marxism in China. Many of the documents that Li Da translated were by Japanese Marxists and socialists; moreover, while the original language of other texts on Marxism translated by Li may not have been Japanese, it was from their Japanese translations that he was largely obliged to work. Li Da, like many other overseas students of the May Fourth generation, had studied in Japan, and it was there that he became fluent in Japanese and familiar with the political context within which Japan's left-wing parties and personalities operated.[123] And it was the response of Japan's left-wing parties and personalities to the problem of the dissemination of Marxism in their own country which was to function as the filter through which Li Da and other Chinese were first to discern the theoretical and political terrain of Marxism. It was the selection of texts for translation by Japanese Marxists and socialists, and their initial interpretation of Marxist concepts and modes of understanding, which were to both orient and limit the perspective of radical overseas Chinese students like Li Da. The concerns of Yamakawa Hitoshi, Takabatake Motoyuki, Sano Manabu, Kawakami Hajime, Sugiyama Sakae and other Japanese Marxists and socialists, as expressed through their political actions and theoretical writings, are thus far from incidental to an understanding of the dissemination of Marxism in China during the 1920s and 1930s.

One of the issues which most exercised Japanese Marxists and socialists was the economic determinism implied in some interpretations of Marxism. As we have seen, Takabatake Motoyuki's *An Overview of Social Problems* alerts readers, through reference to Engels' 1890 formulation, to the possibility of a flexible and dialectical interpretation of the materialist conception of history, one which attributes the various dimensions of the superstructure with a significance greater than that of passive reflection of developments within the economic base. Indeed, the general thrust of Takabatake's book — the employment of social policy to resolve social problems — indicates a belief in the possibility of state intervention to influence the behaviour of the economic realm. The same is true of Kawakami Hajime's *Fundamental Theories of Marxist Economics* which, while commencing from a materialist premise in which the forces of production possess causal priority, allows that the superstructure can possess a reactive influence, and he similarly employs the example of the state to illustrate this point. However, the strongest repudiation of a mechanistic economic determinism is to be found in Sugiyama Sakae's *Introduction to Social Science*. Here, the possibility of superstructural influence within a materialist framework is made abundantly and graphically evident. The response of these Japanese Marxists and socialists to this central problem of Marxist social theory was certainly not lost on Li Da, and it was almost certainly not lost on those Chinese Marxists (and there were very many of them) who read his translations of their writings.

A similar response is to be found in those books which Li Da translated from the Japanese but which were not Japanese in origin. Gorter's *The Materialist Conception of History*, while commencing from a materialist recognition of the causal significance of the forces and relations of production in history, stresses that the materialist conception of history is not a mechanistic theory in which only the economic realm has influence; rather, there is interdependence and reaction between different areas of society, with politics and culture having the capacity to influence economics. Thalheimer's *The Modern Worldview* likewise acknowledges the possibility that consciousness, once created by class, can have a reactive influence; historical materialism does not deny that social groups and parties do possess the capacity for historical influence, although this influence is not of the same order of significance as class.

A clear pattern thus emerges from the texts on Marxism translated by Li Da, whether of Japanese or European origin. In none of them is it accepted that Marxist social theory endorses a mechanistic determinism in which the economic realm is entirely immune from the influence of the superstructure(s). Each of them accepts that the economic base is the most significant factor in historical and social change, but each qualifies this premise of the materialist conception of history through a recognition of the interrelated and interactive nature of society; politics, law, culture, consciousness, art and literature and philosophy are all identified as possessing a capacity to play some role in historical change, as possessing a capacity for reactive influence on the economic base.

The question of "orthodoxy" inevitably arises here. One of the constant themes in Western analyses has been the categorisation of Chinese Marxism, particularly in its manifestation as the thought of Mao Zedong, as heterodox, utopian, idealist and voluntarist for its attribution of influence to the superstructure.[124] Moreover, in order to press home this categorisation, it is assumed, often implicitly, that "orthodox" Marxism is a mechanistic and economistic doctrine which allows little if any role to the superstructure; the basis for an invidious comparison, between an economistic "orthodox" Marxism and its voluntarist "unorthodox" Chinese counterpart, is therefore established. But how valid is this construction of "orthodox" Marxism? It is evident that the authors of the texts on Marxism translated by Li Da would not have endorsed this construction; indeed, it is probable they would have regarded this economistic rendition of the materialist conception of history as little more than a vulgar caricature of Marx's dialectical approach to history. Would they be guilty too of heterodoxy? The answer is, of course, that it depends on the criteria employed to evaluate "orthodoxy". Nevertheless, it is significant that amongst the theorists translated by Li Da are representatives of a number of different currents in the Marxist tradition. Gorter's book received Kautsky's imprimatur, Thalheimer's book was endorsed for use as a textbook in Moscow during the 1920s, and the Japanese authors represent a number of the various theoretical and political strands of Marxism in Japan; yet not one of these authors concurs with the notion that the materialist conception of history is an economistic doctrine within which there is no role for the superstructure; indeed, it is probable that they would have regarded such an interpretation as "heterodoxy," as a mechanistic and undialectical form of materialism. At the very least, Marxists in China had sufficient grounds for rejecting the idea that "orthodox" Marxism was a mechanistic and economistic doctrine, for through Li's efforts, there existed translated texts on Marxism which painted a very different perspective on the materialist conception of history.

Similarly, Li's translations introduced to Marxists in China a wealth of information on the history and content of Marxist philosophy. A number of themes are conspicuous in these translated texts and are significant for the subsequent development of Marxist philosophy in China. First, Chinese Marxists discovered that Marxist philosophy was a significant area of contention within the Marxist tradition, its history characterised by many fierce polemics. Philosophy could be employed as a touchstone in the determination of whether a particular variant of Marxism was "orthodox", and there was consequently a struggle to control both its content and its role. The study of philosophy was thus a legitimate and significant pursuit of the Marxist intellectual. Second, the ubiquity and constancy of motion and change were forcefully impressed on them; the idea of a static or only incrementally changing reality is decisively rejected in favour of a revolutionary perspective which incorporates qualitative change through leaps. Third, they learnt that, although there are at the core of dialectical materialism, several philosophical laws and categories, the law of the unity of opposites stands out as "the most common, the most basic law of dialectics";[125] central to this law is the notion that, while there is identity between contradictions, the struggle between them is absolute. Moreover, in the analysis of the various contradictions within a process, it is necessary to identify the principal contradiction and the principal aspect of that contradiction. Fourth, they were made aware that practice is not only the starting point in the process of knowledge production, it represents the ultimate criterion of truth. Knowledge of an object is not attained through a passive reflection of that object in thought; rather, the human subject must engage in practice in order to identify the essence of the object. The acquisition of knowledge is consequently a dynamic process, with humans interacting continually with their environment, and in so doing transforming both themselves and their environment; of the different forms of practice, production and class struggle are the most significant.

Each of these themes emerges and re-emerges in important texts in the history of Marxist philosophy in China. It is evident, in particular, that Mao Zedong's reading of dialectical materialism incorporates each of these themes; indeed, he endorsed them firmly in "On Contradiction" and "On Practice", essays which have become the cornerstone of Marxist philosophy in China. They are also clearly evident, as we shall see, in Li Da's *Elements of Sociology*, one of the classic works of Marxism in China. Marxist philosophy in China thus has a history with roots firmly embedded in the European and Russian Marxist tradition, but a tradition frequently filtered through the concerns and perceptions of Japanese Marxists and socialists.

Li Da's translations of Marxist texts therefore made a very significant contribution to the dissemination of Marxism in China. His translations acted as one of the important conduits through which information on Marxist movements and ideas reached Marxists in China. However, while Li recognised the importance of providing the early Chinese communist movement with translations of texts on Marxism and was prepared to expend considerable time and energy doing so, he was not prepared to be just a transmitter of the ideas of others. As we have seen, he had, by 1923, achieved a solid reputation as an essayist and propagandist in his own right, and his *Contemporary Sociology* of 1926 established him as one of China's pre-eminent radical theorists. From 1928, Li published a number of books which were to reinforce this reputation, both in China and overseas. His *Zhongguo chanye geming gaiguan* (A General Survey of China's Revolution in Production), drawing inspiration from Lenin's *The Development of Capitalism in Russia* and employing a mass of Chinese and overseas statistical data on the Chinese economy, was published in 1929 and was quickly translated into Russian, Japanese and other languages.[126] A number of other books on economic theory and China's economy followed, and by the mid-1930s he had established a formidable reputation as a political economist. However, alongside this interest in political economy developed a powerful interest in Marxist philosophy, generated by his translation activities in this area, but also by the dramatic upheavals in Soviet Marxist philosophy between 1929 and 1931 which culminated in the formulation of the "new philosophy", which was to capture Li's interest and allegiance. His research on the "new philosophy" was to culminate in 1935 with the publication of the first edition of *Elements of Sociology*, a volume on Marxist philosophy and the materialist conception of history which was to be his crowning theoretical achievement. To a detailed analysis of this important book by Li Da we now turn.

Notes

1. See, however, Arif Dirlik, *The Origins of Chinese Communism* (New York: Oxford University Press, 1989). Further information can be found in *Zhongguo chuban shiliao, pubian* (Materials on the History of Publishing in China) (Beijing: Zhonghua shujiu chuban, 1957).

2. Schram, for example, has used the phrase "hermetic" in relation to Mao's Sinification of Marxism. See Stuart R. Schram, *The Political Thought of Mao Tse-tung* (Harmondsworth: Penguin, 1969, revised edition), p. 114.

3. Interest in Japan in socialism and Marxism dates from the 1870s, and from the 1880s many translations and articles on European socialism were published in Japan. See Martin Bernal, *Chinese Socialism to 1907* (Ithaca and London: Cornell University Press, 1976), Chapter 4. See also Gail Lee Bernstein, "The Russian Revolution, the Early Japanese Socialists, and the Problem of Dogmatism", *Studies in Comparative Communism*, Vol. IX, no. 4 (Winter 1976), pp. 327–48.

4. See Yuan Jinxiang, "Wuchanjieji yijie qianbei Li Da" (Li Da, One of the First Generation of Proletarian Translators), in *Wei zhenli er douzheng de Li Da tongzhi* (Comrade Li Da Who Struggled for Truth) (Wuhan: Wuhan daxue chubanshe, 1985), pp. 169–76. See also Li Da's translator's Preface to Labitos et al., *Zhengzhi jingjixue jiaocheng* (Outline of Political Economy) (Beiping: Bigengtang, 1932), Vol. I, pp. 1–2. Here, Li concedes that he could not speak or read Russian, so had used the Japanese text. The Russian texts he translated had thus been filtered through the process of selection and translation by Japanese Marxists and socialists.

5. Li Da's translation activities concentrated on intepretations of Marxism, rather than texts by Marx and Lenin. He translated only three documents by Marx and Lenin. The first is Karl Marx, "Deguo laodongdang ganglin lanwai piping" (Marginal Critical Notes on the Program of the German Labour Party), translated by Li Da, *Xin Shidai*, no. 1 (April 1923), pp. 1–28. (This document is usually referred to as "The Critique of the Gotha Program)." For analysis of Li's translation of this document, see Yuan Jinxiang, "Wuchanjieji yijie qianbei Li Da", pp. 171–75. The second is V.I. Lenin, "Liening de furen jiefanglun" (Lenin's Theory of the Liberation of Women), translated by Li Da, *Xin Qingnian*, Vol. 9, no. 2 (1921), pp. 1–2. The third is Karl Marx, *Zhengzhi jingjixue pipan* (The Critique of Political Economy), translated by Li Da (Shanghai: Kunlun shudian, 1930).

6. See Wang Shengbing, "Zhongguo Makesizhuyi de yidai zongshi" (Exemplary Teacher of Marxism), in *Wei zhenli er douzheng de Li Da tongzhi*, pp. 25–27.

7. Wang Jionghua, *Li Da yu Makesizhuyi zhexue zai Zhongguo* (Li Da and Marxist Philosophy in China) (Wuchang: Huazhong ligong daxue chubanshe, 1988), p. 27.

8. *Mao Zedong zhexue pizhuji* (Beijing: Zhongyang wenxian chubanshe, 1988), pp. 1–136, 453–92. See also Nick Knight (ed.), *Mao Zedong on Dialectical Materialism: Writings on Philosophy, 1937* (Armonk, New York: M.E. Sharpe, 1990), Introduction.

9. Interview with Yuan Jinxiang, Wuhan, October 1993. Professor Yuan has made a study of Li's translation activities. See "Wuchanjieji yijie qianbei Li Da".

10. Interview with Wang Jionghua, Wuhan, October 1993. For a list of Professor Wang's publications on Li Da, see the Bibliography.

11. Excerpts of "Tantan fanyi" appear in Yuan Jinxiang, "Wuchanjieji yijie qianbei Li Da."

12. Ibid., p. 177

13. Shokai Shungetsu, "Xiandai de Sigandinaweiya wenxue" (Contemporary Scandinavian Literature), translated by Li Da, *Xiaoshuo yuebao*, Vol. 12, no. 4 (June 1921), pp. 1–11. Note that page numbers in these early Chinese journals, as is the case here, often recommenced at 1 with each new article. Li also translated articles on Japanese literature, see Miyajima Shinzo (Shinzaburo?), "Riben wentan zhi xianzhuang" (The Current Situation of the Literary World in Japan), translated by Li Da, *Xiaoshuo yuebao*, Vol. 12, No. 4 (April 1921), pp. 5–15.

14. Takayanagi Matsuichiro, *Zhongguo guansui zhidu lun* (On China's System of Customs and Tariff), translated by Li Da (Shanghai: Shangwu yinshuguan, 1924).

15. Karl Kautsky, *Makesi jingji xueshuo* (The Economic Doctrines of Karl Marx), translated by Li Da (n.p.: Zhonghua shudian, 1921).

16. Leszek Kolakowski, *Main Currents of Marxism: Its Rise, Growth, and Dissolution — Volume II, The Golden Age* (Oxford: Clarendon Press, 1978), p. 33.

17. Wang Jionghua, *Li Da yu Makesizhuyi zhexue zai Zhongguo*, p. 27.

18. See Mikhailovsky, *Jingjixue rumen* (An Introduction to Economic Theory), translated by Li Da (Shanghai: Lehua tushu gongsi, 1930). This is a detailed textbook of 438 pages written from a Soviet perspective. It deals with the economics of capitalism, the theory of surplus value, currency production, labour power, management of enterprises, value and the maturation and collapse of capitalism. See also Labitos et al., *Zhengzhi jingjixue jiaocheng* (A Course on Political Economy), translated by Li Da and Tai Deshan (Beiping: Bigengtang, 1932). This two-volume, 909 page book has contents similar to the text by Mikhailovsky. It has sections on value, the contradictions of commodity economy, the general concept of value, the special capacity of labour to produce value, the forms of value and money, the fetishism of commodities, production of surplus value, relative and absolute surplus value, labour and capital, general concepts of production and accumulation, profit, the cycle of capital and the rate of profit, the tendency of the rate of profit to fall, commercial capital, land rent, and the centralisation of agricultural production. Li Da's translation was based on the 1931 revised edition. The earlier editions of this book had, according to Li, suffered from serious Menshevik errors, but these had been revised, the book now adopting a dialectical materialist and scientific standpoint (see pp. 1–2). See also Kawanishi Taichiro, *Nongye wenti zhi lilun* (Theories on the Agricultural Question), translated by Li Da (Shanghai: Kunlun shudian, 1930). This book contains a detailed study of the agricultural question in Marxist theory, including the writings of Marx, Engels, Kautsky, Liebknecht, Lenin and the Communist International. See also Kawada Shiro, *Tudi jingjixue* (The Economics of the Land), translated by Li Da and others (Shanghai: Yinshuguan, 1930). Li translated the section on rent.

19. See Serge Bricianer, *Pannekoek and the Workers' Councils* (Saint Louis: Telos Press, 1978), pp. 67, 148; also D.A. Smart (ed.), *Pannekoek and Gorter's Marxism* (London: Pluto Press, 1978).

20. Herman Gorter, *Weiwushiguan jieshuo* (An Explanation of the Materialist Conception of History) (n.p.: Zhonghua shudian, 1921), Translator's Preface, appendix, pp. 7–8.

21. Ibid., pp. 1–10.

22. This was the focus of an article by Gorter translated by Li Da and also published in China in 1921. See Hermann Gorter, "Weiwushiguan de zongjiaoguan" (The Materialist Conception of History's View of Religion), translated by Li Da, *Shaonian Zhongguo*, Vol. 2, no. 11 (May 1921), pp. 36–46. Interestingly, Gorter argues that religion is a personal matter, and that it will die away when the appropriate social and economic conditions have been achieved. Until then, politics should not interefere with religious beliefs.

23. Gorter, *Weiwushiguan jieshuo*, pp. 14–15.

24. Ibid., p. 38.

25. Gorter develops this point in considerable detail, providing examples of the discoveries made by various societies throughout history: ibid., pp. 40–45.

26. Ibid., pp. 124–26.

27. It was against the Dutch and German Left, with which Gorter identified, that Lenin had written his famous *"Left-Wing" Communism, An Infantile Disorder.*

28. Wang Jionghua, *Li Da yu Makesizhuyi zai Zhongguo*, p. 33.
29. Takabatake Motoyuki, *Shehui wenti zonglan* (An Overview of Social Problems), translated by Li Da (n.p.: Zhonghua shuju, 1921), 3 volumes.
30. Ibid., pp. 1–162.
31. Ibid., pp. 1–2.
32. Ibid., pp. 4–8.
33. Ibid., pp. 19–20.
34. Ibid., p. 34.
35. Ibid., pp. 116–62.
36. Ibid., p. 100.
37. Ibid., pp. 163–334.
38. Ibid., pp. 214–17.
39. Ibid., pp. 219–20.
40. Ibid., p. 224.
41. Ibid., pp. 225ff.
42. Ibid., p. 241.
43. Ibid., pp. 273–334.
44. Volume 3, pp. 335–488.
45. See, for example, *Li Da wenji*, Vol. 1, pp. 9–23, 128–30, 146–84.
46. Werner Meissner, *Philosophy and Politics in China: The Controversy over Dialectical Materialism in the 1930s* (London: Hurst and Co., 1990), p. 29.
47. Wang Jionghua, *Li Da yu Makesizhuyi zhexue zai Zhongguo*, p. 28.
48. Sugiyama Sakae, *Shehui kexue gailun* (A Survey of Social Science), translated by Li Da and Qian Tieru (Shanghai: Kunlun shudian, 1929), p. 5.
49. Ibid., pp. 18–19.
50. Ibid., pp..34–35.
51. Ibid., pp. 49–71.
52. Ibid., pp. 74–100.
53. Ibid., p. 99.
54. Ibid., p. 100.
55. Ibid., p. 230.
56. See for example the section on "Eastern" (that is Chinese and Indian) dialectics in A. Thalheimer's *Xiandai Shejieguan* (The Modern Worldview), translated by Li Da (Shanghai: Kunlun shudian, 1929), pp. 156–66.
57. Ibid., pp. 1–5.
58. Ibid., pp. 144–48.
59. Ibid., pp. 155–66.
60. Ibid., p. 167.
61. Ibid.
62. Ibid., p. 210.
63. I. Luppol, *Lilun yu shijian de shehuikexue genben wenti* (Fundamental Problems of Theory and Practice in the Social Sciences), translated by Li Da (Shanghai: Xinxian shushe, 1930), Preface.
64. Ibid., pp. 70–75.
65. Ibid., pp. 30–42.
66. Ibid., pp. 156–61. The issue of whether a difference is a contradiction later became a philosophical problem for Mao. In responding to Ai Siqi's *Philosophy and Life*, in which Ai had provided a formulation similar to Luppol's, Mao stated: "if the

principles of development and change are understood then it is known, that under certain conditions, things that are different are able to transform themselves into contradictions. If at the same time and place two definite things begin to act on each other in a mutually exclusive fashion, then they become contradictions." See Nick Knight (ed.), *Mao Zedong on Dialectical Materialism: Writings on Philosophy, 1937* (Armonk, New York: M.E. Sharpe, 1990), pp. 258–60.

67. Kawakami Hajime, *Makesizhuyi jingjixue jichu lilun* (Fundametal Theories of Marxist Economics), translated by Li Da and others (Shanghai: Kunlun shudian, 1930).

68. See Gail Lee Bernstein, *Japanese Marxist: A Portrait of Kawakami Hajime, 1879–1946* (Cambridge, Mass.: Harvard University Press, 1976).

69. Kawakami Hajime, *Makesizhuyi jingji jichu lilun*, p. 46.

70. Ibid., p. 82.

71. Ibid., pp. 85–86.

72. Ibid., p. 93.

73. Ibid., p. 101.

74. Ibid., pp. 105–6.

75. Ibid., pp. 108–19.

76. Ibid., pp. 135–39.

77. Ibid., pp. 154–75.

78. Ibid., pp. 175–212.

79. Ibid., pp. 217–18.

80. Ibid., p. 220.

81. Ibid., p. 240; see also p. 295.

82. Ibid., p. 256.

83. Ibid., p. 269.

84. Ibid., p. 282.

85. On the repetitive character of Soviet philosophy, see Richard De George, *Patterns of Soviet Thought* (Ann Arbor: University of Michigan Press, 1966), p. 193; also Eugene Kamenka, "Soviet philosophy, 1917–1967", in Alex Simirenko (ed.), *Social Thought in the Soviet Union* (Chicago: Quadrangle Books, 1969), p. 95.

86. See Knight (ed.), *Mao Zedong on Dialectical Materialism*, Introduction; also Nick Knight, "Soviet Philosophy and Mao Zedong's 'Sinification of Marxism'", *Journal of Contemporary Asia*, Vol. 20, no. 1 (1990), pp. 89–109.

87. On Ai Siqi's philosophical relationship with Mao Zedong, see Joshua A. Fogel, *Ai Ssu-ch'i's Contribution to the Development of Chinese Marxism* (Cambridge, Mass. and London: Harvard Contemporary China Series, no. 4, 1987); also Ignatius J.H. Tsao, "Ai Ssu-ch'i: The Apostle of Chinese Communism", *Studies in Soviet Thought*, no. 12 (1972).

88. M. Shirokov and A. Aizenberg et al., *Bianzhengfa weiwulun jiaocheng* (A Course on Dialectical Materialism), translated by Li Da and Lei Zhongjian (Shanghai: Bigengtang shudian, 1932). The edition used below is the fourth edition, dated 14 December, 1936. It was the third edition, published June 1935, and this fourth edition which Mao read and annotated. See Knight (ed.), *Mao Zedong on Dialectical Materialism*, pp. 33–35. *A Course on Dialectical Materialism* was prepared by a group of philosophers in the Komakademiia, under Mitin's auspices, for use in the Soviet Communist Party school, and was quickly translated into Japanese. See Joshua A. Fogel, *Ai Ssu-ch'i's Contribution to the Development of*

Chinese Marxism (Cambridge, Mass.: Harvard Contemporary China Series, no. 4, 1987), p. 68.

89. Li talks of his inability to read Russian in his translator's Preface to Labitos et al., *Zhengzhi jingjixue jiaocheng* (A Course on Political Economy) (Beiping: Bigengtang shudian, 1932), Vol. 1, pp. 1–2.

90. Li Da translated Labitos' *Zhengzhi jingjixue jiaocheng*, published in China in 1932, from the Japanese. See ibid., pp. 1–2.

91. Shirokov and Aizenberg, *A Course on Dialectical Materialism*, p. 3.
92. Ibid., p. 4.
93. Ibid., pp. 1–3.
94. Ibid., p. 6.
95. Ibid., p. 7.
96. Ibid., p. 28.
97. Ibid., pp. 22–26.
98. Ibid., pp. 38–39.
99. Ibid., pp. 42–44; see also the critique of Luppol, p. 297.
100. Ibid., pp. 47–48.
101. Ibid., p. 48.
102. Ibid., pp. 52–53; see also the long section pp. 76–100.
103. Ibid., pp. 142–66.
104. Ibid., pp. 184–85.
105. Ibid., p. 189.
106. Ibid., pp. 193–202.
107. Ibid., p. 213.
108. Ibid., p. 232.
109. Ibid., pp. 240–52.
110. Ibid., p. 254.
111. Ibid., p. 261.
112. Ibid., pp. 278–79.
113. Ibid., p. 280.
114. Ibid., pp. 309, 349.
115. Ibid., pp. 321–48.
116. Ibid., pp. 295–97.
117. Ibid., p. 298.
118. Ibid., pp. 349, 385.
119. Ibid., pp. 479–536.
120. Ibid., p. 537–82.
121. See Knight (ed.), *Mao Zedong on Dialectical Materialism*, Introduction; also *Mao Zedong zhexue pizhuji*, pp. 1–136.

122. This is not to undervalue the writings of those, like Li Da and Qu Qiubai, who had lived abroad and who, through their own writings, contributed to the introduction and dissemination of Marxist concepts and forms of discourse in China.

123. Ai Siqi also worked from Japanese texts, although he was able to read Russian. See Fogel, *Ai Ssu-ch'i's Contribution to the Development of Chinese Marxism*, p. 68.

124. Particularly in the writings of Stuart Schram, Maurice Meisner and Frederic Wakeman Jr. See Stuart Schram, *Mao Zedong a Preliminary Reappraisal*

(Hong Kong: The Chinese University Press, 1983), p. 17; also Stuart Schram, *The Thought of Mao Zedong* (Cambridge: Cambridge Univerasity Press, 1989), pp. 5, 17, 54–55, 67, 96, 113, 168, 200. Maurice Meisner, *Marxism, Maoism and Utopianism* (Madison: University of Wisconsin Press, 1982); also *Mao's China and After: A History of the People's Republic* (New York: The Free Press, 1977, 1986). Frederic Wakeman Jr, *History and Will: Philosophical Perspectives of Mao Tse-tung's Thought* (Berkeley: University of California Press, 1973).

125. Thalheimer, *The Modern Worldview*, p. 167; see also Shirokov and Aizenberg, *A Course on Dialectical Materialism*, pp. 189, 280, 285.

126. Li Da, *Zhongguo chanye geming gaiguan* (A General Survey of China's Revolution in Production) (Shanghai: Kunlun shudian, 1929); see also the editor's Preface to Li Da, *Jingjixue dagang* (Outline of Economic Theory) (Wuchang: Wuhan daxue chubanshe, 1985), p. 4.

6

Li Da's *Elements of Sociology* and Marxist Philosophy in China

As we have seen, Li Da had already made a major contribution to the dissemination and popularisation of Marxist theory and philosophy in China during the 1920s and early 1930s. Not only had he, through his translations, made the theoretical tenets of Marxism more widely accessible to Communist Party members and sympathisers than had hitherto been the case, he had, in his *Xiandai shehuixue* (Contemporary Sociology), written one of the first major texts in Chinese to cover most of the theoretical issues of Marxism. Although the section on the philosophy of dialectical materialism in this volume is brief, it nevertheless makes clear that this is *the* philosophy of the "revolutionary class" and the "only correct and appropriate method" for grasping the dialectics of nature.[1] *Contemporary Sociology* also prefigures Li Da's growing preoccupation with the philosophy of Marxism, a preoccupation which was to lead to the composition of his major philosophical treatise *Shehuixue dagang* (Elements of Sociology),[2] hailed by Mao Zedong as "the first Marxist textbook on philosophy to be written by a Chinese", a textbook Mao claimed to have read ten times.[3] Mao also recommended *Elements of Sociology* to comrades at the Yan'an Philosophical Association and the Anti-Japanese Military and Political University[4] and, at the Sixth Plenum of the Sixth Central Committee in October 1938, he called on high-level cadres to study Li Da's book. Over twenty years later, Mao met Li Da at a meeting at Lushan in 1961 and reiterated the important influence of *Elements of Sociology* and proposed that it be revised for publication, for it still had contemporary significance (see Chapter 10).[5] Mao's respect for *Elements of Sociology* consequently ensured this book a secure and esteemed position in the history of Marxist philosophy in China, and its author the status of one of China's leading intellectuals of the twentieth century.[6]

The following two chapters provide a detailed summary and analysis of this important text on Marxist philosophy and theory. In this chapter, the history and influence of *Elements of Sociology* — particularly its influence on Mao Zedong's philosophical thought — are evaluated.

Composition and Publication

Li Da lectured at Beiping University's Legal and Commercial Institute between August 1932 and May 1937, and during this period he studied and taught Marxist economics and philosophy, among other subjects. He also wrote and translated extensively. Important amongst his writings from this period are *Jingjixue dagang* (Elements of Economics), published by the Institute in 1935, a book Mao claimed to have read three and a half times and intended to read ten times,[7] *Shehui jinhuashi* (A History of Social Evolution), and essays on such subjects as dialectical and formal logic. He also translated in 1932, with Lei Zhongjian, Shirokov, Aizenberg et al.'s *Bianzhengfa weiwulun jiaocheng* (A Course on Dialectical Materialism). In the previous chapter, we examined the influence of this and other translations by Li Da on the dissemination and development of Marxism in China. However, Li's translation of *A Course on Dialectical Materialism* is doubly significant in the context of a discussion of *Elements of Sociology* insofar as Li regarded Shirokov and Aizenberg's text as a model in terms of its philosophical approach (although the extent of its influence on Li is disputed by Chinese philosophers, an issue to which we will return).[8]

Elements of Sociology was written over a three- to four-year period, a difficult time for Li as he was harassed by the Guomindang authorities for his suspected connections with the Chinese Communist Party. The first edition was published by the Legal and Commercial Institute at Beiping University in 1935.[9] It ran to some 310,000 characters and was 544 pages in length.[10] Several chapters of this first edition were published in journals in 1935 and 1936. The chapters on dialectical and formal logic, the object of dialectical materialism, and the laws of dialectical materialism, were published in *Faxue zhuankan*, the journal of the Legal and Commercial Institute, in 1935.[11] The chapter on the laws of dialectical materialism was republished in issue no. 1 of *Zhongshan wenhua jiaoyuguan jikan*, and the third chapter, entitled "Dialectics of the Process of Knowledge", was published in issue no. 3 of this same journal.[12] Following the publication of the first edition in Beiping, Li continued to add to and revise the manuscript, and a second revised edition of *Elements of Sociology* was published in Shanghai in May 1937 by the publisher Bigengtang shudian. The book, in this edition, had expanded to 400,000 characters in length, and is, by any estimation, a massive tome (613 pages in the *Collected Writings* edition, more than 800 pages in the original Shanghai edition), one which contains a scholarly summation of virtually all of the various dimensions of the philosophy and social theory of orthodox Marxism. Indeed, O. Briere, in his brief and unfriendly review of Li Da's philosophical writings, commented that *Elements of Sociology* "is according to our knowledge the most learned work published in China on this school [that is, Marxism]".[13]

On the publication of the Shanghai edition, Li sent Mao a copy asking for comments and criticisms. Mao, as we have seen, welcomed the publication of the book with great enthusiasm and, in a letter to its author, referred to Li as a "really good fellow" (*zhenzheng de ren*).[14] Mao's endorsement ensured the book a positive response, and it was regularly republished during the late 1930s, its fourth edition appearing in 1940. In 1939, the chapter dealing with the laws of dialectical materialism was published in Yan'an in a compilation volume on philosophy edited by Ai Siqi,[15] and on Mao's recommendation, the entire book was republished in a slightly revised form in 1948 by Xinhua shudian, with much of the outmoded terminology of early Marxist discourse in China revised to conform to now standardised conventions.[16] The second half of the book, dealing with the materialist conception of history, was also revised and published separately in 1948 in Hong Kong under the title *Xin shehuixue dagang* (An Outline of the New Sociology),[17] and the entire volume was republished on its incorporation into the *Collected Writings of Li Da* in 1981. *Elements of Sociology* has thus been a stubborn survivor in the sometimes fickle world of Chinese Marxism, and it is still, more than half a century after its initial publication, the subject of intense academic scrutiny and debate by scholars in China.

Influences

In terms of influences on Li Da, the date of composition of *Elements of Sociology* is not incidental. Li Da, as we have seen, had written on Marxist philosophy in the 1920s, and in 1930 had collaborated in the translation of the famous Japanese Marxist Kawakami Hajime's *The Fundamental Theory of Marxist Economics*. This translation, published in 1930, contained a section entitled "The philosophical basis of Marxism", which incorporated analysis of the fundamental premises and laws of dialectical materialism, and which traced its historical development.[18] He had also translated works on Marxist philosophy by Thalheimer and Luppol. By the beginning of the 1930s, Li Da was, therefore, already familiar with the history and structure of orthodox Marxist philosophy as it had developed to that time.

In 1931, however, there occurred a significant shift in both the tenor and political significance of dialectical materialism. In April of that year, the interpretation of Marxist philosophy which had enjoyed dominance in the Soviet Union since 1929 came under attack. Abram Deborin, the major exponent and interpreter of dialectical materialism during the 1920s,[19] was criticised along with his supporters by members of the Institute of Red Professors, particularly Mark Mitin, for failing to "give immediate sanction to the Party's practical measures".[20] In an article in *Pravda* in June 1930, the Deborinites were accused of "a lack of party-mindedness", of "extreme formalism and the malicious separation of philosophy from the practical problems of the country", and Deborin's views were finally branded by Stalin as "Menshevising idealism" in December 1930.[21] This repudiation of Deborin signalled not only the complete subordination of philosophy to the demands of the Communist Party of the Soviet Union, but the emergence of a new breed of philosophers, under the leadership of Mitin, who assumed the task of elaborating the variant of dialectical materialism now judged to be orthodox. The texts on philosophy produced following this sea-change of 1931 were distinguished from earlier Soviet philosophy firstly by their more strenuous repudiation of Hegelianism, and secondly, by their greater sense of *partiinost* (or party spirit), the notion that the task of philosophy was to facilitate the goals of the Communist Party.[22] These texts were therefore marked by a rather formalistic recitation of the history, laws and categories of dialectical materialism, there being little scope for innovation given the political dominance of philosophy; indeed, a number of commentators on Soviet philosophy have noted the repetitive character of its texts.[23]

Shirokov and Aizenberg et al.'s *A Course on Dialectical Materialism*, which Li Da translated in collaboration with Lei Zhongjian (Li in fact translated two-thirds of the book and checked the entire translation), was a product of this post-1931 generation of Soviet philosophers. It is quite clear from the translator's preface, written by Li, that he was well aware of the changed circumstances under which the text was written, and the influence that this new stage in the development of Marxist philosophy had had on the philosophical content and political function of dialectical materialism:

> This book ... unifies theory and practice, and integrates philosophy and politics. Setting out from this fundamental standpoint, the authors provide a fresh explanation of the Party character (*dangpaixing*) of philosophy.[24]

Indeed, the first section of *A Course on Dialectical Materialism* elaborates in no uncertain terms the view that philosophy, in the form of dialectical materialism, is the Party's science, one which provides "we Bolsheviks with the standpoint from which the surrounding world can be studied",[25] and that in order for dialectical materialism to effectively fulfil this role it must be revised to make it more "practical"; there must be maintained a unity of theoretical and practical activity.[26]

The comments in Li's translator's preface on Deborin's philosophy also reflect the changed perspective emanating from Soviet philosophical circles. Deborin exposes his "formalism, Hegelian tendencies, and Menshevik colouration", Li suggests, through his uncritical endorsement of Plekhanov and the appearance of abstract Hegelian content in his philosophical writings. Indeed, Li confesses that, in his own recent writings, he had been guilty of uncritically employing the work of Feuerbach, Plekhanov and Deborin, and that he needed to make amends through using *A Course on Dialectical Materialism* as his guide. The task of philosophy must be the integration of the "new practice and theory of the new age" and in this task, this Soviet text "is our model".[27]

While there can be no doubt that Li was heavily influenced in the writing of *Elements of Sociology* by Shirokov and Aizenberg's *A Course on Dialectical Materialism*, perceiving it as his "guide" and "model", it would be mistaken to conclude that this was the only influence. It is evident from reading *Elements of Sociology* that he was familiar with the writings of Mitin and, although he does not cite his sources (a common omission amongst Chinese writers at this time), it is almost certain that he had read Mitin's *Outline of New Philosophy* and possibly *Dialectical and Historical Materialism*. He thus had been exposed to and drew on a number of the central texts of post-1931 Soviet philosophy.[28] This undoubtedly reinforced in Li's mind the content and, perhaps even more importantly, the acceptable limits of the "new philosophy". When he came to write *Elements of Sociology*, he thus had a firm grasp of the discursive terrain on which his own philosophical treatise would be situated and the style of language and exposition which was appropriate; he had, through his familiarity with the Soviet texts on philosophy, acquired a well-developed and acute sense of what could be said and what could not.

A question arises as a result of the significant influence exerted by these Soviet texts on Li's understanding of the content and function of dialectical materialism, and the philosopher's role in its elaboration. That Li was exposed to and influenced by this new wave of Soviet philosophy is not in itself remarkable. After all, there were a number of other Chinese intellectuals involved in the translation and dissemination of Marxist works from the Soviet Union who were influenced by its content.[29] Ai Siqi, in particular, was to translate Mitin's

Outline of New Philosophy and to popularise the often arcane formulations of dialectical materialism through his copious essays and columns.[30] The curiosity lies rather in the fact that at the time Li translated *A Course on Dialectical Materialism* and wrote his own *Elements of Sociology*, he was not a member of the Chinese Communist Party, and therefore not in a formal sense subject to its discipline. That being the case, why did Li conform so fully to the line emanating from Soviet philosophical circles? Was it through a genuine philosophical conviction that the post-1931 Soviet interpretation of dialectical materialism was the correct one; was it the influence of his still-strong connections with the communist movement in China and commitment to its revolutionary program; or was it a mixture of both of these factors? We know that throughout the late 1920s and early 1930s Li continued to maintain close contact with the Chinese Communist Party and to accept tasks from it,[31] and it is very clear from his writings from this period that he remained a fervent supporter of the Chinese revolution. It may be that Li did not perceive his lack of formal membership of the Party as sufficient reason to evade the discipline expected of Party members, and to embellish or challenge the interpretation of the "new philosophy" emanating from the Soviet Union may have seemed tantamount to a breach of discipline. We must keep in mind that Li had been a very early convert to Marxism and a founding member of the Chinese Communist Party, and that his breach with it in 1923 was based on differences over strategy, rather than a rejection of its fundamental theoretical and philosophical doctrines. It may also be the case that Li, seasoned as he was through long association with the communist movement in China, was mindful of the need for flexibility in response to changes in Party line, and the change in the philosophical line which occurred in 1931 was clearly of sufficient magnitude to warrant his observance of it; the alternative would have been a dramatic separation from the philosophical and theoretical activities of the mainstream revolutionary movement and a consequent serious decline in his own influence on and participation within it. By the same token, we should not belittle the possibility that Li did come to recognise, through his exposure to the post-1931 "new philosophy", the danger of conceiving of philosophy as an abstract intellectual pursuit, and also came to accept the consequent need to integrate philosophy with the practical political needs of the revolution. The influence of Shirokov and Aizenberg's *A Course on Dialectical Materialism* on Li may thus have been to convince him *philosophically* that philosophers and philosophy were an integral part of the political and economic struggle, and that the strategies of this struggle would be ultimately determined not by philosophy, but by the Party.

Whatever the reasons, Li's acceptance of the line advocated by the "new philosophy" and his self-criticism for having in the past uncritically utilised the philosophical writings of Deborin and Plekhanov meant that his own writings on philosophy, and in particular *Elements of Sociology*, were to continue to make a very significant contribution to the development and dissemination of Marxist philosophy in China, rather than being side-lined for their independence and lack of commitment. On the other hand, however, Li's observance of the philosophical line emanating from Soviet philosophical circles was to rob his work of the hallmark of originality which might otherwise have set him apart as one of the truly great Marxist philosophers. Acquiescence to the post-1931 line of Soviet philosophy thus brought advantages in terms of continued contact with and influence on the theoretical wing of the revolutionary movement, but exacted a cost in terms of the restrictions imposed by operating within the framework of officially sanctioned Marxist philosophy, restrictions which removed the possibility that Li's considerable capacity for innovative philosophical thought would develop to the extent to which it was otherwise capable.[32]

Li as "Author"

There can be no doubt that Li's high status in China as a Marxist philosopher rested and still rests very heavily on the elaboration of dialectical materialism which appears in *Elements of Sociology*. As we have seen, Mao was to give a ringing endorsement to this book, and its republication as the entire second volume of Li's *Collected Writings* in the early 1980s has ensured it a very significant position in Marxist philosophy in China for some time to come. It is thus necessary for us to explore the contents of this book in some detail, an exercise which will create the basis from which informed judgments may be made about the process of the consumption and dissemination of Soviet Marxist philosophy by the first generation of Marxist philosophers in China. This will hopefully add to our understanding of the genealogy and content of Marxist philosophy in China, as well as its subsequent developmental trajectory. Evaluation of *Elements of Sociology* thus has significance for a comprehension of the structure, content and developmental tendencies of the philosophical dimension of Marxism in contemporary China; it also allows a clearer perception of the textual basis from which Mao was to draw his own understanding of dialectical materialism.

Chapters 7 and 8 are therefore devoted to a detailed summary and analysis of the contents of *Elements of Sociology*. Before the reader turns to these chapters, however, a cautionary word is in order. There is, in light of what has previously been said about the influence of Soviet philosophy on Li, and in particular Shirokov and Aizenberg's *A Course on Dialectical Materialism*, something of a danger in recounting and analysing the contents of *Elements of Sociology* as though it stands alone as a text, rather than as one text in the constellation of texts which collectively constituted the genre of post-1931 mainstream writings on dialectical materialism. The danger lies in giving the impression that the concepts and categories contained in *Elements of Sociology* were Li's brainchild, his own creation, owing little if anything to an already existing body of theory. Such an impression would be a false one. While there is no doubt that Li was the author of *Elements of Sociology* in a conventional sense, he consciously wrote within the confines of a discourse whose parameters were clearly and firmly delineated. Deviation from this discourse could lead to negative sanctions, in particular ostracism by the theoretical wing of the revolutionary movement, although fates more sinister than this were a possibility given the climate of terror which existed in the Soviet Union during the 1930s and the harsh and uncompromising discipline prevailing within Leninist parties. And while Li was not, at the time of writing or publication of *Elements of Sociology*, a formal member of the Chinese Communist Party, it is evident that he continued to operate under a strong sense of identification with and obligation to it. We cannot discern in its pages the motivations of a maverick philosopher such as Ye Qing, one who consciously exploited his position as informed outsider to engage in polemic with a discourse with which he still partially identified.[33] Li's motivation was much more obviously the dissemination of the dominant version of dialectical materialism, the so-called "new philosophy" which he himself fully endorsed; and the vehicle he employed for this task, unlike Ai Siqi whose medium was popularisation through the columns of magazines and journals using everyday language, was a massive textbook which made little if any deference to the conceptual limitations of the reader, a work aimed explicitly at the intellectual. And the overwhelmingly dominant tone of *Elements of Sociology* is one of approval of the "new philosophy". Nowhere to be found within its pages is the quest for originality which implies a degree of scepticism; even the polemical style of language which Li adopts in certain sections of the book to critique those such as Deborin, Plekhanov and Bukharin, whose philosophical views had fallen foul of the approved interpretation of dialectical materialism, is reflective of the style of language to be found in contemporary Soviet texts on philosophy.

What we find in *Elements of Sociology* is erudition, a profound and extremely sophisticated understanding of the complexities of dialectical materialism, and a desire to communicate this to likeminded Chinese intellectuals and, in so doing, to hasten the dissemination of Marxist philosophy in China. *Elements of Sociology* is thus, in the most conventional sense of the term, a textbook, one which draws on an existing body of discourse for its substance and whose purpose is dissemination of information. As pointed out, it is essential to keep this in mind when traversing the summary of Li's volume presented in the following chapters, for one of the implications of exaggerating the originality of *Elements of Sociology* would be to distance Marxist philosophy in China from its Soviet and European counterparts, a tendency already too much in evidence in Western accounts of Marxism in China. The very fact that Li's substantial foray into philosophy was predicated so clearly on the terrain of mainstream Soviet philosophy is in itself highly significant for an understanding of the origins and development of Marxism in China, for it suggests that the philosophical component of Marxism in China is not particularly "Chinese", but shares much with the form of Marxism which was, at one time, widely regarded as possessing universal relevance.

Mao Zedong on Dialectical Materialism: The Influence of *Elements of Sociology*

Between April and August 1937, Mao gave more than 110 lectures at the Anti-Japanese Military and Political University at Yan'an.[34] One of the subjects on which he lectured was the Marxist philosophy of dialectical materialism, and this series of lectures on philosophy was later published under the title *Lecture Notes on Dialectical Materialism*.[35] Two of the most influential texts of Marxism in China ("On Practice" and "On Contradiction") commenced as lectures in this series of lectures. The philosophical influences on Mao at the time of writing these lectures and later, during their revision, is thus of considerable interest. What influence did Li's *Elements of Sociology* exert on Mao during this important period?

We know from Mao's philosophical annotations that, from late-1936, he had embarked on an intensive study of the post-1931 Soviet version of dialectical materialism, and that this was to exercise a profound influence on his own writings on philosophy in 1937. Mao's personal copies of Shirokov and Aizenberg's *A Course on Dialectical Materialism* (which he read and annotated between November 1936 and April 1937), and Mitin's *Dialectical and Historical Materialism* (read and annotated prior to July 1937), are literally covered with his underlinings, summaries and critical annotations, and a comparative analysis of these Soviet texts and Mao's writings on philosophy indicates that he drew on them heavily in writing his *Lecture Notes on Dialectical Materialism*.[36] Although his own copy of Mitin's *Outline of New Philosophy* has not been located, it is safe to assume, according to Chinese Mao scholars, that he also read this in the same intensive way as the other two Soviet texts.[37] Given the direct influence of these Soviet texts on Mao's growing understanding of dialectical materialism, what role might Li Da's *Elements of Sociology* have played?

The answer to this question is complicated by the fact that it is not at all clear whether Mao had read *Elements of Sociology* prior to writing his own *Lecture Notes on Dialectical Materialism* (July, August 1937). On the publication of the revised and expanded Shanghai version of *Elements of Sociology* in May 1937, Li sent Mao a copy. We have direct textual evidence in the form of his annotations and reader's diary (to an analysis of which we will subsequently turn) that Mao did read *Elements of Sociology* between 17 January and 16 March 1938. But had he read it earlier? A number of factors suggest that he had, but the evidence is far from conclusive. First, there is the possibility that Mao had read *Elements of Sociology* before July 1937, but in its first edition which had been published in Beiping in 1935.[38] This is the view of Wang Jionghua, one of China's foremost authorities on Li Da. Wang points to the fact that Mao had repeatedly read Li's *Jingjixue dagang* (Outline of Economic Theory), also published in Beiping in 1935. And even if the 1935 edition of *Elements of Sociology* had not been sent to Yan'an, Mao might still have read parts of it in other sources; its second chapter, "The Laws of Dialectical Materialism", and its third chapter, "Dialectics of the Process of Knowledge", had already been published in issues 1 and 3 (1936) of the journal *Zhongshan wenhua jiaoyuguan jikan*, and in *Faxue zhuankan*, the journal of the Legal and Commercial Institute.[39] Second, Mao later claimed to have read *Elements of Sociology* "ten times", a considerable feat, since it extends to more than 420,000 characters in the 1937 Shanghai edition (310,000 in the 1935 Beiping edition).[40] Even allowing for some hyperbole on Mao's part, this suggests a considerable engagement with this complex text over a significant length of time, quite possibly extending back to before the writing of his own *Lecture Notes on Dialectical Materialism*. A third consideration is the subject matter of *Elements of Sociology* and Mao's own writings on dialectical materialism. Wang Jionghua argues that, while Mao did not plagiarise *Elements of Sociology*, the contents of "On Practice" and "On Contradiction" are "consistent with it".[41] This is not, given the intertextual congruence of the Soviet texts on philosophy and their influence on both Li's and Mao's understanding of dialectical materialism, a particularly convincing argument, for there was a strong element of consistency between all of these texts. Xu Quanxing rejects Wang's assertion of consistency between *Elements of Sociology* and Mao's writings on dialectical materialism, arguing that there is "no direct relation in terms of writing" between them.[42]

There thus exists the possibility that Mao had read *Elements of Sociology* before mid-1937. However, the basis of this supposition is circumstantial and there is not agreement amongst Chinese scholars over this issue. The available documentary evidence allows us only to be certain of the fact that Mao did indeed read and annotate *Elements of Sociology* in early 1938.

Mao's Annotations to *Elements of Sociology*

When we turn our attention to Mao's annotations to *Elements of Sociology*, we notice from the pagination that the edition in Mao's possession in early 1938 was the 1937 Shanghai edition. As with the Soviet texts on philosophy in his possession, he covered its margins and spaces with numerous annotations, and the text of the book is heavily scored with underlinings. The most numerous of the annotations occur in the first section, that which deals with dialectical materialism in the history of human thought (for a summary of Li's exposition, see Chapter 7). These annotations are significant, for they tell us something of Mao's familiarity with the major themes and figures of Western philosophy. It is clear from them that Mao endorsed Li's premise that dialectical materialism must be examined historically: "we must employ an historical perspective (*lishizhuyi*)," Mao comments, "to examine the process of emergence and development of materialist dialectics".[43] Mao's annotations then loosely parallel the content of Li's analysis of the development of dialectical materialist themes in Western philosophy, commencing from the appearance of animistic thought in early primitive societies. The two characteristics of primitive thought were, Mao suggests, "first, that nature, as with humankind, is living, and second, that nature and humankind can transform into one another".[44] For Mao, this was an example of primitive dialectics. The development of the labour process, even in these early times, had the effect of both transforming nature and human beings, and as this occurred language developed: "language is a product of labour," Mao notes, "a means of communication, and the premise of knowledge. It is only with concepts that can be expressed as language, that thought can commence." Similarly, the development of the human brain was a product of labour.[45] The relationship between labour and the development of human thought in primitive society is developed by Mao in the following lengthy annotation:

> The means for the struggle with nature are transformed, as is the way in which life is lived, because of the continual cognition of new aspects of nature during the process of production. Where production is in surplus, technology is improved, and human control over nature is expanded. At this time, animism emerged in the system of thought, and this allowed the division of the world into matter and spirits. This was the earliest attempt by humanity to know nature, and the commencement of a conscious struggle with nature.46

Mao notes that, with increasing human understanding of nature, one of the main sources of religious inspiration declines; on the other hand, however, the emergence of class society brought on by the development of the process of production is the cause of the emergence of philosophy, initially a pastime of the economically dominant, and therefore leisured, class. In the first instance, the form of class society was based on slavery, and it was the slave-owning class, especially of ancient Greece, which introduced philosophy which contained materialist themes:[47]

> Why was it that materialist philosophy could emerge during the Greek era and not before? First, knowledge of the laws of nature must attend progress in the techniques of production, and it is only when this has occurred that humans can gradually discern the character of nature, can start to employ perspectives different to those of religion to explain the world. Second, only when there are handicrafts and commerce, and a commercial slave-owning class which has time and money, is there the motivation for there to emerge sophisticated scholarship. Third, only with the experience of commodity exchange is there generated the capacity for abstract thought, and only then can philosophy be engaged in. Fourth, only when the leading nationalities came into contact and geographical vision was extended, could there be an enlargement of the field of vision of the spirit. Fifth, only when there had been a preliminary development of the natural sciences, and thus the foundation of knowledge, could those factors which constitute necessity and which are universal be determined and a philosophy of nature established. These all represented the new anti-religious worldview, namely the historical foundation of the ancient philosophy of nature. Prior to this, humankind was restricted by the oppression of the forces of nature and society, and could only employ spiritual or supernatural concepts to explain the world; and materialist thought consequently could not appear.[48]

Having established the basis on which materialist forms of philosophy emerged in ancient Greece, Mao turns his attention to individual Greek philosophers. The first of these is Thales who was, according to Mao, the first to offer a natural explanation for the emergence of the universe. For Thales, the universe emerged from water, which was the source and true noumenon of all things in reality; and this perspective which saw all matter as constituted of a simple thing allowed that there could be transformation of one thing into another. This was the first manifestation of materialism and dialectics, although in an extremely simple form.[49]

The second philosopher of ancient Greece considered by Mao in his annotations is Heraclites. Heraclites was also a materialist, perceiving the universe as constituted of four elements (water, fire, air and earth), but of these he designated fire as the basic element, and Mao suggests that in this can be perceived the monism of Heraclites' materialism. However, the main importance of Heraclites, as far as Mao is concerned, lay in his discovery of the two fundamental concepts of dialectical thought: that there is constant change of all things in reality, and that change emanates from the internal struggle of opposites. Heraclites also perceived the universe as limitless in time and space and in a constant state of change, and that in the internal struggle of opposed entities, one form could change into another. Contradiction, for Heraclites, was central to the process of change, and Mao quotes the Greek philosopher to the effect that "struggle is the father of all things in reality". Heraclites can thus be designated, according to Mao, as the "father of dialectics".[50]

The main achievement of Democrites, the next Greek philosopher considered by Mao, was his materialist atomic theory. Mao comments that while Democrites' materialism was a very primitive and mechanistic one, his atomic theory has had a major influence, one in which science is seen to be guided by philosophy. Democrites proposed that matter is constituted of extremely small and impenetrable particles, namely atoms; the various dissociations and associations of these atoms in space create the multifarious character of the material world, one in which the myriad things of reality have their own particular and relative forms. For Democrites, there were only atoms and the void of space; he consequently negated spirit. Motion could not be separated from matter, and space was the condition for the motion of matter. Although his views on the motion of matter were mechanistic, Mao suggests, he perceived the basic laws for the transformation of matter, perceived the causal necessity of the universe, and sought the basic reasons for motion from within matter itself.[51]

Mao here pauses to consider the reasons for the emergence of idealist forms of thought representative of the reactionary aristocracy in ancient Greece. He lists six "historical reasons" why materialism was supplanted by idealism:

1. The deterioration of the Greek slave economy and the production of deep class divisions and struggle led to an ideological struggle between

the aristocratic mentality and democracy, the former becoming the basis for idealist philosophy.
2. Because the system of slavery impeded technological progress, the slave-owning class did not concentrate its attention on natural phenomena which may have had the effect of improving technology, concentrating rather on social phenomena; this gave rise to moral philosophy and state theory.
3. Because those divorced from manual labour denigrated it and exaggerated spiritual matters, there arose idealist philosophy.
4. Consequently, in the realm of consciousness, the aristocracy belittled a philosophy which studied "base matter", considering that only idealist philosophy represented the truth.
5. Because materialist philosophy had been limited by the level of science achieved at that time, it could not avoid naivety and internal contradictions, and was thus derided by idealist philosophers.
6. Due to the fact that materialist philosophy had only involved itself with the dialectics of objective reality and had given no attention to the dialectics of subjective thought, idealism — which did emphasise this — displaced materialism.[52]

Mao then turns his attention to Socrates, the first of the idealist philosophers to struggle against materialism. Mao credits Socrates with raising the issues of moral philosophy and epistemology, and of taking philosophy into the realms of society and thought; in moral philosophy, Socrates spoke of the dialectical relationship between knowledge and action, and in epistemology, he referred to the dialectics of the relationship between the universal and the particular. Nevertheless, Mao judges his moral philosophy to be reactionary, for Socrates had supported the traditional aristocratic system and had rejected the newly emergent democracy. Mao also condemns Socrates' idealism, for he had asserted that knowledge determines action. Mao suggests, rather, that action (practice) is the basis which determines knowledge and the criterion for the determination of what constitutes knowledge. Mao allows that Socrates' epistemology was partially correct insofar as he had perceived the purpose of knowledge as the movement from the particular at the level of perception to the universal at the level of reason; however, he was idealist in believing that the latter constituted the basis for the former.[53]

The last of the ancient Greek philosophers considered by Mao in his annotations to Li Da's *Elements of Sociology* is Plato. Following Li, Mao notes that Plato's thought was idealist, reactionary and incorrect. Plato had believed that only concepts (*linian*) had permanent and real existence, and that they had existed prior to the world and humankind; both the world and human thought were a product, a reflection or shadow, of concepts. He consequently created conceptual logic, advocating that the object of thought is concept, not the perception of the world, and that the method of knowledge was to engage in thought on the basis of concepts empty of any material substance. However, it is in Plato's conceptual logic that his positive contribution lies; for his conceptual logic expressed the function of concepts (*gainian*) in relation to thought.[54]

Mao's annotations dealing with ancient Greek philosophy and philosophers are interesting for a number of reasons. First, although Mao had annotated Shirokov and Aizenberg's *A Course on Dialectical Materialism* and Mitin's *Dialectical and Historical Materialism* far more extensively than Li Da's *Elements of Sociology*, he made no substantial annotations regarding the philosophy of ancient Greece on these two Soviet philosophical textbooks. The reason for this is simple: neither of these Soviet texts contains sections which dwell at any length on ancient Greek philosophy. The Soviet text which does contain such a section is Mitin's *Outline of New Philosophy*, and there are indeed considerable similarities between the content of this section in *Outline of New Philosophy* and that in Li's *Elements of Sociology*, this suggesting the possibility that Li had drawn on this source in compiling his own volume.[55] Mao's own copy of *Outline of New Philosophy* has not survived, but the likelihood is that he read and annotated it in the same way as these other texts on philosophy; however, it may well be the case that Mao had not concentrated on or annotated this particular section of *Outline of New Philosophy*, and consequently concentrated his annotations on the section dealing with ancient Greek philosophy in Li's book when he later came to read it. This suggestion is strengthened by the fact that Mao's own *Lecture Notes on Dialectical Materialism* do not contain any extensive reference to ancient Greek philosophy of the sort contained in Li's volume; if it is the case that Mao read *Elements of Sociology* after he wrote *Lecture Notes on Dialectical Materialism*, we have here a possible explanation for this omission.

Mao's annotations concerning ancient Greek philosophy are also significant, for they demonstrate that Mao had accepted one of the basic premises of dialectical materialism, and that is that philosophy and developments within philosophy can only be understood by reference to the social conditions of the time, and in particular the mode of production and the extent to which this limits or encourages the development of production and technology. As we have observed, Mao invokes this premise when explaining both the flowering of philosophy in ancient Greece and the rise of idealist forms of philosophy there.

Finally, Mao's annotations are interesting insofar as they represent one of the few instances where Mao discusses themes and figures from ancient Greek philosophy. While his other writings on dialectical materialism contain plentiful references to the philosophy of Kant and Hegel and other later philosophers, they do not delve into the early history of Western philosophy to anywhere near the extent of these annotations to Li's *Elements of Sociology*. While these annotations do not suggest any great depth of erudition on Mao's part, they do indicate a familiarity with the subject matter and an interest in the subject sufficient to expend time and energy jotting down these quite extensive annotations.

Mao's remaining annotations to Li's *Elements of Sociology* are far less extensive and consist for the most part of occasional cryptic comments, question marks and vigorous underlining of the text. It is interesting that the bulk of these remaining annotations appear in the section of *Elements of Sociology* concerning the laws and categories of dialectical materialism, and that the second half of the book — that dealing with the materialist conception of history, the economic structure of society and ideology — is almost unannotated. We know that Mao had read the section on dialectics (that is, the first half of the book) from 17–31 January 1938, prior to commencing his "Reading diary", and that he recorded his progress through the latter section of the book in his diary and completed his reading of the book by 16 March. The sections of *Elements of Sociology* that Mao read and recorded in detail in his "Reading diary" thus correspond to the latter half of the book, the part hardly graced by an annotation. The answer to this imbalance in Mao's annotations to *Elements of Sociology* is to be explained by his deep interest at this time in the philosophical dimensions of Marxism and his deeply felt need to achieve mastery of the history, laws and categories of dialectical materialism. The same picture emerges in his annotations to the Soviet philosophical texts by Shirokov and Aizenberg, and Mitin; it is the sections on dialectical materialism in these texts which attracted Mao's attention and his most copious annotations.[56]

Although Mao's annotations to the section of *Elements of Sociology* dealing with the laws and categories of dialectical materialism are rather sparse and cryptic, some do bear consideration. In one of these, next to a section dealing with the emergence of materialism through a process of struggle in the realm of philosophy, one which reflects the struggle in the political arena, Mao commented that "struggle is dialectical".[57] Further on, Mao jotted the annotation "contradiction, that is, motion"[58] and alongside a passage dealing with antagonism as a stage in the development of a contradiction he wrote, "we must acknowledge the universality of the law of leaps".[59] A number of annotations also appear next to a section in which Li had stressed the importance of perceiving and grasping possibility through a correct analysis of objective forces and subjective conditions. Here, Mao notes, somewhat pessimistically, "in the anti-Japanese war both the objective and subjective conditions are insufficient" and he follows this with the comment, "at the time of the Xian incident we grasped cooperation between our Party and the Guomindang, and after the July Seventh Incident [1937] we pursued guerilla war".[60] Mao's annotations dealing with epistemology are also interesting. Li had written that, when analysing the process of knowledge, it is first necessary to explain the dialectics of the movement (*tuiyi*) from matter to consciousness, and second the dialectics of the movement from perceptions to thought. Next to this, Mao wrote: "Third, it is necessary to explain the dialectics of the movement from thought to matter, namely testing and further knowledge."[61]

What conclusions can be drawn from Mao's annotations to Li Da's *Elements of Sociology*? The most important conclusion is that this text on philosophy, although regarded by Mao as "the first Marxist textbook on philosophy to be written by a Chinese", had the effect of reinforcing in Mao's mind the essential message he had already drawn from reading the Soviet texts on philosophy. The fact that the author of *Elements of Sociology* was Chinese was, from the perspective of content, of little consequence, for there is no attempt whatsoever by Li to illustrate the formulations of dialectical materialism by reference to Chinese examples.[62] Indeed, the book remains from start to finish an abstract treatise, Li making no concession to the possibility that his message may have been more comprehensible, more palatable and more relevant had he attempted (as Ai Siqi had done) to illustrate the "new philosophy" with examples drawn from everyday Chinese life. It was, as we have observed, a book whose target audience was intellectuals; and its purpose was to communicate to the reader the contemporary Soviet interpretation of Marxist philosophy. And it was because it so ably achieved this goal that Mao praised its author, and expended a great deal of time and intellectual energy reading and annotating it.

Mao's few schematic annotations to *Elements of Sociology* which actually introduce Chinese examples are reflective of his often-repeated view that it is necessary to apply the methodology of dialectical materialism to the task of discovering the particular characteristics of Chinese reality, rather than learning the formulations of this complex philosophy as an abstract theoretical exercise. In this respect, his annotations here parallel (although far more modestly) his annotations to *A Course on Dialectical Materialism* and *Dialectical and Historical Materialism*; for these earlier annotations contain numerous examples of Mao attempting to apply dialectical materialism to the Chinese context. We can thus see that Mao was an active reader, one who interrogated texts not just to comprehend their content, but to disclose their utility for the achievement of the goals of the Chinese revolution. We have no evidence that the abstract nature of *Elements of Sociology* and its lack of Chinese content left Mao dissatisfied, but it is quite clear from the general tenor of his writings, on philosophical as well as political and military issues, that he regarded the study of theory for theory's sake as a distinct waste of time.[63] *Elements of Sociology* was thus very useful to Mao insofar as it explained the philosophy of dialectical materialism, but the next stage — and without doubt the more important stage for Mao — was the application of this philosophy to the concrete tasks of the revolution in China.

Elements of Sociology: The View from China

Before his death on 24 August 1966, Li Da had been attacked for his outspoken criticism of Lin Biao's ideas which were, Li believed, "opposed to dialectics and science", ideas which "no one could agree with". Li was branded by Lin the "most ferocious (*xionge*) enemy of Mao Zedong Thought" and a "traitor" by Kang Sheng.[64] During the late 1960s and early 1970s, Li Da's contribution to Marxist philosophy in China consequently remained under a cloud, and it was not until 1978 that a positive reassessment began. However, it was the rapid and widespread development of the field of Mao studies in China, predicated on the Sixth Plenum's "Resolution on certain questions in the history of our Party since the founding of the People's Republic of China" of June 1981, that has served as the major premise for renewed and sustained interest in Li Da's philosophical writings, for one of the important themes of this "Resolution" was that Mao Zedong Thought is a scientific system to which many Chinese Party leaders and theorists (among whom Li Da could be numbered) had made a significant contribution.[65] Evaluations of *Elements of Sociology* in China in the 1980s were thus linked to a wider preoccupation with Mao Zedong Thought, and in particular a renewed interest in the origins and content of Mao's philosophical thought.[66]

There is virtual unanimity amongst Chinese scholars that Li Da's *Elements of Sociology* is an outstanding work of Marxist scholarship, one which made a major contribution to the dissemination of Marxist philosophy in China. The judgment rendered by the 1982 edition of the *Chinese Philosophical Yearbook* is typical in this regard. *Elements of Sociology*, it says, has the following characteristics and strengths:

1. It is a treatise which relatively completely and systematically elaborates Marxist philosophy, one which incorporates the general laws of nature, society and human thought. 2. On the basis of its direct explication of Marxist philosophy, it also provides a very clear elaboration of the other philosophical schools and the boundaries between them. 3. It is an

embodiment of the fine style of study which links theory and practice. When utilising the philosophical principles of Marxism to study concrete problems, the author emphasises that abstract analysis is not appropriate and that there must be concrete analysis of concrete circumstances. 4. It upholds the spirit of critical struggle. In its discussions, *Elements of Sociology* carries out analysis and criticism of the viewpoints of idealism and metaphysics, and upholds the principle of the party character of philosophy. 5. The material in the book is quite substantial. It absorbed the definite conclusions of contemporary natural science, to a great extent employed materials regarding the history of philosophy, and in elaborating problems did everything possible to work directly from the sources; in doing these things, *Elements of Sociology* is of great assistance to those readers who have not systematically studied the history of philosophy.[67]

While there is thus general agreement amongst Chinese philosophers on the significance of *Elements of Sociology*, there is nevertheless considerable disagreement on many aspects of interpretation. One of the most vigorous debates occured between Professor Wang Jionghua (of Huazhong University of Science and Technology in Wuhan) and Professor Xu Quanxing (of Beijing University) in the pages of the *neibu* Shanghai journal *Mao Zedong zhexue sixiang yanjiu dongtai* [Trends in the Study of Mao Zedong's Philosophical Thought] from 1984 to 1986.[68] The debate centered on the relationship between *Elements of Sociology* and Mao's "On Practice" and "On Contradiction", but traversed virtually all of the major interpretive issues concerning Li's book. What makes this debate so interesting is that there is almost no agreement between these two well-known scholars.[69]

Concerning the core issue of the relationship between *Elements of Sociology* and Mao's two philosophical essays, Wang Jionghua defends the possibility that Mao could have read Li's book prior to mid-1937 when he wrote "On Contradiction" and "On Practice". As we have seen, he points to the fact that the first edition of *Elements of Sociology* had been published in 1935, and significant portions of it dealing with the laws of dialectical materialism had been republished in journals; Mao may thus have had access to the text, either directly or indirectly, prior to mid-1937. Moreover, Li is known to have sent Mao a copy on the publication of the Shanghai edition in May 1937. But had Mao read it by July and August 1937, when he wrote his *Lecture Notes on Dialectical Materialism* from which the two famous essays on philosophy were taken? Xu Quanxing suggests that the chance Mao had read *Elements of Sociology* by then is "slight" and that it is safer to accept that he read it only after completing the writing of his own essays. This contention is strengthened, according to Xu, by the fact that there is no direct textual relationship between Mao's essays and *Elements of Sociology*; and this also makes the viewpoint that Mao had plagiarised Li's volume, a view shared by a number of Chinese and Japanese scholars,[70] quite untenable. While Wang agrees with Xu that Mao did not plagiarise *Elements of Sociology* in writing his *Lecture Notes on Dialectical Materialism*, he does not accept that there is no direct relationship between Mao's and Li's writings, and he provides a number of examples in which concepts contained in Li's volume also appear in Mao's philosophical essays; there is thus a "consistency" between the two sets of documents. Wang concedes, however, that both Li and Mao had been exposed to a common stock of Soviet philosophical texts, and it is this fact which makes his argument regarding "consistency" less than convincing; indeed, Xu is adamant that the origin of the concepts to be found in "On Contradiction" and "On Practice" is not *Elements of Sociology*, but Leninism via the Soviet texts on philosophy. He moreover maintains that Mao was not influenced by *Elements of Sociology* when revising his two philosopical essays for publication in the early 1950s.

There is also disagreement between Wang and Xu over the extent to which Li was dependent on Soviet texts on philosophy in authoring *Elements of Sociology*. Xu suggests that Li's volume was largely a "reprint" or "reproduction" (*fanban*) of the Soviet texts, and in particular *Outline of New Philosophy* and *Dialectical and Historical Materialism*, both by Mitin. Wang counters by pointing out that these two latter Soviet texts had only been published in translation after June 1936, by which time the first edition of *Elements of Sociology* had already been published; and because the basic structure of the two versions of Li's book remained largely the same, this puts out of court the argument that it could have been only a thinly disguised copy of these Soviet texts. However, Wang's response does ignore the fact that Li had conceded that he had employed Shirokov and Aizenberg's *A Course on Dialectical Materialism* as a model for his own writings on dialectical materialism. Nevertheless, while there is, in my view, no doubt that Li's interpretation of the "new philosophy" drew heavily on Soviet philosophical texts, Xu's charge that *Elements of Sociology* is merely a "reproduction" or "reprint" of them is going too far, for this implies that Li did little more than plagiarise the Soviet texts, which is certainly not the case.

This area of contention bears on the related issue of the degree of originality demonstrated by Li Da in *Elements of Sociology*. Wang charges Xu with denying the "creative contribution" made by this volume, and argues that, while Li did employ many of the concepts and materials contained in the Soviet texts, he did perform "creative labour" to provide *Elements of Sociology* with characteristics that were particularly Li's own. Indeed, Wang suggests that Li's achievement lies not only in providing a comprehensive explanation of Marxist philosophy in *Elements of Sociology*, but in "developing" (*fahui*) some of

Marxist philosophy's basic viewpoints. Xu counters that it would be very difficult to establish the originality of *Elements of Sociology* as many other texts on philosophy from that period were saying the same sorts of thing. For Xu, the achievement of *Elements of Sociology* lies not in its originality but in the fact that it is "China's first relatively complete introduction to Marxist philosophy". This is not the case, responds Wang, pointing to volumes written by Qu Qiubai in the 1920s (*Shehui zhexue gailun* and *Xiandai shehuixue*) and Li's own *Xiandai shehuixue* of 1926; similarly, translations of works such as Bukharin's *Historical Materialism*, Luppol's *The Theory and Practice of the Fundamental Issues of the Social Sciences* (which Li Da had translated), and Shirokov and Aizenberg's *A Course on Dialectical Materialism* (also translated by Li) had already provided comprehensive coverage of Marxist philosophy to a Chinese audience.

Finally, Xu suggests that *Elements of Sociology*'s achievement was limited insofar as it did not integrate Marxist philosophy with China's "reality". One must have some sympathy here for Xu's judgment for, as the summary contained in the next two chapters demonstrates, there is no attempt to illustrate his exposition of dialectical materialism through reference to examples from Chinese life. We know that Li had intended to include a sixth section which would incorporate study of China's society, but this remained incomplete by May 1937 and was not included.[71] However, Li probably felt less compulsion to attempt the "sinification" of dialectical materialism in this volume as he had, in so many of his other books and writings, already provided detailed analyses of a number of very significant problems from China's society and history.[72] Xu's judgment here must therefore be tempered by placing *Elements of Sociology* in the broader context of Li's writings which, in total, reveal an impressive attempt to render a materialist interpetation of Chinese society.

Conclusion

The debate between Wang Jionghua and Xu Quanxing over Li Da's *Elements of Sociology* throws into sharp focus the problematic nature of any attempt to arrive at a definitive interpretation of the origin, history and influence of this text. However, the task of evaluation is made somewhat easier if the criterion of originality is diminished in importance — or indeed, set aside to allow a contemplation of this text from other perspectives. For the major significance of *Elements of Sociology*, I would argue, lies not in its development of the concepts or forms of argument of orthodox Marxist philosophy as this was understood in the early 1930s. Rather, its significance lies in what the text can tell us about the origins and development of Marxism in China. Many interpretations of Marxism in China stress the heterodoxy of its content, emphasise the conceptual distance which separates it from Soviet and European forms of Marxism. However, here we have, in *Elements of Sociology*, one of the most influential texts of Marxism in China, its author universally praised among contemporary Chinese scholars for his role in the dissemination of Marxist theory in China; and yet the contents of this volume are orthodox to a fault. Nowhere in the pages of this massive tome does Li test the limits to orthodoxy, and indeed he goes out of his way to ensure the reader that he has expunged from his own thinking ideas (such as Deborin's excessive Hegelianisation of the dialectic) now deemed heretical in the new climate of the subordination of philosophy to politics. If *Elements of Sociology* is accepted as a model of orthodoxy, does this serve to problematise and weaken the mainstream viewpoint that continually underscores the unorthodox character of Marxism in China? I contend that it does. While there are limits to the argument I am pressing here, and I will turn to these qualifications shortly, the point remains that blanket judgments regarding the idiosyncratic and heterodox character of Marxism in China do not stand up to close scrutiny alongside a close reading of Li Da's *Elements of Sociology* — or Mao's writings on dialectical materialism, for that matter.

This argument is further reinforced when we consider the relationship between *Elements of Sociology* and Mao's understanding of Marxist philosophy. It is not at all clear that Mao had read Li's book by the time, in mid-1937, when he wrote his *Lecture Notes on Dialectical Materialism*, although he certainly did so, as we noted above, in the first few months of 1938. The important aspect of this relationship is not so much the direct relationship between Li's and Mao's writings on dialectical materialism; it is, rather, the relationship both sets of writings shared in common with a limited number of post-1931 Soviet texts on philosophy. These texts — *A Course on Dialectical Materialism, Outline of New Philosophy, Dialectical and Historical Materialism* — conveyed to both Li and Mao information on the content of the "new philosophy" and it is clear from Mao's own extensive writings on dialectical materialism that, in large measure, he drew on and adopted the concepts, modes of logic and forms of discourse contained in these books. The effect of *Elements of Sociology* on Mao was thus to reinforce the interpretation of dialectical materialism already drawn from his assiduous study of the Soviet texts in late 1936 and the first half of 1937. *Elements of Sociology* was thus to become one of a constellation of overlapping and interlocking texts whose essential function was the same: explanation and dissemination of the new orthodoxy in the realm of Marxist philosophy.

The abiding influence of this constellation of texts can be perceived in the way in which dialectical materialism is propounded in textbooks on philosophy published in China in recent years.[73] These primers invariably read like regurgitations of the Soviet philosophy which Li helped disseminate through the pages of *Elements of Sociology*, and which Mao endorsed in his essays "On Contradiction" and "On Practice". It is consequently necessary to recognise the significant influence of post-1931 Soviet philosophy if the genealogy of Marxist philosophy in contemporary China is to be understood. How otherwise are we to explain the continually repeated articulation of this interpretation of Marxist philosophy in China? *Elements of Sociology* is thus significant insofar as it sheds light on the origins of the philosophical aspect of Marxism in China as well as the developmental trajectory it has subsequently traversed.

Finally, while I have emphasised the high level of orthodoxy contained in *Elements of Sociology* and Mao's writings on dialectical materialism, it is important not to fall into the trap of consequently assuming an equal level of orthodoxy across the entire spectrum of the themes and concepts which constitute the totality of Marxism in China. Our analysis of *Elements of Sociology* and its relationship to Mao's philosophical thought allows only the conclusion that the philosophical dimension of Marxism in China is not unorthodox when judged by the orthodoxy which prevailed in Soviet philosophical circles in the early to mid-1930s. The genealogies of other concepts and themes of Marxism in China cannot be assumed, but need to be subject to specific calculations; in this way, blanket generalisations which serve only to disguise the complex pattern of development of Marxism in China would be avoided.

In the next chapter, we embark on a detailed analysis of the contents of Li Da's *Elements of Sociology*. The reader will thus be able to judge the degree of orthodoxy of Li's elaboration of the philosophy of dialectical materialism.

Notes

1. *Li Da wenji* (Collected writings of Li Da) (Beijing: Renminchubanshe, 1981), Vol. I, p. 514.

2. *Elements of Sociology* was the English title given to Li Da's *Shehuixue dagang* by O. Briere. See *Fifty Years of Chinese Philosophy, 1898–1948*, translated from the French by Laurence G. Thompson (New York: Praeger, 1965), p. 76. A good reason

for persisting with this translation of *Shehuixue dagang* is that in the very year the first edition of Li's book was published (1935), a translated book was published with the same title in Chinese. Its English title, *Outlines of Sociology*, would be an alternative translation for Li's book. See Blackmar and Gillin, *Shehuixue dagang* (Outlines of Sociology), translated by Wu Zelin and Lu Deyin (Shanghai: Shejie shuju, 1935). In contrast to Li Da's *Shehuixue dagang*, this latter volume presents a conventional Western, non-Marxist interpretation of sociology.

3. *Zhongguo zhexue* (April 1979), Vol. I, p. 364.

4. Ibid.

5. Wang Jionghua, "Mao Zedong yu Li Da" (Mao Zedong and Li Da), *Xinhua wenzhai*, no 2 (1992), pp. 132–35; see also the biographical introduction to Volume I of *Li Da wenji*.

6. A chapter on Li Da is included in a compendium of China's most influential intellectuals. See *Zhongguo dangdai shehui kexuejia* (China's Contemporary Social Scientists) (Beijing, 1983), pp. 111–30; see also the section on Li Da in *Zhongguo zhexue nianjian 1984* (The 1984 Yearbook of Philosophy in China) (Beijing, Zhongguo dabaike quanshu chubanshe, 1984), pp. 489–99.

7. See the biographical introduction to *Li Da wenji*, I.

8. See Li's translator's preface to Shirokov and Aizenberg et al., *Bianzhengfa weiwulun jiaocheng* (A Course on Dialectical Materialism) (Shanghai: Bigengtang shudian, 1936), p. 4.

9. Wang Jionghua, "'Dagang' de chuangzaoxing gongxian ji 'lianglun' yu ta de guanxi" (The Creative Contribution of *Elements of Sociology* and its Relationship with "On Practice" and "On Contradiction"), *Mao Zedong zhexue sixiang yanjiu dongtai*, no. 1 (1984), pp. 20–23.

10. This 1935 edition of *Elements of Sociology* was only "discovered" by librarians at Beijing University in 1981 and announced to Chinese philosophical circles in the 1982 *Philosophical Yearbook*. See *Zhongguo zhexue nianjian 1982* (The Chinese Philosophical Yearbook 1982) (Shanghai: Zhongguo dabaike quanshu chubanshe, 1982), p. 179. See also "Li Da de 'Shehuixue dagang' zui zao banben de faxian" (The Discovery of the Earliest Edition of Li Da's *Elements of Sociology*), *Zhexue yanjiu*, no. 3 (1982).

11. See Li Da, "Bianzheng luoji yu xingshiluoji" (Dialectical and Formal Logic), *Faxue zhuankan*, no. 5 (1935); Li Da, "Weiwu bianzhengfa duixiang" (The Object of Materialist Dialectics), *Faxue zhuankan*, no. 6 (1935); and Li Da, "Bianzhengfa de jige faze" (Several Laws of Dialectics), *Faxue zhuankan*, no. 7 (1935).

12. "Li Da de 'Shehuixue dagang' zui zao banben de faxian".

13. *Fifty Years of Chinese Philosophy*, p. 76.

14. *Zhonguo zhexue*, no. 1 (1979), p. 364.

15. See Huang Nansen et al. (eds), *Makesizhuyi zhexue shi (diliujuan)* (A History of Marxist Philosophy (Vol. 6)) (Beijing: Beijing chubanshe, 1989), p. 277.

16. See the biographical introduction to *Li Da wenji*, I; also the author's preface in *Li Da wenji*, II, p. 8. Examples of the change in terminology are *demokelaxi* (democracy) becomes *minzhuzhuyi*, *guannianlun* (idealism) becomes *weixinlun*, and *puluoliedaliya* (proletariat) becomes *wuchanjieji*.

17. *Zhongguo zhexue*, no. I, p. 372.

18. Mao read and annotated this section of Li Da's translation of Kawakami Hajime's book at some time during the Yan'an period. See *Mao Zedong zhexue pizhuji*

(The Philosophical Annotations of Mao Zedong) (Beijing: Zhonyang wenxian chubanshe, 1988), pp. 453-92; see also Shi Zhongquan, "A New Document for the Study of Mao Zedong's Philosophical Thought: Introducing *The Philosophical Annotations of Mao Zedong*", translated by Nick Knight, in Nick Knight (ed.), *The Philosophical Thought of Mao Zedong: Studies from China, 1981-1989* (Armonk, New York: M.E. Sharpe, Chinese Studies on Philosophy, 1992), pp. 127-31.

19. For a biographical commentary on the life and ideas of Deborin, see Rene Ahlberg, "The Forgotten Philosopher: Abram Deborin", in Leopold Labedz (ed.), *Revisionism: Essays on the History of Marxist Ideas* (London: George Allen & Unwin, 1962), pp. 126-41.

20. Eugene Kamenka, "Soviet Philosophy, 1917-67", in Alex Simirenko (ed.), *Social Thought in the Soviet Union* (Chicago: Quadrangle Books, 1969), p. 95.

21. Ibid.

22. For analysis of Soviet philosophy at this time, see Gustav A. Wetter, *Dialectical Materialism: A Historical and Systematic Survey of Philosophy in the Soviet Union* (New York: Praeger, 1958); also Richard T. de George, *Patterns of Soviet Thought* (Ann Arbor: University of Michigan Press, 1966); Herbert Marcuse, *Soviet Marxism: A Critical Analysis* (New York: Vintage Books, 1961); Kamenka, "Soviet Philosophy, 1917-67"; Loren R. Graham, *Science and Philosophy in the Soviet Union* (New York: Alfred A. Knopf, 1972); Z.A. Jordan, *The Evolution of Dialectical Materialism: A Philosophical and Sociological Analysis* (London: Macmillan, 1967); David Joravsky, *Soviet Marxism and Natural Science, 1917-1932* (New York: Columbia University Press, 1961); Loren R. Graham, *The Soviet Academy of Sciences and the Communist Party, 1927-1932* (Princeton: Princeton University Press, 1967). For an evaluation of philosophy in the Soviet Union by a Soviet writer, see W.N. Khosokov, *Sulian Makesi Lieningzhuyi zhexueshi gangyao (sanshi niandai)* (An Outline History of Marxist-Leninist Philosophy in the Soviet Union (the 1930s)), translated by Xu Xiaoying and Wang Suqin (Beijing: Qiushi chubanshe, 1985). The original Russian text was written in 1978.

23. See De George, *Patterns of Soviet Thought*, p. 193; also Kamenka, "Soviet Philosophy, 1917-1967", p. 95.

24. Shirokov and Aizenberg, *Bianzhengfa weiwulun jiaocheng*, p. 1.

25. Ibid., p. 8.

26. Ibid., p. 14.

27. Ibid., p. 3.

28. For a contrasting Chinese point of view, see Zhao Dezhi and Wang Benhao, *Zhongguo Makesizhuyi zhexue qishinian* (Seventy Years of Marxist Philosophy in China) (Liaoning: Liaoning daxue chubanshe, 1991), p. 113. These authors suggest that, although *Elements of Sociology* did absorb some of the conclusions from the Soviet texts on philosophy, more important were the ideas that Li had himself developed in the course of his own study of Marxism.

29. See Werner Meissner, *Philosophy and Politics in China: The Controversy over Dialectical Materialism in the 1930s* (London: Hurst and Co., 1990).

30. See Joshua A. Fogel, *Ai Ssu-ch'i's Contribution to the Development of Chinese Marxism* (Cambridge, Mass. and London: Harvard Contemporary China Series, no. 4, 1987); also Ignatious J.H. Ts'ao, "Ai Ssu-ch'i: The Apostle of Chinese Communism", *Studies in Soviet Thought* no. 12 (1972).

31. See the biographical introduction to *Li Da wenji*, Vol. I.

32. Briere comments "needless to add ... one should not look for the least originality of thought in these (Li Da's) works". As we shall demonstrate, however, a text may have considerable significance and influence without possessing "originality" of the type sought by Briere. See *Fifty years of Chinese Philosophy*, p. 77.

33. See Meissner, *Philosophy and Politics in China*.

34. Wu Jun, "Mao Zedong shengping, sixiang yanjiu gaishu" (Comment on Research on Mao Zedong's Life and Thought), *Mao Zedong zhexue sixiang yanjiu dongtai*, no. 1 (1987), pp. 52–58.

35. For a detailed analysis and translation of this document, see Nick Knight (ed.), *Mao Zedong on Dialectical Materialism: Writings on Philosophy, 1937* (Armonk, New York: M.E. Sharpe, 1990).

36. Ibid., esp. pp. 80–83.

37. Tian Songnian, "Dui ji ben zhexue shuji de pizhu" (On the Annotations on Several Texts on Philosophy), in Gong Yuzhi et al. (eds), *Mao Zedong de dushu shenghuo* (Mao Zedong's Life as a Reader) (Beijing: Sanlian shudian, 1986), p. 71.

38. This suggestion is strengthened by the fact that Mao recalled, in a conversation with Li Da in August 1961, that he had read and annotated *Elements of Sociology* but had unfortunately lost it while travelling. It is quite possible that Mao had annotated and then lost the 1935 edition of *Elements of Sociology*, for his annotated 1937 edition has survived. See Sun Qinan and Li Shizhen, *Mao Zedong yu mingren* (Mao Zedong and the Famous) (Jiangsu: Jiangsu renmin chubanshe, 1993), Vol. 1, p. 333.

39. Wang Jionghua, "Du tan 'Lianglun" yu 'dagang'" (A comment on "On Practice" and "On Contradiction" and *Elements of Sociology*), *Mao Zedong zhexue sixiang yanjiu dongtai*, no. 3 (1986), pp. 39–40; see also Wang Jionghua, *Li Da yu Makesizhuyi zhexue zai Zhongguo* (Li Da and Marxist Philosophy in China) (Huabei: Huazhongli da xue chubanshe, 1988).

40. *Zhongguo zhexue*, no. 1 (1979), pp. 34, 364.

41. Wang Jionghua, 'Dagang de chuangzaoxing gongxian ji 'lianglun' yu ta de guanxi", pp. 20–23.

42. Xu Quanxing, "Zai tan 'lianglun' yu 'Shehuixue dagang' — fu Wang Jionghua tongzhi" (Once Again on "On Practice" and "On Contradiction" and *Elements of Sociology* — A response to Wang Jionghua), *Mao Zedong zhexue sixiang yanjiu dongtai*, no. 3 (1985), pp. 24–29.

43. *Mao Zedong zhexue pizhuji*, p. 210.

44. Ibid., pp. 211–12.

45. Ibid.

46. Ibid., pp. 212–13.

47. Ibid., pp. 214–16.

48. Ibid., pp. 217–18.

49. Ibid., p. 219.

50. Ibid., pp. 220–22.

51. Ibid., pp. 222–24.

52. Ibid., pp. 225–27.

53. Ibid., pp. 227–30.

54. Ibid., pp. 230–31.

55. Xu Quanxing has compared *Elements of Sociology* and *Outline of New Philosophy* and suggests that their treatment of the basic laws of dialectical materialism is also very similar, but not amounting to plagiarism on Li's part. See "Zai tan 'liang lun' yu 'Shehuixue da gang' — fu Wang Jionghua tongzhi," pp. 24–29.

56. For a translation of some of these annotations, see Knight (ed.), *Mao Zedong on Dialectical Materialism*, pp. 267–80.

57. *Mao Zedong zhexue pizhuji*, p. 232.

58. Ibid., p. 240.

59. Ibid., p. 250.

60. Ibid., pp. 262–63. The July Seventh incident saw the commencement of the Sino-Japanese War.

61. Ibid., pp. 265–66.

62. Although to be fair to Li, it must be noted that he had originally conceived *Elements of Sociology* as containing a sixth section which would concentrate on the study of Chinese society. However, he never completed the writing of this section. See *Li Da wenji*, Vol. II, p. 5.

63. See in particular Mao's essays "Reform our Study", "Rectify the Party's Style of Work" and "Oppose Stereotyped Party Writing", in *Selected Works of Mao Tse-tung* (Peking: FLP, 1965), Vol. III, pp. 17–26, 35–52, 53–68.

64. *Zhongguo dangdai shehui kexuejia*, pp. 129–30.

65. "Resolution on Certain Questions in the History of our Party since the Founding of the People's Republic of China", in *Resolution on CPC History (1949–1981)* (Beijing: FLP, 1981), pp. 1–86.

66. See Knight (ed.), *The Philosophical Thought of Mao Zedong: Studies from China, 1981–1989*, Introduction.

67. *Zhongguo zhexue nianjian 1982*, pp. 178–79.

68. See no. 1 (1984), pp. 20–23, no. 3 (1985), 24–29, and no. 3 (1986), pp. 39–40.

69. Although Professor Wang Jionghua informed me that Xu Quanxing had subsequently conceded many of the points in their debate. Interview, October 1993, Wuhan.

70. Wang Jionghua, "'Dagang' de chuangzaoxing gongxian yu 'lianglun' yu ta de guanxi", p. 23, note 2. See also Fogel, *Ai Ssu-ch'i's Contribution to the Development of Chinese Marxism*, p. 108, note 33, where he cites the Japanese Mao scholar Takeuchi Minoru who claims that the section "On Consciousness" from Mao's *Lecture Notes on Dialectical Materialism* was plagiarised from *Elements of Sociology*. The problem with Takeuchi Minoru's suggestion is that Li, in turn, derived much of the section on consciousness from Lukachevsky (Lukajiefusiji)'s *A Course on Atheism* (Wushenlun jiaocheng), Chapter 2. (See *Elements of Sociology*, p. 212) The point is that Mao and Li both relied heavily on Soviet texts on philosophy and social theory for their ideas. It is thus somewhat pointless to identify similarities between Mao's writings and those of Li Da, or Ai Siqi (as Fogel does, pp. 68–71), and assume that Mao derived his understanding of dialectical materialism from those Chinese sources.

71. *Li Da wenji*, Vol. II, p. 5.

72. See in particular the many articles and books dealing with a wide number of problems in China's history and society which appear in Volume I of *Li Da wenji*. See also Li Da, *Zhongguo chanye geming gaiguan* (A General Survey of China's Revolution in Production) (Shanghai: Kunlun shudian, 1929).

73. See for example, Xiao Qian et al. (eds), *Bianzhengweiwuzhuyi yuanli* (Principles of Dialectical Materialism) (Beijing: Renmin chunbanshe, 1981); also Li Deyang et al. (eds), *Bianzhenweiwuzhuyi yu lishiweiwuzhuyi* (Dialectical and Historical Materialism) (Wuhan: Hubei renmin chubanshe, 1983); and *Bianzhengweiwuzhuyi yanjiu* (The Study of Dialectical Materialism) (Beijing: Qiushi chubanshe, 1986).

7

Elements of Sociology: The History, Laws and Categories of Dialectical Materialism

Introduction

Elements of Sociology is divided into five sections. The first section, that dealing with dialectical materialism, is the longest and extends to more than 270 pages in the *Wenji* (Collected Writings) edition. The remaining sections cover the materialist conception of history, the economic structure of society, the political structure of society and social consciousness. This and the following chapter are devoted to a detailed summary and analysis of the section on dialectical materialism. This is necessary for a number of reasons. First, virtually none of Li Da's writings on philosophy (or any of the many topics on which he wrote, for that matter) has been translated into English. This paucity of English translations of Li's work has no doubt contributed to the unwarranted neglect of Li in English language commentaries on the dissemination and development of Marxism in China.[1] The summary which follows is intended to rectify that situation, even if only partially. Second, the philosophical subject matter discussed by Li in *Elements of Sociology* is extremely complex, even for those whose Chinese extends to the arcane terminology of dialectical materialism. The summary offered here will, I hope, serve as a less onerous (if only partial) substitute for tackling the original Chinese document. Third, there can be no doubt that Li's reputation in China as a Marxist philosopher rests very heavily on the erudition displayed in *Elements of Sociology*. If we are to evaluate Li's importance to Marxist philosophy in China, it is vital that we do so on the basis of a careful and thorough reading of this pivotal text.

Finally, this summary is intended to reinforce the contention that any understanding of Marxism in China, and particularly its philosophical dimension, must be based on a familiarity with the premises, categories, laws, epistemology and the forms of logic, argumentation and terminology of dialectical materialism. Here we have a philosophical system of considerable complexity, one making fundamental ontological and epistemological assertions. The dismissive treatment meted out to dialectical materialism (often by commentators who give the strong impression that they have made little effort to read and come to grips with what is being said by that philosophy)[2] prevents a clear perception of its significance to the development of Marxism in China. By providing the reader with a detailed account of the contents of *Elements of Sociology*, not only is the breadth of Li Da's understanding of dialectical materialism made abundantly clear, but it becomes evident that we are dealing here with a complex philosophy, the forceful arguments and logic of which have persuaded many Chinese intellectuals, Mao Zedong among them; their adherence to this belief system is incomprehensible if dialectical materialism is lightly dismissed as erroneous, or treated as nothing more than an epiphenomenon of the struggle in the political arena.[3]

In the summary of Li Da's *Elements of Sociology* which follows, I have attempted to capture all of the major lines of argument and the links within these arguments. My purpose is to provide a thorough yet accessible account of Li Da's explication of dialectical materialism.

Before turning to this task, it is appropriate to recall the cautionary note raised in the previous chapter which problematises the notion of Li as author. While we are not for a moment suggesting that Li did not write *Elements of Sociology*, we must keep in mind that the concepts, categories, laws and forms of argument and logic which appear in this substantial volume are not, for the most part, original formulations; by and large, these derived from Soviet Marxist philosophy of the early 1930s (see Chapter 2). One of our aims is to situate the writings of Li Da and Mao Zedong within the general theoretical context of the time, and in so doing make possible an informed judgment of the extent to which both Li and Mao were in the debt of contemporary Soviet texts on philosophy for information on the approved interpretation of dialectical materialism; in other words, we are concerned with the link between Marxist philosophy in China and Marxist philosophy elsewhere, and particularly its relationship to "orthodox" Soviet Marxism. The task is thus to compare *Elements of Sociology* with the Soviet texts on philosophy which were his main source of inspiration, and to evaluate the extent of overlap between them. As we peruse the contents of *Elements of Sociology*, we must keep in mind that Li did not aspire or lay claim to any great originality in writing this volume. It is therefore not originality we seek, but genealogy; it is the substance and style of Li's explication of an already existing philosophy which is of significance here.

Before turning to the contents of *Elements of Sociology*, a comment on its general structure is necessary. Li commences with a survey and analysis of materialist and dialectical themes in the history of human thought, moves on to a consideration of dialectical materialism as a science and, on this basis, considers in some detail the laws and categories of dialectical materialism; his explication concludes with a detailed analysis of the issues of epistemology and logic. In terms of the mode and order of presentation, the structure of *Elements of Sociology* clearly parallels that to be found in the Soviet philosophical texts; indeed, some sections utilise the same sub-headings.[4] Specific comparisons between *Elements of Sociology* and the Soviet texts on philosophy and Mao's writings on dialectical materialism will be provided below, but to avoid interrupting the flow of Li's explication, these will be largely confined to the endnotes.

Dialectical Materialism in the History of Human Thought

Li commences by reiterating the formula that the "only scientific method of sociology is dialectical materialism".[5] It is, he argues, the only method capable of providing a dynamic, lively and organic explanation of society. Although now the weapon of the proletariat and its party in the struggle to realise a socialist society, dialectical materialism can be traced back to the earliest attempts at philosophy in human history. However, the level of development of the various economic structures which have characterised the progress of human society established limits on the extent to which materialist or dialectical ideas have been able to flourish. Primitive societies, for example, gave rise to "primitive dialectics" in the form of animism. This was dialectical, Li suggests, insofar as it was premised on an appreciation of movement and change in the external world; however, such incipient dialectics could not, because of the limitations imposed by the low levels of social and economic development, transcend the religious and superstitious elements of consciousness. Nevertheless, the philosophies of ancient societies such as Greece marked a development in the history of dialectical thought; based on developments in such things as technology, handicrafts, trade and navigation, human thought generated a greater awareness of nature, one which encouraged progress in the various branches of natural science such as mathematics and geography. Li singles out Heraclites for his contribution to dialectical thought, for Heraclites perceived in contradiction the explanation for constant change in the universe; "the struggle of opposites is the initiator and primemover of all change and development, and this is a fundamental idea of dialectics"; for this insight, Heraclites is described as the "father of dialectics".[6]

Li continues that, despite the advances made by the philosophy of ancient Greece, the limitations imposed by the level of economic development — and in particular the nature of the class structure and struggles of slave society — meant that idealist forms of dialectics became prominent at the expense of materialism. A similar explanation is given by Li for the failure of later philosophers, and in particular Kant and Hegel, to link the dialectical themes within their philosophies to materialism. Kant, for example, although seeming to acknowledge the existence of an objective material world, actually negated it when explaining the process of knowledge, falling back on an idealist and metaphysical emphasis on the *a priori* knowledge of the subject of cognition.[7] This was a result of the limitations imposed by the feudal society in which Kant lived. Similarly, Hegel, although bringing dialectics to its highest point, is perceived by Li as a product of the environment created by the bourgeois revolution and class struggle of Germany in the early years of the nineteenth century; the contradictions in Hegel's philosophy — between its progressive and reactionary aspects and between its method and system — are explained by this.[8] His reference to a "world spirit" as the demiurge of change and progress meant that his dialectics could be no more than idealist in character; nevertheless, his recognition of the unity and struggle of opposites within phenomena as the cause of change and development established his idealist dialectics as a precursor of dialectical materialism.[9]

Li suggests that it was only with the emergence of capitalist society, with its inherent contradictions between capital and labour, and between the organised and planned character of production at the level of the enterprise and the anarchic state of production at the level of society, that earlier strands of dialectical and materialist thought could coalesce to create dialectical materialism. Marx and Engels, themselves strongly influenced by the idealist dialectics of Hegel and the materialism of Feuerbach in their early writings, had, by 1844–45, formulated the philosophy of dialectical materialism, a philosophy which overcame the metaphysical materialist shortcomings of Feuerbach's philosophy and the idealism of Hegel. The crucial factor in this development, Li argues, was a recognition of the pivotal role of the emergent industrial proletariat in the structure and development of capitalist society, and a recognition, in such works as *The German Ideology*, that the material conditions of human existence represented the locus from which sprang all historical change and development.[10] From this premise was to come the concomitant recognition that the economic structure of society, incorporating the labour process, constituted the basis (*jichu*) of legal relations and state forms.[11]

In terms of epistemology (an issue he returns to in considerable detail), Li emphasises the role of practice as the basis of the process of knowledge production. The unity of the historical and natural perspectives within dialectical materialism is, he suggests, premised on social practice: the practice of labour, material production and social struggle determined mental artifacts such as ideas and concepts.[12] Li distances the epistemology of dialectical materialism from that of the old-style (or "metaphysical") materialism of Feuerbach; the latter merely perceived knowledge as a reflection of objective reality in the brain of the observer; dialectical materialism, however, went beyond this passive reflection theory to stress practice as the motive force in the development of knowledge.[13]

When Li turns his attention to the development of dialectical materialism, he makes the observation that this philosophy had emerged through a process of philosophical struggle; "philosophical struggle is a reflection of political struggle; this is the key to our understanding of the emergence and development of dialectical materialism".[14] Li then proceeds to demonstrate how certain of the philosophical texts of Marx and Engels (such as *The Poverty of Philosophy* and *Anti-Dühring*) emerged through a process of struggle against the detractors of "scientific socialism". Similarly, Lenin's development of dialectical materialism (in his *Materialism and Empirio-Criticism* and *Philosophical Notebooks*) was related to the political struggles of his time.

Li's elaboration of the position of dialectical materialism in the history of human thought thus sets the scene for a conception of philosophy which is linked to broader political and social struggles, its emergence through struggle serving to explain the often polemical tone in which the philosophy of Marxism has been couched. Li's elaboration also serves as the premise for his conception of the function of dialectical materialism in the "current stage": "to guide the life and struggle of the progressive classes".[15]

The Philosophical Science of Dialectical Materialism

Li proceeds to detail the major problems and issues of dialectical materialism. He deals first with the basic problem of philosophy, the relationship between matter and spirit.[16] The responses of the various philosophies to this problem have, he argues, situated them in one of two camps: materialism or idealism.[17]

Materialism endorses the view that matter comes first in the world and that spirit comes later; matter is thus the primal cause, and spirit emerges from matter. Matter exists objectively and independently of spirit; spirit depends on matter, matter does not depend on spirit. This principle, Li continues, applies equally to society, which can be divided into its material and spiritual components. Spiritual life is a reflection of material life. Material life is the basic cause, it is the base (*jichu*), while spiritual life emerges from it; spiritual life progresses on the basis of progress in material civilisation. Materialism's basic premise is thus that existence determines consciousness, and that consciousness does not determine existence; it therefore follows that social existence determines social consciousness.

Idealism, on the other hand, endorses the view that spirit comes first in the world and that matter comes later. From this perspective, the world is the product of spirit. An example is Hegel's reference to the "absolute spirit" which is presumed to have existed prior to the material world. Idealists, according to Li, thus conceive of the world in thought, and assume that thought creates the material world. Spirit therefore changes first, and changes and developments in the material world precede spiritual change. Idealists perceive the history of humankind as a product of thought; as thought changes, society also will change. The fundamental premise of idealism is: consciousness determines existence, existence does not determine consciousness; applied to history and society, this results in the view that social consciousness determines social existence.

Dualism, which attempts to integrate and unite matter and spirit, cannot, Li asserts, be accounted a separate philosophy, for it actually belongs in the idealist camp. The entire history of philosophy is thus the history of the development and struggle of materialism and idealism. This struggle between materialism and idealism is, he argues, a reflection of actual historical struggles, for those who create philosophy belong to definite social groups. Any philosophical theory reflects the circumstances of the economic life of the era, reflects the level of knowledge of the natural sciences, and reflects the interests and aspirations of definite social groups. In the history of philosophy, idealism has frequently represented the consciousness of conservative classes; materialism, on the other hand, has frequently represented the consciousness of the progressive classes, and these latter have always employed materialism to oppose the spiritual products of the conservative classes. Li portrays the proletariat as the progressive class of the present era which consistently supports materialism and continually struggles against idealism.

And what of truth? Li asserts that truth is on the side of materialism. The history of human practice and the history of human science verify the truth of materialism and expose the erroneous nature of idealism; the more social production expands, the more science progressively reveals the secrets of nature, and the more the truth of materialism is consolidated.

Li then deals with dialectical materialism's role in overturning the dominance of idealism.[18] He suggests that the origins of idealism are to be found in the distinction between mental and manual labour, and the division of society into classes. With the emergence of class society from primitive society, mental labour became the prerogative of the dominant class, while manual labour became the lot of the dominated class. Because the members of the dominant class did not engage in manual labour, they had no direct connection with the real world, and could not therefore correctly reflect the real world in their thinking. The mode of thought characteristic of idealism (which speaks in terms of the "absolute spirit") is entirely consistent with the views of religion on spirit and God. Religions, such as Christianity and Buddhism, have their origin in animism, and religion has the same social function as idealism, the oppression of the lower classes by the dominant class.

Dialectical materialism, Li continues, has drawn on the tradition of materialism, but has overcome the formalistic elements of materialism to emphasis the dialectical theme. Its system sets out from the assumption of a material world which exists independently of thought, and which exists eternally in time and space. Central to this perspective is the concept of motion. The material world is the unity of the various concrete forms of the motion of matter. Thought, for Li, is also a form of motion, and is a special characteristic of the material world, a reflection of the development of the world in the brain of humankind within society.

The origins of development are not external, Li insists, but are to be found in internally generated motion (*ziwo yundong*).[19] The origin of this internally generated motion is contradiction; the struggle of opposites are mutually complementary and at the same time mutually incompatible. The transformation of a thing into its opposite is manifest through leaps, through qualitative change brought on by quantitative changes. Dialectical materialism is the only scientific worldview in that it reflects the truth of all the contradictions in contemporary society, it reflects all of the progress in contemporary science, and reflects the demands of the progressive social classes. It is a synthesis of the entire history of human knowledge.

Ontology: Matter and Motion

When Li turns his attention to the ontology of dialectical materialism,[20] he poses the basic question: what is matter? In response, he refers to the fact that humans daily come into contact with the natural world in countless ways; they experience many aspects of the material world. All of these aspects have a universal and determining characteristic: they all exist independently of our consciousness and are at the same time the source of our perceptions. The totality of these various material entities is referred to by dialectical materialism as matter. Thus, while matter is a philosophical concept, it is an objective reality which exists beyond thought and yet which is reflected in thought. Matter is a general concept which incorporates the most highly organised material categories, one of which is thought; thought is matter. The opposition of thought and matter is thus conditional, and only has significance when raised in the context of epistemology.[21]

Li then argues that the material concepts of philosophy represent absolute truth. However, the material concepts of natural science are frequently only relative truth; this is because the material concepts of natural science progress as the physical and chemical sciences progress, and can only be as correct as these are. This is is where the primary error of contemporary mechanistic materialists lies: they do not make the distinction between the concept of matter in philosophy and the concept of matter as this is used in natural science. They conflate the two and substitute the latter for the former, and thus recommend that natural science replace philosophy. The general significance of matter (which is the province of philosophy) must be distinguished from its particular significance (the province of natural science), and not conflated.

Li continues his exposition of the ontology of dialectical materialism by asserting that the primary form of the existence of matter is motion. Matter and motion are inseparable. It follows from this premise, he suggests, that there is no such thing as absolutely immobile or static matter. Metaphysical idealists of the past have talked of the natural world as though it were in a permanent state of rest and as if there consequently could be no development. Dialectical materialism, on the other hand, recognises immobility as one form of motion, a particular form; it is relative immobility, whereas the motion of matter is absolute. Dialectical materialism also recognises complex forms of motion, in contrast to mechanical materialism which reduces all motion to one simplified, mechanistic form.

Motion can also not be separated from time and space.[22] Time and space are themselves basic forms of the existence of matter, and without them there could be no matter in motion; these, like matter, exist independently of human consciousness. The objective reality of time and space is constantly developing and changing, and the manifestation of this as a reflection in human thought is relative and developmental. Idealists, such as the Kantians, Hegelians and Machists, advocate the view that time and space are merely concepts, and negate their objective character, a perspective which, Li makes clear, is quite erroneous.

The Object of Dialectical Materialism

Li then turns his attention[23] to the object of dialectical materialism. Dialectical materialism is first and foremost, he asserts, a worldview, a scientific worldview which studies the general principles of development of the world. The world is, however, divided into natural and social components, and the sciences which study the particular laws of development of these different components are the various natural and social sciences; their object is the disclosure and elaboration of these particular laws of development. The object of philosophy, on the other hand, is to discover the general principles, categories and laws of the world, and the general laws of development and interconnectedness of the phenomena of the world. Important to this task, Li suggests, is the unity of theory and practice. After all, the laws of nature and society revealed by their respective sciences are products of social practice. The verification of these laws comes through practice, as does the veracity of philosophy. Philosophy is not, however, just about explaining the world, but changing it; it must therefore be a unity of theory and practice.

The worldview which incorporates the results of the various sciences, Li informs us, is a dialectical materialist worldview. This worldview is first of all materialist in that the knowledge contained in the various sciences is a reflection of objective reality and verified through practice. It is, secondly, dialectical in that the nature of development has been revealed by the natural and social sciences to be dialectical in character; dialectics in thought is a reflection of objective dialectics. Dialectical materialism is a dialectical synthesis of the general and particular, of thought and reality, of theory and practice, and of empirical and theoretical science. The philosophy itself is dialectical insofar as it constitutes a developing and dynamic worldview.

There is an intimate connection, Li continues, between the dialectical materialist worldview and the development of science. Without the development of the various sciences to a high level, a scientific worldview could not have been established. By the same token, dialectical materialism is, as well as a worldview, a methodology; it provides a method for research of the various concrete phenomena through its incorporation of the objective world's general phenomena. Philosophy thus provides a general method for the various sciences; it incorporates general principles, categories and laws which the sciences can apply to the particular objects within their domain. However, dialectical materialism is not simply a method of knowledge, it is at the same time a method of practice; knowledge emerges through practice, is verified by practice and guides practice.

The object of dialectical materialism is thus the general laws of development of the world, namely the general laws of development of nature, society and human thought. Dialectical materialism is also, Li claims, an epistemology and a form of logic. He proceeds to elaborate the identity of dialectics, epistemology and logic through analysis of the errors of those who had attempted to separate them.[24] One of these was the dualist Kant, who attempted to separate philosophy into epistemology, logic and ontology; within epistemology he studied the origins and content of human thought separate from logic, in which he studied forms of thought, its laws of development and its concepts. Hegel recognised Kant's error by perceiving the identity of epistemology, logic and dialectics. However, Hegel's philosophy was idealist, and his advocation of the identity of these three was premised on idealist notions such as the logical development of the absolute spirit. The founders of dialectical materialism (that is, Marx and Engels) premised the identity of dialectics, epistemology and logic on a materialist transformation of Hegel's ideas. They perceived the history of thought as a reflection of material practice in the minds of humankind; the identity of dialectics, epistemology and logic results from the fact that they are all the result of this same history of thought. However, while Marx and Engels recognised this point, it was Lenin who developed it.

Lenin's era, according to Li, was the era of imperialism in which class struggle had become particularly acute.[25] The influence of bourgeoise philosophy, in the form of Machism and neo-Kantianism, permeated the labour movement and gave rise to revisionist tendencies. Surprisingly, within the ranks of dialectical materialists there were also those who suggested that dialectics is not an epistemology. An example is Deborin who, in his 1923 monograph *Marx and Hegel*, placed dialectics in opposition to epistemology.[26] The characteristics of the stage in philosophy opened up by Lenin are, for Li, the development of a dialectical materialist epistemology and Lenin's elaboration of the identity of dialectics, epistemology and logic. Lenin also emphasised that the law of the unity of opposites is the kernel of dialectics.[27] These ideas permeate Lenin's *Materialism and Empirio-Criticism* and his *Philosophical Notebooks*. He pointed out that the basic problem of philosophy, namely the problem of the relationship between thought and existence, was at the same time the fundamental problem of epistemology; the materialist explanation of this fundamental problem of philosophy thus became a materialist epistemology. Knowledge is a reflection of existence in thought, and the concepts in our brain are reflections of actually existing objects (although Li later qualifies this rather passive conception of reflection to provide it a dynamic quality in which practice becomes central). This reflection theory is the epistemology of materialism, an epistemology which is also dialectical; there is thus an identity between epistemology and dialectics.

Li then turns his attention to the concept of the unity and development of the world.[28] The development of the world, he argues, is an historical process, and it therefore follows that human knowledge of the world (of nature and society) is also an historical process; the science of dialectical materialism is constituted of the philosophical conclusions of the history of humankind's knowledge of nature and society. This gives rise to a unified world view which at the same time guides the natural and social sciences to reveal new dimensions of the world, and this in turn confirms the correctness of dialectical materialism while supplementing its content to provide a continually developing and unified world view. A unified world view is a unified view of the development of the material world. According to Li, dialectical materialism endorses the view that the world is a unified material entity, that consciousness is a small part of the material world and a product of the process of development of matter. In the material world, all things are in motion, developing, and at the same time interrelated. Li illustrates this by reference to the relationship between atoms to constitute molecules, and the movement of electrons within atoms which can be likened to a solar system in miniature; the conclusion is that the very basic building blocks of the material world evince the characteristics of motion and interrelatedness which are so evident in nature and society more generally.

The complexity of the material world is illustrated by Li through reference to the principles by which the solar system and the earth came into being. In both cases, their processes of emergence reveal change and development, reveal certain common patterns. Similarly, the emergence of life on earth can be explained from a materialist perspective by reference to the formation of complex molecules which constituted the basis of life; certain conditions of temperature and atmosphere altered these to bring about the earliest forms of life. Humankind is the highest expression of the process of evolution from these early life forms.

The Laws and Categories of Dialectical Materialism

The Law of the Unity of Opposites

Having established that dialectical materialism represents a philosophical science which encompasses knowledge of a developing, unified and interrelated material world, Li turns his attention to the various laws of dialectical materialism. This chapter in *Elements of Sociology* is very significant for it sheds light on the status and function he attributed to the laws of dialectical materialism, and it soon becomes clear that Li's exposition, based as it is firmly on the elaboration of the laws of dialectical materialism to be found in the Soviet texts on philosophy from the early 1930s, reflected the orthodox view of the preeminence of the law of the unity of opposites amongst the laws of dialectical materialism. This was a perspective which was to have a profound influence on the way in which Mao Zedong was to interpret dialectical materialism, and the stress on the law of the unity of opposites in Li's philosophical writings could only have served to reinforce the understanding Mao took from the Soviet philosophical texts by Mitin, and by Shirokov and Aizenberg, that the law of the unity of opposites is *the* fundamental law of dialectical materialism.[29]

Li commences his elaboration[30] of the unity and struggle of opposites by referring to the metaphysical conception of development. This is mistaken, he asserts, in its negation of the universality of motion and change in nature and society; it explains change and development by reference to expansion and contraction, or repetition. The dialectical materialist view of development, on the other hand, acknowledges that an essential character of the world is motion and change. Change is permanent and motion is constant, and the reasons for change and development of a thing are determined by the particular characteristics internal to that thing, and especially the contradictions which are inherent in all things. From the atom to the complex phenomena of social life to human thought, all things and phenomena contain internal contradictions. All of these things contain opposed elements which generate their contradictions; all things and phenomena are thus a unity of opposites.

Motion, too, is contradiction, Li continues. This can be seen in the association and dissociation of atoms in chemical motion, in the biological realm in the unity of life and death, and in the development of society through the contradiction between the forces and relations of production. These objective contradictions are in turn reflected in human consciousness to become subjective or conceptual dialectics. The contradictions of necessity and chance, absolute and relative, abstract and concrete, and general and particular, are reflections of objective contradictions in the material world. The cause of motion in a thing is its internal contradictions. Idealists explain the cause of motion through reference to ideas such as the absolute spirit; mechanists see the cause of motion as external to a thing. Both are profoundly mistaken, Li states, and while dialectical materialism does not negate the external context of change, it believes external contradictions must operate through internal contradictions to effect change.

Li then makes the judgment that the law of the unity of opposites is *the* fundamental law of development of the objective world and of human thought. The unity of opposites represents the interpermeation and identity of opposed entities, but the unity of opposites is conditional, temporary and relative, whereas the struggle of opposites is absolute; this is because the imperative for negation and rejection on the part of the contradictory entities is absolute, eternal and unconditional. The resolution of the struggle between opposites leads to a change in the contradictions within a thing, and thus to the emergence of new entities. Change takes the form of continuous change (that is, incremental quantitative change) and discontinuous change (that is, in the form of qualitative change, of leaps). At certain stages in development, the relationship between contradictions can become antagonistic, although Li is at pains to point out that contradictions are not invariably antagonistic (mechanists like Bukharin are charged by Li with wrongly conflating the concepts of contradiction and antagonism); antagonism emerges only at a particular stage in the development of the struggle between opposites, and the resolution of the struggle between antagonistic contradictions comes through qualitative change, through a leap in development, as a new entity emerges.

The object of dialectical materialism is thus, according to Li, the study of the concrete contradictions within nature, society and thought. The general principle of the law of the unity of opposites must be applied to disclose the many contradictions which exist in complex phenomena and processes (such as social classes); as the context or process is different, so will be its defining contradictions, and so too will be the method of their resolution.

The fundamental law of dialectics, Li repeats, is the law of the unity of opposites; it is the kernel of dialectics.[31] This fundamental law incorporates the other laws of dialectics — quantitative and qualitative change, the negation of the negation, causality, form and content, etc. — and is crucial to an understanding of all of these other laws; all of them can be explained by reference to the law of the unity of opposites. Li states that Marx and Engels took the concept of the unity of opposites and transformed it, placing it on a materialist foundation such that it could become the law of development of the objective world and its reflection in thought; this law is thus a thread which runs through the entire corpus of their works. Lenin, too, endorsed the notion that this law is the essence of dialectics, to the extent that all other laws of dialectics are a manifest form of this fundamental law.[32]

Li reminds the reader that, in applying this law, it must be remembered that the development of an object is determined by its essential (*benzhi*) contradiction, and that the other contradictions grow out of this. Analysis must grasp the role of this essential contradiction from start to finish in the process of development.

The Law of the Mutual Transformation of Quantity and Quality

The fundamental law of dialectical materialism is, therefore, the law of the unity of opposites. A manifest form of this law, Li informs us, is the law of the mutual transformation of quantity and quality.[33] On the basis of the development of the law of the unity of opposites, the form of change which becomes manifest is gradual quantitative change which ultimately results in qualitative change in the form of a leap; following this qualitative leap, change within the new phenomenon returns to a gradual quantitative form.

What is quality? Li responds that quality refers to different things, phenomena or processes. The multiplicity of different types of quality can be explained by reference to particular forms of the motion of matter; these different forms of motion have their own particular qualities, but are nevertheless related insofar as, in all types of motion, the process is from simple, low-level forms to complex, high-level forms. Whatever the object of our study, we must, according to Li, grasp the qualitative character of that object, namely the particular and determining form of motion, and only by doing so can we reveal its laws of development. The category of quality incorporates the interrelatedness of different qualities, and also the distinctions between them; one starts from simple distinctions and simple characteristics in order to arrive at an understanding of the specific qualities which characterise phenomena. For example, in general terms, change in society is a function of change in the mutual relations between humans. Different societies manifest this quality differently; the changing relationship between capitalists and labourers in a capitalist society is a particular manifest form of this general quality.

As well as the determining characteristic of quality in an entity, there is also the determining character of quantity. Examples provided by Li include size, speed of motion and range of temperature; these sorts of things must be known in order to understand the quantitative dimensions which characterise an entity. At first glance, he suggests, the quality and quantity of things may not appear related. Things with the same quality may be of different sizes; and the same quantity may appear in qualitatively different entities. For example, factories of a certain size in a capitalist state are capitalist enterprises; factories of the same size in a socialist state are socialist eneterprises; size is not significant in looking at the differences in qualitity between them. When coming to know a thing, we must first, according to Li, grasp the quality that determines the character of that thing, and only then be concerned with its quantitative characteristics; without a prior understanding of the qualitative character of a thing, knowledge of its quantitative dimensions would have no significance.

Li continues that when quantitative change reaches a certain limit it leads to qualitative change.[34] There is mutual interpermeation of quality and quantity of the opposites within a thing, and there emerges change from quantity to quality, and from quality to quantity; the result is that the thing changes from one form to another. The law of the mutual transformation of quantity and quality is thus a law which describes how new things emerge and develop; it describes the process whereby a leap occurs in the development of a thing to produce a new, qualitatively different thing. This law is thus, according to Li, one of the fundamental laws of methodology.

Li then proceeds to provide examples from the worlds of nature and society to illustrate the process whereby quantitative change culminates in a leap through which qualitatively new phenomena emerge. He stresses that this law is fundamental to an understanding of the stages in the development of a thing. As an illustration, he gives the example of the distinction between the stages in the development of capitalism of free competition and imperialism; these are qualitatively different stages and have to be analysed as such.

Li then turns his attention to a specific analysis of the theory of leaps.[35] A leap occurs as a result of a quantitative evolution, of change which is gradual and continuous; the leap itself is abrupt change, change which disrupts the continuous incremental evolution, and it is change which causes a definite qualitative change as a thing is transformed into its opposite. Evolution and leap thus become a unity of opposites, and actual development is a unity of evolution and leaps. Quality of whatever sort, Li continues, develops according to internal contradictions, and the resolution of those contradictions occurs through leaps. When a qualitative limit has been reached, when the tension between the contradictions has become most extreme, that is the point at which the resolution of the contradictions commences. It is this transformation through leaps which distinguishes dialectical materialism from a simple evolutionary view, one which perceives development as a simple process of increase or decrease in size, or of repetition. All things, according to the evolutionary view, develop through a slow, evolutionary pattern of development. This view underpins the approaches taken by reformism which believes that the new society can be achieved through reform and gradual change.

The Law of the Negation of the Negation

Li proceeds to an analysis of the law of the negation of the negation.[36] This law is, he suggests, a concrete manifestation of the law of the unity of opposites. The law of the mutual transformation of quantity and quality explains the process of change and development, and the reason for stages in this process. The law of the negation of the negation is a further concrete elaboration of the way the unity of opposites develops to bring about change in a purposeful manner.

All things contain contradictions, and in the process of development of these contradictions, the lower stage of development is a preparation for the negation of this stage — a preparation for a transformation to an opposed, new and higher stage. This higher stage overcomes — negates — the lower stage, yet retains the positive elements of the lower stage. This higher stage is in turn negated by the next higher stage in development, which in turn is itself negated as development proceeds. Consequently, the first stage (affirmation) is negated by the second stage (negation), and this second stage is in turn negated by the third stage (negation of the negation). The law which describes this process covers all forms of development, whether from the natural or social worlds.

Put simply, Li continues, dialectical negation involves a stage (that is, the stage of affirmation) in the process of development in which one aspect of the contradiction emerges to overcome the old elements which are characteristic of that stage. However, while these old elements are negated, the synthesis which is produced still retains elements of the old. The three stages can thus be referred to as affirmation, negation and negation of the negation, and it is the persistence of positive elements from the first stage of affirmation and the negation of negative elements which gives the process of development its purposeful character and ensures that development proceeds from simpler to more complex forms, from lower to higher. The whole process is driven by the existence of contradictions which permeate each stage in the process of development, and it is the resolution and struggle between the contradictions and their aspects which drives the process through stages in a purposeful direction, and which ensures that qualitatively new and more advanced things emerge.

Li then turns to a critique of those who have misinterpreted the law of the negation of the negation.[37] Although this law originated with Hegel, he approached it from an idealist perspective, believing that the three stages in thought — thesis, antithesis, synthesis — determined development of reality. Dialectical materialism inverted Hegel, liberating the notion of the three stages from its mystical form and placing it on a materialist basis. The mechanists, such as Bogdanov and Bukharin, are criticised by Li for conflating quantity and quality, perceiving development only in terms of quantitative change to which can be applied the laws of mechanics. Rather than perceiving change in terms of the negation of the negation involving a transformation of quality, the mechanists perceive development as moving through stages of equilibrium and disequilibrium to a new equilibrium. Formalists, such as Deborin, are also guilty of a similar error, and their position is more characteristic of a synthesis of Feuerbach and Hegel's views.

Essence and Phenomenon

The three laws discussed by Li — the laws of the unity of opposites, mutual transformation of quantity and quality and negation of the negation — are the three fundamental laws of dialectics. Of these three laws, the law of the unity of opposites is, Li reminds us, the most fundamental law, the kernel of dialectics; the other two are manifestations of this law in different forms. The law of the unity of opposites in fact incorporates these other two laws.

The law of the unity of opposites also incorporates many other categories such as essence and phenomenon, content and form, necessity and chance, and reality and possibility. All of these opposed categories are concrete forms of the law of the unity of opposites.

Li argues that, when science attempts to discover the laws of development of objective things, it confronts first of all their outer appearances.[38] The complexities of things are reduced to common categories through an increasing understanding of their essences, through a deeper and deeper analysis of their internal connections, of their uniformities and dissimilarities, and of their essential contradictions. However, essence is not immediately apparent when we attempt to know a thing; it is not directly manifest on the phenomenal surface of that thing. A contradiction thus exists between phenomenon and essence, and it is not sufficient in coming to know a thing to stop at the level of phenomenal appearances; it is necessary, rather, to move beyond this to discover its essence.

Li proceeds to compare this approach of dialectical materialism to the approach of the empiricists who believe that only phenomenal appearance is accessible to knowledge, and indeed all that is necessary; the concept of an "essence" is not accepted by empiricism. Subjective idealists are also influenced by empiricism, but in dissociating phenomenon from essence come to doubt the possibility of knowing reality and lapse into agnosticism. Kant, in advocating limiting the scope of knowledge to the realm of the phenomenal, was also guilty of agnosticism. Hegel, on the other hand, recognised the intimate connection and dependence of essence and phenomenon, but provided an idealist explanation of essence, for he believed both essence and phenomenon were incorporated in thought.

Li continues that, in contrast to these mistaken views, dialectical materialism establishes the dialectical relationship between essence and phenomenon, and attributes materialist content to the concept of essence. It recognises that both phenomenon and essence exist independently of our consciousness and yet can be reflected in thought as reflections of an objective reality. Phenomenon is directly reflected in perception; reflection of essence, on the other hand, can only be achieved through the application of thought. Phenomenon cannot exist apart from essence, and there is no essence apart from phenomenon; the essence of a phenomenon is its relatively fixed and stable internal dimensions (*cemian*). Li illustrates the distinction and connection between essence and phenomenon by reference to Marx's analysis of capitalism in *Capital*. Marx discovered that the essence which linked commodities — the obvious, universal and myriad phenomena of capitalism — was value, and that the basis of value was labour. It is thus the task, in the process of knowledge production, to move beyond phenomenon to grasp the underlying essence; in complex phenomena, this means moving from an understanding of first-order essences to grasp second-order essences.

Basis and Condition

Having explained the unity of opposites of essence and phenomenon, Li moves directly to an explanation of the dialectics of basis and condition, for they are related categories.[39] The category of basis and condition represents, like the other categories of dialectical materialism, a concrete form of the law of the unity of oposites.

Li explains that, of the interconnections or contradictions which are internal to a thing, one constitutes the starting point for the emergence, development and manifestation of the others. This is referred to by dialectical materialism as the basis, for it constitutes the determining factor for these other interconnections or contradictions. Li points to the many contradictions and interconnections within society; these include relations of production, political and legal relations, and other ideological relations. However, of these relations, the most fundamental are the relations of production, for these constitute the economic base on which resides the superstructure of politics and law and to which correspond definite forms of social consciousness. At a specific stage in the development of the relations of production (as a result of the contradiction between the forces and relations of production), they constitute the basis, and the elements of the superstructure are determined by it.

Between the basis and those things determined by the basis, there is both relative opposition and identity. Moreover, that which is determined by the basis can itself be transformed to constitute the basis for other contradictions. An example here is the political superstructure which, while determined by the relations of production, constitutes a concentrated expression of economics and thus becomes the basis for consciousness.[40]

In terms of the relationship between basis and condition, the development of the basis from embryonic to phenomenal form can only become manifest under definite conditions. The conditions are the most important factor in the development of the basis, but the basis is itself instrumental in creating those conditions. The development of a thing thus relies not only on the basis, but on the conditions created by the basis. Li gives the example of the commodification of labour power as an essential condition for capitalism, one which is generated by the contradiction between social production and private property (that is, within the relations of production, the basis).

Condition, Li continues, assumes two different forms, namely essential and non-essential. Whatever becomes the condition for the development of a thing is the essential condition; the rest are non-essential conditions. The latter can, in certain circumstances, change into the former, for there is a definite relation between them. For example, the centralised organisation of labour was not the essential condition prior to the first Soviet Five Year Plan; however, it became the essential condition as industrial development got underway.

Basis and condition also constitute an identity of opposites. In the process of development, basis transforms into condition, and condition transforms into basis. The example given by Li to illustrate this point is the transformation of the relations of production under feudalism; the opposition between landlord and peasant constituted the basis of feudal society, but with the emergence of the proletariat and bourgeoisie, it became merely a condition as capitalism supplanted feudalism.

Form and Content

Form and content, like basis and condition, comprise a category of dialectics which constitutes a concrete form of the law of the unity of opposites, one which can guide knowledge to a deeper understanding of the laws of development of the objective world.[41]

All forms, Li argues, are produced by their content and are incorporated in their content. For example, the forms of matter are motion, time and space. Within these general forms, all manner of concrete matter exists, each element having its own particular form. All sorts of mechanical, physical, chemical, biological and social phenomena possess their own particular content of matter in motion and motion which assumes different forms, hence the distinctions between them. Form and content are categories in opposition, and these are reflected in our consciousness. Any object has a definite content and form. Form normally has a definite content and ceases to exist if divorced from that content; form is created by content. Content is thus the basis of the unity between these two opposites.

Although, as Li explains, form is produced by content in the process of development, it does not remain static, but exercises a dynamic function in the development of content. Form constitutes both the internal and external structure of content, and it is thus in a position to facilitate or impede the development of content. Nevertheless, content has dominance over form, it is determinative. And in its perpetual forward development it eventually comes into conflict with form, and in the struggle which ensues, content overcomes the resistance of form, rejects it and adopts a new form appropriate to its own development. Li gives the famous example of the obstruction of the development of the forces of production by the relations of production; when this occurs, a struggle ensues between them in which the old relations of production are rejected in favour of new relations of production which are appropriate to the forces of production.

The category of form and content is closely related to the category of phenomenon and essence. Li suggests that, when we analyse any thing or process, we must expose the definite content of the essence within the definite form of the phenomenon. Content and form cannot be separated; to do so is to make the error of metaphysics and idealism. Kantianism and neo-Kantianism are formalist in that they divorce form and content and are concerned only with issues of form. While Deborin has been branded a formalist for wrongly stressing form over content, the mechanistic materialists perceive form as static and stable, rejecting the idea that form plays a dynamic role — one that is reactive on its content. Dialectical materialism, in contrast to these mistaken approaches, grasps the dialectical character of form and content.

Chance and Necessity

Knowledge of the categories of chance and necessity is, Li asserts, equally as important as knowledge of the dialectics of essence and phenomenon.[42] Commencing from phenomenon to move to a deeper understanding of essence is akin to the disclosure of necessity (or inevitability) from within chance; to achieve this disclosure we must, Li suggests, comprehend the dialectical connection between chance and necessity.

Li commences his explanation by reference to chance and necessity in the writings of Engels. In the *Dialectics of Nature*, Engels had pointed to two approaches to the problem of chance and necessity in the history of philosophy. The first suggests chance and necessity are two extremely opposed entities. A thing, relation or process can be either a result of chance or of necessity, but cannot be both; aspects of nature are a function of chance, while others are due to necessity. Engels rejected this view on the grounds that it suggests that those things that cannot be known by science and included amongst its laws are dismissed as a product of chance; but the function of science, Engels insisted, is to discover those things which we do not know; it is therefore faulty to address ourselves only to those things which demonstrate necessity. The second view dismisses chance and recognises only direct necessity; from this viewpoint, nature is a function of simple, direct necessity. The cause and result of each incident in nature, as in society, are a result of actual and definite necessity. This approach does not appreciate that chance can be explained by reference to necessity; rather it rejects chance. Hegel, to his credit, rejected these two viewpoints, and accepted the dialectical connection between chance and necessity, but he did so from an idealist perspective which saw chance and necessity as concepts and not as reality.

Dialectical materialism, according to Li, recognises that chance and necessity are objectively existing things. Actual chance and necessity are given to our perceptions, but perceptual knowledge cannot go beyond chance, and it requires the application of thought to disclose necessity, to discover objectively given necessity within chance. Necessity consists of those unavoidable factors which, complying with certain laws, occur in a process of development or a thing. Chance, on the other hand, is supplementary to necessity, and is constituted of those factors which are not unavoidable in the entire process of development, factors which are external or peripeheral to the process; chance is the externally manifest form of necessity, and it is necessity which represents the internal, central dimension of a thing or process. Li gives the example of the process whereby plants germinate through a definite process of time and conditions; this constitutes necessity. But the fate of individual plants, their germination rates and their growth to maturity are down to chance.

The definite order of the development of necessity occurs through a series of chances. For example, necessity within revolutionary war develops through countless chances and fortuitous circumstances; while these things give rise to necessity, they are also incorporated within the process of the development of necessity. Necessity is the pattern which emerges. In contrast, chance is the manifest form of necessity, it is one juncture or moment of necessity. In the objective world, chance exercises an extremely important function; it is the fabric of necessity, and when it develops it can transform into necessity. An example provided by Li is of primitive commodity exchange which had the characteristic of chance; however, with the development of the forces of production and the emergence of private property, this took the form of necessity.

Chance is a category in opposition to necessity, but it is not in opposition to the concept of causality. Chance too has its causes, and without cause chance could not exist; all chance phenomena have countless causes and conditions, not all of which can be known, although they do in fact objectively exist. Metaphysicians oppose causality and chance, rejecting those things which have no apparent cause as chance; the mechanists make a similar error, rejecting the catageory of chance. However, chance happenings do have their own causes. The Menshevik idealists, such as Deborin, make the opposite error; while recognising the existence of chance, they assert that chance is something determined by external conditions. But the truth is, Li suggests, that external and internal things are interconnected; something that is external to one process is internal to another. Chance can be described as external necessity, as an external manifestation of necessity, but chance also can emerge internally within a process, again as a manifest form of necessity.

Chance, Li concludes, is not an absolute thing, and in the investigation of complex, developing phenomena, one must not start from the assumption of an immediate, perfect and complete reflection of its laws; in terms of the implications for practice, chance must, under all conditions, be overcome in order to transform chance into necessity.

Laws and Causality

The final purpose of all scientific knowledge, Li argues, is to reveal the laws of development of the objects which science studies.[43] When we come to know a particular object, we base ourselves firstly on the law of the unity of opposites and, setting out from the category of quality and quantity, move progressively through the various concretised forms of the law of the unity of opposites: negation and subsequent negation, essence and phenomenon, basis and condition, form and content, chance and necessity, and so on. In so doing, we come to know all of the interconnections of the various phenomena of our object of study. Laws are reflections of the internal, objective tendencies of development of the interconnections of phenomena, and are a manifestation of the necessary relationships between two or more phenomena; laws are thus the reflection of the essence of the process of development of a thing. Law and essence are thus related concepts.

Laws, Li continues, cannot capture the limitless and extremely varied content of phenomena, but can only apprehend it generally, incompletely and approximately. Laws are thus, in comparison with concrete phenomena, a "weak" version of reality; they are limited in that they describe, on the one hand, phenomena at rest, while on the other hand attempting to achieve a deeper, ever more correct and complete reflection of the phenomena in motion. This is a contradiction in the concept of law which mirrors the contradiction between essence and phenomenon in knowledge. The concept of law, because of this internal contradiction, has an essence which is changeable and developmental; it becomes, like other concepts, a moment or stage in human understanding of the world. Only through many years of material production does humankind come to know the laws of the objective world, but these laws are acquired gradually, only relatively completely and correctly, and are approximations. Thus, although laws are reflections of phenomena at rest, such reflections are relative, not absolute. Laws, Li repeats, are developmental; they are historical, as are the phenomena they seek to describe.

Although all laws have this relative characteristic, laws can also have a universal dimension. Laws which reflect the perpetual motion of the development of matter are universal in character. An example here is dialectical materialism's law of the unity of opposites and its various concretised forms; this is a universal law, one that is absolute and eternally relevant. Because of the eternal and absolute motion of matter, the law of the unity of opposites which reflects this absolute character of motion in matter is a general law of development of the objective world, it is a law which is itself dialectical and historical. This is an absolute and objective truth of science and technology, and of the entire history of human thought. The absoluteness and relativeness of laws is a dialectical and not a metaphysical opposition, and these things can only be determined and verified by humankind through lengthy practice.

It is imperative, Li argues, to address the question of causality in the context of a discussion of dialectical materialism's perspective on law. All phenomena, he suggests, emerge from transformations in the phenomena which preceded them. All phenomena have their causes of emergence and are the effects of those causes. The relationship between cause and effect is what can be described as causality, and to explain causality, we must first of all explain interaction (*xianghu zuoyong*). The world is a composite process of the infinite motion of matter. A series of phenomena emerges as a result of the self-movement of matter, and there exists between these phenomena countless interconnections and interactions; these interactions are internal to the process. At the same time, there are interconnections and interactions with other processes; these are external. In our investigations of the objective world, we must not simply investigate interaction but, from the motion of matter and its interconnections, grasp the relationships of cause and effect, and express these in the form of laws. In the process of the motion of matter, there is motion which is dynamic and active, and there is motion which is a function of this dynamic and active motion. The active, dynamic motion can be regarded as the cause; motion which is initiated by this can be seen as an effect. These two sorts of motion constitute the concept of causality, and knowledge of this contributes to our understanding of the law-like nature of the object of investigation.

However, Li continues, the concept of causality can only ever be a relative, one-sided and incomplete reflection of the general interconnectedness of a process; our understanding of causality can thus only constitute a small part of interconnected, objective and general determinations. It is for this reason that causality is a stage in coming to know the law-like character of the general interconnections of real processes.

Cause and effect, founded on interaction, constitute a unity of opposites; on the basis of interaction, cause changes into effect, effect becomes cause, and the two transform into each other and change position. For example, in terms of social phenomena, the economic base is the determining cause of the political superstructure, but politics at the level of the superstructure reacts back on the economic base, and becomes one of the causes of change within the economic base. Although there is interaction between cause and effect, the basis (*jichu*) of this interaction must be identified; for example, when speaking of the interaction between politics and economics, it must be indicated that economics is the basis; and in the interaction between the relations of production and the forces of production, the forces of production are the basis.[44]

The concept of causality is, Li then argues, the foundation of scientific knowledge. When we investigate objects at the level of practice, we perceive their interaction, their causes, and under what conditions a particular form changes into another. The discovery of this relationship of causation allows us to predict the developmental tendencies of the object, and allows the possibility of practical action which will achieve its goals. If we know the conditions within which the motion of a particular object occurs, it is possible for practice to create those conditions and thus create the object. Human practice thus verifies the criteria of causality. This goal-directed practice of humankind, based on knowledge of causality, allows humans to transform the world; it is in itself an effect of human knowledge of causality in the objective world.

Possibility and Reality

Last among the categories and laws of dialectical materialism considered by Li is the category of possibility and reality.[45] This again is a concretised form of the law of the unity of opposites which reflects the deep and multifarious connections of the objective world. The category of reality reflects the entirety of interconnections of the objective world and reveals its law-like character. Reality incorporates essence and phenomenon, basis and condition, form and content, chance and necessity, and so on. Objective, concrete truth is constructed of all the dimensions of reality.

Li explains that possibility is also objective reality. Although the conditions of existence for an object might be present, that does not indicate the necessary existence of that object, and here we have possibility. There is an intimate connection between reality and necessity: reality emerges from necessity. But there are definite limits to possibility; a definite reality manifests a particular process of necessity, and its internal essence, basis and developmental tendencies determine the possibility of the emergence of its stages. Possibility is thus real possibility; it is not sufficient to talk only of necessity. It is important, however, to make a distinction between real possibility and abstract possibility. For example, utopianism endorsed the view that cooperatives could bring about socialism, and this is an example of abstract possibility; but under the conditions prevailing in Soviet Russia, cooperatives are the only possible road for the socialist transformation of the peasant economy. Abstract possibility can thus change into real possibility. A further example provided by Li is that of the first capitalist countries which, through social revolution, had the possibility of transforming into socialist states; this was real possibility. But the present very backward non-capitalist countries cannot directly achieve socialism via social revolution. The transformation of abstract possibility to real possibility is a function of concrete conditions and the general pattern of development; it is not a foregone conclusion that all abstract possibility will transform into real possibility.

Li continues that, when we investigate the transformation of possibility into reality, we must investigate a definite object and the definite conditions under which it will transform into a different form.

Because of the motion and change of the interconnections of object and condition, possibility can be transformed into reality. The significance of this is very great, according to Li. In the sphere of human history, the thing that facilitates the movement from possibility to reality is conscious, goal-oriented and planned social practice; at the political level, this is a concentrated expression of the practice of social groups. All historical phenomena are the result of positive human activity, and human history is created by humankind itself. For example, the transformation of the possibility of socialism into a reality requires a series of conditions, particularly economic conditions; but these conditions on their own are not sufficient to bring about this change, and what is needed is intervention in the form of practice on the part of progressive social groups. These must understand the laws of development of contemporary society, know and select those real possibilities, actively shoulder the burden of their historical mission, formulate theory that will guide practice, build the appropriate organisations and concentrate their activities politically; only in this way will this possibility be transformed into reality.

The real conditions under which possibility can become reality include both objective and subjective conditions. For example, economic conditions are objective conditions; the conscious, goal-oriented and planned practice of progressive social groups is the subjective condition. Objective circumstance is an amalgam of these objective conditions and the strength of the connections between these social groups. To succeed, objective circumstance must be analysed correctly, a correct estimation made of the subjective conditions, and attention paid to the relationship of each part to the whole in the entire process of development. In sum, Li concludes, social practice is an important factor in the transformation of possibility into reality, and to ignore it is to adopt the fatalism of the mechanists who do not understand the various conditions of possibility, or the appropriate unity of subjective conditions and objective circumstance; they consider the transformation of possibility into reality to be a necessary process, something dictated by nature, not needing particular conditions or the efforts of human beings.

Elements of Sociology and Intertextual Congruence

Li thus completes this section on the laws and categories of dialectical materialism with a reassertion of the dynamic and central role of human practice in the process of social change. This is a theme which he elaborates in considerable detail in the following section on the epistemology and logic of dialectical materialism, and we will turn, in the next chapter, to a summary and analysis of Li Da's explication.

Before doing so, however, it is important to return briefly to the important point that the explanation articulated by Li drew heavily on the discourse of dialectical materialism as this appeared in a number of key Soviet texts on philosophy. Virtually every section of Li's book summarised thus far mirrors a section in these Soviet texts, even to the extent of employing the same title. Comparative references have been supplied, in the footnotes to this chapter, to the relevant sections of these Soviet texts, and these make it abundantly clear that there is considerable textual overlap between Li's book and the Soviet sources he employed in writing it, and between the Soviet texts themselves. All of the texts examined contain sections on the history of dialectics and materialism in Western philosophical thought, although the explication contained in *Outline of New Philosophy* by Mitin is the closest in structure and content to that contained in *Elements of Sociology*. Each of the texts also contains detailed consideration of the laws and categories of dialectical materialism, and the form of their elaboration is very similar in each case. Indeed, it is difficult — if not impossible — to identify any significant disparity between these texts, whether in terms of the structure of presentation, the mode of language and explication employed, or the philosophical content.[46]

This high degree of textual congruence underscores the enormously important influence that the contemporary Soviet interpretation of dialectical materialism had on Li Da in the writing of *Elements of Sociology*, and also on Mao Zedong in the compilation of his own *Lecture Notes on Dialectical Materialism*. More generally, this tells us something of great significance in terms of the genealogy of the philosophical dimension of Marxism in China. Philosophers and theorists like Li Da and Ai Siqi, who constituted the first wave of Chinese Marxist philosophers and who were instrumental in the process of the interpretation and dissemination of Marxist philosophy in China, derived their understanding of dialectical materialism largely from Soviet sources. Not only were these philosophers prepared to defer to and accept the orthodoxy claimed so aggressively by these Soviet texts, they virtually reproduced the mode of discourse contained in them. The emergence of a new orthodoxy in Soviet philosophical circles after 1931, its largely uncritical dissemination throughout the Chinese revolutionary movement by philosophers like Li Da during the 1930s, and Mao's endorsement of this reading of Marxist philosophy through the publication of his own writings on dialectical materialism were thus to have a profound and lasting influence on the structure and content of the philosophical dimension of Marxism in China. And while this is but one dimension of Marxism in China, the extent of its orthodoxy, as judged by the standards of international communism of the 1930s, calls into question the view that Marxism in China is to be viewed largely as an Oriental, idiosyncratic and distant cousin of mainstream (that is, European and Soviet) Marxism. The textual evidence, as we have seen, suggests otherwise.

Notes

1. Meissner, for example, vitually ignores Li Da. See *Philosophy and Politics in China: The Controversy over Dialectical Materialism* in the 1930s (London: Hurst and Company, 1990).
2. An example is Schram's throw-away line regarding the "extraordinary low level" of the Soviet theoretical writings of the 1930s: *The Political Thought of Mao Tse-tung* (Harmondsworth: Penguin, 1969, rev. edn), p. 88. For a detailed and sympathetic reconstruction of dialectical materialism, see Loren R. Graham, *Science and Philosophy in the Soviet Union* (New York: Alfred A. Knopf, 1972), esp. Chapter 2.
3. See in particular Werner Meissner, *Philosophy and Politics in China*.
4. This is particularly the case with the treatment of epistemology to be found in *Outline of New Philosophy*, see pp. 341–420.
5. *Li Da wenji* (Beijing: Renmin chubanshe, 1981), Vol. II, p. 9.
6. Ibid., p. 17. We have noted in the previous chapter the interest Mao took in this section of *Elements of Sociology*, writing substantial annotations on such Greek philosophers as Thales, Democrites, Heraclites, Plato and Socrates. In turn, we can see that Li Da was able to derive information on Greek philosophy from a dialectical materialist standpoint from the Soviet philosophical texts of the early 1930s. In particular, *Outline of New Philosophy*, by Mitin et al. contains a section on the dialectical and materialist themes in ancient Greek philosophy which covers virtually all of the material referred to by Li. See *Xin zhexue dagang* (Outline of New Philosophy) (Beiping: Dushu shenghuo chubanshe, 1936), pp. 1–26.
7. *Elements of Sociology*, p. 37.
8. Ibid., p. 38.
9. Ibid., pp. 40–41. Sections on Kant and Hegel, written from exactly the same perspective, appear in all of the Soviet texts on philosophy. See Mitin, *Outline of New Philosophy*, pp. 70–108; M.B. Mitin (ed.), *Dialectical and Historical Materialism* (n.p.: Shangwu yinshuguan, 1936), pp. 90–154; and Shirokov and Aizenberg, *A Course on Dialectical Materialism* (Shanghai: Bigengtang, 1932), pp. 120–65.
10. *Elements of Sociology*, pp. 48–54.
11. Ibid., p. 57.
12. Ibid., p. 60.
13. Ibid., p. 61.
14. Ibid., p. 62.
15. Ibid., p. 68.
16. Ibid., pp. 70–76.

17. The view that the basic problem of philosophy is the relationship between matter and spirit, and that there exist only the two philosophical camps of idealism and materialism, is propounded in the Soviet texts, and also by Mao in his *Lecture Notes on Dialectical Materialism*. See Mitin, *Outline of New Philosophy*, pp. 183–89; Mitin (ed.), *Dialectical and Historical Materialism*, pp. 47–60; Shirokov and Aizenberg, *A Course on Dialectical Materialism*, pp. 48–75; Nick Knight (ed.), *Mao Zedong on Dialectical Materialism: Writings on Philosophy, 1937* (Armonk, New York: M.E. Sharpe, 1990), pp. 86–87.

18. *Elements of Sociology*, pp. 76–83.

19. Ibid., p. 83.

20. Ibid., pp. 84–90.

21. Ibid., p. 85. Cf. Knight (ed.), *Mao Zedong on Dialectical Materialism*, pp. 101–10; Mitin, *Outline of New Philosophy*, pp. 201–14; Mitin (ed.), *Dialectical and Historical Materialism*, pp. 160–71.

22. Cf. Knight (ed.), *Mao Zedong on Dialectical Materialism*, pp. 110–12; Mitin, *Outline of New Philosophy*, pp. 201–14.

23. *Elements of Sociology*, pp. 90–97. Cf. Knight (ed.), *Mao Zedong on Dialectical Materialism*, pp. 96–101; Mitin, *Outline of New Philosophy*, pp. 190–200.

24. *Elements of Sociology*, pp. 97–105.

25. Cf. Knight (ed.), *Dialectical and Historical Materialism*, pp. 33–46, 472–531; also Mitin, *Outline of New Philosophy*, pp. 147–67; also Mitin (ed.), *Dialectical Materialism and Historical Materialism*, pp. 21–31.

26. *Elements of Sociology*, p. 98.

27. Ibid., p. 102.

28. Ibid., pp. 105–14.

29. Cf. Mitin, *Outline of New Philosophy*, pp., 231–45; also Shirokov and Aizenberg, *A Course on Dialectical Materialism*, pp 281–308; also Mitin (ed.), *Dialectical and Historical Materialism*, pp. 212–37; also Knight (ed.), *Mao Zedong on Dialectical Materialism*, p. 154.

30. *Elements of Sociology*, pp. 123–31.

31. Ibid., pp. 131–35. Cf. Knight (ed.), *Mao Zedong on Dialectical Materialism*, p. 154.

32. *Elements of Sociology*, p. 133.

33. Ibid., pp. 135–44. Cf. Mitin (ed.), *Dialectical and Historical Materialism*, pp. 238–45; also Shirokov and Aizenberg, *A Course on Dialectical Materialism*, pp. 271–76; Mitin, *Outline of New Philosophy*, pp. 246–59; Knight (ed.), *Mao Zedong on Dialectical Materialism*, pp. 123, 161.

34. *Elements of Sociology*, pp. 144–48.

35. Ibid., pp. 148–52.

36. Ibid., pp. 152–61. Cf. Mitin, *Outline of New Philosophy*, pp. 260–71; Shirokov and Aizenberg, *A Course on Dialectical Materialism*, pp. 321–48; Mitin (ed.), *Dialectical and Historical Materialism*, pp. 246–57; Knight (ed.), *Mao Zedong on Dialectical Materialism*, pp. 123, 160–61.

37. *Elements of Sociology*, pp. 161–63.

38. Ibid., pp. 163–72. Cf. Mitin (ed.), *Dialectical and Historical Materialism*, pp. 246–57; Shirokov and Aizenberg, *A Course on Dialectical Materialism*, pp. 349–64; Mitin, *Outline of New Philosophy*, pp. 260–71; Knight (ed.), *Mao Zedong on Dialectical Materialism*, p. 124.

39. *Elements of Sociology*, pp. 172–77. Cf. Mitin, *Outline of New Philosophy*, pp. 284–93; Shirokov and Aizenberg, *A Course on Dialectical Materialism*, pp. 433–39; Knight (ed.), *Mao Zedong on Dialectical Materialism*, p. 124.

40. Li derives the concept of politics as the "concentrated expression of economics" from Lenin. It also figures prominently in Mao's social philosophy during the Yan'an period. See Nick Knight, "'On Contradiction' and 'On New Democracy': Contrasting perspectives on causation and social change in the thought of Mao Zedong", *Bulletin of Concerned Asian Scholars*, Vol. 22, no. 2 (April–June 1990), pp. 18–34.

41. *Elements of Sociology*, pp. 177–83. Cf. Mitin (ed.), *Dialectical and Historical Materialism*, pp. 258–76; Shirokov and Aizenberg, *A Course on Dialectical Materialism*, 385–98; Mitin, *Outline of New Philosophy*, pp. 294–303; Knight (ed.), *Mao Zedong on Dialectical Materialism*, p. 124.

42. *Elements of Sociology*, pp. 183–91. Cf. Mitin, *Outline of New Philosophy*, pp. 304–13; Shirokov and Aizenberg, *A Course on Dialectical Materialism*, pp. 458–69; Mitin (ed.), *Dialectical and Historical Materialism*, pp. 299–305; Knight (ed.), *Mao Zedong on Dialectical Materialism*, p. 124.

43. *Elements of Sociology*, pp. 191–201. Cf. Mitin, *Outline of New Philosophy*, pp. 304–13; Mitin (ed.), *Dialectical and Historical Materialism*, pp. 277–98.

44. *Elements of Sociology*, p. 198.

45. Ibid., pp. 201–7. Cf. Mitin (ed.), *Dialectical and Historical Materialism*, pp. 306–15; Shirokov and Aizenberg, *A Course on Dialectical Materialism*, pp. 440–57; Mitin, *Outline of New Philosophy*, pp. 327–40; Knight (ed.), *Mao Zedong on Dialectical Materialism*, p. 124.

46. The repetitive character of Soviet philosophical writings from the 1930s is frequently commented on by Western analysts. See Eugene Kamenka, "Soviet Philosophy, 1917–67", in Alex Simirenko (ed.), *Social Thought in the Soviet Union* (Chicago: Quadrangle Books, 1969), p. 95; also Richard T. De George, *Patterns of Soviet Thought* (Ann Arbor: University of Michigan Press, 1966), pp. 107–8.

8

Elements of Sociology: Epistemology and Logic

Epistemology has constituted one of the core philosophical issues of Marxism in China, and there have been a number of heated debates, frequently spilling over into the political arena, about the nature of the knowledge process and the appropriate criteria for the evaluation of truth. In particular, the role of practice in the determination of truth has preoccupied Marxist philosophers in China, and was the subject of one of Mao Zedong's most influential essays on philosophy.[1] The genealogy of the concepts and categories employed in the epistemological writings of Marxism in China is thus of considerable interest. Li Da's *Elements of Sociology* is important in this context, for it reveals much about the source and nature of the epistemology of Marxist philosophy in China. Our contention, as in the previous chapter, is that orthodox Soviet philosophy of the early 1930s was to have a major impact on the interpretation of Marxist epistemology and logic by Marxist philosophers in China, and that their comprehension of Marxist philosophy was consequently quite orthodox as judged by this prevailing Soviet orthodoxy. A reading of Li Da's *Elements of Sociology* will demonstrate this point.

In this chapter, we look in some detail at Li Da's explication of epistemology and logic as this appears in Chapter 4 of *Elements of Sociology*. Comparisons with Soviet texts on philosophy and Mao's writings on dialectical materialism will be largely provided in the endnotes. It is evident from even a cursory examination of the Soviet texts on philosophy from the early 1930s that these were the primary source of Li Da's explication. In particular, there is considerable similarity between Mitin's *Xin zhexue dagang* (Outline of New Philosophy) and Li's *Elements of Sociology*, even to the extent of Li employing the same headings and sub-headings. Considerable intertextual congruence also exists between Li's book and Shirokov and Aizenberg's *Bianzhengfa weiwulun jiaocheng* (A Course on Dialectical

Materialism) and Mitin's *Bianzhengfaweiwulun yu lishiweiwulun* (Dialectical and Historical Materialism), texts heavily employed by Mao Zedong in the writing of his own essays on dialectical materialism. We will return to the issue of the sources and influence of *Elements of Sociology* at the end of this chapter, and consider again the significance of this volume for an understanding of the developmental trajectory of Marxism in China.

The Epistemology of Reflection Theory

Li Da commences his explication by reminding the reader that dialectics, logic and the epistemology of dialectical materialism constitute a unified philosophy.[2] When he turns his attention to the epistemological dimension of this unified philosophy,[3] he asserts that human knowledge is a process; it is a process of development moving from matter to perceptions and from perceptions to thought; it is a dialectical process which proceeds from practice and returns to practice. This process has, he suggests, its own particular laws of development, laws which dialectical materialism must elaborate. Only then will we be able to understand correctly the reflection of historical objects in logic, their internal connections and historical development.[4]

Epistemology is dialectics, according to Li, and the process of the motion of knowledge is a dialectical process. Although knowledge is a human reflection of objective things, this knowledge is not a simple, direct or complete reflection, but a process whereby abstractions, concepts and laws take form; however, these abstractions, concepts and laws are conditional approximations of the perpetual and developmental law-like character of the universal elements of nature. The self-motion of the process of knowledge reflects the self-motion of the objective world. The various moments (*qiji*) of the process of knowledge (perceptions, ideas, concepts, etc.) are originally reflections in thought of the moments in the objective world. The development of knowledge therefore reflects the development of the objective world. However, the bearers of knowledge are humans, humans who are both social and historical, and the knowledge that humans bear is the highest form of existence of the development of the material world. Knowledge can only emerge with the development of material production in history, and this means perceiving the human subject of cognition as more than a biological organism; the human subject is, rather, a being who, in certain stages of development, engages in labour and struggle. Dialectical materialism attempts to comprehend the unity of subject and object, of knowledge and existence, on the basis of an evaluation of the process of knowledge which is rooted in social and historical practice, and in particular the practice of labour.[5]

According to the reflection theory of dialectical materialism, Li continues,[6] consciousness is a reflection of the objective world in the human brain; in other words, consciousness is an image of objective reality. But how is consciousness created?

Li explains that the existence of the human nervous system is the premise of human consciousness, and that there is an indivisible relationship between the nervous system and human spiritual (that is, psychological) activities. Li then provides a detailed elaboration of the physiology of the nervous system and brain of the advanced primates, including humankind, the point of which is to demonstrate that consciousness within humans is anchored in — and indeed is itself — matter. This extends even to those with mental disorders, which are in actuality, according to Li, disorders of the nerves and brain. Consciousness can thus be perceived as the highest level form of matter, a product of the nervous system. Li argues, in line with Soviet theorists, that the levels and forms of consciousness exhibited by animals other than humans are appropriate to the level of development of their nervous systems; the more complex their nervous systems, the more capable they are of complex forms of thought. But is there no distinction between the consciousness of humankind and that of animals? Li responds that human consciousness has achieved a higher level than that of animals, and this is because the human brain is more highly developed. Also, the human nervous system has developed through countless years of social life; humans have thus developed a much more varied array of conditioned responses to the environment. Complex social arrangements have led to the development of language and abstract thought and concepts, and this has allowed humans the capacity to gain knowledge of objects and to create images of them. Language in particular has been most significant in the capacity of humans to reflect objects in consciousness.[7]

The consciousness of human beings is thus, for Li, a product of the process of development of the material world. Consciousness does not exist outside of matter; rather, consciousness depends on matter, and emerges from it. Consciousness is thus a particular form of matter, one which emerges with the development of language in social life, and following the development of material production.

Perception as the Source of Knowledge

Li then poses the question of the origin of knowledge.[8] He responds that the perception of objective reality reflected in the nervous system is, of the various phases and forms of the process of knowledge, the earliest phase and the earliest form. All human knowledge proceeds from perception; in setting out to investigate the process of knowledge, we must therefore first analyse perception. But how does perception emerge?

Li explains that the systems of perception and the nervous system are integrated. The various perceptions — sight, hearing, taste, smell and touch — are transmitted to the brain via the nervous system.[9] Consciousness of a particular object proceeds from the body's perception of the function of that object; and our consciousness has a recollection of that object, even when it is absent, for it is stored in the brain. It is experience which allows the accumulation of perception. The variegated nature of the external world and the variegated character of the nervous system, including the multifarious functions of the brain, create the multifarious nature of perception. The various aspects of external objects are interconnected, as are the external and internal elements of the body's nervous system; consequently, when an external object acts on the nerves, it causes a perception which reflects, internally and in an interconnected way, the external object.

All things in the world, Li reminds us, are developmental, and so too are human perceptions. The laws of development of perceptions are only a particular form of the general laws of development. The development of perceptions has an intimate relationship with social and historical practice. This is illustrated by the difference between the perception of humans and animals. Li contends that animals perceive such things as light and temperature in ways different to humans; human perceptions are, in general, of a higher order than those of animals, and this is because of the superior nervous system of humans. In the process of production, humans extend their control over nature, and also develop their own nervous systems. Li also points to the distinction between the nervous systems of primitive and modern humans. The former have little capacity to perceive distinctions of size and distance in external objects, whereas the latter have more complex nervous systems and hence perceptions; modern humans are also able to use machines and technology (such as thermometers and telescopes) to gain ever more precise perceptions of the external world. The distinction between primitive and modern humans is the result of social and historical production, for as this has developed, so too has the capacity of humans to perceive the complexity of reality in ever more complex ways. Concrete practice of humans in society determines the development of perceptions.[10]

Li reiterates that the starting point of knowledge is perception. When humans come into contact with the various dimensions of reality, these are reflected in the brain as perceptions. Perceptions allow us to understand the truth of objects in the external world. However, Li emphasises that we cannot infer from this that human perceptions are invariably correct; sometimes reality provides humans with impressions which are false, and thus perceptions are mistaken. An example is the perception that the sun is smaller than the earth, which is of course false.

For Li, the development of perceptions is a process. He states that although perceptions are images of the objective world, true reflections in the form of perceptions cannot be achieved completely, or entirely correctly, or unconditionally, or immediately; rather, our perceptions are approximations of true reflections of objective truth. Practice is the basis of the process of knowledge which commences with perceptions and finishes with thought. We come to know the unified laws of the objective world on the basis of perceptions, for perception is the raw material of thought, and it is thought which abstracts the laws of development of the objective world. Since ancient times, all science has proceeded from perceptions which are reflections of the external world; perception is the bridge by which humans come to know the external world.

Perceptions and Thought

From perception to thought is a process in the motion of the deepening of knowledge.[11] Li explains that human knowledge of the objective world must go through many different moments and stages, and between the stages of perception and thought exists a dialectical connection. In the relationship between perceptions and thought, perceptions are the first moment, the first stage; thought is the final moment, the highest stage in the process of knowledge. The distinction between the two is relative, and Li admits that there is no distinct boundary between them. Thought is based on perceptions; it emerges as the internal connections of the perceptions of the countless objects of external reality, and it expresses their essential form.

Li continues that the totality of objective things is necessarily reflected as perceptions, but such reflections are knowledge only at the level of the senses. It is therefore insufficient to rely on them in attempting to comprehend the law-like character, causality and mutual dependence of objective things; the sort of knowledge required here is logical knowledge, knowledge which is deeper and at a higher level than immediate sense perceptions. But perceptual and logical knowledge are mutually conditional: logical knowledge is a deepening of perceptual knowledge, for thought and perceptions mutually develop and enrich each other's content. The change from perceptual knowledge to thought and the preservation of perceptions in thought are, Li suggests, the key issues of the epistemology of dialectics. He responds to these key issues by suggesting that thought seeks out the interconnections amongst the multifarious perceptions, but it does not create them, and this ability to develop to the stage of thought is dependent on human practice.

Both thought and perceptions are reflections of objective reality in human consciousness: perception is a reflection at the stage of sense perceptions, whereas thought is a reflection at the stage of logic. At this point in his elaboration, Li distances dialectical materialism from the crude notion of a mirror reflection in which perception and thought are merely images planted in the brain of the passive human subject.[12] This, he says, is the incorrect view of mechanistic materialists. It must be remembered, he continues, that human beings are active subjects who through their practice change the world and themselves. The reflection that is achieved in the human mind is thus a dynamic reflection, and knowledge which results from it is a product of historical and social practice. The relationship between perceptions and thought, and the change from the former to the latter, are thus heavily dependent on this dynamic character of the human subject, one which has the capacity to create knowledge, to raise it to the higher level of logical knowledge. But this can only occur through the medium of social and historical practice; practice is the foundation for the deepening of knowledge. In the process of practice, humans observe constant repetition of phenomena, the elimination of one phenomenon and the emergence of another, and the synthesis of many objects in the process of constant material production. This is, according to Li, the basis for the movement of knowledge.

To illustrate this movement of knowledge, Li refers to the well-known example in which the proletariat moves from being a "class in itself" (a phase in which it appreciates only the superficial characteristics of capitalism — it knows it only perceptually) to being a "class for itself" (a phase in the movement of knowledge in which it sees and understands the various connections, contradictions, and regularities of capitalism).[13] In other words, the proletariat gains a deeper, logical knowledge of capitalism through its social practice, and in particular its struggles with the bourgeoisie.

Li then distances the epistemology of dialectical materialism from the various forms of empiricism which advocate the notion that knowledge derives primarily if not solely from the experience of perceptions. All of these viewpoints err, he suggests, in not recognising

Elements of Sociology: Epistemology and Logic

the dynamic role of the human subject who, through social practice, discerns repetitions and interconnections in the myriad perceptions, and from this transforms knowledge to a higher level, the level of logical knowledge. Reflection is not passive, Li repeats, but dynamic and active.[14]

Ideas and Concepts

Li then addresses the vital issue of the process of the movement of perceptions to thought[15] — that is, the movement from perceptions to concepts. He divides this process into two stages, the first being the movement from perceptions to ideas, ideas being an intermediate stage between perceptions and concepts.[16]

Ideas, for Li, are the earliest particular form of the generalisation of the perceptions of objects. Ideas are recollections; they are memories of the various dimensions, aspects and characteristics of an object, brought into a unified form as ideas. Ideas move a considerable distance from the actual object of perception, but move closer to the essence of that object, its law-like behaviour and interconnections. The emergence of ideas is part of the dynamic process of knowledge production; ideas incorporate direct sense perceptions, and on the basis of multifarious past perceptions of an object, derive the essential character of the object, and reflect it more correctly and objectively. Ideas also give the object a distinct and complete form somewhat separate from sense perceptions; ideas can thus provide a deeper reflection of the external world. In this process, the generative (or creative) capacity of the human brain (*tounao de chuangzaoli*) and human practice are interconnected. Practice is the basis for the change from perception to ideas; in their practice, humans not only investigate the change in things, they investigate the direction of that change. Because of the repetition of phenomena, and the repeated production of phenomena in the process of practice, the generative capacity of the human brain develops, and the brain is able to generate ideas regarding the internal connections of things. There is a direct connection between the life of humanity and the construction of ideas of objects.

However, the movement of knowledge, Li asserts, does not cease at the stage of ideas. Ideas are merely the first stage in the generalisation of perceptions and are not able to grasp the developmental laws of the process of development of an object. The deeper reflection of this is achieved at the level of concepts, and this can only be achieved through the movement from the stage of ideas to the stage of concepts in the process of knowledge.[17]

Perceptions and ideas cannot arrive at the essence of objects, and in order to do this and to get at the interrelated internal laws of an object, the movement of knowledge must move beyond perceptions and ideas, and advance to the stage of thought. It is at the stage of thought, according to Li, that the essence of objects is discovered; thought generalises to the highest level from perceptions and ideas. Concepts are a moment in the movement of knowledge; they are a form of thought which reflects objective reality. But the concepts of dialectical materialism are different to those of formal logic. All things are constituted of a unity of opposites, but in formal logic this unity is explained as an abstract identity or mechanical collectivity; from this perspective, things are perceived as completely abstract, as static and without movement or connection. Formal logic's concepts are thus divorced from reality, and without content. In contrast, the concepts of dialectical materialism are a form of thought which reflects the content of the perpetual development of the real world. Dialectical abstractions are able to reflect objective reality comparatively deeply, truly and completely; they are thus a unity of opposites of subjective and objective, and of thought and existence.

All things of the objective world are connected and in motion. Consequently, when we come to know any object, Li suggests, we must study every dimension of it, study it in all its connections — that is, we must grasp the object's various internal aspects and the totality of its complex relationships with external aspects. We must also grasp the process of development of the object, and then come to know its laws of development. Interconnectedness and motion are thus essential in the reflection of objective things as concepts.

Li explains that any concept is in motion and develops as a result of the law of the unity of opposites, and that the perpetual process of the emergence and resolution of contradictions is essential to an explanation of how knowledge of objective reality is achieved. The motive force for the movement of human thought is internal contradictions, the struggle of opposites. Concepts and categories are themselves in opposition. Consequently, there emerges in the movement of thought the following interpermeating opposites: phenomenon and essence, form and content, chance and necessity, possibility and reality, cause and result and so on. And in the motion of these categories is to be discovered their laws of development. The concepts of dialectics are concrete and are constructed through analysis of specific differences and the abstraction of what is universal; indeed, the specific and the universal both exist objectively, and there cannot be one without the other. Concepts reflect the universal which is made up of the various dimensions of the specific, but this universal is itself concrete for it incorporates the rich content of what is universal in the specific or particular.

Concrete objects emerge in our perceptions as a totality of limitless and complex dimensions and relationships. It is only through the exercise of our analytical capacity, Li argues, that we can abstract from these dimensions and relationships the most simple and essential determination (that is, the universal), and only then can we understand the object in its entirety. In this transformation from the specific to the universal, chance becomes necessity, and phenomenon becomes essence. But it is not possible for humans to know concrete things in their absolute entirety; the movement of knowledge must be dialectical and continual, so that knowledge becomes progressively deeper and develops, and does so in line with reality. In concrete concepts, therefore, the particular and the universal permeate each other to achieve identity. Although when coming to know an object we must on the one hand perceive its universality, we must on the other grasp the particularity of the various stages in the process of development of that object. Only if we have knowledge of the dialectical relationship between the universal and the particular will we have concrete knowledge, and only then will we achieve concrete truth.

Li again emphasises that practice is the basis of knowledge, and that knowledge is a reflection of the unity of objective reality, but this reflection is a positive, dynamic reflection. In the process of practice, Li suggests, humankind comes into contact on countless occasions with things in the external world, and gains impressions and perceptions of them which accumulate in the brain. Because of the generative function of the brain, logical order is created out of these perceptions and impressions. The generative capacity of the brain universalises perceptions to create ideas, and universalises ideas to create concepts. But this is a developmental process, one which moves gradually from lower to higher levels; the development of human knowledge is thus manifested in logical concepts and categories. Dialectical materialism explains the development and interconnection of concepts by reference to the development and interconnection of the objective world; it perceives concepts developing in line with the laws of development of reality. The movement of concepts is thus a reflection of the motion of objective things; it is a reflection of the motion of the objective world and human practice, and a reflection of the unity of opposites of subjective and objective, of thought and existence. This reflection is itself a developmental process.

However, Li cautions that the laws of motion and interconnectedness of objective things cannot be reflected in concepts immediately, completely, correctly or unconditionally; as in the process whereby relative truth becomes absolute truth, the reflection of concepts moves from a lower to a higher stage to achieve ultimately a complete reflection. Consequently, the laws of development, whereby concepts reflect the objective world, are conditional, relative and approximate. In their practice, humans continually reveal new contradictions and new interconnections between the objective world and subjective ideas; from the rich perceptions and ideas which emerge from this, richer and deeper concepts are created through the application of logic, consequently moving a step closer to the reflection of the laws of development of the objective world. These new contradictions and interconnections are thus reflected to become the new contradictions and interconnections in concepts, and this pushes forward the motion and development of concepts.

Judgment

Having considered concepts within dialectical materialism, Li argues that it is necessary (in terms of the sequence of logic) to move to a discussion of judgment (*panduan*) and inference (*tuili*), which are forms of thought.[18] Judgment and inference are, like concepts, reflections in thought of the general laws of the development of the objective world and human knowledge. Judgment and inference are forms of the movement of thought, forms of the movement of concepts.

Li first turns his attention to judgment. He quotes Engels as arguing that the development of forms of judgment in logic is the result of the historical development of human knowledge of nature. According to Li, the basic characteristics of a theory of judgment premised on dialectical materialism are as follows. First, correct judgment is a form of reflection of the interconnections of the laws of objective reality. Second, judgment must be oriented towards the content rather than the form of the object under investigation. Third, the classification of forms of judgment is dependent on the classification of forms of concepts; judgments are interrelated, and higher level forms of judgment develop on the basis of lower level forms of judgment. Judgment, like concepts, must incorporate the individual instance, the particular, and the universal. Fourth, judgment is a form of the motion of thought — it is motion and is based on the law of the unity of opposites. Judgment is the determiner of concepts, and the existence of concepts must be founded on judgment; a judgment is the connection of two opposed concepts, which is a unity of opposites. Judgment consists of two moments, the first of which identifies the object of the judgment, the second of which designates the category within which the object should be placed; both are reliant on each other, and there is an identity between them. There is also a contradiction between the particular and the universal, and it is this contradiction which is the source of the motion of judgment, moving from the individual case to the more general and finally to the universal. Fifth, the motion of judgment is linked to the development of human practice and science. For a judgment to disclose a concept's internal moments, inner connections and relationships, there must be definite scientific knowledge and human practice as the premise. Previous knowledge is essential; without it there can be no new knowledge and judgments cannot be made. Similarly, if humans do not come into contact with an object through practice, the perceptions and experience necessary to create knowledge are absent.

Inference

When Li turns his attention to inference, he argues that it constitutes the highest form of the motion of thought; for just as judgment is a development of concept, inference is a development of judgment.[19] Inference is thus a unity of concept and judgment.

Li suggests that, while the valuable kernel of Hegel's theory of inference can be accepted, dialectical materialism rejects its idealism which perceives inference (or concept) as creating its object. In contrast, Marxism's philosophy of dialectical materialism places inference on a material basis. First, dialectical materialism perceives inference, like judgment and concept, as a reflection of the interconnected laws of the objective world; inference is, however, an even more profound reflection than judgment and concept, and at a higher level. Second, from a dialectical materialist perspective, the nub of the theory of inference is the reflection of content in the form of inference; only if inference correctly utilises induction and deduction does it conform to the principles of dialectical materialism and provide a correct reflection of content. Third, the highest form of inference is necessary inference; this is a reflection, in the form of thought, of the necessary motion, tendencies, relationships and connections in the development of the internal essence and self-motion of objective things. The process of inference must reflect the conclusion of this process of development, not only its present connections, but also its future developmental tendencies. Only conclusions derived in this way constitute concrete truth. Fourth, from a dialectical perspective, necessary inference establishes the dialectical relationship between the particular (or individual) and the universal; it reflects the motion from individual things to those which are universal, and draws out the general tendencies and laws of motion from the mass of concrete individual things. In this can be seen the employment of inductive inference; although induction allows scientific conclusions and predictions, inference must also employ deduction (from the universal to the particular) in analysing new phenomena. Fifth, inference sets out from practice and returns to practice. The experience accumulated by humans through the practice of social production constitutes the basis of inference; the truth of the conclusions of inference must be verified through practice and move to practice.

Analysis and Synthesis, Induction and Deduction

Li continues that the construction of concepts, and the making of judgments and inferences, necessarily follows the unified process of analysis and synthesis, namely the process of the movement from perceptual to logical knowledge.[20] Humans firstly analyse ideas, Li suggests, at the level of perception and abstract from them the simplest determinative essence; this abstraction is a materialist abstraction, but it is also an analytical abstraction. The essence of analysis is to reduce things to their simplest element (as in commodity and commodity exchange in the case of Marx's *Capital*). The task of analysis is to discover the universal in the individual instance, and in phenomena discover essence and law.

However, scientific knowledge does not cease at this stage, according to Li, but must recreate the object in thought. To do this it must move from the simplest determinations and relationships to complex determinations and relationships. Synthesis applied to the laws of development of the content of the simplest relationships arrives at a rich totality of multifarious determinations and relationships. In *Capital*, Marx set out from commodity relationships, the simplest form of relationship, and, through synthesis, was able to reveal the laws of emergence and development of contemporary society and its various contradictions. There is a dialectical unity between analysis and synthesis; analysis is the premise for synthesis, and synthesis guides analysis.

Li proceeds to argue that induction and deduction are, from a dialectical materialist point of view, an individisible unity; inductive logic (from particular to universal) and deductive logic (from universal to particular) are not separate, as formal logic claims.[21] Inductive logic cannot explain or comprehend change and development, and its conclusions are partial, unresolved and neither necessary nor universal. Deductive logic, on the other hand, draws conclusions from general premises. The three stages of formal logic are based on deduction; they are premised on axioms and fundamental theorems. These are often the result of countless years of the social practice of humanity, and so deductive inference is often correct; premises which are not verified through practice are, however, subjective and lead to incorrect conclusions. But major premises of deduction (such as "all humans must die") are themselves derived through inductive inference, and so induction and deduction cannot be separated. Dialectical materialism perceives induction and deduction as both being inferences, but the two are not separate methods; they are dialectical moments, a unity within dialectics.

Li again reiterates the point that human knowledge emerges from practice; humans are a part of the material world, and through their struggle to change nature they change themselves. Humans establish a definite relationship between themselves and nature, one in which they know the distinctions and relationships between themselves and nature; at the same time, the various relationships of the natural world continually appear in human perceptions and ideas. Consequently, humans are able to know the laws of development of the natural world, and to actively transform it. In the same way, through social practice, humans also come to understand the laws of development of society, and can therefore move to change society in a positive way. In social practice, the development and motion of the relationships of the objective world ceaselessly act on humans, and are accumulated in perceptions and ideas to become the raw material of thought; in the same way, thought has a dynamic and positive relationship with the objective world. In the abstract process of thought, humans analyse and at the same time synthesise the direct and concrete; in the unified process of analysis and synthesis, the motion of the relationship between the concepts we employ reflects the process of development of the objective world. That which impels the motion of concepts is internal contradiction (such as those between phenomenon and essence, individuality and universality, form and content and so on), but these oppositions are dialectical and interpermeating. Consequently, within the process of thought, the change from phenomenon to essence, form to content, and so on, reflects the reality of the development of the objective world, and arrives at knowledge at the level of synthesis. Thought must then move again to practice.

It is only practice, Li reaffirms, which can verify the knowledge of the laws of development of the history of the objective world; it is only practice which can grasp the concreteness of historical objects. But practice and knowledge are an indivisible unity. Practice is the basis of knowledge; knowledge is the impetus behind practice. Practice verifies the truth of knowledge and actively changes the objective world.

According to Li, therefore, knowledge of the objective world adopts the following sequence: practice —> direct concrete —> abstract thought —> intermediate concrete —> practice. This develops through a cyclical form of motion, a dialectical form of development. Knowledge develops as the objective world develops and along with social practice. New contradictions, relationships and dimensions are constantly revealed in the process of the history of social practice, and these impinge on human consciousness to create new contradictions between objective and subjective this impels new movement in thought, pushing it to a higher stage in which thought grasps the objective world more fully, profoundly and concretely; at the same time, social practice actively and dynamically changes the world. This cyclical motion of thought is thus a developmental process from relative to absolute truth.

Critique of Formal Logic

There are, according to Li, two approaches to the methodology of thought:[22] formal logic and dialectical logic.[23] He argues that all metaphysicians and idealists have employed formal logic, venerating it as a scientific approach for the methodology of thought. It is, they claim, a tool which is applicable in any era, any country and for all people; it can also supposedly be applied to any science, any problem or any happening.

Formal logic, Li explains, recognises three basic laws of thought — the laws of identity, contradiction and excluded middle — and perceives these three laws to be the basis of the construction of concepts and the making of judgments and inferences. Without these laws, formal logic claims, human thought would be entirely impossible. The law of identity in formal logic has the formula "A is A" or "A is equivalent to A". In other words, a thing or concept has identity with itself or an equivalent thing or concept. This makes for a static view, according to Li, one which does not allow for development or change. This law expresses an abstract identity, one which excludes or rejects all identities which are different. The second law of formal logic, that of contradiction, has the formula "A is not not-A". This is another manifestation of the law of identity, but expressed in negative form. This law only expresses abstract difference, Li suggests, for formal logic cannot know identity or difference on the basis of the unity of identity and difference; it cannot perceive the identity between different things, it cannot perceive the moment of negation in affirmation and the moment of affirmation in negation, and therefore does not allow that things can at the same time be both affirmation and negation. The third law of formal logic is that of excluded middle. Its formula is "A is B or is not-B". According to this law, where there are two mutually opposed judgments, one must be the truth and the other must be incorrect. It does not allow the possibility of a third judgment — for example, in mathematics, the debate about whether a line is or is not straight should allow the possibility that both views are correct. The law of excluded middle expresses abstract opposition, Li charges, and rejects opposition based on the unity of opposites; however, all things in the objective world are a unity of opposites. Each aspect of an opposition constitutes the premise for its opposite, and in fact demands the existence of that opposite; at the same time, each aspect is the negation of its opposite and demands that its opposite not exist. Therefore, each aspect affirms and negates its opposed aspect, and there is a relationship of both affirmation and negation between opposed aspects. The struggle between contradictory things can only be resolved through struggle; if we wish to understand the necessity of things, we must understand their internal relationships, understand their unity of opposites. The law of excluded middle, on the other hand, recognises only one aspect of the contradiction and negates the other, thus expressing only a formal opposition. In objective reality, however, abstract oppositions do not exist.

Li's critique of formal logic has four dimensions. First, formal logic is subjectivist; it does not penetrate into the content of things, and provides only a one-sided, superficial and abstract reflection of the relationships of a complete entity, providing instead laws of thought which perceive things as eternally unchanging. The truths it provides are thus abstract truths, truths which allow a consistency between truth and the laws of thought, but not between thought and the real world. Second, formal logic completely lacks a developmental perspective, seeing stasis and immobility as the basis for coming to know things; this view does not allow for the growth or extinction of things. Third, formal logic completely lacks a perspective on interconnectedness; things are themselves or not, and there are no relationships. It thus provides a one-sided and partial perspective, seeing things in isolation. Fourth, the principles of formal logic are isolated from social practice. Whether human thought is or is not in conformity with the objective world is a matter for social practice; formal logic's laws of thought are thus abstract constructions separate from the real world, formulae without content which cannot be verified through social practice.

Li continues that, in contrast to formal logic's approach to the construction of knowledge, the logic of dialectical materialism is premised on the materiality of the objective world, a world which is changing and developing as a result of contradictions internal to things and processes. The logic of dialectical materialism perceives the interconnectedness of things, and recognises that the identity which exists between things is conditional, temporary and relative. The laws it generates are not, like those of formal logic, abstract laws, but laws which reflect development and change in reality. Dialectical logic, unlike formal logic, can constitute the method of science.

Li then turns to a critique of Plekhanov's interpretation of the relationship between formal and dialectical logic. While Plekhanov had defended dialectical logic, he believed that it was appropriate to employ formal logic to study things which were immobile and at rest, and that dialectical logic should be employed to study things which were moving and changing. Li points out that immobility is merely a phase in the process of change and development of a thing; immobility is thus a temporary and relative condition, and this condition must also be observed from a dialectical perspective. Plekhanov's mistake lay in not understanding the law of the unity of opposites and in endorsing the validity of the abstract law of identity.

Another error identified by Li is the separation of theory and practice, perceiving theory as the domain of dialectical logic and practice the domain of formal logic. However, practice is the foundation for the development of knowledge; practice is therefore also the premise for knowledge arrived at through dialectics. Li concludes by suggesting (and here he follows Engels and Lenin) that formal logic does have a role to play. However, that role is limited to abstract forms of knowledge, such as mathematics.

Historical Materialism

The second half of *Elements of Sociology* returns to the theme, extensively canvassed in Li Da's earlier writings on historical materialism, of the relationship between the economic structure of society, the political and legal superstructures, and forms of consciousness and ideology. We will not tarry here, for the burden of what Li has to say on these issues is in large part a reiteration and expansion of his already established viewpoint that there exists a dialectical causal interaction between the various levels of the social totality, but that the economic structure or base retains overall dominance.[24] Li stresses that humans are "social animals" and that their lives are intimately connected with the forms of economic production which prevail in their society.[25] In societies characterised by hostile class formations, humans have no alternative but to belong to one or other of the classes, and their political activities and consciousness are inevitably a function of class. However, politics and consciousness are not merely passive social entities, mechanically created by society's economic structure; they are dynamic, and capable of exerting an influence on the economic structure. Li's explication stresses the interaction between base and superstructure, but at the same time emphasises the continuing causal dominance of economics:

As stated above, the economic structure is the base of society, and the political, legal superstructure and the ideological superstructure are established on this base and are determined by it. However, these two superstructures, while determined by the base, exert a definite reactive influence on the base. In the process of development of society, the political and legal superstructure and ideological superstructure are not only dependent (shoudong) social phenomena; both exert an influence, and indeed influence the development of the economic structure and consequently become dynamic social phenomena. This is the reactive influence of the superstructure on the base. However, the reactive influence of the superstructure on the base, when looked at from the perspective of origins and results, definitely does not exert the same influence as does the base on the superstructure. The possibility of a reactive influence of the superstructure on the base derives from the developmental force (fazhan liliang) which the superstructure derives from the base.[26]

For Li Da, therefore, politics could exert a significant influence on economic development, either positively or negatively. But this capacity to facilitate or hinder economic development derived from developments occurring within the economic base. The same was true of ideology. When ideology correctly reflected the economic structure and political superstructure, it could reveal their laws of development, thus allowing humans to transform economics and politics and thus facilitate social progress; in the same way, ideology which did not accurately reflect the laws of development of economics and politics could hinder social and economic progress. The task of the revolutionary science of historical materialism was, however, to perceive ideology in its social and economic context, and to make a distinction between "material change" and "ideological forms", for the latter had to be explained by reference to the contradictions of material life, and especially "the contradiction between society's forces and relations of production".[27]

Elements of Sociology and Marxism in China

Elements of Sociology stands as one of the classic works of Marxist philosophy in China. It traverses virtually all of the substantive problematic theoretical issues addressed by Marxist philosophers and theorists in Europe and the Soviet Union, and provides a solid theoretical foundation on which other Marxists in China, including Mao Zedong, could build. This contribution to the development of Marxism in China has been widely acknowledged in China, and Li Da is recognised as one of the pre-eminent Chinese Marxist intellectuals of the twentieth century. The very limited recognition received by Li Da and his *Elements of Sociology* in Western interpretations of Marxism in China reveals only too clearly the incomplete and selective nature of those interpretations. And this selectivity is not without implications, for a close analysis of the writings of Li Da can tell us much about the early influences on Marxist philosophy and theory in China. In particular, it demonstrates that Marxism in China had strong genealogical links with European and Soviet Marxism and was not, therefore, as aberrant and idiosyncratic as many Western interpretations would have us believe. It is evident, as I have suggested in the course of the the last three chapters, that the most significant influence on Li Da's *Elements of Sociology* was orthodox Soviet philosophy of the post-1931 period. This is not to say that Li Da was entirely dependent on Soviet philosophy for his understanding of Marxist philosophy. Indeed, we saw in Chapter 5 that Li had, prior to 1931, studied and translated the works of many Japanese, European and Russian Marxist theorists. Nevertheless, by Li's own testimony, the post-1931 Soviet texts on philosophy constituted the model after which *Elements of Sociology* was fashioned; and a comparison of the texts by Mitin, and by Shirokov and Aizenberg, with *Elements of Sociology* indicates just how powerful that influence was.

Elements of Sociology thus stands not only as a testimony to Li Da's stature as a Marxist theorist, but as evidence of the powerful and pervasive influence exercised by orthodoxy on his understanding of Marxism. The significance of this for the development of Marxism in China is great indeed. As we saw in Chapter 6, *Elements of Sociology* constituted one of the major texts to influence Mao Zedong's understanding of Marxist philosophy. The rendition of Marxist philosophy found in *Elements of Sociology* served to complement and reinforce the message Mao derived from the writings of Mitin, and Shirokov and Aizenberg, which Mao read and annotated so assiduously in 1936–37. Mao's endorsement of this interpretation of Marxist philosophy in his own writings on philosophy, and in particular "On Contradiction" and "On Practice", has meant that the influence of post-1931 Soviet philosophy on Marxism in China has been an enduring one. Indeed, for the most part, this interpretation of Marxist philosophy is still accepted in China as the correct and orthodox version. It is no coincidence that Li Da's *Elements of Sociology* has been accorded high praise by Party theorists in post-Mao China; for its explication of Marxist philosophy is still perceived as valid and accurate some sixty years after its composition.

The significance of *Elements of Sociology* to the development of Marxism in China is thus twofold. First, this massive tome on dialectical and historical materialism represented, as Mao himself pointed out, the first major text on Marxist philosophy to be written by a Chinese scholar. Its authorship by a Chinese lent it a cachet in China which the translations of foreign texts on Marxist philosophy could not hope to achieve. Second, while its author was Chinese and this fact did much to add legitimacy to the book and reinforce its popularity, Li Da's interpretation of Marxist philosophy was not, in itself, particularly Chinese. On the contrary, Li's purpose in writing *Elements of Sociology* was to bring to Chinese readers a comprehensive analysis of Marxist philosophy as this was represented in post-1931 Soviet philosophical discourse. In doing so, he contributed significantly to the dissemination in China of concepts and modes of thought characteristic of the form of Marxism which had achieved dominance in the international communist movement, and which had universal pretensions. *Elements of Sociology* thus represented a conduit through which ideas from beyond the Chinese context could pass into the parlance and thinking of Marxists in China. And while *Elements of Sociology* was not the only such medium for the transmission of Marxist ideas to Marxists in China, it was one of the most influential.

Li Da wrote *Elements of Sociology* in the early 1930s while not a member of the Chinese Communist Party. His continued commitment to the cause of the dissemination of Marxist theory in China remained unabated despite his departure from the Party which he had helped found. His status as an independent, non-Party Marxist intellectual gave him a degree of autonomy which he might otherwise not have enjoyed, and his most productive years were those spent outside the Party. By temperament, Li was ill-suited to meek obedience to authority which he perceived as mistaken. How then would he respond to the victory of the Chinese Communist Party in 1949 and his readmission to the Party? How would he react to the new orthodoxy — Mao Zedong Thought — and his role of explicating and disseminating this new orthodoxy? In the following two chapters, we will evaluate Li's post-1949 writings on philosophy and theory, paying particular attention to his philosophical and personal relationship with Mao Zedong. This relationship, for the most part a cordial one, had its darker side, for Li was more than a little dubious about the ideological direction China took in the late 1950s and early 1960s. Initially, however, he was the post-1949 regime's faithful servant, and his explications of Mao Zedong

Thought of the early 1950s did much to disseminate and popularise the ideology of China's new leader.

Notes

1. See Nick Knight (ed.), *Mao Zedong on Dialectical Materialism: Writings on Philosophy, 1937* (Armonk, New York: M.E. Sharpe, 1990), pp. 132–53; also *Selected Works of Mao Tse-tung* (Peking: FLP, 1965), Vol. I, pp. 295–309.
2. Li Da, *Elements of Sociology*, in *Li Da wenji* (Collected Writings of Li Da) (Beijing: Renmin chubanshe, 1981), Vol. II, p. 208; cf. M.B. Mitin, *Xin zhexue dagang* (Outline of New Philosophy) (n.p.: Dushu shenghuo chubanshe, 1936), pp. 341–43.
3. *Elements of Sociology*, pp. 208–11.
4. Cf. Shirokov and Aizenberg, *Bianzhengfa weiwulun jiaocheng* (A Course on Dialectical Materialism) (Shanghai: Bigengtang, 1932), p. 193.
5. The importance of conceiving of the process of knowledge production from a social perspective which stresses the practice of the human subject also appears in Shirokov and Aizenberg, *A Course on Dialectical Materialism*, pp. 191–203; also Mitin, *Bianzhengfaweiwulun yu lishiweiwulun* (Dialectical and historical materialism) (n.p.: Shangwu yinshuguan, 1936), pp. 195–206.
6. *Elements of Sociology*, pp. 211–23.
7. Cf. Mitin, *Dialectical and Historical Materialism*, pp. 172–86; also Mitin, *Outline of New Philosophy*, pp. 341–61.
8. *Elements of Sociology*, pp. 223–32.
9. Cf. Mitin, *Outline of New Philosophy*, pp. 347–48.
10. Cf. ibid., pp. 351–54.
11. *Elements of Sociology*, pp. 232–39.
12. Cf. Mitin, *Dialectical and Historical Materialism*, pp. 173–75.
13. Cf. ibid., p. 155–56.
14. It is very probable that Li Da drew much of his information for this entire section on perceptions from Mitin, *Outline of New Philosophy*, pp. 341–61; but cf. also Shirokov and Aizenberg, *A Course on Dialectical Materialism*, pp. 193–222. In this latter source, the practice of the human subject is particularly emphasised.
15. *Elements of Sociology*, pp. 239–49.
16. Cf. Mitin, *Outline of New Philosophy*, pp. 361–65.
17. On concepts in the epistemology of dialectical materialism, see Mitin, *Outline of New Philosophy*, pp. 365–73.
18. *Elements of Sociology*, pp. 249–55. On judgment and inference in the epistemology of dialectical materialism, see Mitin, *Outline of New Philosophy*, pp. 373–97.
19. *Elements of Sociology*, pp. 255–60.
20. Ibid., pp. 261–67. Cf. Mitin, *Outline of New Philosophy*, pp. 397–406.
21. Induction and deduction are discussed in Mitin, *Outline of New Philosophy*, pp. 406–13.

22. An editorial note explains that Li was not satisfied with this section on formal logic and revised it in 1961 in *Weiwubianzhengfa dagang* (Outline of Dialectical Materialism). For more on *Outline of Dialectical Materialism*, see Chapter 10.

23. *Elements of Sociology*, pp. 267–80. Cf. Mitin, *Outline of New Philosophy*, pp. 413–18. See also Knight (ed.), *Mao Zedong on Dialectical Materialism*, pp. 159–63 for Mao's critique of formal logic.

24. Li's views on this subject also appear in his *Jingjixue dagang* (Elements of Economic Theory) (Wuhan: Wuhan daxue chubanshe, 1985), first published in 1935. See especially Li Da's Preface.

25. *Elements of Sociology*, pp. 286–89.

26. Ibid., p. 292.

27. Ibid., pp. 292–93.

9

Li Da and Mao Zedong Thought

The period between the publication of the Shanghai edition of *Elements of Sociology* in 1937 and his readmittance to the Chinese Communist Party in December 1949 was the least productive in Li Da's otherwise long and highly productive career. After the relative stability of his years in Beiping, Li's life was overtaken by the turmoil and instability of the anti-Japanese War and the civil war which followed, and this was to have a significant impact on his ability to research and write.

Between 1937 and the end of 1938, Li held positions at Guangxi University and at the Zhongshan University in Guangdong, and in January 1939 he moved to Chongqing where, at the bidding of the Communist Party, he again lectured on dialectical materialism to Feng Yuxiang and his research centre. From the autumn of 1940 to July 1941, he re-assumed his position at Zhongshan University, but as a result of interference from the Guomindang educational authorities, he lost his job, and for the next six years he was without a university position, living mainly in his native Lingling county in Hunan province. In the spring of 1947, he gained a teaching position at Hunan University, but was given teaching duties in the university's law department. While he was less familiar with the subject of law than philosophy or economics, he threw himself into this new task with his characteristic enthusiasm and tenacity. The result was the publication in 1947 of his lectures on law under the title *Falixue dagang* (Elements of Jurisprudence).[1] This 250,000 character monograph analysed the essence and function of law from the perspective of historical materialism, and is uncompromisingly Marxist in its approach.[2]

With his readmittance to the Chinese Communist Party in December 1949, a new chapter opened in Li Da's life as a philosopher and theorist. Not only was he now an active participant in the political life of the new People's Republic of China, but the facilities necessary for the realisation of his immense potential as a theorist were now also available to him. Between 1950 and his death in 1966, a steady stream of articles, chapters, books, pamphlets, published lectures, newspaper and magazine columns, addresses and reports flowed from his pen. His writings from this post-Liberation period traverse a large variety of subjects, but as with his pre-1949 writings, focus primarily on philosophy, social science and the law.

Li's readmittance to the Party was also significant insofar as he was now regarded as one of the Party's senior intellectual figures, and an authority on the Party's theoretical and ideological system. He was once again *inside* the Party, with all that that implied for what could and could not be said and written. Before 1949, Li had been preoccupied with the elaboration of Marxist philosophy and theory and its dissemination within China; he had been particularly concerned that the interpretation of Marxism which reached the revolutionary movement was the correct, the orthodox version. We noted in a previous chapter the shift in Li's approach to dialectical materialism as a result of the shifting orthodoxy in the Soviet Union between 1929 and 1931, and his own *Elements of Sociology* contained a very comprehensive elaboration of the orthodoxy then current in Soviet philosophical circles. Moreover, many of his writings of the early 1920s had adopted a polemical tone in pursuit and defence of the orthodox Marxist interpretation of the materialist conception of history. But Li had not just propagated orthodoxy because it was orthodoxy, but because he held it to be true; where truth and orthodoxy intersected, Li had been relentless in its propagation. He had shown himself prepared, at great personal cost, to distance himself from an official line which he believed to be incorrect or anti-Marxist; his departure from the Party in 1923 is the obvious example. Li's relationship with orthodoxy was thus an ambiguous one. He was its faithful and relentless servant as long as he held it to be true, and in the past he had been prepared to face the chill winds of political disfavour rather than speak false.

But could Li's personal integrity survive his readmission to the Party in 1949 and the enormous power and authority wielded by the originator of China's new orthodoxy, Mao Zedong? It is clear that Li's ability to adopt an independent position shrank considerably in the 1950s and 1960s, and although he occasionally held strong dissenting views on theory and politics, he limited himself to an oral expression of these rather than committing them to paper. For example, his heated verbal disagreement with Mao over the Great Leap Forward finds no expression in his writings of that time; similarly, his adamant refusal to accept the new orthodoxy of Lin Biao in the early 1960s is not reflected in his writings. The changed climate of power after 1949 and Li's prominent position within its intellectual hierarchy thus created opportunity and challenge, as well as serious restrictions. The most significant challenge faced by Li was how to respond to the elaboration of Mao Zedong Thought. As we will see in the course of this and the next chapter, Li worked energetically to propagate the theoretical system of Mao Zedong Thought, but would demur in private from some of its more radical implications, particularly when these transgressed Li's understanding of the materialist conception of history.

Li Da, Mao Zedong and Mao Zedong Thought

Li's association with Mao Zedong[3] commenced at the time of the establishment of the Chinese Communist Party, though Li's reputation had reached Mao earlier through his articles and translations, particularly those in *The Communist*, and it is evident that Mao thought highly of Li as a theorist and educator (Li having been appointed the principal of the Party's school for girls [*pingmin nuxiao*] in 1921).[4] In 1922, Mao wrote to Li, inviting him to take up the position of principal at the Hunan Self-Study University, and to edit the university's journal, *New Age*. As Li's Chinese biographies recount, Li and Mao were then constantly in each other's company, discussing questions of Marxist theory and the Chinese revolution, and they formed a "militant friendship" (*zhandou de youyi*).[5] This early friendship between Li and Mao was to survive Li's break with the Party in 1923, and it is evident that Mao retained his respect for Li's qualities as a propagandist and theorist. In August 1936, in a letter to another Hunanese friend, Yi Lirong, Mao asked whether Yi had kept in contact with Li Da and his wife, Wang Huiwu. He also mentioned that he had read Li's translation (presumably of the Soviet text *A Course on Dialectical Materialism*) and expressed admiration for it; he also expressed the hope that Yi could maintain cordial relations with Li and his wife.[6] Following the publication of the Shanghai edition of *Elements of Sociology* in May 1937, Li sent a copy to Mao. As we observed in Chapter 6, Mao was highly impressed with this volume, reading and annotating it many times. He wrote to Li to congratulate him and to ask him to send ten more copies of the book to Yan'an.[7]

At the beginning of the Yan'an Period (1936–47), Mao's thought had not yet become the dominant ideology of the Chinese Communist Party as it would in the early to mid-1940s, particularly following the Seventh Party Congress in 1945. While Mao's leadership position was much more secure following his decisive victory at the Zunyi Conference in January 1935, his influence in matters of doctrine extended primarily to military tactics and questions of political strategy, and even here, Mao's views on such issues were certainly not beyond dispute. There was no cult of Mao or his thought, and he had not yet gained the reputation as philosopher which he would later acquire. Indeed, Mao undertook, in late 1936 and early 1937, a period of intensive study of dialectical materialism in order to broaden and deepen his understanding of this politically important and sensitive area of Marxism.[8] As we observed earlier, a major source of influence at this time were the post-1931 Soviet texts on philosophy translated by Chinese intellectuals like Li Da and Ai Siqi; moreover, the writings of these two Chinese intellectuals, also heavily influenced by contemporary Soviet philosophy, were themselves to become an integral part of the constellation of texts which Mao read and drew, either directly or indirectly, into his own essays and lectures on philosophy. Mao's philosophical writings of 1937 thus bear the unmistakable imprint of these Soviet sources and the Chinese texts inspired by them. Mao's "On Practice" and "On Contradiction" (July and August 1937), essays which were to become the cornerstone of Chinese Marxism after 1949, were thus the vehicle whereby the concepts, categories, laws and modes of thought characteristic of orthodox Soviet philosophy of the 1931–36 period, were drawn into mainstream Chinese Marxism. And while Mao may have developed certain of the ideas in the Soviet texts, and provided Chinese illustration of the abstract formulations of dialectical materialism, the consistency between his writings on Marxist philosophy and those of the Soviet philosophical texts is quite apparent.

This consistency was a major factor predisposing Li Da to expend considerable energy elaborating the content of Mao's "On Practice" and "On Contradiction" following their revision and official publication in the early 1950s. Li could undertake this task with good conscience, not just because Mao's philosophical essays were the new orthodoxy, but because they accorded with his own understanding of Marxist philosophy.

Li's explanatory notes for reading "On Practice" and "On Contradiction" were originally written and published in instalments in the journal *Xin Jianshe* (New Construction), but were later combined into two separate booklets, and in 1979 published as a single volume (of 342 pages).[9] Indeed, it was Mao himself who suggested to Li, in a letter of 27 March 1951, that he assemble his "Explanations" into "a single pamphlet so that it can be widely circulated".[10] It is clear from Mao's two letters to Li of March 1951 and September 1952 that Li had kept closely in touch with Mao regarding his explanatory notes, sending drafts to Mao for his comment. According to Chinese sources, Mao did make some fairly substantial suggestions, actually adding a paragraph of five lines to Li's elaboration of "On Practice".[11] The general tenor of Mao's response is, however, positive and congratulatory: "This explanation is excellent and will play a great role in disseminating materialism via popular language ... In the past, little has been done in disseminating dialectical materialism in popular language, and this is what the broad masses of working cadres and young students urgently need. I hope you will write more articles."[12]

Reading Mao Zedong's "On Practice"

The laudatory comments with which Li Da introduces his *"Shijianlun" jieshuo* (An Explanation of "On Practice") set the tone for his subsequent exegetical treatment of Mao's essay. "On Practice" is, he asserts:

> a development of the Marxist-Leninist theory of practice; it is the foundation of Mao Zedong Thought, and integrates basic principles of dialectical materialism with the concrete practice of the Chinese revolution. It is a theory of action for the Chinese revolution, and is the scientific summation of Mao Zedong's methodology of thought and work.
> "On Practice" particularly points out the two most outstanding characteristics of dialectical materialism, namely its class character and its practicality, and it makes clear that dialectical materialism is the philosophy of the proletarian revolution.[13]

"On Practice" makes it very clear, Li continues, that practice is the only criterion of truth. Li does not, however, delve too deeply into why it is that some people's practice seems to be correct and leads to success, whereas others' is incorrect and leads to failure. The problem, he suggests, is that there has not been a correct reflection of the laws of the external world in the minds of the latter, and consequently they cannot achieve the objectives they anticipated. How this "correct reflection" is to be achieved, however, we are not told, although we should not expect too much of these explanatory notes when Mao's own essay is (for good reasons) largely silent on this problem as well.[14] Nevertheless, Li repeats the point made in his opening remarks that "On Practice" represents a development of Marxist-Leninist epistemology. It is a development, he asserts, insofar as Mao had emphasised the dialectical character of the process of knowledge: setting out from reality and practice, gaining perceptions of reality, from there moving to the realm of thought, and from thought moving back to reality and practice, the entire process continually repeated with knowledge becoming more complete with each cycle in the process. Mao's identification of the unity of theory and practice, with practice as its basis, was thus a major contribution to Marxist philosophy.[15]

The exegetical section of Li Da's "Explanation" adopts the form of a detailed elaboration of each paragraph of Mao's "On Practice". The language used is relatively simple, and illustrations and explanations are provided of each point made in Mao's essay. Rather than attempting to summarise each of Li's elaborations, several examples are provided below in translation following their relevant sections (in italics) of "On Practice". This will provide the reader with a sense of the style adopted by Li to explicate Mao's interpretation of the epistemology of dialectical materialism. However, the following extracts have been chosen not only because they demonstrate the explicatory style adopted by Li, but also because they bear on one of the important themes we have pursued thus far through Li's writings: his understanding of the materialist conception of history and, in particular, the relationship between economic base and superstructure.

Above all, Marxists regard man's activity in production as the most fundamental practical activity, the determinant of all his other activities. Man's knowledge depends mainly on his activity in material production, through which he comes gradually to understand the phenomena, the properties and the laws of nature, and the relations between himself and nature; and through his activity in production he also gradually comes to understand, in varying degrees, certain relations that exist between man and man. None of this knowledge can be acquired apart from activity in production. In a classless society every person, as a member of society, joins in common effort with the other members, enters into definite relations of production with them and engages in production to meet man's material needs. In all class societies, the members of the different social classes also enter, in different ways, into definite relations of production and engage in production to meet their material needs. This is the primary source from which human knowledge develops.[16]

(Explanation) Dialectical materialism extended from the realm of nature to the realm of society to become historical materialism. The general points of historical materialism are: The most important and basic task of humans living in society is the acquisition of the aspects of material life necessary to keep them alive. Consequently, before people can engage in political activities and other spiritual and cultural activities, they must first engage in productive activities to satisfy the requirement for the necessities of life such as clothing, food, shelter, and so on. If humans are to obtain the necessities of life, they must participate in social production. In the process of social production, there emerges amongst them definite and necessary relationships which do not change at will; in other words, relations of production appropriate to the level of development of the material productive forces prevailing at that time. The totality of these relations of production constitutes the base (*jichu*) of society. The viewpoints of politics, law, religion, art and literature, and philosophy, and the systems appropriate to these, are the superstructure which is determined by the base. Although there are many forms of social practice, Marxists consider the productive activities of humans to be the most fundamental practical activity, and the one which determines all other activities.

Human beings, since their evolution from the higher primates to primitive people, have collectively extracted from nature the necessities of life with which to sustain their existence. In this process, they came into contact with countless objects of the natural world, realising firstly that they are themselves different from these objects of nature. Over a long period of productive activity, they gradually came to know water, fire, wind, snow, clouds, rain, movement, plants, air and other natural phenomena; they perceived the movement of the sun and the moon, the alternation of day and night, the annual growth and maturation of plants, and so on; they thus came to comprehend the characteristics and laws of natural objects, and moreover, in conformity with their characteristics and laws were often able to use nature, to overcome and transform it. There was thus an exchange of matter between activity and the natural world, with humans using their labour power on the objects of nature and the natural world giving humans the things that they needed. Humans accordingly come to realise that they dwell in nature, and a constant and mutual relationship emerged between humans and nature. Humans moreover recognise that, within productive activities, they must form definite relations for the mutual exchange of their labour, for only by so doing will they be able to extract from nature the necessities of life. These mutual relations are relations of production. All other social relations emerge on the basis of these relations of production. Over a long period of productive activity, humans were able gradually and to varying degrees to recognise the definite relations between humans, namely to recognise the relations of production and the other social relations which have developed on these relations of production. All of this knowledge of the relations between humans and nature, and between humans themselves, is derived in the process of production, and has moreover been used to guide productive activities and to promote production.

In primitive classless society, all humans toiled and each was his or her own master. Initially, they knew that, in order to obtain the necessities for life, it was necessary to divide the work of gathering and hunting according to distinctions in age and gender. With the change from a nomadic to a settled existence, and from a gathering economy to one based on production, they formed clans and, on the basis of a definite division of labour, exchanged their labour and formed relations of production which were equal; they ran agricultural activities and raised livestock, and subsequently operated handicrafts as well. The forces of production consequently gradually developed and material life became more prosperous. However, subsequent to the division of labour and the emergence of private property, there began to emerge in society a distinction between a slave-owning and a slave class, and society then changed into the earliest class society, which was a slave society.

Class society has passed through slave society, feudalism and capitalism. These three class societies have all been divided into two great opposed classes. The relations of production in these societies are basically a function of the relationships between their classes. In slave society, the relations of production formed between slave-owners and slaves was a system in which the slave-owners not only owned the means of production, but also the slaves; in feudal society, the feudal masters owned the land, and the peasants, fixed to the land, were feudalism's principal labour; in capitalist society, the capitalists own the machines, workshops, raw materials, and the workers sell their labour power. Although the form of the relations of production established in these various class societies is different, they are each a manifestation of the relationship between exploiter and exploited. On the one side is the exploiting class, namely the slave-owning class, the landlords and the capitalists; they monopolise society's means of production, do not participate in productive labour, and through the exploitation of their opposite class, live prosperous lives. On the other side is the exploited class, namely the slaves, the peasants and the proletariat. Because they have been deprived of the means of production, they have no alternative but to toil for the exploiting class, obtaining the bare necessities of life and leading an inhuman existence. The exploiting class knows that the exploited class is vastly in the majority; so in order to suppress opposition from the exploited masses, it organises the power of the state as an institution for the oppression of the antagonistic class and to protect the fiscal and legal forms of the relations of production. This all constitutes a system of exploitation. However, under its inhuman living conditions, the exploited class gradually comes to an awareness of this system of exploitation, and recognises that the institution of the state reinforces this system of exploitation; it then realises that it must unite to overthrow the exploiting and oppressing class, and there then breaks out the revolt of the slaves, the revolution of the peasants, and the proletarian revolution. And the knowledge which allows the exploited class to recognise the system of exploitation and initiate class struggle is obtained through the process of production.[17]

Man's social practice is not confined to activity in production, but takes many other forms — class struggle, political life, scientific and artistic pursuits; in short, as a social being, man participates in all spheres of the practical life of society. Thus man, in varying degrees, comes to know the different relations between man and man, not only through his material life but also through his political and cultural life (both of which are intimately bound up with material life). Of these other types of social practice, class struggle in particular, in all its various forms, exerts a profound influence on the development of man's knowledge. In class society everyone lives as a member of a particular class, and every kind of thinking, without exception, is stamped with the brand of a class.[18]

(Explanation) There are many aspects of social life in class society, particularly in capitalist society, and many people participate in these real life activities. Speaking generally, besides activity in production which is a fundamental form, there are the forms of political activity, science and art, and all of these are forms of class struggle. Class relations are, in origin, relations of production, and class struggle emerges and develops in the process of production. Because the means of production have been appropriated, the proletariat has, under a wage system, no option but to sell their labour power to the capitalist and to produce surplus value for the capitalist. However, in the process of production they come to recognise the exploitative system of capitalism, and subsequently realise they must unite and initiate a struggle against the bourgeoisie. At first, this struggle is economic, a struggle to gain improved conditions of labour, but as it proceeds they initiate a political struggle and organise for revolution. Revolution must grasp the correct revolutionary theory. Consequently, the spirit of class struggle must permeate all areas of spiritual culture, such as theory, the arts, philosophy, and this becomes a theoretical struggle. Because reactionary bourgeoise thought is consistently dominant in all these realms, the bourgeoisie can employ all reactionary theory, arts and philosophy as spiritual weapons to rule the proletariat; similarly, the bourgeoisie relies on economic and state power as a material weapon to rule the proletariat. In order to overthrow capitalist society and establish a socialist society, the proletariat must establish the theory, arts and philosophy of its own class, thoroughly purge reactionary bourgeois thought and eradicate the disguised and harmful poisons of the enemy. Within class society, each of the opposed classes has its own class thought which emanates from life in a definite class.

For more than a hundred years, the minds of the Chinese people have been poisoned by feudal, bureaucrat-capitalist and imperialist thought, so that for a long time the revolutionary people were not able to establish correct revolutionary thought. Over the last thirty years, the thought of the people's leader Mao Zedong, forged gradually in revolutionary practice, has become the revolutionary guiding ideology of the people of the entire country, and has permeated the political, economic and cultural realms; and this is Mao Zedong Thought. On the basis of Mao Zedong Thought, we must now, from the realms of science, the arts and philosophy, thoroughly "eradicate feudal, comprador, and fascist thought, and develop thought which serves the people". In particular, we must love our country, love the people, establish a new patriotism, eradicate the influence of imperialist invasion on Chinese culture, overcome national inferiority, and strengthen national self-respect and self-confidence, and this will be manifest in the Chinese people also standing up on the ideological front as well.[19]

It can be seen from these two excerpts from *An Explanation of "On Practice"* that Li was in complete agreement with Mao that the starting point for an understanding of social structure and social change was the productive activities in which humans engage in order to pursue their livelihood. Li's elaboration of the emergence of classes and the passage of history through various modes of production with their characteristic class relationships is no more than a summary of the conventional interpretation of historical materialism. There is nothing new here — and, indeed, one would not expect novelty in an elaboration of this sort. A number of points about this passage are, however, noteworthy. First, Mao makes it clear in "On Practice", one of his most widely read essays, that it is the realm of production which has causal priority in the process of social change; the class relationships into which humans enter at the point of production have a dominating effect, not only on economic relationships, but on political and intellectual relationships as well. All human thought is influenced by class; as Mao insists, "every kind of thinking, without exception, is stamped with the brand of a class". It is often suggested that Mao's understanding of Marxist theory was unorthodox because he failed to recognise sufficiently the materialist (that is, productive and class) underpinnings of human behaviour and thought, and yet it is difficult to reconcile this suggestion with the passage we have just examined, for Mao is here doing little more than reiterating one of the most basic premises of historical materialism. Moreover, Mao (as we have seen from his correspondence to Li of the early 1950s) agreed entirely with Li's more extended elaboration which also stresses the productive base of society as the origin of politics, culture and philosophy. Neither Mao nor Li believed, however, that the causal relationship between economics, on the one hand, and politics, culture and ideology on the other, was a one-way affair, with economics immune from the influence of the superstructure; rather, there was a dialectical interaction between these different areas of the social formation, although causal dominance resided in the economic realm. We will pursue this link in the chain of Mao and Li's ratiocination shortly, when we turn to Li's elaboration of the appropriate passage of "On Contradiction".

Second, Li's elaboration raises, as he had done in his previous writings on historical materialism, the issue of ideology as a technique of class domination. The bourgeoisie not only employs its control of economic resources and the political power of its state to force compliance to its will, it uses the various realms of "spiritual culture" (theory, arts, philosophy) to disseminate and reinforce its class perspective; "reactionary bourgeoise thought" is dominant in all of these realms, and unless the proletariat is able to formulate and propagate an alternative conception of the world, one which conforms to its own class interests, it will be unable to resist and ultimately overthrow the domination of the bourgeoisie. From this perspective, "spiritual culture" assumes increased importance as an arena of class struggle. "Spiritual culture" is not merely a reflection of the economic life of a class; once formed, it becomes a mode of contention between the competing classes. Consequently, the establishment of correct revolutionary theory by the proletariat becomes an urgent necessity, for without it, its struggle will lack direction and coherence. Li's call for the Chinese to adopt an anti-imperialist patriotism was thus premised on the view that successful prosecution of class struggle requires attention to the ideological realm as well as to the economic and political realms. For Li, historical materialism was a theory which recognised the interaction and interdependence of the various dimensions of social life, but such interaction and interdependence was ultimately built on the primacy of the realm of production, and it was this recognition of the significance of production which prevented the analysis of ideology from lapsing into an idealist preoccupation with the role of ideas separate from their material origins. As he points out, "each class has its own thought which emanates from life in a definite class".

This recognition of the interactive character of the different realms of the social formation had been a significant theme in Li Da's earlier interpretive writings on historical materialism. He had never accepted the view that belief in a materialist perspective precluded a belief in the historical significance of politics or "spiritual culture". From his earliest writings, he had accepted the possibility — indeed, the desirability — of a political revolution, and his many years of painstaking elaboration and dissemination of Marxist theory reveals only too clearly his belief in the importance of struggle in the realm of "spiritual culture", of ensuring that the theory employed in revolutionary struggle was correct. Li perceived in Mao's "On Practice" a similarly appropriate recognition of the significant contribution correct theory could make to the successful prosecution of struggle; he also approved of Mao's recognition of the interrelated and interactive character of social life. Li consequently felt no qualms in writing this detailed elaboration of "On Practice", for Mao's interpretation was compatible with Li's own understanding of Marxist theory and philosophy; not only was Mao's thought, as contained in this essay, the new orthodoxy, it was orthodox by the standards of the Marxist philosophy which both Li and Mao had studied so assiduously in the 1930s. There was thus, at this stage at least, a meeting of minds on how to interpret historical materialism.

Reading Mao Zedong's "On Contradiction"

The reference in "On Practice" to the interrelated character of the different realms of the social formation is repeated and expanded in Mao's "On Contradiction". Here Mao reaffirms, in the name of a dialectical rather than mechanistic materialism, that the relations of production, theory and the superstructure do exert a reactive influence "in certain conditions" and indeed can "manifest themselves in the principal and decisive role", although he qualifies this by reasserting that the productive forces, economic base and practice generally do play "the principal and decisive role". As I have analysed this controversial passage in considerable detail elsewhere,[20] let us turn directly to Li Da's elaboration of it. We commence, as before, with the passage from "On Contradiction" in italics. Li's extended explanation then follows.

Some people think that this is not true of certain contradictions. For instance, in the contradiction between the productive forces and the relations of production, the productive forces are the principal aspect; in the contradiction between theory and practice, practice is the principal aspect; in the contradiction between the economic base and the superstructure, the economic base is the principal aspect; and there is no change in their respective positions. This is the mechanical materialist conception, not the dialectical materialist conception. True, the productive forces, practice and the economic base generally play the principal and decisive role; whoever denies this is not a materialist. But it also must be admitted that in certain conditions, such aspects as the relations of production, theory and the superstructure in turn manifest themselves in the principal and decisive role. When it is impossible for the productive forces to develop without a change in the relations of production, then the change in the relations of production plays the principal and decisive role. The creation and advocacy of revolutionary theory plays the principal and decisive role in those times of which Lenin said, "Without revolutionary theory there can be no revolutionary movement." When a task, no matter which, has to be performed, but there is as yet no guiding line, method, plan, policy, the principal and decisive thing is to decide on a guiding line, method, plan or policy. When the superstructure (politics, culture, etc.) obstructs the development of the economic base, political and cultural changes become principal and decisive. Are we going against materialism when we say this? No. The reason is that while we recognize that in the general development of history the material determines the mental and social being determines social consciousness, we also — and indeed must — recognize the reaction of mental on material things, of social consciousness on social being and of the superstructure on the economic base. This does not go against materialism; on the contrary, it avoids mechanical materialism and firmly upholds dialectical materialism.[21]

(Explanation) The principal and non-principal aspects of a contradiction undergo mutual transformation, and we have given above many examples to explain this. However, those who hold mechanist materialist opinions assert that the aspects of a contradiction do not undergo mutual transformation. For example, there are those who say that in the contradiction between the forces of production and relations of production, the forces of production are the principal aspect, and that the two aspects do not undergo a mutual transformation. This opinion does not accord with dialectical materialism. From a dialectical materialist perspective, in the contradiction between the forces of production and the relations of production, the forces of production are the most active, most revolutionary element in production, and they are the determinative element in the process of the development of production. The relations of production are compatible with the level of development of the relations of production. "As are the forces of production, so will be the relations of production." "First there is change and development of society's forces of production, and then the relations of production of the people, and their economic relationships, which are dependent on these changes, give rise to changes which are compatible with the changes in the forces of production." (*Dialectical and Historical Materialism*) It is evident that the forces of production occupy the principal position in relation to the relations of production. On the other hand, the relations of production also influence the development of the forces of production; and the forces of production are also dependent on the relations of production. Although the relations of production develop as do the forces of production, the relations of production at the same time have a reactive influence on the forces of production; and this is because society's forces of production are constantly developing. When the relations of production are compatible with the nature and condition of the forces of production and give the forces of production room to develop, they can assist the development of the forces of production. Conversely, when the relations of production are incompatible with the nature and condition of the forces of production and give them no room to develop, they then obstruct the development of the forces of production. This is the reactive influence of the relations of production on the forces of production. At such times, the relations of production occupy the principal position in relation to the forces of production. However, such a situation cannot be protracted, for the relations of production cannot continue to hold back the development of the forces of production, and sooner or later the relations of production must become appropriate to the level of development of the forces of production, become compatible with the nature of the forces of production; that is to say, the forces of production still occupy the principal position in the contradiction. However, how are the relations of production able to obstruct the development of the forces of production? It is because the forces of production settle what sort of instruments of production the people use in order to produce their material needs, whereas the relations of production settle the question of ownership, that is, whether there is social or individual ownership. In class society, the means of production are monopolised by a particular class to the detriment of other classes. For example, in capitalist society, the means of production are monopolised by the bourgeoisie, while the proletariat owns nothing apart from its labour power. Therefore, the relations of production of capitalism are the relations between the bourgeoisie and proletariat, are the relations between exploiter and exploited; they are property relations. The relations of production of capitalist society obstruct the development of the forces of production; that is, the property relations of the capitalists perform an obstructive function. An example of this sort of obstruction of the development of the forces of production is the economic crisis which occurs in capitalist countries. Because the capitalist private ownership of the means of production is the common characteristic of the process of production, there then occurs an economic crisis. In order for there to be smooth development of the forces of production, the relations of production of capitalism must be destroyed, and relations of production established which are compatible with the common characteristics of the process of production, and which are compatible with the nature of the forces of production, and these are socialist relations of production. This must be achieved by the proletarian revolution. The economic law that the relations of production must be compatible with the nature of the forces of production still applies in socialist society; the relations of production will still however exercise an effect, namely the fact of the relations of production falling behind the development of the forces of production still exists objectively. However, with social ownership of the means of production as its base, the contradiction between the relations of production and the forces of production in socialism is non-antagonistic; when people discover that the relations of production are incompatible with the development of the forces of production, they can then alter those relations of production so that they become compatible with the nature of the forces of production, and consequently accelerate the development of the forces of production.

There are those who suggest that, in the contradiction between theory and practice, practice is the principal aspect of the contradiction and that the respective positions of theory and practice cannot be mutually transformed. This viewpoint is similarly mistaken. Revolutionary practice certainly occupies the principal position in relation to revolutionary theory; but if revolutionary practice does not have the guidance of revolutionary theory, it can change into blind practice and will inevitably suffer defeat. Lenin said: "Without revolutionary theory there can be no revolutionary movement." Therefore, when the proletariat wages revolution but lacks the guidance of revolutionary theory, the establishment and advocacy of revolutionary theory exercises the principal and determinative function. This can be observed from the hundred and more years of the revolutionary history of the Chinese people. From the Opium War of 1840, through the Taiping Rebellion, the Sino-French War, the Sino-Japanese War of 1894–95, the Reform Movement of 1898, the Boxer Rebellion, the 1911 Revolution, and down to the May Fourth Movement, the revolution of the Chinese people to oppose imperialism and feudalism has been waged unyieldingly and continuously. However, because there was not established a revolutionary theory integrated with the concrete practice of the Chinese revolution, victory could not be achieved. During that period, "Chinese progressives went through untold hardships in their quest for truth from Western countries. Hong Xiuquan, Kang Youwei, Yan Fu and Sun Yat-sen were representative of those who had looked to the West for truth before the Communist Party of China was born." "The Chinese learned a good deal from the West, but they could not make it work and were never able to realise their ideals. Their repeated struggles, including such a country-wide movement as the Revolution of 1911, all ended in failure." ("On the People's Democratic Dictatorship)"[22] However, since the October Revolution in Russia transmitted to us the universal truths of Marxism-Leninism, which have been tested around the world and shown to be correct, the appearance of the Chinese revolution has changed. Comrade Mao Zedong said: "For a hundred years, the finest sons and daughters of the disaster-ridden Chinese nation fought and sacrificed their lives, one stepping into the breach as another fell, in quest of the truth that would save the country and the people. This moves us to song and tears. But it was only after World War I and the October Revolution in Russia that we found Marxism-Leninism, the best of truths, the best of weapons for liberating our nation. And the Communist Party of China has been the initiator, propagandist and organiser in the wielding of this weapon. As soon as it was linked with the concrete practice of the Chinese revolution, the universal truth of Marxism-

Leninism gave an entirely new complexion to the Chinese revolution." (*Selected Works of Mao Tse-tung*, vol. 3, p. 754)[23] And the integration of the universal truths of Marxism-Leninism and the concrete practice of the Chinese revolution is truly none other than Mao Zedong Thought. Because the revolution of the Chinese people has had the guidance of Mao Zedong Thought, it has been able to go from one victory to another. This is the best illustration of the exercise of the principal and determinative function of revolutionary theory in relation to revolutionary practice.

Also, when we are involved in work of whatever kind (that is, practice), there must be a definite orientation, program, plan and policy to guide the work. The orientation, program, plan and policy become, in relation to that work, principal and determinative. At present, our new state is preparing for large-scale economic construction, and is in the process of formulating a major economic plan which will establish the objectives for the struggle of the people of the entire country. The principal and determinative function of the plan in relation to construction is very evident.

There are those who say that, in the contradiction between economic base and the superstructure, the economic base is the principal aspect of the contradiction, and the position of the two aspects cannot be mutually transformed. This opinion is also incorrect. "The base is the economic structure of society at the given stage of its development. The superstructure is the political, legal, religious, artistic, philosophical views of society and the political, legal and other institutions corresponding to them." (Stalin, *Marxism and Problems of Linguistics*)[24] The base is primary, and the superstructure is secondary and is produced by the base. When Stalin talked of the base as the economic structure of society at the given stage of its development, he was referring to the totality of the relations of production compatible with the level of the forces of production in a given stage of development. When the forces of production develop to a higher stage, the relations of production subsequently develop to a higher stage; that is, the economic system of society is transformed into an economic system of a higher stage. Therefore, the economic base of society changes and develops as do the forces of production. Because of the change of society's economic base, the superstructure, which is created by and is compatible with the economic base, also gives rise to change. The superstructure serves the economic base. In antagonistic societies, the superstructure is established to consolidate the economic system which serves the interests of the class which monopolises the means of production; the superstructure is a class instrument used to control the means of production this class has seized. This instrument of domination can be divided into material and spiritual dimensions. The material instruments of control include the agencies of coercion such as the state, the courts, and the police. The spiritual instruments of control include political, legal, religious, art and literary, as well as philosophical viewpoints. The political and legal systems of these agencies of coercion are compatible with these viewpoints. For example, the imperialist state, in order for the bourgeoisie to dominate the proletariat, not only employs the courts and the police (sometimes mobilising troops) to crush the resistance of the proletariat, it also uses schools, bookstores, newspaper houses, the church, theatres, film companies, radio, and so on, to disseminate bourgeoise thought in the attempt to anaesthetise the broad masses of the proletariat, and hence maintain the capitalist system of private ownership. The superstructure of capitalist society therefore reflects, and moreover serves the capitalist economic base.

That the economic base occupies the principal position in relation to the superstructure is an evident truth. However, while the superstructure is created by and reflects the base, that is not to suggest that the superstructure is completely passive and negative towards the base. After the superstructure is established, it possesses dynamic and active strength in relation to the base. Stalin said: "The superstructure is a product of the base, but this by no means implies that it merely reflects the base, that it is passive, neutral, indifferent to the fate of its base, to the fate of the classes, to the character of the system. On the contrary, having come into being, it becomes an exceedingly active force, actively assisting its base to take shape and consolidate itself, and doing its utmost to help the new system to finish off and eliminate the old base and the old classes. It cannot be otherwise. The superstructure is created by the base in order to serve it, to actively help it to take shape and consolidate itself, to actively fight for the elimination of the old, moribund base together with its old superstructure." (*Marxism and Problems of Linguistics*)[25] Therefore, once the superstructure is established, it becomes an exceedingly active force, one which can accelerate or retard or obstruct the development of society. For example, after the bourgeoisie overthrew feudal society, the superstructure it established was compatible with the capitalist economic system — the organs of the bourgeoise state and the viewpoints of bourgeoise politics, law, religion, art and literature, philosophy and so on — and these actively helped the formation and consolidation of the capitalist economic system; moreover, it adopted all methods to assist the capitalist system destroy and eliminate the system of feudalism and the feudal classes, and in so doing allowed the further development of capitalism. However, when the forces of production develop to a definite point, when they come into conflict with capitalist relations of production, the capitalist relations of production obstruct the development of the forces of production; consequently, the capitalist economic base weakens and goes into decline. However, the bourgeoisie uses the capitalist superstructure to suppress the proletarian revolutionary movement, and attempts to arrest the decline in the capitalist economic base. The superstructure of capitalism thus obstructs the development of society. Thereupon, on the basis of the conflict of the new forces of production and the capitalist relations of production, there emerged Marxism. Marxism mobilised and organised the proletariat. Once the proletariat became organised, it became a powerful revolutionary force, one capable of overthrowing the capitalist superstructure, establishing revolutionary power, and using all its might to eliminate the capitalist economic system and establish a socialist economic system. The relations of production of semi-colonial and semi-feudal China have obstructed the development of new forces of production for many years; the feudal, compradore and fascist superstructure did its utmost to protect the rotten and declining economic base. However, the working class and its command post, the Chinese Communist Party, armed with Mao Zedong Thought, organised the people's democratic united front which, under the leadership of the working class and with the worker–peasant alliance as its basis, and uniting with the petty bourgeoisie and national bourgeoisie, became a powerful revolutionary force which finally overthrew the reactionary Guomindang government, established a state of the people's democratic dictatorship, eliminated the semi-colonial and semi-feudal economic system and established a socialist economic system. It can thus be seen that, although the superstructure is produced by the economic base, once it has been created, it becomes a powerful and positive force.

It can be seen from the explanation given above that the forces of production, practice, and the economic base in general perform the principal and determinative role, and of this there can be no doubt. However, it must also be acknowledged that the relations of production, theory, and the superstructure, under definite conditions, can alter to take on the principal and determinative role. This explanation conforms to dialectical materialism, and this is because we acknowledge that in the general development of history, the material determines the spiritual, and social existence determines social consciousness. In other words, we acknowledge that the material life of society and social existence are the principal phenomena, and that the spiritual life of society and social consciousness are secondary phenomena. Spiritual life is a reflection of material life, and social consciousness is a reflection of social existence. In sum, social thoughts, theories, viewpoints and so on, are a reflection of the conditions of the material life of society. We must set out from the conditions of the material life of society in explaining social thoughts, theories and viewpoints; we cannot commence from social thoughts, theories and viewpoints to explain the material life of society. We must explain social consciousness by reference to social existence; we cannot explain social existence by reference to social consciousness. Therefore, social existence plays the determinative function in relation to social consciousness. However, we cannot consequently say that social consciousness plays no reactive role in relation to social existence. In the history of society and in social life, social consciousness performs a positive, reactive function. In antagonistic societies, there are old social thoughts, theories and viewpoints as well as new social thoughts, theories and viewpoints. The former serve the interests of the rotten reactionary class, and the reactive role they play is the obstruction of the development of society; the latter serve the interests of the newly emerged revolutionary class, and the reactive role they assume in relation to the old society is the elimination of the old society and the establishment of a new society. Therefore, when the decline of the old society commences, and when the conditions of the material life of society have already posed new tasks for society, the newly emerged social thoughts, theories and viewpoints become a spiritual weapon of the newly emerged revolutionary class, become a material force able to destroy the old social order and establish a new social order. Once Mao Zedong Thought, which is a reflection of the laws of development of Chinese society, grasped the broad masses of the people, it became a powerful material force and China's people's revolution went from victory to victory. The reactive influence of social consciousness on social existence is very significant.[26]

The first point to be made about this interesting passage is that Mao Zedong had read it and regarded it as a valid elaboration of his views on the relationship between forces and relations of production, between theory and practice, and between economic base and superstructure; and because Mao had read and approved Li's interpretation, it can safely be regarded as virtually an extension of Mao's own writings on Marxist theory. Here was an interpretive passage written by an old friend, one with the deserved reputation of China's foremost Marxist theoretician; Mao respected what Li wrote, and we know that he gave his blessing to these explanatory writings. While the passage obviously mirrors Li's views, its purpose was to expand and illustrate Mao's understanding of the aetiology of social change in Marxist theory. This passage thus possesses a double significance: it is not only indicative of Li's understanding of essential features of the new orthodoxy of Mao Zedong Thought, it also provides the possibility of an extended insight into Mao's views on the philosophical and theoretical dimensions of Marxism.

Second, it is important to emphasise that both Li and Mao decidedly rejected a mechanistic interpretation of historical materialism, one which perceived the forces of production, the economic base, and practice as invariably performing the principal and determinative function. This interpretation was mechanistic insofar as it failed to give sufficient emphasis to the interrelated and interactive character of the various dimensions of the social formation; from this perspective, forces of production always determine the relations of production, the economic base always determines the superstructure, and practice always determines theory. Li and Mao both felt this view failed to grasp the complexity of the social formation and the process of social change. It was also bad Marxism, for it failed to apply the basic premises of Marxist philosophy to the interpretation of society; if the laws of dialectics are universal, they must be applicable to the relationships existing within the social formation. The relationship between forces of production and relations of production is therefore necessarily dialectical; while the former normally retains dominance, the two are bound in a relationship in which the latter, on occasion, can exert a reactive influence on the former. Such a view does not attribute unbridled license to the relations of production to dictate the direction or pace of historical change, for its autonomy to act is circumscribed by the existence of the forces of production, its opposite and normally superordinate number in the contradiction, and without which it could not exist. The capacity of the relations of production to influence the forces of production was limited; in those circumstances in which the forces of production were developing, the relations of production could act to impede their further development or, after significant change, to facilitate their further development. Ultimately, causal dominance resided with the forces of production, for it was the imperative for constant development within them which drove the whole process of social change.

The same form of analysis can be provided for Li and Mao's views on the relationship between economic base and superstructure, and between theory and practice. Ultimate dominance resides with the economic base and practice, but the superstructure and theory, in certain historical circumstances, have the capacity to influence their opposite number, although that influence is temporally limited. Mechanistic materialism's portrayal of these relationships is condemned by Li and Mao for its undialectical quality. The process of social change is, they stress, complex, interactive and developing, it is dialectical; to think otherwise is to go against the fundamental premises of Marxist theory. It is thus something of an irony that judgments of Mao's Marxism (and Marxism in China more generally) have frequently adopted the criteria of mechanistic materialism, accepting the invariable dominance of the forces of production and the economic base as the standard of Marxism, and consequently branding Mao an idealist or voluntarist for allowing a role in social change to both the relations of production and superstructure.[27] A reading of Marxism rejected by Mao himself is thus mobilised to underscore his heterodoxy; yet the appeal to this mechanistic Marxist "orthodoxy" by such critics is threadbare indeed. Mao's two philosophical essays and Li's elaboration of them establish quite different criteria for Marxist orthodoxy. Indeed, in his elaboration, Li invokes the writings of Soviet Marxist philosophy from the early 1930s, which had greatly influenced both he and Mao, to reinforce the orthodoxy of their critique of mechanistic materialism and to reinforce their dialectical perception of the process of social change. What Li and Mao are saying is not new and, as we have seen in previous chapters, has a long genealogy stretching back to the major theoretical figures of European and Soviet Marxism.

Before leaving Li Da's explanatory notes on Mao's "On Contradiction", it is worth pointing briefly to Li's reassertion that the law of the unity of opposites is the most fundamental law of dialectical materialism. It will be remembered that Li, following the practice of Soviet philosophy of the early 1930s, had made the same point in his *Elements of Sociology*. Li could therefore happily reinforce and expand Mao's introductory comment that the "law of contradiction in things, that is, the law of the unity of opposites, is the basic law of materialist dialectics".[28] Li points to the writings of Marx and Engels which are, he suggests, thoroughly permeated by this law; Marx's *Capital* and Engels' *Anti-Dühring* and *Ludwig Feuerbach and the End of Classical German Philosophy* "also developed the spirit of this law". Lenin, too, brushing aside the neo-Kantian distortions of Bernstein and the later errors of Plekhanov, explained and developed the law of the unity of opposites, describing it as the "most fundamental and most important law of dialectics, and the law with greatest determinative significance". Li continues that, following in the footsteps of Marx, Engels, Lenin and Stalin, Mao Zedong "studied the experience of the world proletarian revolution, absorbed the new achievements of contemporary science, and fully, thoroughly, and clearly 'explained and developed' the theory of the law of the unity of opposites; moreover, he concretely, flexibly, and ingeniously applied this theory to the problems of the Chinese revolution, established China's revolutionary theory and policies and, using the experience of personally leading the people's revolution, enriched and developed this theory. 'On Contradiction', like 'On Practice,' is truly the valuable theoretical result of the integration of the universal truths of Marxism-Leninism and the concrete practice of the Chinese revolution."[29]

How to Study Mao Zedong Thought

As well as this lengthy commentary on Mao's two essays on philosophy, Li wrote a number of other articles whose purpose was to guide the reader in the study of Mao Zedong Thought. One of the first of these was an article, published first in *Renmin Zhoubao* [People's Weekly] in the latter half of 1951 and subsequently republished in several other sources.[30] "Read Comrade Mao Zedong's Four Articles from 1926–1929" deals with four of the first five documents in Volume 1 of *The Selected Works of Mao Zedong*. Li introduces these documents by asserting that "the glory, greatness and correctness of the Party cannot be separated from the guidance of Mao Zedong Thought" and states that this guidance is expressed in concentrated form in the writings published over the years by Mao. In the first of the articles from the 1926–29 period, "Analysis of the Classes in Chinese Society" (March 1926), Mao had addressed the most significant question of the Chinese revolution: how to differentiate between the enemies and friends of the revolution. Using the class theory of Marxism-Leninism, Mao had analysed the various classes of semi-colonial, semi-feudal China, pointing out most importantly that the bourgeoisie in China differed from the bourgeoisie in capitalist countries; for in China there existed a division between the compradore bourgeoisie, the spokesman of imperialism, and the national bourgeoisie, which had a revolutionary character but which was also willing to collude with imperialism. However, the fact that one of its two characters was revolutionary (desiring the establishment of an independent bourgeoise state) allowed the possibility of a united front between the national bourgeoisie, together with the petty bourgeoisie and semi-proletariat (particularly the large mass of the stratum of poor peasantry) under the leadership of the proletariat. Mao thus very early on arrived at a political formulation which would hold good for the period of the New Democratic revolution. Similarly, Mao discerned very early in the revolutionary process that, within the framework of the united front led by the proletariat, the peasantry constituted the most important ally of the Chinese revolution. This was the essential thrust of his 1927 "Report on an Investigation of the Peasant Movement in Hunan", which established the theoretical basis for the worker–peasant alliance and the relationship between the Party and the peasantry. Mao again discerned economic distinctions within the peasantry: in the struggle to eliminate the landlords, the 70 per cent who were poor peasants could be mobilised for the revolution, the 20 per cent who were middle peasants had to be united with, and the 9 per cent of rich peasants had to be neutralised. Mao also discerned that it was necessary to form peasant associations to strike politically at the landlords, and to arm the peasants for defence of their rights. In the third document from this period, "Why is That Red Political Power can Exist in China" (October 1928), Mao elaborated the reasons why the communist revolution could survive in China despite the serious setbacks of 1927. Of these, the divisions among the enemy (the "whites") stood out, as did the establishment and development of the Red Army which could take armed struggle to the enemy; under the correct leadership of the Party, and relying on the organisation of the peasants and workers and the establishment of revolutionary base areas, "red political power" could not only survive in China, but prosper as well. However, with the establishment of the Red Army, a new set of problems was created for the Chinese revolution, and this was the subject of Mao's "On Correcting Mistaken Ideas in the Party" (December 1929). Here Mao stressed that the Red Army was subject to the control and discipline of the Party, for it was impermissable for a purely military viewpoint to emerge which did not recognise the political objectives for which the Red Army fought. Mao also established certain necessary organisational modes of conduct, including criticism and self-criticism, linking with the masses, and the study of Marxism-Leninism and its application to the concrete practice of the Chinese revolution. Li Da concludes by asserting that these four documents by Mao established the theoretical premises for the revolutionary struggle in China, premises which gradually led to victory. These documents are thus an expression of Mao's "great revolutionary genius".

Li wrote other articles which elaborate and extol specific documents written by Mao.[31] Others exhort the study of Mao's writings in general and also urge the application of Mao's thought to particular fields. An example of the latter is an article written at the height of the Great Leap Forward which called for a leap forward in the study of philosophy.³² Li acknowledged that the study of Marxist-Leninist philosophy had made great strides since Liberation, but there were deficiencies. One of these was that "many comrades" were unwilling to go beyond Stalin's formulations, relying rather on a rather bookish and dogmatist approach to philosophy.³³ The result was philosophical research which bore little relationship to the reality of China's revolution and socialist construction. This dogmatism was in turn manifest in a style of teaching in the area of philosophy which emphasised rote learning and the writing of formalistic, empty essays. Li called for a change, suggesting that a reading of Mao's writings, especially on philosophy, could encourage a great leap forward in philosophy. Not only should the "scientific content" of Mao's essays be studied, Li asserted, but also Mao's "scientific method for linking theory and practice". After all, Mao was the "great craftsman (*dajiang*) of dialectical materialism", and each of his writings used dialectical materialism to analyse historical and revolutionary reality, and was a model for the resolution of the major problems of Chinese revolution and construction. Philosophers had to learn from Mao's ability to write articles on philosophy which were readily understood by the masses and which had consequently become a material force for change; to effectively emulate this style, philosophers should go to the villages and factories and become as one with the masses, participating in production and class struggle.

Due to ill-health, Li wrote little after the Great Leap Forward, although he was heavily involved in the early 1960s in supervising the revision of his *Elements of Sociology* (see the next chapter). One of his last published essays (1960) was entitled "How Should Mao Zedong Thought be Studied?"³⁴ Li commences this essay by extolling the virtues of Mao Zedong Thought; Mao's writings, he says, all use Marxism-Leninist theory to study the specific characteristics of China's history and culture, and the economic and political situation. Mao had created a completely Sinified Marxism, a scientific theory for revolution and socialist and communist construction. All theoretical and practical workers should study Mao Zedong thought. But how should they study it? Li suggests that those studying Mao Zedong Thought should first commence with "Reform our Study" and "Rectify the Party's Style of Work", for these essays deal with the method for studying Marxism, a method which can in its turn be employed to study Mao Zedong Thought. The important message in these essays was to study the attitude (*taidu*) of Marxism, first and foremost of which was "to seek truth from facts". Having studied the problem of attitude, it was next necessary to study the ideological method (*sixiang fangfa*) of Mao Zedong Thought; to do this, it was necessary to study Mao's writings on epistemology. These contained three fundamental principles:

1. the integration of the universal truths of Marxism-Leninism with the concrete practice of the Chinese revolution;
2. dialectical materialism, namely the use of contradictions and class as an analytical method; and
3. an emphasis on practice in the process of knowledge.

Li Da particularly stresses the last principle, seeing it as the basis of knowledge and the criterion of truth. Li again concludes by suggesting that the materials for study come from the masses, and that it is therefore necessary for theoretical workers to go to factories and villages to learn from workers and peasants. Above all, philosophers and social scientists, cultural workers and educators must strive "to establish the proletarian world view and thoroughly eliminate the bourgeoise world view, and to study Mao Zedong Thought and thoroughly integrate Mao Zedong Thought in scientific research and the work of education".

Conclusion

The rather extravagant praise accorded Mao's essays and thought by Li reveals only too clearly the changed relationship between the two. Li was now expending considerable energy elaborating Mao Zedong Thought, something he had not done at all prior to 1949, whereas Mao had earlier assiduously studied Li's philosophical and economic writings; indeed, Mao's understanding of Marxist philosophy owed much to Li Da's interpretation of dialectical materialism and his translations of Soviet sources. Similarly, although Li's explanatory notes on Mao's philosophical essays do attempt to situate Mao's philosophical thought in the broader context of the development of Marxist theory rather than portraying them as the spontaneous creation of a genius, his elaboration does culminate by hailing Mao's thought as a development of Marxism-Leninism; and the rather extravagant language in which he does so says much about the changed political relationship between Li and Mao, as well as Li's new role as one of the new communist state's pre-eminent intellectuals and theorists. Li's period in the political wilderness may have ended, but his readmission to the Party brought not only the potential for theoretical and political influence, but limitations and restrictions as well. He could no longer write or act as he liked, for his life was now intimately linked to the Party, whose demands set the agenda for both his theoretical work and political activities. His personal relationship with Mao, dating back three decades, also complicated this scenario. As we will observe in the next chapter, Li's attempt to persist with his life's mission of the elaboration and transmission of Marxist theory in China was complicated by the problem of China's new orthodoxy. Li was no longer dealing with Marxism-Leninism, complex and sensitive enough on its own, but with Marxism-Leninism-Mao Zedong Thought; and the creator of Mao Zedong Thought was, in the 1950s and 1960s, not only alive and well but carefully monitoring what others said of his contribution to Marxism. To the extent that Li agreed with Mao's interpretation of the ontology and epistemology of dialectical materialism, he was able in good conscience to provide the detailed elaboration of "On Contradiction" and "On Practice" required of him in the early 1950s. After all, Li recognised in Mao's essays the strong influence of the Soviet Marxist philosophy which had likewise influenced him in the early 1930s.

But what would Li's reaction be if required to provide theoretical elaboration and support for a viewpoint with which he disagreed? After all, he had shown himself to be a man of high principle in the past, one not at all afraid to incur the displeasure of the mighty should his views not coincide with theirs. However, the option of standing on his dignity and quitting the Party, as he had in 1923, was no longer a realistic option in the 1950s and 1960s; such a move would have been tantamount to an act of self-destruction. Initially, however, the ambivalence of his situation was lessened by the fact that he was able to give virtually unreserved support to Mao and the Party in their pursuit of socialist construction. Li's views coincided with the temper of the times. The new Chinese state was committed to a form of Marxist theory and practice which he understood and supported; moreover, his talents and experience as an educator and philosopher were clearly in demand. By the mid-1950s, however, Li was becoming involved in the controversial campaigns against those intellectual figures who had earned Mao's enmity. Left to his own devices, would Li have felt moved to write bitter criticisms and denunciations of Hu Shi, Liang Shuming, Fei Xiaotong and others, something for which he is now criticised in China? It seems unlikely. Similarly, given a free hand, would Li have reacted more openly to his perception of the excesses of the Great Leap Forward? Li's writings of the late 1950s suggest total support for Mao, his criticisms reserved for a private and fiery exchange with him. Moreover, confronted by Lin Biao's theory of Mao Zedong Thought as the pinnacle of Marxist theory in the early 1960s, Li's reaction was dismissive, although again he did not air his views in print. Nevertheless, the problem of Mao Zedong Thought (how to evaluate its position in the development of Marxism-Leninism) would not go away and greatly complicated, and ultimately compromised, Li Da's last major philosophical project, the revision of his *Elements of Sociology*.

In the next chapter, we will turn to a consideration of these final episodes in Li's life. It will become evident that, like other intellectuals in Mao's China, Li was not a free agent; not only was he sometimes obliged to lend his talents to purposes he may not wholly have approved, he could not, even in those projects initiated by him, write exactly what he wished. Yet the services rendered by him to Mao and the Party were in the end not enough to save him, and he was swept away by the maelstrom of the Cultural Revolution, his privately voiced objections to Mao's policies and to Lin Biao's attribution of infallibility to Mao Zedong Thought sufficient to condemn him.

Notes

1. Excerpts of *Falixue dagang* can be found in *Li Da wenji*, Vol. 1.
2. The information in this paragraph is taken from Li Siju et al., "Li Da yijiusijiu nianqian lilun huodong ji zhuzuo biannian" (Chronicle of Li Da's Pre-1949 Theoretical Activities and Writings), *Zhongguo zhexue*, No. 1 (1979), pp. 370–72.
3. I explored the relationship between Li Da and Mao Zedong during extensive discussions (in September 1993) with Li Junru, Director of the Mao Zedong Thought Research Centre at the Shanghai Academy of Social Sciences and the editor of the journal *Mao Zedong zhexue sixiang yanjiu* (Research on the Philosophical Thought of Mao Zedong). According to Li Junru, the relationship between Li Da and Mao Zedong went through four stages. The first was 1921–27. During this period, Mao and Li first met at the First Congress of the CCP, although Mao had undoubtedly read Li's writings previously. After the First Congress, a close relationship developed on the basis of their shared Hunanese origins and their interests in theory. At this stage, Li's capacity as a theorist was superior to Mao's, Li already having studied Marxism for several years. During Li's spell as the principal of the Self-Study University in Changsha, the relationship between them developed. The second period in their relationship was from 1927–47. During this period, Mao was developing his own strategy for revolution in the realm of practice, and solving in practice the problem of the Sinification of Marxism, something which Li did not solve. However, during this second phase, Mao continued to learn from Li in the realms of philosophy and social science, and was particularly influenced by Li's translation of Shirokov and Aizenberg's *A Course on Dialectical Materialism*, as well as Li's *Elements of Sociology*. The third phase was from 1947–57, during which their relationship changed dramatically. During this period, Li now learnt from Mao. Li expended considerable energy in disseminating Mao's thought, but this thought was no longer the thought of just an individual; instead, it was the guiding ideology of the Party and the new state. Having rejoined the Party, Li Da was now one of a number of intellectuals involved in disseminating and popularising the ideology of the new ruling group. The

relationship between Mao and Li was thus influenced by the power factor; still influenced by their earlier personal and friendly relationship, it was now strongly mediated by the changed power equation between the two. It was no longer a matter of Li writing what he liked, for the new guiding ideology was Mao Zedong Thought. The fourth period in the relationship between Li Da and Mao lasted from 1957–66. From 1957, Mao began to stress the dynamic subjective readiness of the masses for change in a way which Li could not accept, for it went against his understanding of Marxist materialism. Li felt that Mao's policies were mistaken and told Mao so. However, Li continued to carry out Mao's bidding when he felt it to be correct. An example was his willingness to revise *Elements of Sociology* in the early 1960s (see the next chapter). For Li Junru's writings on Mao Zedong Thought, see Li Junru, *Mao Zedong yu xiandai Zhongguo* (Mao Zedong and Contemporary China) (Fuzhou: Fujian renmin chubanshe, 1991). For other analysis of the relationship between Li Da and Mao, see Sun Qian and Li Shizhen, *Mao Zedong yu mingren* (Mao Zedong and the Famous) (Jiangsu: Jiangsu renmin chubanshe, 1993), Vol. 1, pp. 315–34.

4. *Li Da wenji*, Vol. 1, p. 5.

5. Ibid., p. 9.

6. *Mao Zedong shuxin xuanji* (Selected Letters of Mao Zedong) (Beijing: Renmin chubanshe, 1983), p. 47.

7. Li Siju et al., "Chronicle of Li Da's Theoretical Activities", pp. 363–64; also Guo Huaruo, "Mao zhuxi kangzhan chuqi guanghui de zhexue huodong" (Chairman Mao's Glorious Philosophical Activities During the Early Period of the Anti-Japanese War), *Zhongguo zhexue*, Vol. 1 (1979), p. 34.

8. See Nick Knight (ed.), *Mao Zedong on Dialectical Materialism: Writings on Philosophy, 1937* (Armonk, New York: M.E. Sharpe, 1990), Introduction.

9. The first in the sequence of articles on "On Practice" was originally published in *Renmin Ribao* (People's Daily) on 1 February 1951, but was quickly republished in *Xin Jianshe*.

10. Michael Y.M. Kau and John K. Leung (eds), *The Writings of Mao Zedong, 1949–1976: Volume 1, September 1949–December 1955* (Armonk, New York: M.E. Sharpe, 1986), p. 179.

11. See *Mao Zedong shuxin xuanji*, pp. 407–8, 445; for translations of Mao's letters to Li Da, see Kau and Leung (eds), *The Writings of Mao Zedong, 1949–1976*, Vol. 1, pp. 179–80, 285–86.

12. Ibid., p. 179.

13. Li Da, *"Shijianlun" " Maodunlun" jieshuo* (An Explanation of "On Practice" and "On Contradiction") (Beijing: Sanlian shudian, 1979), p. 1.

14. Ibid., pp. 3–6.

15. Ibid., pp. 6–9.

16. Ibid., p. 15; translation taken from *Selected Works of Mao Tse-tung* (Peking: FLP, 1965), Vol. I, pp. 295–96.

17. Li Da, *"Shijianlun" "Maodunlun" jieshuo*, pp. 16–18.

18. Ibid., p. 18; the translation is from *Selected Works of Mao Tse-tung*, Vol. 1, p. 296.

19. Li Da, *"Shijianlun" "Maodunlun" jieshuo*, pp. 19–20.

20. Nick Knight, "*On Contradiction* and *On New Democracy*: Contrasting Perspectives on Causation and Social Change in the Thought of Mao Zedong", *Bulletin of Concerned Asian Scholars*, Vol. 22, No. 2 (April–June 1990), pp. 18–34.

21. Li Da, *"Shijianlun" "Maodunlun" jieshuo*, pp. 262–63; translation taken from *Selected Works of Mao Tse-tung*, Vol. 1, pp. 335–36.

22. The translation of the quote is from *Selected Works of Mao Tse-tung*, Vol. 4, pp. 412–13.

23. Translation taken from ibid., Vol. 3, pp. 17–18.

24. Translation of this quote taken from J.V. Stalin, *Marxism and Problems of Linguistics* (Peking: FLP, 1972), p. 3.

25. Ibid., p. 5.

26. Li Da, *"Shijianlun" "Maodunlun" jieshuo*, pp. 262–70.

27. See for example, Stuart R. Schram, *The Thought of Mao Tse-tung* (Cambridge: Cambridge University Press, 1989), pp. 5, 17, 54–55, 67, 96, 113, 168, 200.

28 *Selected Works of Mao Tse-tung*, Vol. 1, p. 311.

29. Li Da, *"Shijianlun" "Maodunlun" jieshuo*, pp. 120–21.

30. Li Da, "Du Mao Zedong tongzhi 1926–1929 de sipian wenzhang" (Read Comrade Mao Zedong's Four Articles from 1926–1929), *Renmin zhoubao*, No. 36 (1951); also in *Renmin ribao*, 30 August 1951, and *Changjiang ribao*, 9 September 1951. Also *Li Da wenji*, Vol. 4, pp. 135–47.

31. See, for example, Li Da, "Mao Zedong sixiang de weida shengli — jinian dang chengli sanshi zhounian he 'Lun renmin minzhuzhuanzheng' fabiao er zhounian er zuo" (The Great Victory of Mao Zedong Thought — Commemorating the Thirtieth Anniversary of the Founding of the Party and the Second Anniversary of the Publication of 'On the People's Democratic Dictatorship'), *Changjiang ribao*, 2 July 1951.

32. Li Da, "Renzhen xuexi Mao zhuxi de zhuzuo, gaizheng xuefeng, jioafeng he wenfeng" (Conscientiously Study Chairman Mao's Writings, and Rectify Study, Teaching and Writing), *Zhexue yanjiu*, No. 7 (1958), pp. 1–2.

33. There is some irony in Li's position here, as he had tried as best he could to reconcile the philosophical differences between Mao and Stalin in his explanatory notes on "On Practice" and "On Contradiction". (See *"Shijianlun" "Maodunlun" jieshuo*, pp. 121–23.) Here Stalin was spoken of in a reverential manner.

34. Li Da, "Zenyang xuexi Mao Zedong sixiang" (How Should Mao Zedong Thought Be Studied?), *Wuhan daxue renwen kexue xuebao*, No. 1 (1960), pp. 1–3; also in *Li Da wenji*, Vol. 4, pp. 738–43.

ical thought of Mao Zedong, was considered in the previous
10

Writings on Marxist Philosophy and Theory of the 1950s and 1960s

As we observed in the previous chapter, the tone and content of Li Da's philosophical and theoretical writings changed significantly in the post-Liberation period. Prior to his readmission to the party in 1949, Li had not written a single article which focused on Mao Zedong's thought, yet during the 1950s and early 1960s the explication and dissemination of Mao's thought became a major preoccupation for Li. This change is to be explained by reference to the changed political climate within which Li wrote and to his altered status from sympathetic outsider to highly esteemed Party theorist and philosopher. Li was no longer disseminating only Marxist and Leninist philosophy, but the thought of the new leader of China, Mao Zedong. It is apparent from his writings of the 1950s and early 1960s that Li genuinely considered Mao's thought to be a development of Marxism-Leninism and that he was consequently prepared to play an active role in its explication and dissemination. His numerous writings from the the post-1949 period traverse, as usual, a wide range of topics, but the focus remains on Marxist theory, of which Mao Zedong's thought had now become a highly significant component.

Li Da's writings on theory and philosophy of the 1950s and 1960s can be divided into four categories. The first of these, Li's explication of the philosophical thought of Mao Zedong, was considered in the previous chapter. The second incorporates Li's polemical writings from the 1950s, in which he critiqued other intellectuals whose philosophical and theoretical views were deemed by the Party to be erroneous and a threat. The third includes his writings of the period of the Great Leap Forward (1958–60). Despite his serious reservations about this campaign, it prompted Li to write a series of interesting articles which return to the issue of the materialist conception of history and how this should be interpreted in the context of a socialist society. The fourth involved his revision, under the prompting of Mao Zedong, of *Elements of Sociology*, his classic work from the 1930s. This latter project remained incompleteat the time of Li's death, the first section being formally published only in 1978; it nevertheless represents a fitting swansong, as the history of the project reveals something of the tensions confronted by this strong-minded intellectual in the context of a changing orthodoxy. Li had resolved this sort of problem in 1923 by leaving the Party; in the early 1960s, with the cult of personality emerging around Mao and the storm clouds of the Cultural Revolution gathering on the horizon, that option was not open to Li. His refusal to accept that Mao Zedong Thought was, as Lin Biao asserted, the pinnacle of Marxist-Leninist thought, created a dilemma not only for the revision of *Elements of Sociology*, but for Li's professional and personal life as well. The dilemma ended, without resolution, with his death in August 1966.

Polemical Writings of the 1950s: Hu Shi

In the heady days following Liberation and his readmission to the Party, that dilemma lay in the future. With his characteristic enthusiasm and appetite for hard work, Li threw himself into the task of elaborating Mao's theoretical and philosophical thought, for Mao's thought, as it had developed to 1949, was in Li's estimation a valid development of Marxism-Leninism, and a valid and successful application of its universal principles to the Chinese context. His explication of "On Practice" and "On Contradiction" reveals, as we have seen, no area of disagreement with Mao's philosophical thought, the intention of his explication being only to flesh out and illustrate Mao's precepts in accessible language.

Li Da's support for Mao Zedong's thought during the early 1950s was made manifest not only through his writings directly on it, but also through his contribution to a number of campaigns whose purpose was the criticism of intellectual figures to whom Mao and the Communist leadership were hostile. Li lent his considerable philosophical and literary talents to criticisms of a number of noted philosophers and social theorists, including Hu Shi and Fei Xiaotong.[1] While the motivation for Li's critiques was overtly political and their style polemical, they cannot for this reason be dismissed as the mere pamphleteering of a once-famous intellectual compelled by changed circumstance to play the role of the philosophical court jester, for these polemical writings reveal the considerable philosophical and theoretical erudition of which Li had demonstrated himself capable in his pre-1949 writings.

In 1954, the famous Chinese philosopher Hu Shi became the target of a virulent campaign whose purpose was to discredit him politically and to weaken the appeal of his pragmatic philosophy. Li wrote a number of articles in 1954–55 contributing to this campaign which were subsequently expanded into two pamphlets, *Hu Shi fandong sixiang pipan* (A Critique of Hu Shi's Reactionary Thought) and *Shiyongzhuyi: diguozhuyi de yuyong zhexue* (Pragmatism: The Philosophical Tool of Imperialism).[2] Li commences the first of these (a sizeable pamphlet of 53,000 characters) with a candid admission that he had not read Hu Shi's articles and books in his many years at universities in the "white" areas (that is, those controlled by the Guomindang).[3] In order to write this critique, Li was thus obliged to spend a month of "patient work" studying Hu Shi's philosophy. It is also clear from the second of these two pamphlets that he devoted considerable attention to Hu Shi's English and American predecessors in the tradition of pragmatic philosophy: Charles Pearce, John Dewey, William James and Ferdinand Schiller.[4]

Li's critique focuses on a number of presumed deficiencies in Hu Shi's philosophy of pragmatism. The first of these is pragmatism's response to the fundamental question of philosophy, the relationship between matter and consciousness. Materialism, Li asserts, regards matter as primary and consciousness as secondary. Pragmatism, while appearing to endorse this proposition through its emphasis on experience, in effect lapses into subjective empiricism by rejecting the relationship between experience and the objective world, recognising only the relationship between individual experience and one's own perceptions and feelings (*qinggan*). It suggests (and here is similar to Machism) that experience is the integration (*jiehe*) of matter and consciousness; perceptions and experiences are thus not reflections of the objective world, but things contained in human consciousness. Consequently, while physical objects (facts, things, existence, the universe, the material world) and mental objects (perceptions, truth, inference, thought, knowledge) are both portrayed as incorporated within "pure experience", mental objects are in effect dominant. The process of knowledge is confined to experience, the objects of knowledge being themselves within experience, rather than possessing an objective existence independent of human thought; reality is thus something which humans create. For Li, this runs counter to dialectical materialism, which stresses the objective existence of reality, but which emphasises the knowability of reality by human thought through the agency of human practice; experience of reality is gained through practice, through production and class struggle. This experience is reflected in the human nervous system, leading to perceptions and the accumulation of "perceptual experience", which creates the material for thought. Through a process of cognition, ideas and concepts are created which must themselves be tested in production and class struggle to determine whether they are correct. Li charges pragmatism with neglecting the role of social practice (the struggle for production, class struggle and scientific experimentation); pragmatism's so-called "practice" is based on thoughts and concepts subjectively manufactured and put into practice (*shixing*), but the results of this "practice" merely demonstrate the compatability of subjective and subjective, rather than subjective and objective.[5] Pragmatism therefore lapses into a form of agnosticism, one in which the possibility of ascertaining the truth of the objective world and its laws of development is denied.[6] When it speaks of "truth", pragmatism refers to something which is created by humans, and this is because "knowledge" is knowledge of subjective experience, rather than of the objective world;[7] subjective experience can "know" only itself, and cannot employ practice to discover the laws of development of the objective world, but only to verify the compatibility of thought and subjective experience.[8]

Pragmatism secondly perceives experience as something which is continually evolving, for the world and the universe are themselves continually evolving, although incrementally, rather than through dramatic change. Li criticises this as a vulgar evolutionist view, one deriving from the simplistic application of Darwin's views to human history, and one which leads to a rejection of revolution and an acceptance of reformism, for even the major revolutions of history are perceived by Hu as part of a gradual evolutionary process.[9] The advocation of gradual reform does not, however, threaten the capitalist system, and indeed contributes to its maintenance; Hu Shi is thus guilty of disseminating a philosophical view which reinforces capitalism. An example of Hu's reformism cited by Li is his call for "good government" in the early 1920s. At a time when the Communist Party was actively engaged in struggle against the reactionary warlord government, Hu issued an appeal for a constitutional and open government, one based on "planned politics". This reformist appeal was not only futile, but served to distract attention from the necessity for resolute struggle, and thus reinforced rather than weakened the warlord government and its supporters.[10]

According to Li, in terms of methodology, pragmatism takes the idealist path. Hu Shi, following John Dewey, reduced philosophy to a method of thought for the solution of human problems; because this method no longer recognises the philosophical struggle between materialism and idealism, it in effect abandons philosophy for science, which alone is held capable of studying the specific problems which humans confront. But this method is capable of making no philosophical judgment regarding morals or values, and does not attempt to do so; the major ills of society are thus ignored in favour of investigation of social minutiae, for individual problems are the appropriate object of investigation.[11] However, in its presumed but false neutrality, pragmatism becomes in effect a philosophy of the bourgeoisie, for it fails to recognise that social problems are not isolated but derive from the structural characteristics of capitalism, with its class system based on the exploitation of the working class. In stressing the study of individual problems, pragmatism opposes Marxism, for the latter philosophy opposes a piecemeal approach, perceiving the major problems of society as related to production and class relations. Consequently, Marxism, in contrast to pragmatism, stands openly opposed to capitalism and imperialism, for it recognises the interrelated character of these systems of oppression.[12]

From Li's perspective, one of the major weaknesses of Hu Shi's method is his belief that society is composed of "individuals". With this belief, Hu Shi cannot but reject the concept of class and its implications for revolutionary social change; his perception ignores the distinction between capitalist and worker and between landlord and peasant, for all are just "individuals". In his attempted refutation of Hu Shi's emphasis on individuals, Li lapses into a rather formulaic recitation of the causal sequence between the elements of the social structure:

> Our perspective is that Hu Shi's is an entirely bourgeois formalistic social view. We know that the history of human society produces the sequence of the five stages of primitive society, slave society, feudal society, capitalist society, and socialist society, and is now moving towards a communist society. The societies of these specific stages are a function of the particular totality of their relations of production. On this foundation (in a commercial society, its class relations), there is a superstructure which is compatible with it; this superstructure represents the social views on politics, law, religion, art and literature, and philosophy, including the political and legal systems which are compatible with those views. This then is the social structure. The contradiction between the forces and relations of production is the motive force for social development. When the relations of production are compatible with the forces of production, the social structure is stable; but when the relations of production are out of step with the forces of production, the social structure becomes unstable, and there occurs social revolution. The progressive revolutionary class rises to overthrow the old relations of production and to establish new relations of production which are compatible with the development of the forces of production. Therefore, the law that the relations of production must be compatible with the forces of production is a general law covering all stages of the development of society.[13]

Li qualifies this statement by concluding that "each stage of society has its own specific laws of development",[14] and by later talking of the "relative independence" of philosophy from economic determination,[15] but there is no reference here to the dynamic reactive role that the superstructure can play. As we shall observe, however, he does return to this theme in his writings of the period of the Great Leap Forward, and here the superstructure once again assumes the active role it had in his earlier writings.

Li is also extremely critical of Hu's deprecating attititude towards China and his esteem for American values and achievements. Hu had studied in the United States under the American philosopher of pragmatism John Dewey, and this had influenced him, both philosophically and politically, to adopt a sympathetic attitude towards the intentions of America and other foreign countries in China, as well as towards the forces of reaction within China which supported or condoned imperialist aggression. Hu had thus advocated acceptance of Japan's Twenty-one Demands by the Yuan Shikai government, and had joined Chiang Kai-shek's "traitorous clique".[16] From first to last, he had opposed the Communist Party, opposed the anti-imperialist and anti-feudal struggle, and demonstrated that he was nothing more than an "American cultural compradore".[17] Li sneers at Hu Shi's description of himself as a "citizen of the world"; he is, rather, a "citizen of the United States of America", one who advocated the necessity of American development of China, for China's culture was inferior to world culture which in effect was dominated by America. Hu was thus easily identified by Li as a proponent of the "wholesale Westernisation" of China (although it is doubtful that Hu meant by this slogan anything more than a conscientious absorption of Western skills and values in all areas, rather than the indiscriminate transplantation of things Western and the rejection of everything Chinese).[18]

It is Hu Shi's genuflexion to the West, one suspects, that is the real motivation for Li's attack. Although Li Da presents an accessible critique of Hu's pragmatic philosophy from a dialectical materialist perspective, the distinction between the epistemology of pragmatism and that of dialectical materialism would no doubt have been rather too finely drawn for some of Li's readers. Both philosophies, after all, employ the concepts of experience; both philosophies oppose formal logic.[19] Indeed, Li is hard-pressed to persuade his readers that dialectical materialism has a more logical solution than pragmatism to the problem of how perceptual sensations are transformed into concepts and thoughts; there is no attempt by Li to present any theoretical advance in this problematic area for dialectical materialism, and he falls back on a recitation of the properties and virtues of its epistemology. It is, rather, Li's critique of the political and social implications of pragmatism which carries the most force He is able to demonstrate clearly that pragmatism's endorsement of individualism entails a rejection of class as the focus for the study of social problems, and that this rejection serves to strengthen the hand of the capitalist class, for pragmatism's focus on "social problems" does not incorporate consideration of the exploitation of the working class and the "toiling masses", and consequently is no threat to capitalism's structure of exploitation. Similarly, although Li's attack on Hu Shi's affinity with America relies heavily on *ad hominem* invective, he is effectively able to draw from it the conclusion that Hu has played the role of cultural comprador for American interests; Hu's pragmatism had thus become "the philosophical tool of imperialism".[20]

Li's critique of Hu Shi was not, of course, a personal vendetta, for prior to 1954, he had taken no interest in Hu Shi's philosophical writings or personal life. It is to be understood rather as part of a wider campaign to discredit Hu Shi and to oppose American imperialism which, in the early 1950s, loomed as the largest threat to China's security. Many other intellectuals were drawn into this campaign, and it would have been virtually impossible for Li, with his pre-eminent stature in China's philosophical world, to stand aloof. It would, however, be incorrect to give the impression that Li's participation in the campaign was unwilling, for once the catalyst of the campaign had triggered his interest in Hu Shi and the philosophy of pragmatism, he committed his considerable skills as a philosopher and propagandist to its success. He even went so far as to send several of his articles on Hu Shi to Mao Zedong for comment. In his letter of response, Mao clarified a number of problems with Li's exposition of pragmatism, but enthusiastically endorsed the general tenor of Li's critique of pragmatism:[21]

> Your writings are in popular language and easy to understand. This is good. When you write again, I suggest that you make use of appropriate occasions to explain certain basic concepts in philosophy so that cadres in general can read and understand them. We must use this opportunity to help the millions of cadres, both inside and outside the Party, who have no knowledge of philosophy, to understand some Marxist philosophy. What do you think? My respects.
>
> Mao Zedong
28 December 1954

The political climate, in which Li's involvement in the campaign to criticise Hu Shi was made virtually unavoidable, was thus reinforced by Mao's personal endorsement of his participation. Should he have resisted these pressures? Li's biographer, Wang Jionghua, while obviously sympathetic to his subject, is very critical of this aspect of Li's philosophical career; he was guilty, Wang suggests, of "arbitrariness" (*duduanzhuyi*), for he ignored or gave insufficient emphasis to Hu's positive contributions.[22] In response, we might suggest that Wang's judgment gives insufficient consideration to the political and social climate within which Li operated in the early 1950s. Even had he wished to avoid participation in the campaign or to write a more "even-handed" critique of Hu's philosophical thought and career (and there is no evidence that either of these was the case), the point remains that Li was, like all other prominent Chinese intellectuals at the time, not a free agent and could not have chosen to do so without serious personal consequences. The cost of his re-entry to the Party in 1949 was acceptance of Party discipline and all that that implied; and one significant implication was that Li could not stand aloof from the Party's campaigns against its intellectual enemies.[23]

Polemical Writings of the 1950s: Fei Xiaotong

Li Da's attack on Fei Xiaotong (b. 1911) in the wake of the Hundred Flowers movement is now largely ignored in post-Mao China. It is as though this attack on the social theories of this prominent and now highly respected ethnologist and anthropologist was an indiscretion best ignored. Li's polemic is, however, of some interest, for it demonstrates that his opposition to mainstream sociology, manifest as early as the 1920s, had not faltered. His own understanding of sociology, articulated in his *Contemporary Sociology* and *Elements of Sociology*, was premised on the precepts of historical materialism. Consequently, anthropologists and sociologists such as Fei who did not employ the concepts of forces and relations of production as their point of departure, relying rather on Western "capitalist sociology", were in effect guilty of employing a "compradore sociology".

In his pamphlet *A Critique of the Compradore Sociology of Fei Xiaotong* (written in 1957 and published in May 1958), Li accuses Fei (a non-Party intellectual who had been branded a "rightist") of attempting a restoration of "capitalist sociology" through the establishment of a "sociology working party" which planned to found sociology departments in universities and cadre schools.[24] Li regards this as a general strategy to seize control of the academic world and to oppose Marxism's historical materialism. The purpose of Li's pamhlet is to pose the following questions: What in actuality is Fei Xiaotong's "capitalist sociology"? Is it a science? What class does it serve? And what dangers does it pose for "our socialist state"?[25]

In answering these questions, Li looks first at the origins of "capitalist sociology". This first originated, he suggests, in France, with the writings of August Comte, the positivist philosopher who believed that concepts (*guannian*) were the basis for the entire social structure, and who used the history of the development of knowledge to explain the history of the development of society. Capitalist society, which had emerged during the last, positivist, phase in the development of human thought was thus perceived by him to be the most rational and progressive of societies. He consequently felt that the consolidation of "order" in capitalist society was an absolute necessity, and that the capitalist class should be supported in its struggle against both the feudal aristocracy and the newly emergent proletariat. His sociology was perceived as assuming this function. This pro-capitalist, anti-proletarian theme in sociology was then carried forward in the biological sociology of Herbert Spencer, which perceived society as akin to the animal kingdom, the division of society into the exploited and the exploiters, the oppressors and oppressed, being a manifestation of the laws which governed nature. Capitalism thus possessed no internal contradictions, and the notion of class struggle was rejected. One branch of biological sociology, the Social Darwinists, perceived the domination of the proletariat by the capitalists, and of small nations by imperialism, as in conformity with the natural laws of competition. Another branch perceived race and nation as the basic factors in history, and the struggle between them as the motive force in history; this sociological persuasion perceived the white race as the creators of culture, and therefore having the right to oppress and exploit the black and yellow races.[26]

However, the most important strand of "capitalist sociology" during the era of imperialism was social psychology. This brand of sociology regarded society as constructed by the mutual interaction of human psychologies, and it was this which constituted the appropriate object for sociological study. Those individuals or nations possessing superior psychologies were able to dominate others. As human knowledge, from this perspective, was the prime motive force in social change, any attempt to reform society must be premised on the transformation of the will of the people (*renxin*), and this could only be achieved through education; however, the educators would, Li retorts, be those who possessed superior knowledge, while those being "educated" would be the proletariat and toiling masses.[27]

In addition, "capitalist sociology" includes Malthusian population theory and what Li terms "formal sociology". Despite these divisions within "capitalist sociology", they all possess the following characteristics:

1. They all adopt an idealist social perspective, employing social ideas to explain social existence.
2. Because they are afraid of the objective laws of social development, they reject them, attempting to verify that the capitalist system will last forever.

3. They oppose Marxism, and in particular historical materialism.
4. They oppose the proletarian revolution, and advocate reformism.
5. They justify the dominance and exploitation of the proletariat by the bourgeoisie.
6. They create theories which justify imperialist invasion.

At odds with "capitalist sociology" is historical materialism, which is the only science which recognises the laws of development of society, which unifies a scientific social perspective and methodology, and which unifies social theory and practice. The experience of the communist parties in the Soviet Union, China and other countries verifies, according to Li, the truth of historical materialism.[28]

The "Chinese sociology" of Fei Xiaotong is, according to Li, "capitalist sociology" with a Chinese flavour. Fei's sociological research can be split into two themes: village sociology and the analysis of the social structure. For Fei, the model for the Chinese social structure was provided by Confucius, with ethical relations as its standard and personal relations as its foundation; the historical sequence of this society was dependent on "the rites" (*li*). Moreover, China's economic structure was "an economy of deficiency", one with an abundance of human beings but poor in resources, and one which typified the Malthusian population theory. Because the Chinese people had absorbed the Confucian emphasis on rites, they did not have an attitude towards nature which allowed science and technology to develop, and this led to economic stagnation and deficiency. Fei saw no hope of economic modernisation, and for that reason perceived China as merely a market for the industrialised nations. The only hope Fei perceived for economic growth was in China's villages with the establishment of small factories and enterprises. Nevertheless, because of its longevity, Fei perceived the traditional Chinese social structure as superior to those of Western nations.[29]

Li is critical of the derivative character of Fei's "Chinese sociology". It derives, he suggests, largely from the writings of Liang Qichao who had similarly stressed the importance of rites, ethical standards and personal relations to traditional Chinese society.[30] Both Liang and Fei employed an idealist conception to oppose the Marxist view of Chinese history and society; both rejected the objective laws of social development, and the existence of class and class struggle. Politically, both had opposed the communist-led revolution against imperialism and feudalism. On the eve of Liberation, at a time when large-scale land reform was being carried out in the liberated areas, Fei had opposed the seizure of the land by the peasants and had advised the landlords to shift their capital from land into industry.[31]

Li then turns his critical scrutiny to Fei Xiaotong's social investigations. Fei is, Li asserts, a disciple of Bronislaw Malinowski, an anthropologist who had employed a functionalist perspective to analyse the social system, customs and habits of colonial peoples.[32] Fei's use of Malinowski's approach is presented as grim irony by Li; for here is a Chinese cultural sociologist using a method employed to study colonial peoples to investigate village life in socialist China. The result is a treatise on China's villages which speaks of the dissatisfaction of the peasants with co-operativisation, which regards the land reform as a mistake, and which in effect broadcasts the superiority of semi-colonialism and semi-feudalism. Li argues, however, that Fei's depiction of China's village life is inaccurate, and he points to empirical evidence which verifies the proposition that the life of China's peasants had indeed improved as a result of Liberation and the rural policies pursued since by the Communist Party.[33] The same holds true, Li adds, for Fei's analyses of China's national minorities, which are informed by Malinowski rather than Marx.[34]

Like his attack on Hu Shi, Li's critique of Fei Xiaotong contains its share of invective. For example, Li presents in a rather sinister light Fei's motives for writing such books as *Peasant Life in China* in English and publishing them in England and the United States; these are, he asserts, the actions of one whose target audience is the intellectuals of the colonial powers.[35] Fei is also branded as one seeking to be perceived as the "saviour" of landlords and rich peasants.[36] This invective aside, Li's critique of Fei's sociology does represent a serious, if rather polemical, attempt to discredit a theory standing in opposition to Marxism's historical materialism. Just as Li had expended considerable energy studying Hu Shi's pragmatic philosophy, it is clear that Li had also studied Fei's sociological writings in an attempt to understand their premises and methodology. Nevertheless, Li's polemic against Fei is a product not only of his staunch intellectual adherence to Marxism, but of the political climate prevailing in the wake of the failure of the Hundred Flowers campaign of 1956–57. Fei Xiaotong was one of China's most prominent social scientists, having been vice-president of the Chinese Institute of Ethnic Studies and deputy director of the Specialists Bureau of the State Council; he had also been a member of the Standing Committee of the Democratic League. In March 1957, Fei had published an article in *People's Daily*, entitled "The Early Spring Weather of the Intellectuals", in which he pointed out, on the basis of a tour of the country, that China's intellectuals feared the political "early spring weather" — in other words, they distrusted the invitation to "bloom and contend" for they had found through experience that the political climate was liable to alter suddenly, and that the mild weather of spring could rapidly return to hard frost. For this and other activities, Fei was subsequently denounced as a "big Rightist" by Mao, although Mao himself suggested that thought reform through labour would not be appropriate for a "big intellectual" like Fei whose "shoulders can't carry anything", whose "hands can't lift anything".[37] Fei's punishment was rather to be lambasted by intellectuals like Li Da who had not wavered in their support of the Party, and who rallied to the cry to oppose revisionism and right-wing opportunism.[38]

Theoretical Writings of the Great Leap Forward

In hindsight, Li Da's polemical writings of the 1950s appear as something of an irony in light of the fate that befell him with the onset of the Cultural Revolution in 1966, for he was in turn to become the subject of a vicious campaign of vilification in which he was denounced as "an anti-Party, anti-socialist representative of the bourgeoisie who is opposed to Mao Zedong Thought".[39] Indeed, the attack on Li Da was to be worse than anything that he had himself inflicted on others, for although Li's critiques of Hu Shi and Fei Xiaotong were polemical, they were based on a thorough study of their writings and a careful and logical attempt to repudiate their philosophy and theory. Li received no such consideration, and his more than four decades of service to the elaboration of Marxism and its dissemination in China were to be swept aside in a tide of invective and abuse.

But that lay in the future, when the orthodoxy for which Li was previously prepared to commit his talents and energy had been transformed into what Li believed was a caricature of its previous self. Li's doubts about the wisdom of the direction Mao Zedong's thought was taking first emerged with the onset of the Great Leap Forward. As we observed in Chapter 1, his frank and heated exchange with Mao in October 1958 centered on the propriety of giving excessive emphasis to the role of subjective forces and the superstructure in initiating social change, something Li accused Mao of doing. While Li had never espoused a mechanistically economistic interpretation of the materialist conception of history, he did demur at the notion that the subjective enthusiasm of the masses was, in the absence of appropriate material conditions, sufficient to achieve social change of the magnitude desired by Mao. Li's reservations regarding the theoretical premises and practical implications of the Great Leap Forward were not, however, made public. Indeed, during the years 1958–60 he wrote a booklet and a series of articles, published mainly in the journal *Lilun zhanxian* (Theoretical Front), which elaborated the materialist conception of history and applied it to the context of socialist transition. These writings contain a strong affirmation of the policies of socialisation and cooperativisation carried out since Liberation, and could be read too as a defence of the Great Leap Forward.[40] For, as we shall see, Li attributes the superstructure with a dynamic capacity to react on the economic base, and to facilitate the establishment, consolidation and development of the base; he moreover describes the relations of production, in the context of socialism, as a significant motive force for rapid development of the forces of production.[41] Mao would have quarrelled with neither of these views.[42] Nevertheless, in Li's careful and quite detailed interpretation of historical materialism, one can perceive a repudiation of the view that the superstructure and human consciousness possess a virtually unfettered capacity to initiate major social change; they can only possess what Li terms a "relative independence" from economic determination. The divergence between Li and Mao was thus not over whether the superstructure possessed a dynamic role, for both agreed that it did; the disagreement centered rather on the extent of this role, and the extent to which the superstructure was constrained by the developments within the economic base.[43]

A number of themes stand out in Li's theoretical writings from the Great Leap Forward. First, Li reiterates the standard view that all societies, impelled by universal laws of development, pass through certain modes of production: primitive, slave, feudal, capitalist, socialist, and from there to communism. He qualifies this historical timetable by arguing that each nation's development is also determined by its own specific conditions; the universal laws of development and the specific conditions are linked. Such specific conditions might include the historical stage reached by that nation, its internal and external conditions, and the influence of other nations with which it has come into contact. Li gives the example of the primitive Germanic peoples who were able to progress directly to feudalism on the basis of the semi-feudal, semi-slave society engendered by the economic changes following the collapse of Imperial Rome. Similarly, in the era of capitalism, European powers had used military force to vanquish "backward" nations, compelling them to become not only colonies but forcing them into a capitalist form of development; with the emergence of the socialist camp, the more powerful socialist societies had helped "backward" societies, such as Mongolia, to move directly from feudalism to socialism.[44]

There are, Li continues, general laws, independent of human volition, which govern the socialist transition of all nations; all nations, for example, must establish socialist democracy, institute a dictatorship of the proletariat and eliminate the old society's system of oppression. However, each nation has its own characteristics, and the forms that these laws take will differ as the conditions differ; these include such things as the level of industrialisation, size of population, strength of the old exploiting classes, geographical conditions, the nature of traditions and the psychology of the people. The policies to be pursued for socialist construction will therefore obviously differ from one nation to the next, but such policies must be in conformity with the general laws which are shared in common by all societies making this transition. Consequently, the experience of socialist revolution and construction in the Soviet Union had been comprised of a fundamental experience which was of relevance to other countries, as well as experiences which were specific to the Soviet Union. The basic thrust of China's experience of revolution (armed struggle, worker–peasant alliance under the leadership of the Communist Party) and socialist construction (socialisation of industry, cooperativisation of land, elimination of exploitation) had mirrored the fundamental experience of the Soviet Union, but these of course had been made manifest in accord with China's own specific characteristics. A communist party of any country had to steer a path between underemphasising its nation's specific characteristics and giving them undue emphasis; the former strategy exhibited a tendency towards dogmatism, while the latter was a revisionist tendency. To avoid these pitfalls, a Marxist party had to employ dialectical materialism to investigate problems, and carry out a comprehensive and concrete analysis, and so achieve a unity of theory and practice.[45]

A second and important theme in Li's writings of the Great Leap Forward is the causal relationship existing between the economic base and the superstructure. The object of historical materialism, Li argues, is the discovery of the general laws of social development, and these laws concern first and foremost the causal significance of the various realms of society. Commencing from the materialist premise that social existence determines social consciousness, historical materialism perceives society as a "socioeconomic formation" (*shehui jingji xingtai*). This concept is, Li asserts, a fundamental concept of historical materialism, for it allows the discovery of the developmental tendency of the material foundation of the process of history. The totality of the relations of production generated by the material forces of production constitutes the economic structure of society, and this is the social base (*shehui jichu*). On this social base, and reliant on it, is established a legal and political superstructure; corresponding to this are definite forms of social consciousness, namely philosophy, natural science, social science, literature, art, morality, religion and so on. The socioeconomic formation, with the relationship between its various components, is depicted diagrammatically by Li in a manner clearly reminiscent of

Sugiyama Sakae's depiction of the 1920s, and translated into Chinese by Li (see Chapter 5).[46]

Although it appears from the diagram below that there is a reciprocal level of influence between the base and superstructure, Li stresses that within the socioeconomic formation, the base has causal dominance; it possesses a "determinative function" (*jueding zuoyong*). The superstructure is clearly not a passive reflection, however, for it has the capacity to react on the base, and the base is subject to the definite influence of the superstructure (*shi jichu shoudao yiding de yingxiang*). Nevertheless, Li stresses that the capacity of the superstructure to influence the base is itself generated by the base, and if the base alters, the superstructure also must alter, and the entire character of society changes as the social formation is transformed into a higher form. The replacement of one socioeconomic form by another is a consequence of the contradiction between the forces and relations of production which manifests itself as class struggle. However, Li is once again at pains to point out that the manifestation of this general law of historical development is subject to the particular characteristics of each society, and what historical materialism analyses is the history of actual

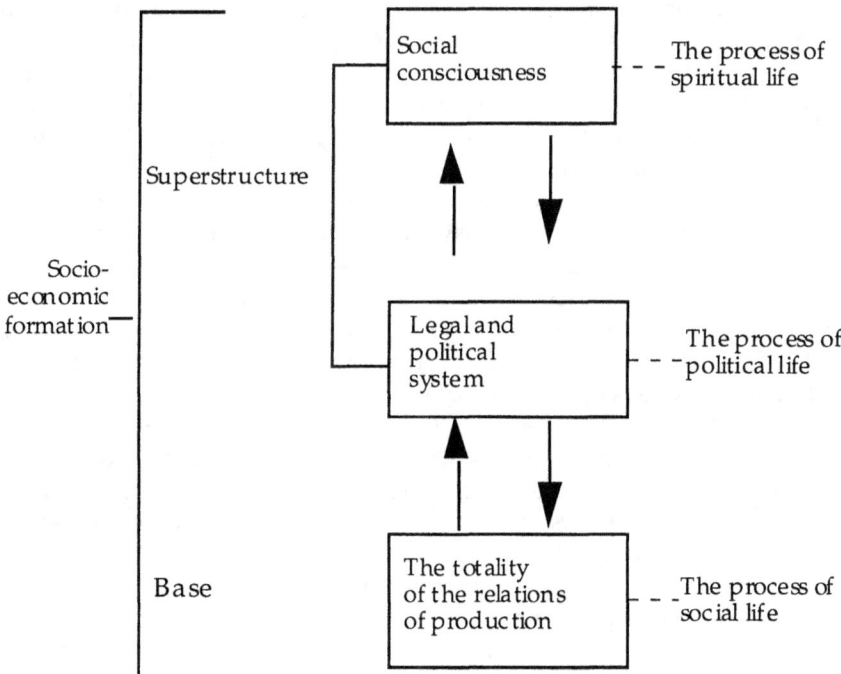

FIGURE 10.1   Li Da's Concept of the Socio-economic Formation

societies during definite stages of development; the object of analysis is the unity of particular and general laws of development.[47]

Li proceeds to identify the various dimensions of the economic base. The forces of production can be defined, following Marx, as the labour process. This incorporates labour power (the productive experience and skills of the labourer), the instruments of labour (the tools of production to which the experience and skill of the labourer are applied) and the objects of labour (the material resources from which products are created by the labourer using appropriate instruments). The labour process is an integrated process in which each of these three facets must be present; if one is absent, humans will be unable to engage in production, and they must, moreover, be present in appropriate dimensions. Moreover, the labour process can only proceed in the context of definite social relations; the two are indivisible, for the forces of production represent the content of particular class relations, while the relations of production represent the form of the development of the forces of production. It is the combination of the forces and relations of production which constitutes the economic base.[48] A unity thus exists between the forces and relations of production, and within this unity, the relations of production can exert an influence on the forces of production (in either an obstructive or accelerative role). The relations of production, once created by the forces of production, possess a "relative independence", but the forces of production ultimately occupy the dominant position in the unity of opposites which exists between them.[49] The forces of production are in constant development, and the relations of production which emerge are appropriate to this development, although any harmony between them can only be a temporary phenomenon; there is ultimately a clash between them as the formerly appropriate but now increasingly anachronistic relations of production become obstructive of further development of the forces of production. The contradiction between forces and relations of production is the motive force impelling change to a higher productive form.[50] This contradiction exists in all societies. The distinction lies between those societies which are antagonistic and those which are not; in the former, the contradiction between forces and relations of production will be antagonistic and can only be resolved through violence and class struggle; in socialist societies, however, because of public ownership and "comradely" mutual cooperation, this contradiction assumes a non-antagonistic form.[51]

Li stresses that the relations of production do not exist in pure form. Marx had abstracted from the experience of a number of capitalist societies to provide his analysis of "pure" capitalist relations of production, but he was well aware, according to Li, that the economic structure of any society is exceedingly complex, with remnants of previous economic forms persisting into subsequent eras. The mixture of classes existing within the relations of production varies from one social formation to another. The American social formation differed from the British in that, although both were dominated by a capitalist mode of production, their class relations differed; America possessed no feudal remnants as did the British social formation, but had possessed a form of production based on slavery; however the dominant class relationship in both cases, and the one which defines capitalism as a distinct economic form, is the relationship between capitalists and proletariat. Nevertheless, Li emphasises that it is essential to grasp the complexity of the economic structure of society, with its variegated and diverse class composition, for only then is it possible to comprehend the complexity of the superstructure and the complexity of political and ideological struggles. The view that the superstructure of a society is solely the domain of that society's dominant class is without foundation, for there are other class influences at work which generate forms of behaviour and modes of thought within the superstructure.

The contradictions existing within the economic base are reflected in the superstucture, and in class societies, this contradiction is antagonistic in character. Li provides the example of the political influence exerted by the proletariat in some capitalist countries; this influence had been sufficient to detabilise the superstructure and to compel the capitalist class to mobilise the state and armed forces (themselves elements of the superstructure) to defuse the threat in the realm of the superstructure. Similarly, forms of consciousness are reflections in the superstructure of the relations of production, but once created are capable of influencing the outcome of the struggle between the classes. In capitalist countries, those who dominate in the economic realm tend to dominate too in the realm of consciousness. The capitalist class employs all of the organs of propaganda (schools, newspapers, radio, broadcasts, films, the church) to disseminate reactionary thought to weaken the revolutionary will and determination of the proletariat and the people; it employs the tactic of encouraging reformism amongst the labour aristocracy. But the struggle in the superstructure becomes intense as the proletariat moves from being a "class-in-itself" to being a "class-for-itself", one with a coherent consciousness of its historical role and objectives.[52]

Li argues — and this is reminiscent of his own experience — that one of the first tactics which must be employed by the party of the proletariat to implement revolutionary struggle is to disseminate and propagandise Marxism amongst the proletariat and the masses of the people; only when this has been achieved is it possible to mobilise and organise them for the attack on the power of the capitalist class. Once the proletariat has seized power, it must continue the task of disseminating Marxism in order to weaken the influence of capitalist thought and to increase receptivity to socialist ideas, for it is only when the socialist line has prevailed over the capitalist line on the ideological front that the dictatorship of the proletariat can be consolidated and a socialist society established.

Given the particular conditions prevailing in China, the superstructure assumed enhanced significance for the seizure of power. The Party, which Li terms the "principal element and leading force" of the superstructure, assumed the task of establishing and consolidating socialist relations of production. Indeed, without the Party's intervention and guidance, a socialist economic base could not have been established. In this respect, the capitalist and socialist revolutions differed. The former was a result of the gestation of capitalist relations of production in the womb of feudal society; the seizure of power by the capitalist class facilitated the development of the already existing class relationships characteristic of capitalism. Socialist relations of production, on the other hand, could not develop in the womb of the old society; as a result, the task of the proletarian revolution was not only the seizure of power, but the use of this power to establish, "from the bare earth", socialist relations of production. Here Li draws heavily on Lenin, whom he quotes as saying "politics takes precedence over economics" (*zhengzhi youxian yu jingji*), for, in the context of socialist transition, when the Party adopted certain economic measures and organised economic work, it had to do so from a political standpoint which, if deviated from, would lead to chaos. In China, the system of the dictatorship of the proletariat established after Liberation represented an advanced superstructural form; China's national economy was, however, "backward". This contradiction could only be resolved through the development of China's economy.[53]

Li stresses, however, that China's superstructure following Liberation was not uniformly advanced. The Party and its state structure, the dictatorship of the proletariat, were historically advanced, but there were many aspects of the superstructure which were not so, and indeed which attempted to obstruct — and were capable of doing so — the consolidation of socialist relations of production and further economic advance. In China, although the economic contradiction between the people and reactionary classes had lost much of its anatagonistic character as a result of socialist transformation, the influence of the reactionary classes remained strong in the superstructure. The former landlords and compradores had been overthrown, but still existed, their mouthpiece (*dailiren*) being the bourgeois rightists; and the national bourgeoisie and its intellectuals were only gradually accepting socialism.[54] The influence of these classes and class fractions persisted in the political superstructure in the form of right-wing elements like Liang Shuming within China's democratic parties; these elements could not accept that their cause was lost, opposing the Communist Party and striving for a restoration of capitalism.[55] In the realm of ideology, they openly espoused bourgeois thought in an attempt to overturn the leading role of Marxism, and in the fields of science and education they also attempted to weaken the influence of Marxism and the leading role of the Party.[56] Consequently, not only had the antagonisms not weakened in the superstructure, they had intensified, and there was thus a need for a socialist revolution in the political and ideological realms. The Party had responded to this problem through the education of intellectuals to rid them of bourgeois thought, and had attempted to disseminate socialist thought amongst China's peasants. However, the problem remained, for although the socialist transformation of China's economy had been basically completed by 1956, the victory of the socialist revolution in politics and ideology was, as the right-wing attacks on the Party and socialism in 1957 attested, far from completed.[57]

Li thus asserts the necessity of a socialist revolution in the superstructure; he also emphasises the "positive significance" that the Party has for the establishment of socialist relations of production. Given the importance he attributes to the superstructure, could his explanation be misinterpreted as a metaphysical theory, as one which attributes complete autonomy to the superstructure? On several occasions, Li recognises that his viewpoint could be so interpreted.[58] He is, however, at pains to correct this impression, emphasising yet again that any independence of the superstructure can only be relative; this relative autonomy emerges most clearly during those historical periods when there is not only a contradiction between base and superstructure, but sharp contradictions as well within the superstructure, between positive superstructural forces working for the consolidation of the socialist economic base and negative superstructural elements attempting to undermine this policy. This was precisely the situation in China; China's class structure had been exceedingly complex, and although this had changed as a result of the socialist transformation of the early 1950s, former classes and strata still existed and their influence persisted in the superstructure. An explanation of this influence would be impossible without mounting a materialist analysis which examined the previous and current structure of China's relations of production.

Li concludes that when we observe history (and the period of socialist transition is no exception), we must examine two aspects, the economic on the one hand, and the legal, political and ideological on the other; it appears on occasion as though these two aspects are unrelated. However, Li insists that if we dig deeper the behaviour of an apparently independent superstructure can still be explained by reference to changes and developments within the base. This is particularly the case with the state and the legal system which are often claimed to be independent of the interests of the dominant economic class, neutral arbiters of society's conflicting interests. However, they are, in fact, a concentrated expression of economics; they are created by the base and are a reflection of it.[59]

We can perceive in Li Da's elaboration of the materialist conception of history from the period of the Great Leap Forward a basic reaffirmation of the views that he had held for almost four decades. The importance he attributed in the early 1920s to the "political revolution" (see Chapter 3) was readily transposable to the need for a revolution in the superstructure in the context of socialist China in the late 1950s.[60] And in neither case did Li perceive his recognition of the significance of the superstructure as a denial of the materialist premises of the materialist conception of history. Rather, the economic base was the dominant force for historical change, but its relationship with the superstructure was mediated by a host of factors (manifestations of particular laws) which meant that the relationship could take on a complex character in which the superstructure became capable of playing a dynamic role and exerting a considerable influence. Li clearly believed that China's socialist transition was just such an instance, China having experienced a period of change in which the rapidity of economic transformation and development had generated a contradiction with the superstructure, some sections of which not only now lagged behind the economic base but which attempted either to forestall further change or achieve a dismantling of China's socialist economic institutions and relationships. Li was in no doubt that these forces for reaction in the superstructure, because of the fluid nature of the historical context, could play a serious negative role, and had to be struggled against. It is in this context that the reasons for Li's willing participation in the campaigns to criticise Hu Shi, Fei Xiaotong, Liang Shuming and others become clearer, for his call for a revolution in both science and culture was premised on a perception that any great leap forward in production would be seriously compromised if there were no concomitant leap forward in these other areas; the struggle against reactionary political ideas, philosophies and social science methodologies was thus, for Li, an urgent necessity.[61]

Li's conception of the materialist conception of history was thus founded first and foremost on a conception of the interrelated character of the socioeconomic formation, one in which "the process of social life", while retaining overall causal dominance, was itself subject to the influence of other non-economic realms. It is clear too that Li recognised that the socioeconomic formation was not a unified totality, but was founded on a series of contradictions (among others, between relations and forces of production, and between base and superstructure). The actual characteristics of these contradictions and the manner of their unfolding had to be the subject of concrete analysis, for each socioeconomic formation, while governed by universal laws of development, possessed its own particular laws, and these had to be understood through both investigation and practice. Li makes it clear that it is not sufficient to assume the appropriateness of models which, for purposes of analysis, abstract the essential features of a particular mode of production from its concrete socioeconomic formation, from its historical setting. While such models (such as Marx's critique of capital) were of immense importance in delineating the principal structural configuration and developmental tendencies of a mode of production, real-world socioeconomic formations were inevitably an untidy amalgam of forms of production, institutions, practices and relationships characteristic of a number of modes of production and, in the ideological sphere, different modes of thought appropriate to previous eras persisted in complex relationship with newer and more progressive ideas. These specificities and complexities of a concrete socioeconomic formation had to be grasped through investigation, but such investigation, to avoid being overwhelmed by the myriad concrete data, had to be premised on an understanding of the universal laws of development, of the big historical picture.

Li's disagreement with Mao over the policies of the Great Leap Forward centered, therefore, not on whether the superstructure could exert an influence, for both agreed that it did. Indeed, Li makes it very clear that the complex and rapid economic changes which the Chinese socio-economic formation had experienced had accentuated the contradiction between economic base and superstructure; for the latter still harboured modes of thought (from traditional ideas and customs to modern Western sociology and philosophy) which opposed the economic changes achieved since 1949 and resisted further change. In this concrete context, the superstructure became a highly significant site for struggle, for without an attenuation of the strength of ideas resistant to progress, the consolidation and further development of the socialist economic base were threatened. Li felt that he had played his part, through his polemical and theoretical writings and educational activities, in the struggle to weaken the hold of what he termed "reactionary thought" in the realm of the superstructure. By the same token, Li recognised — perhaps more so than Mao — the stubborn character of old ideas. It was not a question of sweeping these aside in one or even several campaigns; it was, rather, a question of long-term, painstaking education and propaganda, precisely the tasks Li had pursued since his first acquaintance with Marxism in the late 1910s, for without widespread comprehension and acceptance of the theory which underpinned change, the viability of change in the long term was in doubt.

Li must, therefore, have had reservations regarding the subjective readiness of the masses for a change of the magnitude of the Great Leap Forward; moreover, he was not convinced that the material foundations were in place for such a change. Had the prior development of the forces of production been extensive enough to suggest that a radical campaign of change was necessary or would succeed? While his writings of the 1958-60 period indicate in the main a strong public endorsement of the Great Leap Forward and provide a theoretical rationalisation of sorts for its policies,[62] it is clear from the record of his conversation with Mao that Li had his doubts, and his later support for Peng Dehuai in his tussle with Mao over the wisdom of the Great Leap Forward is further evidence of this.[63] For Li, the subjective readiness of the Chinese people was an important factor, and he recognised that the superstructure could play a significant role in historical change. But a failure to analyse the material premises for change and to consequently exaggerate the dynamic capacity of the superstructure to initiate and effect change was tantamount to lapsing into a metaphysical reading of the process of history, something he decidedly rejected.[64]

Elements of Dialectical Materialism and Mao Zedong's Contribution to Marxist Philosophy

Despite his expressed reservations on the policies of the Great Leap Forward, Li's friendly association with Mao, dating back to the early 1920s, continued apparently unabated. In August 1961, Li travelled to Lushan for prolonged rest following the discovery that, as well as the medical conditions from which he had previously suffered (gastric ulcer, high blood pressure and diabetes), he now had coronary heart disease which had developed to an edematous stage.[65] Mao was then at Lushan for a conference, and on the afternoon of the 25th, sent a car to bring Li to his own residence so that they might talk. After inquiring about Li's health and work, Mao turned to questions of theory. After conversing on problems of formal logic, Mao expressed the view that Li's *Elements of Sociology* was a particularly profound work which had had a major impact in the 1930s and was still significant. It should, he opined, be revised and a new edition published. Li demurred, citing his poor health as a reason why such a major task of research and writing was impossible.[66] "You have a Philosophy Department at Wuhan University, don't you?" Mao retorted. "You can find a couple of competent assistants to help you do it, and you can direct the project." Li thought Mao's suggestion a good one, and agreed to undertake the task.[67] The following day, Li telegrammed his assistant Tao Delin to come to Lushan where Li informed him of the Chairman's project. Li decided to abandon his convalescence in order to commence work on the project immediately. He wrote to Yu Zhihong, then Head of the Philosophy

Department at Wuhan University, informing him of the task Mao had set them and of the need to recruit a number of research assistants.[68] A Mao Zedong Thought Research Centre (*yanjiushi*) was subsequently established within the Department, and Tao Delin appointed to head the team of researchers whose task was the production of a major treatise on Marxist philosophy, one based on Li Da's *Elements of Sociology*, but incorporating major philosophical developments within the Marxist tradition.[69] This completed work would be entitled *Makesizhuyi zhexue dagang* (Elements of Marxist Philosophy), and Li Da would act as its editor.

Between late 1961 and 1965, when a draft of *Elements of Dialectical Materialism* (the first half of *Elements of Marxist Philosophy*) was completed, this research group under Li Da struggled with the politically sensitive task of revising *Elements of Sociology* to incorporate developments in Marxist philosophy since the mid-1930s. Of these, the most sensitive was Mao's own philosophical thought. To what extent had Mao been responsible for developing Marxist philosophy; how original was his contribution? After considerable controversy,[70] Li and his research associates eventually and perhaps inevitably responded by not only attributing to Mao a major role in the development of Marxist philosophy, but by drawing heavily on the structure and content of his philosophical writings. Mao's contribution to the development of dialectical materialism is listed (chronogically following the contributions of Marx, Engels and Lenin) in a way which suggests strongly that Mao's philosophical thought represented the high point of Marxist philosophy. *Elements of Dialectical Materialism* asserts that Mao Zedong Thought

> is, in the era when imperialism is heading for collapse and socialism moving towards victory, and in the great revolutionary struggles of the Chinese people, the integration of the universal truths of Marxism-Leninism with the concrete practice of revolution and construction; it is a synthesis of the historical experience of the struggles of the proletariat both internationally and domestically, and it creatively develops Marxism-Leninism.[71]

Elements of Dialectical Materialism proceeds to detail Mao's "glorious contributions" to materialist dialectics as follows. First, Mao raised the philosophical level of the intra-Party struggle between the correct and incorrect lines, and provided a method for the resolution of such struggles which guaranteed the victory of the correct line.[72] Incorrect "left" and right opportunist lines are both forms of subjectivism (idealism and metaphysics) which stand in opposition to dialectical materialism, and in his two celebrated philosophical essays, "On Practice" and "On Contradiction", Mao had critiqued these erroneous tendencies. In "On Practice", Mao had criticised the subjectivism of dogmatism and empiricism. The former placed excessive emphasis on book learning and thoughts hatched in the mind, and rather than proceeding from reality, was guided by subjective aspirations or theoretical formulas. Rather, the criteria for the evaluation of knowledge, Mao had demonstrated, was revolutionary practice, and knowledge develops as practice develops. Empiricism, on the other hand, was not interested in the development of perceptual knowledge to the level of rational knowledge, being satisfied rather with narrow and partial experiences of reality. Mao had pointed out that perceptual and rational knowledge represent two stages in a unified process of knowledge; while rational knowledge depends on perceptual knowledge, the latter, if not developed to the level of rational knowledge, could never achieve the status of "true knowledge".[73]

In "On Contradiction", Mao had critiqued dogmatism and empiricism by pointing out the relationships between universal and the particular, between identity and struggle, and the distinction between antagonism and non-antagonism; without a recognition of the unity of opposites existing between these, it was not possible to analyse a situation correctly. For example, subjectivists are not able to recognise the unity which exists between struggle and identity. The "left" opportunists, during the period of the Democratic Revolution, adopted a position towards the national bourgeoisie of "all out struggle, reject alliance"; right opportunists, on the other hand, adopted the opposite stance of "complete alliance, reject struggle". Because these two incorrect tendencies had not recognised the unity of identity and struggle, the "result was that their knowledge was divorced from objective reality".[74] Mao's two philosophical essays, employing the world view of Marxism-Leninism, had thus provided the Party with a weapon whereby it could investigate revolutionary questions and correctly distinguish between true and false Marxism, and between correct and incorrect practice. Mao's philosophical thought had thus, according to *Elements of Dialectical Materialism*, made a major contribution to the correct resolution of intra-Party struggle.

Second, Mao Zedong was the first to provide a "systematic, profound, concise, and readily understood" elaboration of Marxist philosophy, and in so doing, he concretised it in a way which allowed it to guide the Party's style of work and become a "sharp weapon" which the broad masses could directly grasp. In his various philosophical essays, Mao had not only developed Marxist philosophy, but had done so in a manner which was accessible, using lively, everyday language which was replete with imagery relevant to the experience of the masses. In China, each worker, peasant, soldier, intellectual and cadre was thus able to grasp dialectical materialism; the extent to which Marxist philosophy had become a material force was therefore unprecedented.

Third, in the context in which opposition to feudalism and imperialism was the principal task and in which the peasantry constituted the bulk of the masses, Mao had formulated a theory on colonial and semi-colonial revolution. How could socialism be achieved in a semi-feudal, semi-colonial country? No response to this question could be found in the works of Marxism-Leninism, *Elements of Dialectical Materialism* asserts, but through his integration of the universal principles of Marxism-Leninism and the concrete practice of the Chinese revolution, Mao completely solved this seemingly intractable problem. Using the principles of dialectical materialism, Mao concretely analysed the economic status and political attitudes of China's social classes and strata, and also analysed the many complex contradictions of Chinese society; on this basis, he correctly determined the program, line, strategy and tactics of the Chinese revolution. Of these, the most important was the theory that the revolution was developmental and would pass through a number of stages. Mao correctly distinguished between the different tasks for the stages of the democratic and socialist revolutions, but perceived that there was an intimate connection between these two stages, with the democratic revolution preparing the conditions within which the socialist revolution could occur; following nationwide victory in the democratic revolution, an immediate advance was made towards the goals of the socialist revolution. For Mao, the united front, armed struggle and party-building were the main strategies which would guarantee victory in the democratic revolution; he had been shown to be correct, so his ideas on these themes were thus of universal significance for the peoples of all the countries of the world.[75]

Fourth, following the liberation of China, Mao had applied the principles of dialectical materialism to the new historical conditions, and had been the first to formulate a complete theory of socialist revolution and construction; in so doing, Mao had developed dialectical materialism. One of the crucial problems Mao had had to resolve, according to *Elements of Dialectical Materialism*, was the problem of "capitalist restoration", a problem which no previous Marxist had successfully or systematically addressed. Mao had summed up the practical experience of China's socialist revolution and construction, and had analysed positive and negative international experiences, principally those of the Soviet Union. In his "On the Correct Handling of Contradictions among the People" and other writings, Mao had critiqued the errors of revisionism and had clarified the mistaken views of those within the revolutionary ranks.[76]

Elements of Dialectical Materialism continues that Mao had pointed out that the law of the unity of opposites, the most fundamental law of the universe, was still applicable to socialist society. Even after the socialist transformation of the system of ownership, class contradictions persisted, and throughout the entire period of socialism the bourgeoisie and proletariat persisted; so too did the struggle between socialism and capitalism. In order to defend socialist construction and prevent capitalist restoration, it was necessary to consolidate the dictatorship of the proletariat, and to carry the socialist revolution "through to the end" in the realms of politics, economics, ideology and culture. At the same time, it was necessary to develop rapidly the forces of production, to establish modernised agricultural and industrialised sectors, and to overtake the advanced capitalist countries in the not too distant future. In this way, the material foundation of socialism would be created.

Elements of Dialectical Materialism concludes:

> In the process of applying materialist dialectics to the creative resolution of the extremely complex novel problems of contemporary revolutionary struggles, Mao had of necessity instilled it with new content and independently pushed forward materialist dialectics, raising it to a new stage. Mao Zedong's philosophical thought ... is a great development of materialist dialectics in the current era.[77]

Elements of Dialectical Materialism:
The Laws of Dialectics

Given this accolade to Mao's contribution to the development of Marxist philosophy, it is little wonder that the section of *Elements of Dialectical Materialism* devoted to the laws of dialectics bears a very strong resemblance to "On Contradiction". The subheadings of the chapter entitled "The Law of the Unity of Opposites" indeed virtually replicate the subheadings of Mao's essay. The chapter commences by emphasising that the law of the unity of opposites is the basic law of dialectical materialism; all things contain contradictions, and the relations within a thing and its relations with other things are all contradictions, and these relations are all subject to change.[78] The other laws and categories of dialectics are therefore all manifest forms of the law of the unity of opposites and can only be understood by reference to it; the law of the unity of opposites is thus "the key" to dialectics.[79] For example, the law of qualitative and quantitative change explains that the motion of all things adopts two forms: relative rest (quantitative change) and conspicuous change (qualitative change). The transition from one form of change to the next can only be understood by reference to the way in which the contradictions within the thing in motion behave. The struggle between the aspects of the principal contradiction is continual, but until it reaches an extreme point, the change this generates is only quantitative; when this extreme point is reached, the aspects of the contradiction undergo fundamental qualitative change: the original character of the thing is transformed and a new thing emerges. When this happens, quantitative change immediately recommences within the new thing. Without an appreciation that the law of the unity of opposites, with its description of the behaviour of contradictions, is the fundamental law of dialectics, the law of qualitative and quantitative change would be incomprehensible.

The same is true of the law of the negation of the negation (here given the appelation the law of affirmation and negation).[80] This law reveals that the general developmental tendency is forward, but that the route described by development can be tortuous and winding (*quzhede*). A thing advances through a continuing and unfolding repetition of the process of affirmation and negation which generates a wave-like form of development. Each thing contains elements which serve to maintain its existence; these are the elements of affirmation (*kending de yinsu*). Each thing also contains elements which facilitate its destruction, and these are the elements of negation (*fouding de yinsu*). When the elements of affirmation occupy the principal aspect of the contradiction which defines the thing, the existence of the thing is maintained; this is the stage of affirmation. However, the elements of negation gradually expand, and at the point they come to occupy the principal aspect of the contradiction, the thing changes into its opposite, and becomes something new; this is the stage of negation. This pattern is repeated, as the new thing also contains elements for both affirmation and negation.[81]

Without a comprehension of the law of the unity of opposites, the law of the negation of the negation would make no sense. Other categories of dialectical materialism (essence and phenomenon, content and form, cause and effect, inevitability and chance, possibility and reality) are also all various concrete manifestations of the law of the unity of opposites. As this is the case, *Elements of Dialectical Materialism* logically concludes, it is necessary when studying dialectics to first comprehend the law of the unity of opposites. Using this as its premise, *Elements of Dialectical Materialism* proceeds to an exposition of this law, providing in effect a detailed elaboration of Mao's "On Contradiction". The universality and particularity of contradiction, the principal contradiction and the principal aspect of a contradiction, the identity and struggle of the aspects of a contradiction, and antagonistic and non-antagonistic contradictions are all covered here in a way which draws heavily on Mao's writings on dialectical materialism. *Elements of Dialectical Materialism* does, however, draw in other authorities on dialectical materialism as well as developments in Marxist philosophy since the mid-1930s. This includes reference to Mao's subsequent philosophical writings, and in particular "On the Correct Handling of Contradictions Among the People" (1957), in which the concept of non-antagonistic contradictions is developed.[82] Nevertheless, the overwhelming impression given is that Mao's "On Contradiction" represents the most complete and profound elaboration of the law of the unity of opposites in the history of Marxist philosophy. While there is some acknowledgement of the intellectual ancestry of this law (particularly Engels and Lenin), there is little if any acknowledgement that Mao drew heavily on Soviet philosophical sources of the early 1930s in the writing of "On Contradiction". Li Da was aware — perhaps more so than any other Chinese intellectual (with the possible exception of Ai Siqi)[83] — of Mao's indebtedness to these sources, but in the context of the early 1960s it remained impolitic to address too closely the immediate sources of Mao's writings on philosophy.[84] That project would have to await a different political climate, one in which the authority of the Chairman had been much reduced. By the 1980s, however, Li and Ai Siqi were both long dead, and it fell to a new generation of Chinese philosophers to exploit the relative openness of the post-Mao era to explore this formerly sensitive subject.[85]

Elements of Dialectical Materialism's treatment of the laws of dialectics also reflects the context within which the book was compiled in a number of other respects. One of the most obvious of these is the book's preoccupation with the issue of revisionism, in both its international and Chinese manifestations. Internationally, the Soviet philosophers of the 1960s are of great concern, for they had rejected the notion, so central to Mao's thinking, that contradictions would persist throughout the period of socialist transition; they had consequently rejected the possibility of class struggle, stressing rather the harmonisation of class interests under the leadership of the Communist Party. Soviet philosophers had referred scathingly to the principle of the universality of contradiction as "mystification", "superstition" and an "abstract principle which dogmatically manipulates (*wannong*) contradiction".[86] Why do these philosphers talk such nonsense, *Elements of Dialectical Materialism* inquires. It is because there is a capitalist restoration occuring in their country, and they represent the "rotten and backward element" of the class contradiction existing in socialist society.[87]

Soviet philosophers were guilty too of supporting the idea, touted by China's revisionist philosophers of the early 1960s, that "two combine into one" (*he er er yi*).[88] Soviet philosophers had interpreted the notion of the unity of contradictions to mean that the aspects of a contradiction were indivisible, their identity the equivalent of a common interest. The purpose of studying dialectics, from this perspective, was "to learn how to unite two opposed ideas". But this was fundamentally mistaken, according to *Elements of Dialectical Materialism*. Dialectical materialism had never treated the identity existing between the aspects of a contradiction as only commonality or common interests. Where was the common interest existing between imperialism and oppressed peoples, between imperialist states and socialist states, between the bourgeoisie and the proletariat, and between revisionism and Marxism-Leninism? Similarly, dialectical materialism had never perceived the identity of the aspects of a contradiction as indivisible; rather, under certain conditions, these contradictory aspects inevitably moved towards their opposite. The appropriate dialectical viewpoint was encapsulated in the saying "one divides into two" (*yi fen wei er*), endorsed by Mao as a means of investigating and handling problems, and one which did not negate the struggle of contradictions.[89]

While the incorporation of Mao Zedong's contribution to the elaboration of the laws of dialectical materialism represents a major feature of the revision of Li Da's *Elements of Sociology*, there is attention devoted too to Mao's contribution to the epistemology of Marxism. This section of *Elements of Dialectical Materialism*, revised largely by Tao Delin,[90] reiterates that the epistemology of Marxism is "the dynamic and revolutionary theory of reflection". This theory stands on two premises: one is the recognition that the ultimate source of knowledge is the objective material world; the other is the recognition that knowledge is able to provide a correct image (*yingxiang*) of the objective material world.[91] However, a recognition that the origin of knowledge is the material world does not in itself constitute the reflection theory of dialectical materialism. Central to this theory is the dynamic role of human practice; practice is the foundation of the process of knowledge, a process which observes certain dialectical laws.[92] This process commences with practice which provides perceptual knowledge; there is then a leap from perceptual to rational or conceptual knowledge (thought), which then must be tested in practice, for it is practice which determines whether thought is or is not correct. This cycle is constantly repeated: "practice, knowledge, again practice, and again knowledge".[93] The process of knowledge thus moves dialectically from a superficial to a more profound, from a one-sided to a multifaceted understanding of reality. But to obtain correct knowledge, humans must participate in "revolutionary practice" to change reality. This "revolutionary practice" incorporates not only the productive activities of humans, but also class struggle and scientific experimentation.⁹⁴

It can be seen that the explication of epistemology provided by *Elements of Dialectical Materialism* adds little in substantive terms to that which had appeared in *Elements of Sociology* nearly thirty years before (see Chapter 8). What is new is the deference paid to Mao's writings and his contribution to Marxist epistemology. Mao Zedong, *Elements of Dialectical Materialism* asserts, had:

> employed a general formula to profoundly and comprehensively summarise the limitless process of development of the motion of human thought: "practice, knowledge, again practice, and again knowledge. This form repeats itself in endless cycles, and with each cycle the content of practice and knowledge rises to a higher level." This is a glorious contribution to Marxist epistemology, one which has immense significance for directing revolution and the work of construction.⁹⁵

The Fate of *Elements of Dialectical Materialism*

With the completion of the draft of *Elements of Dialectical Materialism* in 1965, it was sent as a *neibu* (internal) document for comment and criticism to Mao Zedong and other senior Party leaders and intellectuals, including Kang Sheng, Chen Boda, Zhang Wentian, Zhou Enlai, Zhu De and Liu Shaoqi.⁹⁶ Mao's brief annotation to *Elements of Dialectical Materialism* (dated 1965) was first published in 1988, and it suggests that he was in agreement with the mode of explication adopted by Li and his research associates to explain the centrality of the law of the unity of opposites to dialectical materialism.⁹⁷ Mao's annotation reads:

> The kernel of dialectics is the law of the unity of opposites, and other categories such as the mutual transformation of quality and quantity, negation of the negation, connection, development ... and so on, can all be explained by reference to this central law ... All of the categories (and there are perhaps more than ten of these) can be explained by reference to the contradictions within things, by the unity of opposites. For example, what is called essence (*benzhi*) can only be spoken of as the principal contradiction and the principal aspect of a contradiction within a thing.⁹⁸

Events were, however, to overtake plans to publish *Elements of Dialectical Materialism* and to complete the second volume of *Elements of Marxist Philosophy*, a volume to be entitled *Elements of Historical*

Materialism.[99] With the outbreak of the Cultural Revolution, not only was Li to become the target of a vicious campaign of criticism and the research team which had produced *Elements of Dialectical Materialism* dispersed, but the book itself was criticised for having "revised" "On Practice" and "On Contradiction".[100] Li's death in August 1966 was to put an end to any hope that the revision of *Elements of Sociology* could be completed. Following the Cultural Revolution, *Elements of Dialectical Materialism* was lightly edited by Tao Delin and published in 1978. The purpose in publishing the book so long after it was written was, according to one authority, to provide material on Marxist philosophy suitable for study by high-level intellectuals and for use as a textbook by philosophy students at university level; it is still apparently used by "some universities" for that purpose.[101] Nevertheless, it is apparent that the dramatic change in the political climate following Mao's death has rendered *Elements of Dialectical Materialism* largely obsolete. Chinese critics of the book now perceive it, in many respects, as too left-wing, something of an irony given Li's fate during the Cultural Revolution. The book's critique of revisionism in particular is perceived as a symptom of the "politicisation" of Marxist philosophy so prevalent during Mao's lifetime.[102] Moreover, the uncritical glorification of Mao's contribution to the development of Marxist philosophy, so evident in *Elements of Dialectical Materialism*, has been repudiated in post-Mao China; not only have philosophers in China been willing to examine critically the sensitive issue of the immediate sources of Mao's philosophical writings, they have recognised that Mao was not the only Chinese to contribute to the elaboration and dissemination of Marxist philosophy in China.[103]

Li Da had hoped that *Elements of Marxist Philosophy*, when completed, would be a text used in the Third World where texts on Marxism had come primarily from the Soviet Union. Here would be a major Chinese text on Marxist philosophy which could compete with this Soviet influence. This hope has not been fulfilled, however, for *Elements of Dialectical Materialism* has never been translated into a foreign language.[104] The reason for this is, again, that the book would not project to the world the different image of Marxist philosophy embraced by China's post-Mao leadership. It has remained a text for Chinese students and intellectuals, and fewer and fewer of these evince much enthusiasm for this book, written so patently to meet the political goals of another era and the demands of an orthodoxy now largely repudiated.[105]

Notes

1. He also wrote critiques of Liang Shuming and the philosopher Xu Maoyong. See Li Da, "Xu Maoyong duiyu Makesizhuyi zhexue de xiuzheng" (Xu Maoyong's Revision of Marxist Philosophy), *Lilun zhanxian*, No. 2 (1958), pp. 12–17; also Li Da, *Liang Shuming zhengzhi sixiang pipan* (A Critique of the Political Thought of Liang Shuming) (Wuhan: Hubei renmin chubanshe, 1956).
2. Li Da, *Hu Shi fandong sixiang pipan* (A Critique of Hu Shi's Reactionary Thought) (Hankou: Hubei renmin chubanshe, 1955); and Li Da, *Shiyongzhuyi: diguozhuyi de yuyong zhexue* (Pragmatism: The Philosophical Tool of Imperialism) (Hubei: Hubei renmin chubanshe, 1956).
3. Li Da, *Hu Shi fandong sixiang pipan*, pp. 2–3.
4. Li Da, *Shiyongzhuyi: diguozhuyi de yuyong zhexue*, p. 5
5. Ibid., pp. 5–6; also Li Da, *Hu Shi fandong sixiang pipan*, Chapters 1 and 4.
6. Li Da, *Shiyongzhuyi: diguozhuyi de yuyong zhexue*, p. 9.
7. Ibid., pp. 12–13.
8. Ibid., pp. 13–14.
9. Li Da, *Hu Shi fandong sixiang pipan*, pp. 21–22, 61–66.
10. Ibid., pp. 40–41.
11. Li Da, *Shiyongzhuyi: diguozhuyi de yuyong zhexue*, pp. 6–7.
12. Li Da, *Hu Shi fandong sixiang pipan*, Chapters 1 and 4.
13. Ibid., pp. 19–20.
14. Ibid., p. 20.
15. Ibid., p. 64.
16. Ibid., p. 51.
17. Ibid., pp. 51, 72; also *Shiyongzhuyi: diguozhuyi de yuyong zhexue*, pp. 22–25.
18. Li Da, *Shiyongzhuyi: diguozhuyi de yuyong zhexue*, pp. 24–30. For a discussion of the problem of "wholesale Westernisation" in Hu Shi's thought, see Jerome B. Grieder, *Hu Shih and the Chinese Renaissance: Liberalism in the Chinese Revolution, 1917–1937* (Cambridge, Mass.: Harvard University Press, 1970). See also Hu Shih, *The Chinese Renaissance: The Haskell Lectures, 1933* (New York: Paragon Book Reprint Corp., 1963), esp. pp. 24–26, where Hu describes the "diffused penetration" of China's culture by Western values and habits, and how this process "may yet culminate in solving some of our pressing and basic problems of life and culture, and achieve a new civilization not incompataible with the spirit of the new world".
19. Li Da, *Shiyongzhuyi: diguozhuyi de yuyong zhexue*, pp. 16–21.
20. Ibid., pp. 31–36.
21. Michael Y.M. Kau and John K. Leung (eds), *The Writings of Mao Zedong 1949–1976: Volume II, January 1956–December 1957* (Armonk and London: M.E. Sharpe, 1992), p. 506. Translation slightly modified.
22. Wang Jionghua, *Li Da yu Makesizhuyi zhexue zai Zhongguo* (Li Da and Marxist Philosophy in China) (Wuchang: Huazhong ligong daxue chubanshe, 1988), pp. 247–59.
23. It is something of an irony that both Li Da and Hu Shi are now lauded as China's pre-eminent philosopers, and that chapters on both can be found in the same

book. See, for example, Li Zhenxia (ed.), *Dangdai Zhongguo shi zhe* (Ten Philosophers of Contemporary China) (Beijing: Huaxia chubanshe, 1991), pp. 1–49, 423–64.

24. Fei Xiaotong was thus regarded by Li as a leading representative of advocates of "capitalist sociology". For Li's critique of China's other "bourgeois" sociologists and further criticism of Fei, see Li Da, "Zichanjieji shehui xueshuo de pipan" (A Critique of Bourgeois Theories of Society), *Lilun zhanxian*, No. 9 (1958), pp. 29–42.

25. Li Da, *Fei Xiaotong de maiban shehuixue pipan* (A Critique of Fei Xiaotong's Compradore Sociology) (Wuhan: Hubei renmin chubanshe, 1958), p. 1.

26. Ibid., pp. 2–4.

27. Ibid., p. 5.

28. Ibid., pp. 5–6.

29. Ibid., p. 11.

30. Li Da had been highly critical of Liang Qichao in his writings of the early 1920s. See *Li Da wenji*, Vol. I, pp. 57–74.

31. Li Da, *Fei Xiaotong de maiban shehuixue pipan*, p. 13.

32. Fei had, in fact, studied under Malinowski at the London School of Economics as a doctoral student during the late 1930s. For further information, see James P. McGough, *Fei Hsiao-t'ung: The Dilemma of a Chinese Intellectual* (New York: M.E. Sharpe, 1979).

33. Li Da, *Fei Xiaotong de maiban shehuixue pipan*, pp. 16–18.

34. Ibid., p. 20.

35. Ibid., p. 14. One wonders if Li had read this book in its original English, for it had not been translated into Chinese. For a recent reprint of this book, see Fei Hsiao-tung, *Peasant Life in China: A Field Study of Country Life in the Yangtze Valley* (London and Henley: Routledge and Kegan Paul, first published in 1939, reprinted in 1980).

36. Li Da, *Fei Xiaotong de maiban shehuixue pipan*, p. 19.

37. See Roderick Macfarquhar, *The Origins of the Cultural Revolution: I.Contradictions Among the People, 1956–1957* (London: Oxford University Press, 1974), pp. 200, 277; also Michael Y.M. Kau and John K. Leung (eds), *The Writings of Mao Zedong 1949–1976: Volume II, January 1956 – December 1957* (Armonk, New York: M.E. Sharpe, 1992), pp. 600, 662, 665, 733, 735.

38. For further information on the campaign against Fei, see McCough, *Fei Hsiao-t'ung: The Dilemma of a Chinese Intellectual*.

39. Song Jingming and Li Qunde, "Jianchi Makesizhuyi de dianfan: Li Da wannian zai Wuhan de huodong" (A Model for Upholding Marxism: Li Da's Activities in Wuhan During His Later Years), in Xia Peidong (ed.), *Wuhan fengyun renwu* (Persons of Distinction from Wuhan) (Wuhan: Wuhan daxue chubanshe, 1991), p. 39.

40. See, in particular, Li Da, "Woguo xianjieduan de shangcengjianzhu he jingjijichu de guanxi" (The Relationship Between Economic Base and Superstructure in China during the Current Stage), *Xuexi*, No. 12 (1958), pp. 8–10; also Li Da, "Cong shehuizhuyi dao gongchanzhuyi" (From Socialism to Communism), *Lilun zhanxian*, No. 8 (1959), pp. 34–45; also Li Da, "Gongchanzhuyi shehui de liangge jieduan" (The Two Stages of Communist Society), *Wuhan daxue renwen kexue*

xuebao, No. 1 (1959), pp. 1-7, particularly the introductory paragraph; see, however, p. 3 where Li suggests that the transition from socialist to communist society is gradual and does not occur as a result of "revolutionary cataclysm" (*geming baofa*).

41. See, in particular, Li Da, *Zhengfeng yundong de bianzhengfa* (The Dialectics of the Rectification Movement) (Hankou: Hubei renmin chubanshe, 1958), pp. 6-8.

42. For an interpretation of Mao's understanding of the materialist conception of history at this time, see N.J. Knight, *Mao and History: An Interpretive Essay on some Problems in Mao Zedong's Philosophy of History*, Chapter 4. See also Paul Healy, *Mao and Classical Marxism: Epistemology, Social Formation, Classes and Class Struggle in Mao Zedong's post-1955 Thought* (Unpublished Ph.D thesis, Griffith University, 1988).

43. An example of Li's more prudent approach to the Great Leap Forward can be seen in his suggestion that the successful establishment of the People's Communes required three conditions: 1. Implementation of widespread education in communist ideology; 2. planned development of production; and 3. on the basis of the development of production, gradual improvement of the lives of the people. These conditions could be read as a muted criticism of the policies of the Great Leap Forward which failed to implement adequate ideological preparation for the large-scale changes, which failed to manage the development of production in a planned way, and which did not *gradually* improve the lives of the people; indeed, Li felt that the Great Leap Forward had rapidly made the lives of the people worse. See Li Da, "Gongchandang shehui de liangge jieduan", p. 5.

44. Li Da, "Shehuizhuyi geming yu shehuizhuyi jianshe de gongtong guilu" (The Common Laws of Socialist Revolution and Socialist Construction), *Lilun zhanxian*, No. 2 (1958), pp. 35-40. This was also published as a pamphlet under the same title (Hankou: Hubei renmin chubanshe, 1958).

45. Ibid.

46. Li Da, "Lishiweiwuzhuyi de duixiang" (The Object of Historical Materialism), *Lilun zhanxian*, No. 2 (1958), p. 82. Compare this diagram with those in Sugiyama Sakae, *Shehui kexue gailun* (An Introduction to Social Science), translated by Li Da and Qian Tieru (Shanghai: Kunlun shudian, 1929), pp. 100, 150.

47. Li Da, "Lishiweiwuzhuyi de duixiang", pp. 82-98.

48. Li rejects the notion (common among some of his comrades) that the forces of production can be perceived as external to the economic base; the relations and forces of production represent, rather, a unity of opposites and cannot be divided in this manner. See Li Da, "Shengchanli yu shengchanguanxi" (Forces and Relations of Production), *Lilun zhanxian*, No. 5 (1958), pp. 40-48. esp. p. 45. For an analysis of Mao's interpretation of the materialist conception of history which suggests that he too perceived the forces of production as external to the economic base, see N.J. Knight, *Mao and History: An Interpretive Essay on some Problems in Mao Zedong's Philosophy of History*, pp. 265-359.

49. Ibid., p. 46. "The forces of production are the most lively, most revolutionary element of the process of production."

50. Li Da, "Lishiweiwuzhuyi de duixiang".

51. Li Da, "Shengchanli yu shengchanguanxi", p. 47.

52. Li Da, "Lishiweiwuzhuyi de duixiang".
53. Li Da, "Woguo xianjieduan de shangcengjianzhu he jingjijichu de guanxi", p. 8.
54. Li Da, "Cong shehuizhuyi dao gongchanzhuyi", p. 34.
55. See also Li Da, *Liang Shuming zhengzhi sixiang pipan*. Liang Shuming (1894–1977), a former member of the "Third Force" which opposed domination of China by both the GMD and the CCP and a member in the 1950s of the Democratic League, had publicly opposed the industrialisation and agrarian policies of the Chinese Communist Party. For Mao's vitriolic attack on Liang in 1953, see "Criticism of Liang Shu-ming's reactionary ideas" in *Selected Works of Mao Tse-tung* (Peking: FLP, 1977), Vol. 5, pp. 121–30.
56. Li Da, "Woguo xianjieduan de shangcengjianzhu he jingji jichu de guanxi", p. 10.
57. Li Da, "Lishiweiwuzhuyi de duixiang".
58. Ibid; also "Woguo xianjieduan de shangcengjianzhu he jingjijichu de guanxi", p. 8.
59. Ibid. For an analysis of Mao's use of the concept of politics as a "concentrated expression of economics", see Nick Knight, "*On Contradiction* and *On New Democracy*: Contrasting Perspectives on Causation and Social Change in the Thought of Mao Zedong", *Bulletin of Concerned Asian Scholars*, Vol. 22, No. 2 (April–June 1990), pp. 18–34.
60. See, in particular, Li Da, "Shejie wuchanjieji shehuizhuyi geming lun" (On the World Proletarian Socialist Revolution), *Lilun zhanxian*, No. 8 (1958), pp. 36–44. Here Li draws heavily on the Leninist conception of revolutionary change, and in particular the need for a vanguard party, guided by correct revolutionary theory, to carry forward the "political revolution". The first section of this article on the proletarian revolution can be found in *Lilun zhanxian*, No. 6 (1958), pp. 36–45. This section deals with Marx and Engels' views on revolution.
61. See Li Da, *Zhengfeng yundong de bianzhengfa*, pp. 23–26. Li also was conscious of the need to struggle against revisionism abroad. His critique of the Yugoslavian Communist Party examines the economic base, the political superstructure, and forms of consciousness characteristic of the Yugoslavian socioeconomic formation. See Li Da, "Fandui xiandai xiuzhengzhuyi" (Oppose Contemporary Revisionism), *Lilun zhanxian*, No. 5 (1958), pp. 1–4.
62. See, however, Li Da, "Gongchanzhuyi shehui liange jieduan", pp. 5–7.
63. Wang Jionghua, "Li Da: yi wei Puluomixiusishi bohuozhe" (Li Da: A Prometheus who Sowed Fire), in Li Zhenxia (ed.), *Dangdai Zhongguo shi zhe* (Ten Philosophers of Contemporary China) (Beijing: Huaxia chubanshe, 1991), pp. 37–38.
64. See Li Da, "Woguo xianjieduan de shangcengjianzhu he jingjijichu de guanxi", p. 8.
65. Tao Delin, "Li Da yu *Weiwu bianzhengfa*" (Li Da and *Elements of Materialist Dialectics*), in *Wei zhenli er douzheng de Li Da tongzhi* (Li Da Who Struggled for Truth) (Hankou: Wuhan daxue chubanshe, 1985), p. 209. Tao's article was originally published in *Shulin*, No. 2 (1979).
66. According to a number of Li Da's former colleagues at Wuhan University, Li Da's health was so poor at this time that he was unable to write properly because

his hands shook so badly. Any lectures or talks he gave were also difficult to follow as he lacked the energy to speak loudly and clearly. Personal interviews, October 1993.

67. See Sun Qian and Li Shizhen, *Mao Zedong yu mingren* (Mao Zedong and the Famous) (Jiangsu: Jiangsu renmin chubanshe, 1993), Vol. 1, pp. 333–34.

68. A copy of Li Da's letter can be found in *Wei zhenli er douzheng de Li Da tongzhi*, pp. 209–10.

69. Tao Delin is now (1994) Vice Chancellor of Wuhan University. Other members of this research group were Wang Xuanwu, Duan Qixian and Chen Zuhua. The latter two were postgraduate students in the early 1960s and are now Professors at Wuhan University's Philosophy Department. I had the good fortune in October 1993 to discuss with them their participation in the project to revise *Elements of Sociology*.

70. Interview with Professor Duan Qixian, 12 October 1993.

71. Li Da (ed.), *Weiwubianzhengfa dagang* (Elements of Dialectical Materialism) (Beijing: Renmin chubanshe, 1978), p. 151.

72. Ibid.

73. Ibid., pp. 152–53.

74. Ibid., p. 154.

75. Ibid., pp. 156–58.

76. Ibid., p. 158.

77. Ibid., p. 160.

78. Ibid., pp. 242–43.

79. Ibid., p. 245.

80. Stuart Schram has made much of Mao's usage of the term the law of "affirmation and negation" (*kending fouding guilu*) to describe the law of the "negation of the negation", and he has wrongly translated *kending fouding guilu* as "the law of the affirmation of the negation". The correct translation is "the law of affirmation and negation". Schram's intention is to emphasise Mao's heterodoxy and to highlight his nihilistic tendencies. However, *Elements of Dialectical Materialism* clearly asserts that the term *kending fouding guilu* is the equivalent of "the law of the negation of the negation" (see p. 241). See Stuart R. Schram, *The Thought of Mao Tse-tung* (Cambridge: Cambridge University Press, 1989), pp. 138–45; also Stuart R. Schram, "The Marxist", in Dick Wilson (ed.), *Mao Tse-tung in the Scales of History* (Cambridge: Cambridge University Press, 1977), p. 64. For my response to Schram, see Nick Knight (ed.), *Mao Zedong on Dialectical Materialism: Writings on Philosophy, 1937* (Armonk, New York: M.E. Sharpe, 1990), pp. 19–24.

81. Li Da (ed.), *Elements of Dialectical Materialism*, p. 246.

82. The extent to which the concept "non-antagonistic contradictions" has developed Marxist theory has been challenged by Shlomo Avineri. It is, he says, "a bastard term ... meaningless within the framework of Marx's thought". See Shlomo Avineri, *The Social and Political Thought of Karl Marx* (Cambridge: Cambridge University Press, 1968), p. 175.

83. Ai Siqi had been in Yan'an in the late 1930s and was intimately involved in the philosophical study group which formed around Mao.

84. For my own discussion of this issue, see *Mao Zedong on Dialectical Materialism*, Introduction.

85. See Nick Knight (ed.), *The Philosophical Thought of Mao Zedong: Studies from China, 1981–1989* (Armonk, New York: M.E. Sharpe, Chinese Studies in Philosophy, Spring–Summer, 1992), Chapters 1, 4, 5, 6 and 7.

86. Li Da, *Elements of Dialectical Materialism*, pp. 252–54.

87. Ibid., p. 254.

88. However, for Li's reservations about incorporating in *Elements of Dialectical Materialism* discussion of "two combine into one" and "one divides in two", see Wang Jionghua, *Li Da yu Makesizhuyi zai Zhongguo*, pp. 314–15. Wang concludes that, given the historical conditions prevailing at that time, Li had no option but to include discussion of this debate. Tao Delin recalls that Li wrote to him from Beijing specifically instructing him not to include discussion of "one divides into two" and "two combine into one", but given the circumstances, Tao felt he had no option but to include it, and that consequently he must take the responsibility. Tao Delin, "Li Da yu *Weiwubianzhengfa dagang*", pp. 217–18.

89. *Elements of Dialectical Materialism*, pp. 240, 269–70, 273–74.

90. Interview with Professor Duan Qixian, Wuhan, 12 October 1993.

91. *Elements of Dialectical Materialism*, p. 413.

92. Ibid., pp. 414–19.

93. Ibid., p. 481.

94. Ibid., p. 423.

95. Ibid., p. 481. The quote is taken from "On Practice" in *Selected Works of Mao Tse-tung* (Peking: FLP, 1975), Vol. 1, p. 308.

96. Wang Jionghua, *Li Da yu Makesizhuyi zhexue zai Zhongguo*, pp. 288–89. Also interview with Professor Duan Qixian, Wuhan, 12 October 1993.

97. There is, however, some suggestion that Mao's general reception of *Elements of Dialectical Materialism* was not altogether positive. A local Party leader informed Li Da that Mao had complained that the second section, which dealt with the history of Marxist philosophy, contained too much reference to "the ancients, the dead and foreigners". Wang Jionghua, *Li Da yu Makesizhuyi zai Zhongguo*, p. 303 note. Also interview with Professor Duan Qixian, Wuhan, 12 October 1993. Li Da was also apparently criticised for not revising *Elements of Sociology* in line with the suggestion that there was *only one* law of dialectics, the law of the unity of opposites. See Tao Delin, "Li Da yu *Weiwubianzhengfa dagang*," pp. 216–17.

98. *Mao Zedong zhexue pizhuji* (The Philosophical Annotations of Mao Zedong) (Beijing: Zhongyang wenxian chubanshe, 1988), pp. 505–7.

99. A start had been made on *Elements of Historical Materialism*. Indeed, although Li Da had moved to Beijing in 1965 in his capacity as a member of the Standing Committee of the National People's Congress, he returned to Wuhan University early in 1966 to direct work on the research and writing of this volume. See Tao Delin, "Li Da yu *Weiwubianzhengfa dagang*," p. 212.

100. Interview with Professor Duan Qixian, Wuhan, 12 October 1993.

101. Ibid.

102. Wang Jionghua, *Li Da yu Makesizhuyi zhexue zai Zhongguo*, pp. 312–13.

103. See, in particular, Shi Zhongquan, "A New Document for the Study of Mao Zedong's Philosophical Thought: Introducing the Philosophical Annotations of Mao Zedong", in Knight (ed.), *The Philosophical Thought of Mao Zedong: Studies from China, 1981–1989*, esp. p. 139.

104. Interview with Professor Duan Qixian, Wuhan, 12 October 1993.

105. It must be said in Li's defence that he was very troubled by the issue of how to deal with Mao's development of Marxist philosophy in a "scientific" way, one which did not exaggerate the extent of Mao's contribution. Li feared that if Mao's contribution were exaggerated, the book would become a laughing stock among foreigners. Tao Delin recalls that Li's attitude was out of step with the "wind" blowing at that time, and that although he and the other research assistants attempted to implement Li Da's approach, they did not succeed. See Tao Delin, "Li Da yu *Wewubianzhengfa dagang*," pp. 215–16.

11

Conclusion: Li Da and Marxist Philosophy in China

The ambiguity inherent in Li Da's last major philosophical project is, in an important sense, characteristic of his entire philosophical career. For his attempt in the early 1960s to revise *Elements of Sociology* to incorporate developments in Marxist philosophy since the volume was written in the early 1930s was compromised by the overwhelming significance of Mao Zedong Thought in contemporary Chinese political and philosophical life. Li Da did not have a free hand to evaluate the development of Marxist philosophy; the rising tide of the new orthodoxy, which was to culminate in the cult of personality surrounding Mao at the time of the Cultural Revolution, precluded an uninhibited evaluation of Mao's contribution to Marxist philosophy. *Elements of Dialectical Materialism* thus incorporates a glowing account of Mao's philosophical thought, and Mao is numbered as one of the great thinkers in the pantheon of Marxist philosophy. The pressure to conform, to join in the chorus of adulation of Mao, was too much, even for Li, as strong-minded and independent as he was. The laudatory tone adopted by *Elements of Dialectical Materialism* when discussing Mao's contribution to Marxist philosophy was not enough, however, to save either Li or the book, for Li was to die prematurely as a result of ill-treatment incurred for his supposed opposition to Mao. There is irony in the fact that the volume, while published posthumously in 1978, is now regarded in China as too left-wing, as too uncritical of Mao and his philosophical thought.

The dilemma faced by Li Da in the early 1960s was an echo of the previous dilemmas he had faced in his relationship with both the Party and Marxist philosophy. In 1923, he chose to leave the Party rather than submit to policies which he regarded as politically unsound and not grounded in Marxist theory, as he understood it. Yet, unbidden by any political authority, Li altered his conception of Marxist philosophy in the early 1930s to conform to the changes in philosophy in the Soviet Union. One of the most significant of these changes had been the subordination of philosophy to the demands of the Party, to the practical tasks of the moment. That Li should adopt this new conception of the role of Marxist philosophy, even though he had previously demonstrated his unwillingness to subordinate his intellect to mistaken Party direction, can only be explained by his conviction of the appropriateness of this new development in the relationship between philosophy and politics. However, this acceptance of philosophy's subordination to politics was mediated by his belief, at an intellectual level, in the correctness of the content of this new philosophy. Li subscribed to this new philosophy, not merely because it was orthodoxy, not merely because Marxist political leaders asserted it to be truth, but because he himself believed it to be true. And once Li accepted the veracity of this version of Marxist philosophy, he did not thereafter depart from its basic assumptions. This explains his willingness to explicate Mao's philosophy in the early 1950s, for Li recognised that Mao's philosophical thought, as contained in "On Practice" and "On Contradiction", drew heavily on this Marxist orthodoxy. There was thus, initially, no tension between Li's conception of Marxist philosophy and his role as explicator of Mao's thought. By the same token, however, Li recognised that Mao's understanding of Marxist philosophy was, in large measure, derivative, owing much to orthodox Soviet philosophy; the basic premises of "On Practice" and "On Contradiction" had been drawn from the Soviet texts on philosophy of the early 1930s and other Chinese texts, such as *Elements of Sociology*, which had been inspired by the new Soviet philosophy. Li's view of Mao's stature as a philosopher was thus grounded in a realistic appreciation of the debt that Mao owed to orthodox Soviet Marxist philosophy. Yet Li's personal recognition of Mao's limited originality as a philosopher could not, given the political climate of the early 1960s, be given voice in the revised version of *Elements of Sociology*, although there is ample evidence to indicate the tensions this recognition created, both within Li himself and amongst the team of researchers he assembled to complete the revisions to *Elements of Sociology*. The revision of *Elements of Sociology* was not merely a philosophical project; it was a sensitive political task entailing considerable political risk. The penalties for getting it wrong were great indeed, and in retrospect it is evident that, no matter how hard they attempted to arrive at a formulation which was philosophically appropriate and politically acceptable, Li and his team of researchers found themselves literally in a no-win situation.

In this regard, Li's philosophical career is illustrative of the predicament faced by many of China's intellectuals. While they had been supportive of the Party's attempts to construct a socialist society, they chafed at their lack of autonomy for critical reflection which their status as intellectuals assumed. We should not, however, extend the parallels between Li Da and the dilemma of other intellectuals in post-1949 China too far. Li Da was no Ding Ling or Fei Xiaotong, and for much of the 1950s he was the Party's faithful servant. This involved him in serving the Party in ways which have drawn criticism from commentators in post-Mao China. In particular, his participation in the virulent campaigns against Hu Shi, Fei Xiaotong and Liang Shuming are regarded as symptomatic of the excessive subordination of philosophy to politics during the Maoist era, and of Li's own failure of judgment. It was only with the Great Leap Forward that Li's reservations concerning the theoretical underpinnings and practical implications of Mao's policies for socialist transition began to grow. But even then, his public stance was still highly supportive of the Great Leap Forward, his articles of the time suggesting that socialist relations of production had to be developed in China "from the bare earth", a view which could only have served to reinforce the impatient tenor of the Great Leap Forward policies. Rather, presuming on his long and cordial relationship with Mao, Li expressed his reservations in private to the Chairman himself. And while, as we know, this candid criticism did not please Mao, he held great respect for Li's stature as a philosopher and his personal integrity, and did not move against Li. Indeed, Mao subsequently praised Li for his contribution to the development of Marxism in China and invited him to revise his *Elements of Sociology* for republication.

While Li Da had a troubled relationship with orthodoxy and political power, much of his philosophical writing is also concerned with the explication and elaboration of issues which have had a problematic history within the theoretical framework of orthodox Marxism. Of these issues, one of the most difficult for Marxism had been the relationship between society's economic infrastructure (or base) and its political, legal and ideological realms (the superstructure). Mechanistic materialist readings of this relationship had attributed the economic base with complete causal dominance; the superstructure is perceived as merely a reflection of the economic base, having little if any capacity to influence the direction or pace of historical change. This mechanistic conception of the aetiology of social change has, as we observed in Chapter 2, been widely challenged within the Marxist tradition. Not only has this perspective been criticised as endorsing an undialectical conception of the relationship between economic base and superstructure, it has been attacked for its lack of recognition of the significant role that politics and consciousness can play in achieving social change. Marxists as theoretically and practically removed as Plekhanov, Lenin, Gramsci and Althusser have taken issue with mechanical materialism, opting for a perspective on social change which, while allowing a capacity for historical influence to political struggle and human consciousness, has nevertheless insisted on the general causal dominance of the economic base and developments within it. The relationship between economic base and superstructure is not, therefore, a relationship of equals, but a relationship of unequal reciprocity; the superstructure has an influence, but it is a reactive influence, and the capacity for that influence is generated by the economic base.

It is this current within European, Russian and later Japanese Marxism which exerted the most profound influence on Li Da and, through him, Marxism in China. From his earliest writings on socialism and Marxism, Li spoke of the need for a "political revolution", one which could complement and accelerate the impulses for "social revolution" emerging from the economic base. Li saw no contradiction in his espousal of Marxism *and* his endorsement of the "political revolution", for Li's theoretical understanding of Marxism presumed a role for political struggle and human consciousness. It was this conviction which drew Li into the political activities which culminated in the formation of the Chinese Communist Party, and it was this conviction which led, too, to Li's life long commitment to the explication and dissemination of Marxist theory, to the raising of consciousness of the need for socialism. For Li, the capacity of the superstructure to influence the process of social change was an article of faith deeply embedded in Marxism. His acceptance of this article of faith involved no compromise of Marxist orthodoxy; indeed, Li believed, as had many Marxists before him, that orthodox Marxism prescribed a role for political organisation and action in the achievement of historical goals. And he believed, too, that a mechanistic materialism which repudiated political action on the grounds of the evolutionary character of the process of social change had nothing in common with Marxism's commitment to the struggle at all levels — economic, political, ideological — to achieve a more just, a more equitable society.

It is thus something of an irony that Western evaluations of Marxism in China have frequently adopted this mechanistic reading of Marxism as the standard of orthodoxy against which Marxism in China should be judged. The result has been a marked tendency to exaggerate the conceptual and theoretical distance which separates Marxism in China from its European and Soviet counterparts. Marxism in China has thus been characterised as exotic, idiosyncratic, bizarre, an Asian offshoot of an essentially European ideology; it is Chinese Marxism, rather than Marxism in China. A careful genealogy of the sources of Marxism in China does not, however, support this perspective. As we have seen, Li Da, one of the most influential elaborators and disseminators of Marxism in China, was heavily influenced by theoretical and political currents in Europe, Russia and Japan. He was, as his early writings indicate, thoroughly conversant with the history of socialism and Marxism in

Europe and had, even before the establishment of the Chinese Communist Party, translated the writings of Karl Kautsky and Hermann Gorter. Gorter's *An Explanation of the Materialist Conception of History* made it quite clear that Marxism endorsed the possibility — indeed, the desirability — of political organisation and action to achieve historical goals. Similarly, the writings of Japanese socialists and Marxists translated by Li, such as Takabatake Motoyuki, Kawakami Hajime and Sugiyama Sakae, while recognising the materialist premises of Marxism, recognised the capacity of politics and human consciousness to exert an influence on the course of history. The Russian texts on Marxism, such as Thalheimer's, also allowed a role for politics and human consciousness. Is it any wonder, then, that Li Da did not accept the evolutionary and mechanistic reading of Marxism as orthodoxy? For Li, orthodox Marxism emphasised the materialist premises of history (the importance of the labour process and class formations), but it recognised also the interrelated character of human society. Given this interrelatedness, it was impossible to conceive of the political and legal superstructures, and human consciousness, as playing no role in the process of social change; their influence, which could at times be significant, could not, however, approach the level of influence exerted by the economic base, for it was this which dominated the social landscape, and which generated the original impulse for change.

Li's understanding of Marxism did not, therefore, break with its materialist premises. Indeed, his reading of the process of social change remains, in the final analysis, an economistic one; his economism is, however, a far cry from the mechanistic and evolutionary reading of social change within the Marxist tradition which precluded any reactive influence on the part of the superstructure. Li's economism was a flexible and dialectical one. It was the premise on which could be built a lifetime of theoretical and political activity, for without a belief in the significance of raising human consciousness through the agency of theory, of education to inform and mobilise, of political action to combat inequality and injustice, Li's own life would have had no coherence or rationality, dedicated as it was to the pursuit of all of these. By the same token, he recognised the limitations imposed by the materialist conception of history on the efforts of the individual to achieve change. Li saw himself as part of a wider historical movement brought into being by the massive economic and social changes unleashed by the Industrial Revolution and the rise of capitalism in Europe; those changes had resonated round the globe, and it was their impact in China, in the guise of imperialism, which had generated the revolutionary movement of which Li was a part. From his conversion to Marxism in the late 1910s, Li determined that he would do what he could to foster that movement through the dissemination of revolutionary theory and through political action. But, of these two, it was theory which was of greatest significance to Li. His disagreement with Chen Duxiu, which precipitated his departure from the Party in 1923, was as much about the sigificance of theoretical work as the united front strategy. Li believed strongly that what the Party needed above all else was to deepen its theoretical understanding of Marxism, for practice, without the guidance of theory, would inevitably lead to erroneous policies which would set back the cause of revolution. Nevertheless, Li continued, after quitting the Party, to serve the revolutionary movement through his writing, translations, educational activities and the occasional political task. But he remained conscious that the successful outcome of the revolutionary struggle could not be a function of the theoretical and political activities of any one individual. The materialist conception of history precluded such a belief, but it did not preclude the possibility that human action, on a sufficiently wide scale, could influence the direction and result of that struggle. Li recognised that theory, even where correct, was inconsequential unless grasped and acted on by people in sufficient numbers; his own role as elaborator and disseminator of theory would remain a marginal one in the absence of those material forces which motivated people in sufficient numbers to seek out theory for the purpose of achieving political and social change. It was in this context that the role of philosopher and theorist assumed significance. Yet, despite the ebb and flow of the fortunes of the revolutionary movement, Li remained committed to the role of theorist and philosopher which he defined for himself in the late 1910s and early 1920s, and from which he subsequently never deviated. And his efforts were rewarded, as we have seen, by the adoption by the Party and its leaders of the philosophical and theoretical views expressed in his publications and translations of the late 1920s and early 1930s. It was through their acceptance by Mao in particular that Li's elaborations of Marxist philosophy and theory gained wide currency and exerted considerable influence.

Li's philosophical writings exerted an influence, not only because they demonstrated his erudition as a philosopher, but because they drew on and elaborated the philosophical discourse which had become dominant in the Soviet Union since 1931, and which consequently had a profound impact on the member parties of the Comintern, including the Chinese Communist Party. Li was not, of course, the only Chinese philosopher to elaborate Marxist philosophy; also very significant was Ai Siqi. But Li's contribution stood out. In terms of sheer volume, his translations and writings on philosophy dwarfed the contribution of other Chinese philosophers. Not only did he translate several important pre-1931 texts on Marxist philosophy, he co-translated Shirokov and Aizenberg's *A Course on Dialectical Materialism*, a text which was to have such a strong influence on Mao, and through Mao, Marxism in China more generally. Moreover, his own *Elements of Sociology* was to take the elaboration of Marxist philosophy in China to a new plane; not only was it a massive tome covering the entire range of issues covered by dialectical and historical materialism, it was directed explicitly at theorists and intellectuals. This was not a work of popularisation, as so many of Ai Siqi's were. This was an uncompromising text, one which recognised the complexity of Marxist philosophy and theory and which challenged the intellectuals of the revolutionary movement to apply themselves to the difficult task of mastering this complex body of theory. As we have seen, Mao himself rose to this challenge, claiming to have read the book "ten times". Whether or not this was an exaggeration, the point remains that the seal of approval given to *Elements of Sociology* by Mao meant that its level of complexity represented the level of theoretical sophistication to which other Party theorists and philosophers had to aspire. Moreover, the contents of this book and its mode of explication were to become a model for emulation in the philosophical realm.

Elements of Sociology thus represented an important conduit through which post-1931 Soviet philosophical discourse was transmitted to the Chinese revolutionary movement. While it represented only one of several texts to perform this function, it was doubly influential because it had been written by a Chinese scholar. But the content of *Elements of Sociology* was not, apart from the language in which it was written, specifically Chinese. While Li had intended to complete the volume with a section on Chinese conditions, that project was never completed. Consequently the book, as eventually published in the better known second (Shanghai) edition, contains little if any reference to the Chinese economic, social and political context. Li, of course, recognised the importance of a detailed understanding of China's history and contemporary situation; his earlier writings and some of his translations deal with these. Yet *Elements of Sociology* is, first and foremost, a text on Marxist philosophy and theory, a text whose primary function was to inform the reader of the Marxist philosophical discourse deemed orthodox within Soviet philosophical circles. The book has a rather abstract quality, one which underlines its presumption of universal significance; philosophy and theory, it is saying, know no national boundaries. This characteristic of this classic work of Marxism in China underscores, yet again, the coherence of the philosopical and theoretical dimensions of Marxism in China with those dimensions of orthodox Marxism then dominant within the international communist movement. To this extent, Marxism in China was not unique, was not a home-grown product.

Li spoke with authority and deep familiarity of the laws and categories of dialectical materialism, and the philosophical debates within the Marxist tradition. Important here is his assertion that the law of the unity of opposites represented "the fundamental law" of dialectical materialism and that the other laws and categories of dialectical materialism were an expression of this fundamental law. Here Li was reiterating a theme already deeply embedded in Marxist philosophy, and emphasised in the Soviet texts on philosophy which he and others translated into Chinese in the early 1930s. This conception of the relationship between the various laws and categories of dialectical materialism was thus transmitted to Marxism in China, and indeed was to become the cornerstone of Mao's own elaboration of the laws of dialectical materialism. The emphasis Mao placed on the law of the unity of opposites did not preclude an appreciation of the role played by the laws of qualitative and quantitative change and the negation of the negation; this is evident in the text available to us of the pre-Liberation version of "On Contradiction", and Mao's philosophical annotations. However, Mao's endorsement of the pre-eminence of the law of the unity of opposites within Marxist philosophy has ensured its persistence as a central article of faith of Marxism in China; Marxist philosophy in the China of the 1990s, despite the widespread repudiation of much else of Mao's heritage, cleaves to a belief in the law of the unity of opposites as the "fundamental law" of dialectical materialism. Li's part in the process of the development of Marxism in China was thus a highly significant and durable one, for some sixty years after the publication of *Elements of Sociology*, its essential themes still have currency within China's theoretical circles.

It is doubtful, nevertheless, that Li would have been pleased with the scale and consequences of the reform program which China has experienced since the late 1970s. While he may have identified with much of the philosophical research carried out by philosophers in post-Mao China, perceiving in it themes prominent in his own philosophical writings from the 1930s, he would not have approved the widespread embrace of the capitalist measures by Deng Xiaoping's strategy for China's economic revival. It is true that Li held serious reservations about Mao's policies for socialist transition of the late 1950s, and supported (in private) Peng Dehuai's criticisms of the Great Leap Forward. By the same token, there is no evidence to suggest any disquiet on his part at the policies — of the socialisation of industry and the cooperativisation of agriculture — which characterised the first phase of China's socialist transition. Li was, in this respect, a conventional old-style Marxist, one who perceived the socialist transition necessitated the increasing control of the state of the various forms of property. His disagreement with Mao was not on this score, but on the pace of change. Li believed that the Party had to lead China towards its objective of a socialist society, but it had to do this in a way which recognised the constraints on progress; of these, one of the most significant was the educational level of the Chinese people. It is no coincidence that Li devoted much of his life to education; at the village level and the national level, as lecturer at many of China's universities and as vice-chancellor of Wuhan University, Li made a strong personal commitment to the process of education. Li's belief in the importance of education for the achievement of socialism is attested, too, by his belief in the importance of disseminating Marxist theory and his commitment to this task never wavered. Li would thus have identified the answers to China's problems in terms different to those which Deng Xiaoping has employed to construct his economic strategy. In Li's eyes, Deng would be guilty of throwing the baby out with the bathwater, of repudiating those elements of economic and social policy essential to the achievement of socialism. The decay of China's education system during the 1980s and 1990s, especially in China's rural areas, would have shocked Li; he would have been shocked too by the low esteem in which China's modern academics are held. However, Li would have recognised that the transformation of China's economic base to allow foreign capitalist investment, Western management techniques and the massive expansion of the market both within and outside the state sector, could not but have a dramatic impact on China's superstructure, of which the education system was a significant part. While education could play a role in achieving change in the direction of socialism, it could not hope to do so in the absence of the requisite economic conditions.

Thus, while Li Da's philosophical legacy has been an enduring one and still resonates within Marxism in China at a theoretical level, the socialist China which he worked so hard to create appears even further from realisation. Nevertheless, Li's writings and translations of Marxist philosophy and theory did play a very significant part in the dissemination of Marxism in China and helped shape the ideological outlook of the revolutionary movement and the intellectual world of post-1949 China. His life and work thus represent a window through which the origins and character of Marxism in China can be examined and perhaps the most revealing thing this examination reveals is the powerful influence that European and Soviet Marxism exercised on its theoretical dimensions. While Li was Chinese, he was intellectually an internationalist, for the Marxism to which he subscribed claimed to be of universal significance, and was widely accepted as such. It was his philosophical activities which helped ensure that Marxism in China did not become a purely nationalist credo within which Chinese traditional cultural and philosophical currents predominated. The extent to which Marxism in China contained and still does retain a universal dimension therefore owes much to Li Da.

Bibliography

Writings by Li Da

Li Da. "Riben zhengdang gaizao zhi qushi" (The Trend in the Transformation of the Japanese Political Parties). *Xiangdao*, Vol. 1, No. 1 (1922). Pp. 7–8.

——— . "Wei shouhui Luda yundong jinggao guoren" (Inform the People of China About the Campaign to Retrieve Lushun and Dalian). *Xin shidai*, No. 1 (1923). Pp. 1–5.

——— . "Jiu guo hui bu si, da dao bu zhi" (The Old World is Unable to Die, and the Big Thieves Persist). *Xin shidai*, No. 4 (July 1923). P. 1.

——— . "Zhongguo shanggong jieji yingyou zhi juewu" (The Consciousness that the Chinese Merchants and Working Class Require). *Xin shidai*, No. 4 (July 1923). Pp. 1–4.

——— . *Xiandai shehuixue* (Contemporary Sociology). Shanghai: Kunlun shudian, 1926.

——— . *Minzu wenti* (The Nationality Question). Shanghai: Nanqiang shuju, 1929.

——— . *Zhongguo chanye geming gaiguan* (A General Survey of China's Revolution in Production). Shanghai: Kunlun shudian, 1929.

——— . "Zhongguo xiandai jingjishi gaiguan" (A Survey of China's Contemporary Economic History). *Faxue zhuankan*, No. 5 (1935). Pp. 85–112.

——— . "Bianzheng luoji yu xingshi luoji" (Dialectical Logic and Formal Logic). *Faxue zhuankan*, No. 5 (1935). Pp. 1–22.

——— . "Preface" to Lu Zhenyu, *Zhongguo yuanshi shehui shi* (A History of China's Primitive Society), in Cai Shangsi (ed.), *Zhongguo xiandai sixiang shi ziliao jianbian* (Selected Materials in the History of Contemporary Chinese Thought). Zhejiang: Zhejiang renmin chubanshe, 1983. Pp. 759–60. Preface dated April 1943.

——— . "Du Mao Zedong tongzhi 1926–1929 nian de sipian wenzhang" (Read Comrade Mao Zedong's Four Essays from 1926–1929). *Renmin ribao*, 30 August 1951.

——— . *Tan xianfa* (On the Constitution). Hankou: Zhongnan renmin chubanshe, 1954.

——— . *Hu Shi fandong sixiang pipan* (A Critique of the Reactionary Thought of Hu Shi). Hankou: Hubei renmin chubanshe, 1955.

——— . "Zhongguo gongchandang de faqi he diyici, dierci daibiao dahui jingguo de huiyi" (Reminiscences on the Initial Period of the Chinese Communist Party and the First and Second Party Congresses). *Yida Qianhou*. Beijing: Renmin chubanshe, 1980, Vol. 2. Pp. 6–18.

———. *Zhongguo renmin gongheguo xianfa jianghua* (A Discussion of the Constitution of the People's Republic of China). Beijing: Renmin chubanshe, 1956.

———. *Shiyongzhuyi: Diguozhuyi de yuyong zhexue* (Pragmatism: The Philosophical Tool of Imperialism). Hubei: Hubei renmin chubanshe, 1956.

———. *Liang Shuming zhengzhi sixiang pipan* (A Critique of the Political Thought of Liang Shuming). Wuhan: Hubei renmin chubanshe, 1956.

———. *Fei Xiaotong de maiban shehuixue pipan* (A Critique of Fei Xiaotong's Compradore Sociology). Shanghai: Renmin chubanshe, 1958.

———. "Qiyi huiyi" (Reminiscences of the First of July). *Qiyi yuekan*, No. 1 (1958). Pp. 1–5.

———. *Shehuizhuyi geming yu shehuizhuyi jianshe de gongtong guilu* (The Laws in Common of Socialist Revolution and Socialist Construction). Hankou: Hubei renmin chubanshe, 1958.

———. *Zhengfeng yundong de bianzhengfa* (The Dialectics of the Rectification Movement). Hankou: Renmin chubanshe, 1958.

———. "Wo guo xian jieduan de shangcengjianzhu he jingji jichu de guanxi" (The Relationship Between Economic Base and Superstructure in China During the Current Stage). *Xuexi*, No. 2 (1958). Pp. 8–10.

———. "Cong shehuizhuyi dao gongchanzhuyi" (From Socialism to Communism). *Lilun zhanxian*, No. 6 (1958). Pp. 36–45; No. 7 (1958). Pp. 36–44; No. 8 (1959). Pp. 35–45.

———. "Shejie wuchanjieji shehuizhuyi geminglun" (On the World Socialist Revolution). *Lilun zhanxian*, No. 8 (1958). Pp. 36–44.

———. "Shengchanli yu shengchanguanxi" (Forces of Production and Relations of Production). *Lilun zhanxian*, No. 5 (1958). Pp. 40–48.

———. "Zenyang xuexi Mao Zedong sixiang" (How to Study Mao Zedong Thought). *Wuhan daxue renwen kexue xuebao*, No. 1 (1960). Pp. 1–3.

———. "Gongchanzhuyi shehui de liangge jieduan" (The Two Stages of Communist Society). *Wuhan daxue renwen kexue xuebao*, No. 1 (1959). Pp. 1–7.

———. "Zichanjieji shehui xueshuo de pipan" (A Critique of Bourgeoise Theories of Society), *Lilun zhanxian*, No. 9 (1958). Pp. 29–42.

———. "Fandui xiandai xiuzhengzhuyi" (Oppose Contemporary Revisionism), *Lilun zhanxian*, No. 5 (1958). Pp. 1–4.

———. "Renzhen xuexi Mao zhuxi de zhuzuo, gaizheng xuefeng, jiaofeng he wenfeng" (Earnestly Study Mao Zedong's Thought, Transform our Styles of Work in Study, Culture and Education). *Zhexue yanjiu*, No. 7 (1958). Pp. 1–2.

———. "Lishiweiwuzhuyi de duixiang" (The Object of Historical Materialism). *Lilun zhanxian*, No. 2 (1958). Pp. 82–98.

———. "Shehuizhuyi geming yu shehuizhuyi jianshe de gongtong guilu" (The Laws in Common of Socialist Revolution and Socialist Construction). *Lilun zhanxian*, No. 2 (1958). Pp. 35–40.

———. "Xu Maoyong duiyu Makesizhuyi zhexue de xiuzheng" (Xu Maoyong's Revision of Marxist Philosophy). *Lilun zhanxian*, No. 2 (1958). Pp. 12–17.

———. "Yanzhe sheyue geming de daolu qianjin" (Forward Along the Path of the October Revolution). *Zhongguo qingnian*, nos 13 and 14 (1961).

——— . (ed.). *Weiwubianzhengfa dagang* (Elements of Materialist Dialectics). Beijing: Renmin chubanshe, 1978.
——— . *"Shijianlun", "Maodunlun" jieshuo* ("On Practice" and "On Contradiction" — A Commentary). Beijing: Sanlian shudian, 1979.
——— . *Falixue dagang* (Elements of Jurisprudence). Beijing: Falu chubanshe, 1983.
——— . *Jingjixue dagang* (Outline of Economic Theory). Wuchang: Wuhan daxue chubanshe, 1985.
——— . "Li Da zizhuan (jielu)" (Li Da's autobiography (extracts)), in Zhonggong Hunan weidangshi ziliao kezhengji yanjiu weiyuanhui (ed.), *Hunan dangshi renwu zhuanji zike xuanbian* (Selected Materials on the Lives of Persons in the History of the Party in Hunan). Hunan: n.p., 1987, Vol. 2. Pp. 1–11.
——— . "Li Da zizhuan" (Li Da's autobiography), in Zhonggong Hunan weidangshi ziliao kezhengji yanjiu weiyuanhui (ed.), *Hunan dangshi renwu zhuanji zike xuanbian* (Selected Materials on the Lives of Persons in the History of the Party in Hunan). Hunan: n.p., 1987, Vol. 2. Pp. 12–32.
——— . *Li Da wenji* (Collected Writings of Li Da). Beijing: Renminchubanshe, 1981–1988, four volumes.

Translations by Li Da

Abe Iso. *Chan er zhixian lun*. Translated by Li Da. Shanghai: Shangwu yinshu guan, 1928.
Gorter, Hermann. *Weiwushiguan jieshuo* (An Explanation of the Materialist View of History). Translated by Li Da. Shanghai: Zhonghua shuju, 1921. Li Da's translator's preface appears p. 7 of the appendix.
——— . "Weiwushi de zongjiao guan" (The Materialist Conception of History's View of Religion). Translated by Li Da. *Shaonian Zhongguo*, Vol. 2, No. 11 (1921). Pp. 36–46.
Hozumi Shigeto *Falixue dagang* (Elements of Jurisprudence). Translated by Li Da. N.p.: Shangwu yinshuguan, 1928.
Katayama Koson. "Dazhan yu Deguo guominxing ji qi wenhua wenyi" (The First World War and Germany's National Characteristics, Its Culture, and Literature and Art). Translated by Li Da. *Xiaoshuo yuebao*, May 1921. Pp. 20–25.
Kautsky, Karl. *Makesi jingji xueshuo* (The Economic Doctrines of Karl Marx). Translated by Li Da. n.p.: Zhonghua shudian, 1921.
Kawada Shiroo. *Tudi jingjixue* (The Economics of the Land). Shanghai: Shangwu yinshuguan, 1933.
Kawakami Hajime. *Makesizhuyi jingjixue jichu lilun* (The Fundamental Theories of Marxist Economics). Translated by Li Da and others. Shanghai: Kunlun shudian, 1930.
Kawanishi Taichiroo. *Nongye wenti zhi lilun* (Theories on the Agricultural Question). Translated by Li Da. Shanghai: Kunlun shudian, 1929.
Labituosi et al. *Zhengzhi jingjixue jiaocheng* (A Course on Political Economy). Translated by Li Da. Shanghai: Bigengtang shudian, 1933.
Lenin, V.I. "Liening de furen jiefanglun" (Lenin's Theory of the Liberation of Women). Translated by Li Da. *Xin Qingnian*, Vol. 9, No. 2 (1921). Pp. 1–2.

Luppol, A. *Lilun yu shijian de shehui kexue genben wenti* (Fundamental Problems of Theory and Practice in the Social Sciences). Translated by Li Da. Shanghai: Xinxian shushe, 1930.

Marx, Karl. "Deguo laodongdang ganglin lanwai piping" (Marginal Critical Notes on the Program of the German Labour Party). Translated by Li Da. *Xin Shidai*, No. 1 (April 1923). Pp. 1–28. This document is usually referred to as "The Critique of the Gotha Program".

Mikhailevsky, *Jingjixue rumen* (An Introduction to Economic Theory). Translated by Li Da. Shanghai: Lehua tushu gonci, 1932.

Miyajima Shinzoo (Shinzaburo?). "Riben wentan zhi xianzhuang" (The Current Situation of the Literary World in Japan). Translated by Li Da. *Xiaoshuo yuebao*, Vol. 12, No. 4 (April 1921). Pp. 5–15.

no author, "Tuole yan de lang" (The Wolf Who Had a Tooth Pulled). Translated freely from the original (*yishu*) by Li Da. *Xin shidai*, No. 4 (July 1923). Pp. 1–12.

Sakai Toshihiko. *Nuxing zhongxin shuo* (Theories of the Centrality of Women). Translated by Li Da. Shanghai: Shangwu yinshuguan, 1921.

Sano Manabu. "Eguo nongmin jieji douzheng shi" (A History of the Class Struggle of the Russian Peasantry). Translated by Li Da. *Xin Qingnian*, Vol. 8, No. 6 (1921). Pp. 1–11.

Shirokov, M. and Aizenberg, A. et al. *Bianzhengfa weiwulun jiaocheng* (A Course on Dialectical Materialism). Translated by Li Da and Lei Zhongjian. Shanghai: Bigengtang shudian, 1932. Li Da's translator's preface, dated June 1935, appears, Pp. 1–4. The fourth edition (1936) of this work has been used throughout this book.

Shookai Shungetsu. "Xiandai de Sigandinaweiya wenxue" (Contemporary Scandinavian Literature). Translated by Li Da. *Xiaoshuo yuebao*, Vol. 12, No. 6 (June 1921). Pp. 1–11.

Sugiyama Sakae. *Shehui kexue gailun* (An Introduction to Social Science). Translated by Li Da and Qian Tieru. Shanghai: Kunlun shudian, 1929. Translators' preface, Pp. 1–3.

Takabatake Motoyuki. *Shehui wenti zonglan* (An Overview of Social Problems). Shanghai: Zhonghua shuju, 1921, three volumes.

Takayanagi Matsuichiroo. *Zhongguo guanshui zhidu lun* (On China's System of Customs Duty). Translated by Li Da. N.p: Shangwu yinshuguan, 1924. Translator's preface, Pp. 1–3.

Thalheimer, A. *Xiandai shejieguan* (The Modern Worldview). Translated by Li Da. Shanghai: Kunlunshudian, 1929. Translator's preface, Pp. 1–5.

Yamakawa Hitoshi. "Cong kexue de shehuizhuyi dao xingdong de shehuizhuyi" (From Scientific Socialism to Active Socialism). Translated by Li Da. *Xin Qingnian*, Vol. 9, No. 1 (May 1921). Pp. 1–4.

Yamakawa Kikue. *Funu wenti yu funu yundong* (The Question of Women and the Women's Movement). Translated by Li Da. Shanghai: Yundong tushu gongsi, 1929.

———. "Laonong Eguo di jiehun zhidu" (The System of Marriage in Soviet Russia). Translated by Li Da. *Xin Qingnian*, Vol. 8, No. 2 (1921). Pp. 11–21.

Bibliographies and Chronologies

Dai Dingsu (ed.). *Wuhan daxue zhexuexi keyan chengguo mulu* (A Bibliography of the Research Results of the Philosophy Department at Wuhan University). Hong Kong: Zhonghuakeji (guoji) chubanshe, 1991. Pp. 1-32.
Li Siju, Tao Delin et al. "Li Da yijiusijiu nianqian lilun huodong ji zhuzuo biannian" (The Pre-1949 Theoretical Activities of Li Da and a Bibliography of His Writings). *Zhongguo zhexue*, Vol. I (1979). Pp. 345–72.
Song Jingming. *Li Da zhuanji* (The Life of Li Da). Hubei: Hubei renmin chubanshe, 1986. Pp. 176–204.
Wang Jionghua. *Li Da yu Makesizhuyi zhexue zai Zhongguo* (Li Da and Marxist Philosophy in China). Hubei: Huazhong ligong daxue chubanshe, 1988. Pp. 324–40.
Zeng Mianzhi. "Li Da zhuyi yaolu" (Bibliography of Li Da's Writings and Translations), in Zhonggong Hunan weidangshi ziliao kezhengji yanjiu weiyuanhui (ed.), *Hunan dangshi renwu zhuanji zike xuanbian* (Selected Materials on the Lives of Persons in the History of the Party in Hunan). Hunan: n.p., 1987), Vol. 2. Pp. 133–52.
Zhongguo dangdai shehui kexuejia (Social Scientists of Contemporary China). Beijing: Shimu wenxian chubanshe, 1983. Pp. 131–42.

Chinese Language Sources

Burov, V. "Li Da yu Zhongguo de Makesizhuyi shehuixue" (Li Da and Chinese Marxist sociology). Translated from the Russian by Sun Aidi. *Guowai shehuixue*, No. 6 (1986). Pp. 10–14.
Chen Dianyun. "Li Da zai dang qian chuanbo de weiwushiguan ji qi lishi zuoyong" (The Historical Materialism Introduced by Li Da Prior to the Founding of the Chinese Communist Party and its Historical Function). *Qiu Suo*, No. 2 (1983).
Du Peiyan. "Bianzheng weiwuzhuyi zai Zhongguo de chuanbo" (The Dissemination of Dialectical Materialism in China). *Zhonggong dangshi yanjiu*, No. 3 (1988). Pp. 28–34.
Fan Zhaoqi. "Li Da dui chuangjian Zhongguo gongchandang de zhongda gongxian" (Li Da's Enormous Contribution to the Establishment of the Chinese Communist Party). *Xuexi yu yanjiu*, No. 11 (1983).
Gao Lu. "Mao Zedong yu luojixue" (Mao Zedong and the Study of Logic), in Wen Xianzhu (ed.), *Mao Zedong dushu yu xiewen* (On Mao Zedong's Reading and Writing). Beijing: Zhonggong zhongyang dangxiao chubanshe, 1993. Pp. 125–41.
Gui Zunyi and Wang Dong. "Li Da dui Zhongguo Makesizhuyi shixue de gongxian" (Li Da's Contribution to Chinese Marxist Historiography). *Huadong shifan daxue xuebao: zhesheban*, No. 3 (1990).
Guo Huaruo. "Mao zhuxi kangzhan chuqi guanghui de zhexue huodong" (The Glorious Philosophical Activities of Chairman Mao in the Early Years of the Anti-Japanese War). *Zhongguo zhexue*, Vol. I (1979). Pp. 31–37.

Hu Sheng. "Chuanbo Makesizhuyi lilun de xianquzhe: Jinian Li Da tongzhi danchen yibai zhounian" (A Pioneer in the Dissemination of Marxist Theory: Commemorating the Hundredth Anniversary of Li Da's Birth), *Guangming ribao (jing)*, 28 October 1990.
Hu Shengzhu (ed.). *Zhongguo gongchandang de qishinian* (The Seventy Years of the Chinese Communist Party). Beijing: Zhonggong dangshi chubanshe, 1991.
Huang Nansen et al. (eds). *Makesizhuyi zhexue shi (diliujuan)* (The History of Marxist Philosophy), Vol. 6, Beijing: Beijing chubanshe, 1989.
"Huasheng wei xuanchuan Makesizhuyi fendou buxi: shoudu jinian Li Da bainian danchen" (A Life of Continuous Advocacy of Marxism: The Capital Celebrates the Hundredth Anniversary of Li Da's Birth). *Renmin Ribao*, 28 October 1990.
Hunan dangshi renwu zhuanji cailiao xuanpian (Selected Biographical Materials on Persons in the History of the Hunan Communist Party). Hunan: Zhonggong Hunansheng weidangshi cailiao zhengji yanjiu weiyuanhui, 1987.
"Jinian lao xiaozhang Li Da tongzhi" (In Commemoration of Our Former Vice-Chancellor Comrade Li Da). *Wuhan daxue xuebao*, No. 1 (1981). Pp. 1–43.
Jin Yinghao. "Li Da guangrong de yisheng zizi bu juantan zhenli — dang de 'yi da' daibiao" (Li Da, a Glorious Life in Continual Search for the Truth — A Representative at the Party's First Congress). *Dang shi yanjiu yu jiaoxue*, No. 6 (1990).
Kawakami Hajime (trans.?). *Weiwushiguan yanjiu* (Research on the Materialist Conception of History). Shanghai: Shangwu yinshuguan, 1926. German title: *Uber Materialististiche Geschichtsauffassung*.
Keluosikefu, Wei Ni, *Sulian Makesi Lieningzhuyi zhexue shi gangyao (sanshi niandai)* (A Commentary on the History of Soviet Marxist-Leninist Philosophy During the 1930s). Translated by Xu Xiaoying and Wang Shuqiu. Beijing: Qiushi chubanshe, 1985.
"Li Da tongzhi yuanan dedao pingfan zhaoxue" (The Unjust Judgement on Comrade Li Da Overturned), in Zhonggong Hunan weidangshi ziliao kezhengji yanjiu weiyuanhui (ed.), *Hunan dangshi renwu zhuanji zike xuanbian* (Selected Materials on the Lives of Persons in the History of the Party in Hunan). Hunan: n.p., 1987, Vol. 2. Pp. 1–11.
"Li Da de 'Shexuixue dagang' zui zao banben de faxian" (The Discovery of the Earliest Text of Li Da's *Elements of Sociology*). *Zhexue yanjiu*, No. 3 (1982).
Li Qiju. "Zhongguo gongchandang chuangshiren zhi yi: Li Da de jiandang huodong" (One of the Founders of the Chinese Communist Party: Li Da's Party Building Activities), *Henan shifan daxue xuebao*, No. 2 (1981); also in Ren Wuxiong (ed.), *Zhongguo gongchandang chuangjian shi yanjiu wenji* (Research on the History of the Establishment of the Chinese Communist Party). Shanghai: Baijia chubanshe, 1991. Pp. 356–73.
Li Qiju et al. "*Gongchandang yuekan* yu Li Da tongzhi" (The *Communist Party Monthly* and Comrade Li Da). *Guangming Ribao*, 2 July 1979.
———. "Jiandang qianhou de Li Da tongzhi" (Comrade Li Da at the Time of the Founding of the Party). *Lishi yanjiu*, No. 8 (1979).
Li Ji. "Li Da tongzhi zai Zhongguo gongchandang chuangjian shiqi de sixiang tedian chutan" (A Discussion of the Particular Characteristics of Li Da's Thought During the Founding Period of the Chinese Communist Party). *Lingling shizhuan xuebao*, No. 1 (1986).

Li Siju, Wang Jionghua and Zhang Dixian (eds). *Makesizhuyi zhexue zai Zhongguo* (Marxist Philosophy in China). Shanghai: Renmin chubanshe, 1991.

Li Weiwu. *20 shiji Zhongguo zhexue bentilun wenti* (Questions of Ontology in Twentieth Century Chinese Philosophy). Hunan: Xinhu shudian, 1991.

Li Zhenxia (ed.). *Dangdai Zhongguo shi zhe* (Ten Philosophers of Contemporary China). Beijing: Huaxia chubanshe, 1991. Pp. 313–29.

Lin Musen (ed.). *Zanmen de lingxiu Mao Zedong* (Our Leader Mao Zedong). Beijing: Jiefangjun chubanshe, 1992. Pp. 47–50, chapter on Li Da.

Liu Fuhai. "Shilun Li Da de daode lilun" (An Investigation of Li Da's moral theory). *Hunan shifan daxue shehui kexue xuebao (Changsha)*, No. 4 (1991).

Lu Xichen and Wang Yumin. *Zhongguo xiandai zhexue shi xinbian* (New Edition of History of Contemporary Philosophy in China). Jilin: Jilin renmin chubanshe, 1987.

Ma Jihua. "Ai Siqi zai zhexue xianshihua shang de jiechu gongxian" (Ai Siqi's Outstanding Contribution to Making Philosophy Practical). *Mao Zedong zhexue sixiang yanjiu dongtai*, No. 3 (1986). Pp. 35–38.

"Mao Zedong he Li Da de yichang zhenglun" (A Dispute between Mao Zedong and Li Da). *Beijing qinghuabao*, 15 December 1992.

Mao Zedong, *Mao Zedong zhexue pizhuji* (The Philosophical Annotations of Mao Zedong). Beijing: Zhongyang wenxian chubanshe, 1988.

———. *Mao Zedong shuxin xuanji* (Selected Correspondence of Mao Zedong). Beijing: Renmin chubanshe, 1983.

Mitin, M.B. *Bianzhengweiwulun yu lishiweiwulun* (Dialectical and Historical Materialism). Translated by Shen Zhiyuan. N.p.: Shangwu yinshuguan, 1936.

———. (ed.). *Xin zhexue dagang* (Outline of New Philosophy). Translated by Ai Siqi and Zheng Yili. N.p.: Dushu shenghuo chubanshe, 1936.

Qu Qiubai wenji (Collected writings of Qu Qiubai). Beijing: Renmin chubanshe, 1988), Vol. 2.

Song Jingming. "Li Da tongzhi zai jiandang shiqi dui chuanbo Makesizhuyi de gongxian" (Comrade Li Da's Contribution to the Dissemination of Marxism at the Time of the Founding of the Party). *Wuhan daxue xuebao*, No. 3 (1983).

———. "Li Da zhuyao zhuyi shumu" (Li Da's Writings and Translations). *Yinshu qing bao zhishi*, No. 4 (1985).

———. "Li Da yu wusi sheqi de sixiang da lunzhan" (Li Da and the Major Ideological Debates of the May Fourth Period). *Wuhan daxue xuebao (shehuikexue ban)*, No. 4 (1987).

———. "Jianxin MaLie, zhongyu zhenli: xuexi he jicheng Li Da tongzhi de geming jingshen (Steadfast Belief in Marxism-Leninism, Devotion to the Truth: Study and Carry on Comrade Li Da's Revolutionary Spirit), *Wuhan daxue xuebao (shehui kexueban)*, No. 6 (1990).

———. "Zhongshi yu zhenli: Li Da tongzhi de zuigao zhunze" (Fidelity to the Truth: The Highest Standard of Comrade Li Da). *Hubei ribao*, 3 October 1985.

———. *Li Da zhuanji* (The Life of Li Da). Hubei: Hubei renmin chubanshe, 1986.

———. "Li Da zaoqi de aiguo sixiang ji qi xiang Makesizhuyi de zhuanbian" (Li Da's Early Patriotic Thought and His Conversion to Marxism). *Chuhui cong shu* Hubei: Hubei renmin chubanshe, 1981, Vol. 2. Pp. 159–71.

---. "Li Da de jiaoyu shijian he banxue sixiang" (Li Da's Educational Practice and His Ideas on School Management), *Wuhan daxue xuebao (shehui kexueban)*, No. 3 (1984). Pp. 37–44.
Song Jingming and Li Qunde. "Jianchi Makesizhuyi de dianfan: Li Da wannian zai Wuhan huodong" (A Model for Upholding Marxism: Li Da's Activities in Wuhan During His Later Years), in Xia Peidong (ed.), *Wuhan fengyun renwu* (Persons of Distinction from Wuhan). Wuhan: Wuhan daxue chubanshe, 1991. Pp. 27–42.
Song Jingming and He Qianwen. "Mao Zedong yu Li Da" (Mao Zedong and Li Da). *Dangshi tiandi*, nos 1, 2 and 3 (1993).
Song Jingming and Li Lin. "Qingqun de jiaobu: ji zhonggong yi da daibiao Li Da (The Footsteps of Youth: In Memory Li Da, of a Great Representative of the Chinese Communist Party). *Mingren zhuanji*, No. 11 (1991). Pp. 8–22.
Song Jingming and Xiong Chongshan. "Li Da", in Zhonggong Hunan weidangshi ziliao kezhengji yanjiu weiyuanhui (ed.), *Hunan dangshi renwu zhuanji zike xuanbian* (Selected Materials on the Lives of Persons in the History of the Party in Hunan). Hunan: n.p., 1987, Vol. 2. Pp. 33–109.
Song Qinan. "Mao Zedong yu Li Da jiaowang de qianqianhouhou" (The Ins-and-Outs of the Relationship Between Mao Zedong and Li Da). *Qilian xuekan*, No. 4 (1992).
Song Zhiming and Zhao Dezhi. *Xiandai Zhongguo zhexue sichao* (Philosophical Trends in Contemporary China). Beijing: Zhongguo renmin daxue chubanshe, 1992.
Sun Qinan and Li Shizhen. *Mao Zedong yu mingren* (Mao Zedong and the Famous). Jiangsu: Jiangsu renmin chubanshe, 1993, two vols.
Tang Qunyuan. "Shishu Li Da minzhu geming shiqi de tongyi zhanxian sixiang yu shijian" (A Discussion of Li Da's Thought and Practice Regarding the United Front During the Period of the Democratic Revolution). *Lingling shizhuan xuebao*, No. 2 (1987).
---. "Li Da yu faxue" (Li Da and Jurisprudence). *Lingling shizhuan xuebao*, No. 1 (1986).
---. "Li Da yu Furen xiaoxue" (Li Da and Furen Primary School). *Lingling shizhuan xuebao*, No. 2 (1982).
Tao Delin. "Li Da zhuanlue" (The Life of Li Da). *Zhongguo zhexue nianjian* (China's Philosophical Yearbook). Shanghai: Zhongguo dabaike quanshu chubanshe, 1984. Pp. 489–99.
---. "Xuexi Li Da tonzhi zhongyu Makesizhuyi de jingshen: jinian Li Da tongzhi dansheng 100 zhounian" (Study Comrade Li Da's Spirit of Fidelity to Marxism: Commemorating the Hundredth Anniversary of Li Da's Birth). *Wuhan daxue xuebao (shehui kexueban)*, No. 6 (1990).
Tao Delin and Jie Ren. "Li Da", in Meng Qingren (ed.), *Zhuming Makesizhuyi zhexuejia pingzhuan* (Biographies of Famous Marxist Philosophers). Jinan: Shandong renmin chubanshe, 1990. Pp. 291–334.
Wang Jionghua. "'Dagang' de chuanzaoxing gongxian ji 'lianglun' yu ta de lianxi ("On Contradiction" and "On Practice" and the Creative Contribution of *Elements of Sociology*, and the Connection Between These Texts). *Mao Zedong zhexue sixiang yanjiu dongtai*, No. 1 (1984). Pp. 20–23.

―――. "Dutan 'lianglun' yu 'dagang'" (On the Relationship Between "On Practice" and "On Contradiction" and *Elements of Sociology*). *Mao Zedong zhexue sixiang yanjiu dongtai*, No. 3 (1986). Pp. 39–40.

―――. *Li Da yu Makesizhuyi zhexue zai Zhongguo* (Li Da and Marxist Philosophy in China). Hubei: Huazhong ligong daxue chubanshe, 1988.

―――. "Mao Zedong yu Li Da" (Mao Zedong and Li Da). *Xinhua wenzhai*, No. 2 (1992). Pp. 132–35.

―――. "Li Da: yi wei Puluomixiusishi bohuozhe (Li Da: A Prometheus who Sowed Fire), in Li Zhenxia (ed.), *Dangdai Zhongguo shi zhe* (Ten Philosophers of Contemporary China). Beijing: Huaxia chubanshe, 1991. Pp. 313–29.

Wei zhenli er douzheng de Li Da tongzhi (Comrade Li Da who Struggled for Truth). Wuhan: Wuhan daxue chubanshe, 1985.

Wu Liping and Ai Siqi. *Weiwu shiguan* (The Materialist Conception of History). Beijing: Renmin chubanshe, 1983. Co-written and first published in Yan'an in 1938.

Xing Bensi. "Jinian jiechu de Makesizhuyi lilunjia jiaoyujia Li Da tongzhi" (In Memory of the Outstanding Marxist Theorist and Educationalist Comrade Li Da). *Guangming ribao*, 11 February 1990.

Xu Quanxing. "Zai tan 'lianglun' yu 'shehuixue dagang' ― fu Wang Jionghua tongzhi" (Once Again on "On Contradiction" and "On Practice" and *Elements of Sociology* ― a Response to Comrade Wang Jionghua). *Mao Zedong zhexue sixiang yanjiu dongtai*, No. 3 (1985). Pp. 24–29.

―――. "Li Da zai Zhongguo chuanbo Makesizhuyi zhexue de lishi gongji" (The Historical Achievement of Li Da's Dissemination of Marxist Philosophy in China). *Guangming ribao*, 15 October 1990.

Xiu Suhua. "Zhongguo sanshiniandai zhexue lunzhan" (Philosophical Debates in China During the 1930s). *Mao Zedong zhexue sixiang yanjiu dongtai*, No. 1 (1988). Pp. 78–83; and No. 4 (1988). Pp. 70–74.

Yang Bangguo. "Mao Zedong yu Li Da de zhexue jiaowang" (The Philosophical Relationship Between Mao Zedong and Li Da). *Mao Zedong sixiang luntan (Changsha)*, No. 4 (1992). Pp. 49–52.

―――. "Li Da zai Zhongguo gongchandang chuangjian zhong de lishi zuoyong" (The Historical Role of Li Da in the Founding of the Chinese Communist Party). *Nankai xuebao*, No. 4 (1991).

Ye Yonglie. *Hongse de qidian* (Red Beginnings). Shanghai: Shanghai renmin chubanshe, 1991.

Yong Tao. "Jianchi he fazhan MaLiezhuyi Mao Zedong sixiang de dianfan: jinian Li Da tongzhi 100 zhounian danchen" (A Model in upholding and Developing Marxism-Leninism Mao Zedong Thought: In Commemoration of the Hundredth anniversary of Li Da's birth). *Wuhan daxuebao (shehui kexueban)*, No. 6 (1990).

Yu Qingtian et al. *Mao Zedong yu tongshi* (Mao Zedong and Colleagues). Beijing: Renmin daxue chubanshe, 1993, Vol. 2. Pp. 311–42.

Yuan Jinxiang. *Mingjia fanyi yanjiu yu shangxi* (Reasearch on and Appreciation of Famous Translators). Hubei:Hubei jiaoyu chubanshe, 1990. Pp. 167–76.

Zhang Xiyang. "Lun Li Da duiyu Zhongguoshi shehuizhuyi jianshe de tansuo" (On Li Da's Considerations on the Establishment of Chinese-style Socialism). *Tianjin shida xuebao*, No. 3 (1991).

Zhang Xiuying and Ren Wensi. "Zhongguo zaoqi Makesizhuyizhe de chenghu zhi wojian" (My View on How We Should Designate China's Early Marxists). *Zhonggong dangshi yanjiu*, No. 5 (1988).

Zhao Dezhi and Wang Benhao. *Zhongguo Makesizhuyi zhexue qishinian* (Seventy Years of Marxist Philosophy in China). Liaoning: Liaoning daxue chubanshe, 1991. Pp. 48–57.

Zhongguo chuban shiliao, pubian (Materials on the History of Publishing in China). Beijing: Zhonghua shujiu chuban, 1957.

Zhonguo xiandai zhexue shi yanjiuhui et al. *Jinian Li Da danchen yibai zhounian* (Commemorate the Hundredth Anniversary of Li Da's Birth). Changsha: Hunan chubanshe,1991.

Zhongguo dangdai shehui kexuejia (Contemporary Chinese Social Scientists). Shimu wenxian chubanshe, 1983.

Zhuang Fuling (ed.). *Zhongguo Makesizhuyi zhexue chuanbo shi* (A History of the Dissemination of Marxist Philosophy in China). Beijing: Zhongguo renmin daxue chubanshe, 1988.

English Language Sources

Ahlberg, Rene. "The Forgotten Philosopher: Abram Deborin", in Leopold Labedz (ed.), *Revisionism: Essays on the History of Marxist Ideas*. London: George Allen & Unwin, 1962.

Avineri, Shlomo. *The Social and Political Thought of Karl Marx*. Cambridge: Cambridge University Press, 1968.

Bernal, Martin. *Chinese Socialism to 1907*. Ithaca and London: Cornell University Press, 1976.

Bernstein, Gail Lee. *Japanese Marxist: A Portrait of Kawakami Hajime, 1879–1946*. Cambridge, Mass.: Harvard University Press, 1976.

———. "The Russian Revolution, the Early Japanese Socialists, and the Problem of Dogmatism". *Studies in Comparative Communism*, Vol. IX, No. 4 (Winter 1976). Pp. 327–48.

Boorman, Howard L. *Biographical Dictionary of Republican China*. New York and London: Columbia University Press, 1968. Pp. 328–29.

Bottomore, Tom and Rubel, Maximilian (eds). *Karl Marx: Selected Writings in Sociology and Social Philosophy*. Harmondsworth: Penguin, 1963.

Bricianer, Serge. *Pannekoek and the Workers' Councils*. St Louis: Telos Press, 1978.

Briere, O. *Fifty Years of Chinese Philosophy, 1898–1948*. New York and Washington: Frederick A. Praeger, 1965.

Burov, V. "Li Da and the Dissemination of Marxist Ideas in China". *Far Eastern Affairs*, No. 3 (1983). Pp. 102–13.

Carver, Terrel. *Marx and Engels: The Intellectual Relationship*. Brighton: Wheatsheaf Books, 1983.

De George, Richard T. *Patterns of Soviet Thought*. Ann Arbor: University of Michigan Press, 1966.

Dirlik, Arif. *Revolution and History: Origins of Marxist Historiography in China, 1919–1937*. Berkeley: University of California Press, 1978.

―――. *The Origins of Chinese Communism*. New York: Oxford University Press, 1989.
Engels, Frederick. *Anti-Dühring (Herr Eugen Dühring's Revolution in Science)*. Peking: FLP, 1976.
―――. *Dialectics of Nature*. Moscow: FLPH, 1954.
Fei Hsiao-tung. *Peasant Life in China: A Field Study of Country Life in the Yangtze Valley*. London and Henley: Routledge and Kegan Paul, 1939, reprinted 1980.
Fogel, Joshua. *Ai Ssu-ch'i's Contribution to the Development of Chinese Marxism*. Cambridge, Mass. and London: Harvard Contemporary China Series, No. 4, 1987.
Graham, Loren R. *Science and Philosophy in the Soviet Union*. New York: Alfred A. Knopf, 1972.
―――. *The Soviet Academy of Sciences and the Communist Party, 1927–1932*. Princeton: Princeton University Press, 1967.
Grieder, Jerome B. *Hu Shih and the Chinese Renaissance: Liberalism in the Chinese Revolution, 1917–1937*. Cambridge, Mass.: Harvard University Press, 1970.
Healy, Paul. *Mao and Classical Marxism, Epistemology, Social Formation, Classes and Class Struggle in Mao Zedong's Post-1955 Thought*. Unpublished PhD thesis, Griffith University, 1988.
―――. "Reading the Mao Texts: The Question of Epistemology". *Journal of Contemporary Asia*, Vol. 20, No. 3 (1990). Pp. 330–58.
Hoston, Germaine, A. *Marxism and the Crisis of Development in Prewar Japan*. Princeton: Princeton University Press, 1986.
Hu Shih. *The Chinese Renaissance: The Haskell Lectures, 1933*. New York: Paragon Book Reprint Corp., 1963.
Joravsky, David. *Soviet Marxism and Natural Science, 1917–1932*. New York: Columbia University Press, 1961.
Jordan, Z.A. *The Evolution of Dialectical Materialism: A Philosophical and Sociological Analysis*. London: Macmillan, 1967.
Kamenka, Eugene. "Soviet Philosophy, 1917–67", in Alex Simirenko (ed.), *Social Thought in the Soviet Union*. Chicago: Quadrangle Books, 1969.
Kau, Michael Y.M, and Leung, John K. (eds). *The Writings of Mao Zedong, 1949–1976: Volume I, September 1949–December 1955*. Armonk, New York: M.E. Sharpe, 1986.
―――. *The Writings of Mao Zedong, 1949–1976: Volume II, January 1956–December 1957*. Armonk: M.E. Sharpe, 1992.
Knight, Nick (ed.). *Mao Zedong on Dialectical Materialism: Writings on Philosophy, 1937*. Armonk, New York: M.E. Sharpe, 1990.
―――. "Soviet Philosophy and Mao Zedong's 'Sinification of Marxism'". *Journal of Contemporary Asia*, Vol. 20, No. 1 (1990). Pp. 89–109.
―――. (ed.). *The Philosophical Thought of Mao Zedong: Studies from China, 1981–1989*, *Chinese Studies in Philosophy*, Vol. 23, nos 3–4 (Spring–Summer 1992).
―――. "The Marxism of Mao Zedong: Empiricism and Discourse in the Field of Mao Studies", *Australian Journal of Chinese Affairs*, No. 16 (July 1986). Pp. 7–22.
―――. "*On Contradiction* and *On New Democracy*: Contrasting Perspectives on Causation and Social Change in the Thought of Mao Zedong". *Bulletin of Concerned Asian Scholars*, Vol. 22, No. 2 (April–June 1990). Pp. 18–34.

———. *Mao and History: An Interpretive Essay on Some Problems in Mao Zedong's Philosophy of History*. Unpublished PhD thesis, University of London, 1983.
Kolakowski, Leszek. *Main Currents of Marxism: The Founders*. Oxford: Oxford University Press, 1978.
———. *Main Currents of Marxism: Its Rise, Growth and Dissolution — Volume II, The Golden Age*. Oxford: Clarendon Press, 1978.
Korsch, Karl. *Marxism and Philosophy*. London: NLB, 1970.
Krapivin, V. *What is Dialectical Materialism?*. Moscow: Progress Publishers, 1985.
Lefebvre, Henri. *Dialectical Materialism*. London: Jonathon Cape, 1968.
Lenin, V.I. *Materialism and Empirio-Criticism*. Peking: FLP, 1972.
———. *Collected Works*. London: Lawrence and Wishart, 1961, Vol. 38.
———. *What is to be Done? Burning Questions of our Movement*. Peking: FLP, 1975.
Levine, Norman. *The Tragic Deception: Marx Contra Engels*. Oxford and Santa Barbara: Clio Books, 1975.
Lichtheim, George. *Marxism: An Historical and Critical Study*. London: Routledge and Kegan Paul, 1961.
Luk, Michael Y.L. *The Origins of Chinese Bolshevism: An Ideology in the Making, 1920–1928*. Hong Kong: Oxford University Press, 1990.
Lukács, Georg. *History and Class Consciousness*. London: Merlin Press, 1968.
Mao Zedong. *Selected Works of Mao Tse-tung*. Peking: Foreign Languages Press, 1965–1977, five vols.
Macfarquhar, Roderick. *The Origins of the Cultural Revolution: I Contradictions Among the People, 1956–1957*. London: Oxford University Press, 1974.
Marcuse, Herbert. *Soviet Marxism: A Critical Analysis*. New York: Vintage Books, 1961.
Marx, Karl. *Surveys from Exile*. Harmondsworth: Penguin, 1973.
———. *The Revolutions of 1848*. Harmondsworth: Penguin, 1973.
———. *Grundrisse: Foundations of the Critique of Political Economy (Rough Draft)*. Harmondsworth: Penguin, 1974.
———. *Capital: A Critique of Political Economy, Volume One*. Harmondsworth: Penguin, 1976.
———. *A Contribution to the Critique of Political Economy*. London: Lawrence and Wishart, 1971, with an Introduction by Maurice Dobb.
———. "Marginal Notes on Adolph Wagner *Lehrbuch Der Politischen Oekonomie*". *Theoretical Practice*, No. 5 (1972).
Marx, Karl, and Engels, Frederick. *Selected Works in Two Volumes*. Moscow: FLPH, 1951, Vol. II.
—— *Selected Letters*. Peking: FLP, 1977.
McCough, James P. *Fei Hsiao-t'ung: The Dilemma of a Chinese Intellectual*. New York: M.E. Sharpe, 1979.
Meisner, Maurice. "Utopian Socialist Themes in Maoism", in John W. Lewis (ed.), *Peasant Rebellion and Communist Revolution in Asia*. Stanford: Stanford University Press, 1966, Pp. 207–52.
———. "Leninism and Maoism: Some Populist Perpsectives on Marxism-Leninism in China". *China Quarterly*, No. 45 (January–March 1971). Pp. 2–36.
———. *Mao's China and After: A History of the People's Republic of China*. New York: The Free Press, 1977, 1986.

———. *Marxism, Maoism and Utopianism*, Madison: University of Wisconsin Press, 1982.
Meissner, Werner. *Philosophy and Politics in China: The Controversy over Dialectical Materialism in the 1930s*. London: Hurst and Co., 1990.
Party History Research Centre of the Central Committee of the Chinese Communist Party (comp.). *History of the Chinese Communist Party — A Chronology of Events (1919–1990)*. Beijing: FLP, 1991.
Plekhanov, George V. *In Defence of Materialism: The Development of the Monist View of History*. London: Lawrence and Wishart, 1947.
———. *Fundamental Problems of Marxism*. London: Martin Lawrence Ltd, n.d.
———. *Materialismus Militans*. Moscow: Progress Publishers, 1973.
———. *The Materialist Conception of History*. New York: International Publishers, 1940.
Saich, Tony. *The Origins of the First United Front in China: The Role of Sneevliet (Alias Maring)*. Leiden: E.J. Brill, 1991, two vols.
Schram, Stuart R. *Mao Tse-tung*. Harmondsworth: Penguin, 1966.
———. *The Political Thought of Mao Tse-tung*. Harmondsworth: Penguin, 1969, rev. edn.
———. *The Thought of Mao Tse-tung*. Cambridge: Cambridge University Press, 1989.
———. "The Marxist", in Dick Wilson (ed.), *Mao Tse-tung in the Scales of History*. Cambridge: Cambridge University Press, 1977. Pp. 35–69.
———. *Mao Zedong: A Preliminary Reassessment*. Hong Kong: The Chinese University Press, 1983.
Schwartz, Benjamin I. "The Legend of the 'Legend of Maoism'". *China Quarterly*, No. 2 (April–June 1960). Pp. 35–42.
———. *Chinese Communism and the Rise of Mao*. New York and London: Harper and Row, 1951.
———. *Communism and China: Ideology in Flux*. New York: Atheneum, 1970.
Shao Weizheng. "The First National Congress of the Communist Party of China: A Verification of the Date of Convocation and the Number of Participants". *Social Sciences in China*, Vol. 1, No. 1 (March 1980). Pp. 108–29.
Shteppa, Konstantin, F. *Russian Historians and the Soviet State*. New Brunswick: Rutgers University Press, 1962.
Stalin, J.V. *Problems of Leninism*. Peking: FLP, 1976.
Ts'ao, Ignatius J.H. "Ai Ssu-ch'i: The Apostle of Chinese Communism". *Studies in Soviet Thought*, No. 12 (1972).
Wetter, Gustav A. *Dialectical Materialism: A Historical and Systematic Study of Philosophy in the Soviet Union*. New York: Praeger, 1958.
Wittfogel, Karl. "The Legend of 'Maoism'". *China Quarterly*, No. 1 (January–March 1960). Pp. 72–86, and No. 2 (April–June 1960). Pp. 16–34.
Wolin, Sheldin S. "Paradigms and Political Theories", in P. King and B.C. Parekh (eds), *Politics and Experience*. Cambridge; Cambridge University Press, 1968. Pp. 125–52.

Index

aetiology of social change, see social change, aetiology of
affirmation, elements of, 283
Ahlberg, Rene, 45
Ai Siqi, 133, 155, 158, 167, 205, 233, 284, 300
Aizenberg, 48, 87, 1, 22614, 124, 133–39, 152, 154, 155, 156, 158, 159, 165, 166, 170, 190, 209, 300
Althusser, 297
analysis and sythesis, 220
anarchism, 4, 63, 68, 72–73
Anti-Japanese Military and Political University, 151, 159
anti-Japanese War, 1, 17–18, 166, 231
art and literature, in social life, 94
Avenarius, 40
Bai Pengfei, 17, 18
Bakunin, 73
base, 270
    and superstructure, 224, 248, 270–72, 276, 298
basis and condition, 196–97, 201
Beiping, years in, 16–17
Berkeley, 103, 135
Bernstein, 123, 249
bloc within, 9
Bogdanov, A.A., 40, 45, 135, 195
Bolshevism, 72, 75, 85, 123
Bukharin, 45, 50, 124, 133, 158, 195
Capital, 5, 196, 248
capitalism, 100
    as international system, 72
    emergence of; 182
    in China, 78
    overthrow of, 66
capitalist restoration, 282
capitalist sociology, 264–65, 266
causality, concept of, 202–3

cause and effect, laws of, *see* laws of cause and effect
CCP, *see* Chinese Communist Party
chance and necessity, 199–200, 201
Chartists, 122
Chen Boda, 286
Chen Duxiu, 6, 11–12, 13, 85, 90, 300
Chen Gongbo, 12
Chen Wangdao, 6, 113
Cheng Mingren, 19
Cheng Qian, 19
Chiang Kai-shek, 262
Chinese Communist Party, 107
    alliance with GMD, 81
    First Congress, 7
    formation of, 298
    intellectual hierarchy, 232
    Li's dilemma regarding, 295–96
    Li's life outside, 13–16
    Li's relations with, 296–97
    Li's resignation from, 8–13, 76, 90, 108, 258, 295
    Manifesto, 76
    readmission to, 18–19, 227, 231–32, 257, 258, 264
    Second Congress, 9, 10, 76
    sense of identification with, 158; formation, 1, 6–8
    Seventh Party Congress, 232
    Sixth Plenum of the Sixth Central Committee, 151, 168
Chinese Marxism, *see* Marxism in China
Chinese sociology, 266
civil war, 1
class, 98–101
    as economic category, 99
    class-for-itself, 273
    class-in-itself, 273

Index

consciousness, 64, 66
contradictions, 282
formations, 224
opposition between classes, 98
relationships, 32, 64, 80
structure in China, 68–69
struggle, 43, 44, 64, 66, 73, 273, 286
Collected Writings of Li Da, 24, 157
Comintern, 2
commitment to Marxism, 13
commodities
production of, 121
commodity relationships, 220
communism, 62–63
in China, 144
Communist Manifesto, The, 5, 7, 10, 66, 68, 77, 81, 84
Communist Party of the Soviet Union, 107, 133, 154
Communist victory, 1
Communist, The, 6–7, 72, 232
Comte, August, 264
concepts, 164
and ideas, 215
Consciousness, 7
consciousness, human, 101, 104, 125, 126, 211, 212, 214
class, 273
social, 132, 135
Contemporary Sociology, 14, 30, 39, 87, 90, 91–98, 98, 144, 151, 264
contradiction, 35–36, 119, 132, 137–38, 163, 166, 185, 192, 194, 222
contradiction and motion, 42
in reality, 42, 137, 143, 276, 283, 284–85
law of, 222, 223
struggle of, 137
within economic base, 273
correct thought, 131
Course on Dialectical Materialism, A, 48, 114, 124, 133–39, 140, 154, 155, 156, 158, 166, 167, 170, 172, 209–10, 232, 300
influence on Mao, 140, 159
Mao's annotations, 165
translation of, 152

Critique of the Gotha Program, 7, 8, 77, 81, 84, 109
Cultural Revolution, 1, 20, 22–23, 258, 268, 295
impact on Li, 23–24, 254, 268
currency, 105
Darwin, Charles, 260, 265
death, Li Da, 24, 231, 258, 287
Deborin, Abram, 40, 45–46, 47, 50, 54, 106, 107, 124, 130, 132, 133, 134, 135, 137, 154, 155, 157, 158, 172, 188, 200
deduction, and induction, 220
"Deliberation on Social Revolution", 68–71
democracy, 74–75
Democratic Revolution, 280
Democrites, 163
Deng Chumin, 91, 114
Deng Xiaoping, 302, 303
Dewey, John, 260, 262
Dialectical and Historical Materialism, 159, 167, 172, 210
dialectical logic, and formal logic, 224
dialectical materialism, 2, 31, 34, 40, 41, 42, 45, 53–54, 103–6, 126, 130, 131, 133, 138–39, 152, 252
as epistemology, 188
categories of, 166, 179–208, 302
development, 183
dismissive treatment of, 180
history, 161, 181–83
laws of, 152, 166, 179–208, 190–204, 302, *see also individual laws*
Li's interpretation of, 252
Mao's contribution to, 285
Mao's views on, 159–61, 173, 283
methodology, 167
natural perspective, 183
new stage in, 154–55
ontology, 186–87
philosophical science of, 183–85
principles of, 281
textual basis for, 157
worldview of, 188
see also essence and phenonomenon; basis and condition; form and

content; chance and necessity; laws and causality
dialectical negation, 194
Dialectics of Nature, 199
dialectics, 101–6, 129, 130, 131, 132, 136, 152, 166
   categories of, 43, 138
   in Soviet Marxism, 36
   laws of, 35, 36, 43, 138, 143, 282–86
dictatorship of the proletariat, 65
Ding Ling, 297
"direct movement", 70, 72
Dong Biwu, 13
dualism, 184
Duan Qirui, 5, 62
Economic Doctrines of Karl Marx, The, 5, 117–18
economic determinism, 50, 53
economic materialism, 50
economic theory, 16–17
education, 3–4
Elements of Dialectical Materialism, 22, 278–82, 279, 295
   fate of, 286–87
Elements of Economics, 152
Elements of Historical Materialism, 286–87
Elements of Jurisprudence, 99, 231
Elements of Marxist Philosophy, 22, 279, 286
Elements of Sociology, 2, 17, 22, 23, 30, 39, 104, 107, 115, 139, 143, 231, 232, 238, 264, 296, 301, 302
   and dialectical materialism, 179–208
   and intertextual congruence, 204–6
   and Marxism in China, 225–27
   and Marxist philosophy, 151–78
   epistemology and logic, 209–29
   influences on, 153–57
   Mao's comments on, 153, 161–68, 286
   publication, 152–53
   revision, 254, 258, 278–82, 296
   significance, 168–69
   structure, 181
empiricism, 196

Encmen, 45
Engels, Frederick, 10, 41, 42, 46, 48, 51, 53, 75, 122, 124, 127, 131, 132, 182, 183, 199, 224, 248, 249, 279, 284
   on social change and philosophy, 33–39
epistomology, 49–50, 188, 209–29, 286
   of reflection theory, 210–11
essence, 105
   and phenomenon, 195–96, 199, 201, 283
   first order, 196
   second order, 196
European socialist movement, 6
excluded middle, law of, 222–23
Explanation of the Materialist Conception of History, An, 5, 118–21, 299
expulsion from CCP, 23
Fabians, 122
Fei Xiaotong, 55, 253, 258, 264–68, 268, 276, 297
fellow traveller, Li as, 20
Feng Yuxiang, 16, 17, 18, 231
feudalism, 99
Feuerbach, 42, 125, 130–31, 155, 182, 195
Fichte, 122
First United Front, 2, 8
forces of production, 94, 95, 98, 132, 247, 272, 276
   and philosophy, 102–3
   development of, 282
form and content, 198, 201, 283
formal logic, 152, 216
   critique of, 222–24
   laws of, 138
formal sociology, 265
Fundamental Knowledge of Society, 91, 102, 104
Fundamental Problems of Theory and Practice in the Social Sciences, 129–30
Fundamental Theories of Marxist Economics, 130–32, 153
Gang of Four, 23
German Social Democratic Party, 69, 74

Index

GMD, *see* Guomindang
Godwin, 122
Gorter, Hermann, 5, 84, 113, 117–21, 123, 128, 141, 299
Gotha Program, 665
Gramsci, 83, 297
Great Leap Forward, 21, 22, 23, 55, 231, 251, 253, 257, 268–78, 302
    Li's reservations about, 297
    writings of period, 268–78
Greek philosophers, 182
    Mao's views on, 162–65
Guo Dali, 113
Guomindang, 1, 9–12, 90
    alliance with CCP, 2, 81
    harrassment of Li, 152, 231
Harrington, 122
health, 4, 20, 23–24, 251
Hegel, 41, 42, 45, 46, 53, 104, 107, 122, 125, 131, 132, 134, 135, 136, 166, 182, 184, 188, 195
    Hegelian philosophy, 34, 41, 47, 49, 154, 155, 172, 187
    theory of inference, 219
Heraclites, 163, 182
historical materialism, 224–25, 238, 239, 270
    in Soviet Marxism, 44–46
History of Social Evolution, A, 152
History of the Evolution of Society, A, 17
Hou Wailu, 113
"How Should Mao Zedong Thought be Studied?", 251
Hozumi Shigeto, 15
Hu Shi, campaign against, 20–21, 55, 253, 258–64, 268, 276, 297
Hu Xieqing, 3
human relations, 93, 224
Hundred Flowers period, 21, 264
idealism, 36, 104, 125, 135, 163, 165, 184, 191
ideas, 215; and concepts, 215–18
identity, law of, 222
ideology, 225
imperialism, 80
Indonesian Communist Party, 9
induction, and deduction, 220–22

inevitability and chance, 283
inference, 219–20; inductive, 219
Introduction to Dialectical Materialism, 128–29
Japan, hostility to China, 4
Japanese Marxism, *see* Marxism, Japanese
Li Da in, 3
Jiang Chun, 68
judgment, 139, 218–19
    as orthodoxy, 40, 46–51
    in Japan, 51–54
    in Soviet Marxism, 44–46
    philosophy of, 129
July Seventh incident, 167
June Third Movement, 5, 70
Kang Sheng, 23, 168, 286
Kant, 135, 166, 182
Kantianism, 66, 187, 198
Kautsky, Karl, 5, 74, 75, 84, 113, 117–18, 120, 299
Kawakami Hajime, 3, 5, 15, 52, 53, 87, 91, 105, 128, 130–32, 140, 141, 153, 299
Kawanishi Taichiro, 15
knowledge, production, 136–37
    process of, 210, 215, 252
Korsch, Karl, 31
Kropotkin, 4, 73
Kunlun Publishing House (Kunlun Shudian), 15, 114
labour, organisation of, 66–67
    and human thought, 161–62
    process, 272
    socialisation of, 96
    surplus of, 69
language, function of, 95
law, 98–101, 105
    and causality, 200–203
    dialectical materialism on, 201
law of affirmation and negation, 283
law of contradiction, 222
law of excluded middle, 222–23
law of identity, 222
law of leaps, 166
law of qualitative and quantitative change, 282–83

law of the mutual transformation of quantity and quality, 49, 192–94, 196
law of the negation of the negation, 49, 194–95, 196, 200, 283
law of the unity of opposites, 48–49, 138, 143, 188, 190–92, 196, 200, 248, 282, 302
laws of cause and effect, 124–25, 283
laws of development, 217–18
laws of formal logic, 222–23
laws of motion, 34
  and interconnectedness of objective things, 217
laws of the objective world, 219
laws of thought, 222–23
League of Social Scientists, 15
Lecture Notes on Dialectical Materialism, 160, 165, 169, 205
Lei Zhongjian, 152, 154
Lenin, Vladimir, 5, 10, 31, 39, 42–44, 46, 49, 51, 67, 74, 75, 82, 84–85, 130, 132, 144, 188, 224, 248, 249, 279, 284, 297
Li Dazhao, 5, 85, 113, 118
Li Furen, 3, 18
Li Hanjun, 6, 7, 118
Li Haoming, 102
Li Weihan, 19
Liang Qichao, 71–72, 266
Liang Shuming, 253, 274, 276, 297
Lichtheim, 33
life, of Li Da, 1–29
Lin Biao, 20, 23, 24, 168, 232, 253, 254, 258
Liu Shaoqi, 19, 22, 286
Locke, 122
logic, 209–29
  inductive, 220
Lu Xun, 22
Lukécs, Georg, 31
Luppol, I., 91, 106, 124, 128, 129–30, 132
Mach, Ernst, 40, 106, 135, 187, 259
Malinowski, Bronislaw, 267
Malthusian population theory, 95, 265, 266
Manchuria, Japanese invasion of, 5

Mao Zedong, 4, 6, 8, 13, 14, 16, 17, 19, 20, 21–22, 31, 85, 109, 133, 140, 151, 180, 205, 210, 225, 226, 232, 257, 277, 279, 286, 295, 296, 301
  annotations, 161–68
  contribution to Marxist philosophy, 278
  influences on, 159
  Li's relationship with, 227, 232, 232–34, 252, 269, 277
  on dialectical materialism, 159–61, 233
  on Greek philosophy, 162–65
  philosophical thought, 114
  scientific content of essays, 251
  understanding of Marxist theory, 239
Mao Zedong Thought, 23, 24, 85, 116, 168, 227, 253, 254, 279, 295
  ideological method of, 252
  Li Da and, 231–56, 258, 268
  new orthodoxy, 247
  study of, 249
Mao Zedong Thought Research Centre, 279
Marx, Karl, 5, 9, 34, 40, 41, 42, 68, 75, 78, 122, 131, 132, 136, 182, 183, 196, 248, 249, 272, 279
  on social change and philosophy, 33–39
"Marxism Restored", 8, 64, 67
Marxism
  as science, 65
  basic theories of, 112, 151
  degeneration of, 65–66
  economistic reading of, 121
  Elements of Sociology and, 225–27
  genealogy of, 54
  in China, 30–62, 112, 140, 143, 298, 301
  in Europe, 113, 298
  in Germany, 65
  Japanese, 51–54, 140, 141, 298
  Li's conversion to, 112, 114, 299
  orthodox, *see* orthodoxy, orthodox Marxism
  philosophy of, 53, 125
  Soviet, 46–51, 180, 298

Index

textual basis in China, 157
Marxism-Leninism, 23, 24, 116, 234, 249, 250, 251, 253
   universal truths of, 252
Marxism-Leninism-Mao Zedong Thought, 30, 253
Marxist philosophy, 143, 301
   and *Elements of Sociology*, 151–78
   and social theory, 30–62
   dissemination, 140, 151
   genealogy of, 157
   history and content, 142
   Li Da and, 295–304
   Li's explanation of, 64–68
   Li's writings on, 257–94
   Mao's contribution to, 278–82
   Mao's understanding of, 172
Marxist socialism, 73–75
"Marxist Theory and China", 8–9, 75–82, 84–85, 91
Marxist theory, 257–94
   of social change, 38
material conditions of existence, 43
material relations, 93
materialism, 36, 104, 125, 126, 130–31, 135, 184–85, 259
   Marxist materialist theory, 43
   materialist dialectics, 104
   materialist historiography, 43
   materialist interpretation of social change, 37–38
   see also dialectical materialism
Materialist Conception of History, The, 141
materialist conception of history, 53, 79, 83, 84, 92, 119–20, 122–23, 124, 130, 132, 232, 276
materialist epistemology, 189
materiality of reality, 34
matter and motion, 163, 186–87
matter and spirit, 183–84
May Fourth Movement, 5–6, 21, 30, 56, 70, 140
means of production, 132
mechanistic determinism, 141
mechanistic materialism, 46, 106, 107, 297

Menshevising idealism, 47, 53, 133, 134, 135, 136, 154, 155
Mikhailovsky, 40, 41
Minin, 45, 134
Mitin, Mark, 47, 48, 49, 54, 107, 133, 154, 155, 159, 165, 166, 190, 205, 209, 210, 226
Modern Worldview, The, 141
Montesquieu, 122
More, Thomas, 122
motion and matter, 163, 186–87
motion, 282
   and contradiction, 42
motion, concept of, 185, 190–91
nationality, 120
negation of the negation, law of, *see* law of the negation of the negation
negation, elements of, 283
neo-Kantianism, 87, 123, 135, 198, 249
New Age, 8
New Culture Movement, 21
New Youth, 7, 8
new orthodoxy, 227, 232, 253
"new philosophy", 144, 157, 158, 172
new thought movement, 6
1911 Revolution, 3, 80
Northern Expedition, 14
objective world, knowledge of, 221
Oceania, 122
"On Contradiction", 20, 39, 114, 143, 159, 160, 169, 170, 226, 233, 253, 258, 279, 280, 282, 283, 284, 287, 296, 302
   explanatory notes to, 233, 239, 240–49
"On Correcting Mistaken Ideas in the Party", 250
"On Practice", 20, 114, 143, 159, 160, 169, 170, 226, 233, 253, 258, 279, 280, 287, 296
   explanatory notes to, 233, 234–40
"On the Correct Handling of Contradictions Among the People", 281, 284
one divides into two, 285
ontology of dialectical materialism, 186–87

Opium War, 79
Oppenheimer, 124
orthodoxy, concept of, 32
orthodoxy, orthodox Marxism, 39–44, 45, 46–51, 65, 85, 86–87, 106–7, 142–43, 172, 173, 205, 232, 287, 296, 299
  Li and, 54–56, 112
  Soviet orthodoxy, 180, 226
  theoretical framework, 297
  see also new orthodoxy
Outline of Economic Theory, An, 16
Outline of Jurisprudence, 18–19
Outline of New Philosophy, 155, 160, 165, 172, 205, 209
Overview of Social Problems, An, 121–23
Paris Commune, 70
parliamentary strategy, 69
peasantry, economic distinctions within, 250
  dissemination of socialism amongst, 275
Peng Dehuai, 22, 278, 302
People's Publishing House, 7
perception, as source of knowledge, 212–13
  and thought, 213–15
phenomenal appearance, 195–96
phenomenon, 105; and essence, 198
philosophical struggle, 183
philosophy, 94
  and dialectics, 101–6
  and forces of production, 102–3
  as part of economic struggle, 156
  history of, 103
  in post-Liberation China, 19–22
  Party character of, 130, 134
PKI, *see* Indonesian Communist Party
Plato, 103, 164–65
Plekhanov, 39–42, 44, 45, 46, 50, 51, 124, 132, 133, 134, 137, 155, 157, 158, 224, 249, 297
Pokrovsky, 50
polemical writings, 258
political status, of Li, 19–20
politics, 98–101, 225
  in post-Liberation China, 19–22

political life, 127
possibility and reality, 203–4, 283
practice, 221
  as basis of knowledge, 217
pragmatism, 259, 260
primitive dialectics, 181–82
production, mode of, 269
  revolution in, 71
  techniques of, 107
proletariat, as universal class, 31
  oppression of, 80
  proletarian revolution, 64–65, 66, 249
  seizure of power by, 273, 274
property relations, 64, 93
Qian Tieru, 52
Qin Bangxian, 113
Qu Qiubai, 85, 87, 101, 124
quality, 192
quantity, 192
  and quality, 49
  quantitative change, 193
Raltsevich, Vasili, 47
reactionary thought, 277
"Read Comrade Mao Zedong's Four Articles from 1926–1929", 249
reality, nature of, 37
  and possibility, 203–4
Red Army, 250
Red Guards, 23
reflection theory, epistemology of, 210–11
  of dialectical materialism, 211
relations of production, 64, 93, 94, 98, 126, 197, 247, 272, 276
religion, 119
Reng Wuxiong, 11
"Report on an Investigation of the Peasant Movement in Hunan", 250
reputation as author, of Li, 157–59
resignation from CCP, *see under* CCP
Resolution on Certain Questions, 168
revisionism, 65, 66, 74, 281, 284
  in Germany, 84
revolution, causes of, 68
  economic, 100
  political, 100
revolutionary practice, 285

Index 325

Rousseau, 68, 80, 122
Roy, M.N., 9
Russian Revolution, 4, 6, 44, 70
Sakai Toshihiko, 51
Sano Manabu, 140
Save China Association, 5, 62
Scandinavian writers, 117
Schelling, 122
scholasticism, 45
science, 93, 187
Selected Works of Mao Zedong, 249
Self-Study University, 8
sexual equality, 63
Shanghai Committee for the
   Establishment of the CCP, 6, 7
Shirokov, 48, 87, 114, 124, 133–39,
   152, 154, 155, 156, 158, 159, 165,
   166, 170, 190, 209, 226, 300
Sinification of Marxism, 13
Sneevliet, Hendricus, 9, 90
social change, 91–95, 238, 247
   aetiology of, 31–32, 51
   cause of, 132
   human action in, 201
   process of, 299
   theory of, 107
social consciousness, 95, 96–98
   role in social change, 98
social development, 95–98
social formation, 273
social life, process of, 126
social policy, 121
social problems, 121
social revolution, 68–71, 74
   in China, 77–78
   materialist explanation of, 70
social structure, 91, 92–93, 238, 247
social theory, 30–62
   contract, 92
   idealist, 92
   organic, 92
socialism, and communism, 62–63
   characteristics of, 62–64, 122
   history, 63
   Marxist, *see* Marxist socialism
socialist transformation of system of
   ownership, 282
   socialist transition, 275, 276

socialist construction, 282
socioeconomic formation, 272, 276
sociology, as euphemism, 92
Socrates, 164
Song Jingming, 12
Soviet Marxist philosophy, 248
Soviet Union, 3
   1931 watershed in, 116, 124, 154
   economic evolution, 81–82
   Marxism in, 2, 44–46, 79, 248
   philosophical texts of, 133
spirit and matter, 183–84
spiritual culture, 239, 240
spiritual relations, 93, 127
Stalin, Josef, 2, 41, 47, 50, 133, 249, 251
State and Revolution, 5
state theory, 100
state, and society, 99
Stepanov, 45
strikes, 69–70
Sugiyama Sakae, 3, 52–53, 124–28,
   140, 141, 271, 299
Sun Yat-sen, 3, 10
superstructure, 93, 108, 141, 273
   and base, 224, 248, 270–74, 276,
   298
*Survey of China's Revolution in
   Production, A*, 91, 108
Survey of Social Science, 124–28
syndicalism, 72
synthesis, and analysis, 220–22
Takabatake Motoyuki, 5, 121–23, 128,
   140, 141, 299
Takayanagi Matsuichiro, 117
Tao Delin, 22, 23, 278, 279, 285, 287
tariff system, 113
textile industry, 79
Thales, 162–63
Thalheimer, A., 15, 87, 91, 106, 128–29,
   132, 141, 299
"The Labourer and Socialism", 67
The Nationality Question, 91
Theoretical Front, 268
theory and practice, separation of, 224
theory of leaps, 193–94
Thompson, William, 122
thought, function of, 95
   and existence, 189

and perception, 213–15
thought, of Li Da, origins, 30–62
Timiryazev, 45
translation, 112–50
 and dissemination of Marxism, 139–44
 Li's philosophy of, 116–17
 of Japanese texts, 51
 of Marxist texts, 5, 15
 of philosophy, 106
Trotsky, 50, 78
Twenty-one Demands, 4, 262
two divides into one, 284–85
unions, 69–70
United Front, 9–12, 115, 281; see also Second United Front
unity of contradictions, 105
unity of essence and phenomenon, 105
unity of opposites, law of, see law of the unity of opposites
unity of theory and practice, 130, 155, 234
universal laws of development, 269–70, 276–77
Utopia, 122
utopianism, 203
Voltaire, 122
Wang Huiwu, 7, 115, 232
Wang Jionghua, 20–21, 23, 169–71, 263
Wang Yanan, 113
warlords, 10

Weber, 124
Western influence, 69
"Why is It That Red Political Power Can Exist in China?", 250
Women's Voice, 7
women, emancipation of, 2, 123
 socialism and, 64
 status of, 64
 subordination of, 63–64
 women's movement, 113
World of Labour, The, 7
world spirit, 182
Wu Liangping, 113
Xu Quanxing, 169–71
Xu Teli, 3
Yamakawa Hitoshi, 52, 53, 140
Yan'an period, 16, 232
Yan'an Philosophical Association, 151
Ye Qing, 158
Yi Lirong, 232
Yong Yang, see Li Da
Young China, 7
Yu Zhihong, 278
Yuan Shikai, 262
Yudin, Pavel, 47
Zhang Qingfu, 15
Zhang Wentian, 286
Zhang Zhongshi, 113
Zhou Enlai, 18, 22, 286
Zhou Fohai, 12
Zhu De, 286

For Product Safety Concerns and Information please contact our EU
representative GPSR@taylorandfrancis.com
Taylor & Francis Verlag GmbH, Kaufingerstraße 24, 80331 München, Germany